Active Equity Portfolio Management

Edited by

Frank J. Fabozzi, CFA
Adjunct Professor of Finance
School of Management
Yale University

Published by Frank J. Fabozzi Associates

Cover design by Scott C. Riether

This publication is designed to provide accurate and authoritative information in regard to the subject matter covered. It is sold with the understanding that the publisher is not engaged in rendering legal, accounting, or other professional services.

ISBN: 1-883249-30-9

Printed in the United States of America

Table of Contents

Contributing Authors

Paul M. Bagnoli	Sanford C. Bernstein and Company, Inc.
Jon A. Christopherson	Frank Russell Company
Roger G. Clarke	Analytic/TSA Global Asset Management
Bruce Collins	Western Connecticut State University
Harindra de Silva	Analytic/TSA Global Asset Management
Mark Edwards	Plexus Group
Frank J. Fabozzi	Yale University
Gary L. Gastineau	American Stock Exchange
Bruce I. Jacobs	Jacobs Levy Equity Management
Robert C. Jones	Goldman Sachs Asset Management
David Krider	First Quadrant, L.P.
David J. Leinweber	First Quadrant, L.P.
Kenneth N. Levy	Jacobs Levy Equity Management
Christopher K. Ma	KCM Asset Management Group, Inc. and Stetson University
James E. Mallett	Stetson University
Greg M. McMurran	Analytic/TSA Global Asset Management
Joseph J. Mezrich	Salomon Brothers Inc.
Keith L. Miller	Salomon Brothers Inc.
Robert F. Ploder	IBM Retirement Funds
Eric H. Sorensen	Salomon Brothers Inc.
Peter Swank	First Quadrant, L.P.
Wayne H. Wagner	Plexus Group

Chapter 1

Investment Management: An Architecture for the Equity Market

Bruce I. Jacobs, Ph.D.
Principal
Jacobs Levy Equity Management

Kenneth N. Levy, CFA
Principal
Jacobs Levy Equity Management

INTRODUCTION

Anyone who has ever built a house knows how important it is to start out with a sound architectural design. A sound design can help ensure that the end product will meet all the homeowner's expectations — material, aesthetic, and financial. A bad architectural design, or no design, offers no such assurance and is likely to lead to poor decision-making, unintended results, and cost overruns.

It is equally important in building an equity portfolio to start out with some framework that relates the raw materials — stocks — and the basic construction techniques — investment approaches — to the end product. An architecture of equity management that outlines the basic relationships between the raw investment material, investment approaches, potential rewards and possible risks, can provide a blueprint for investment decision-making.

We provide such a blueprint in this chapter. A quick tour of this blueprint reveals three building blocks — a comprehensive core, static style subsets, and a dynamic entity. Investment approaches can also be roughly categorized into three groups — passive, traditional active, and engineered active. Understanding the market's architecture and the advantages and disadvantages of each investment approach can improve overall investment results.

The authors thank Judith Kimball for her editorial assistance.

1

Exhibit 1: Equity Market Architecture

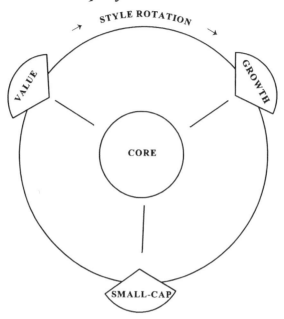

AN ARCHITECTURE

Exhibit 1 provides a simple but fairly comprehensive view of the equity market.[1] The heart of the structure, the core, represents the overall market. Theoretically, this would include all U.S. equity issues. (Similar architectures can be applied to other national equity markets.) In line with the practice of most equity managers, a broad-based equity index such as the S&P 500 or (even broader) the Russell 3000 or Wilshire 5000, may proxy for the aggregate market.

For both equity managers and their clients, the overall market represents a natural and intuitive starting place. It is the ultimate selection pool for all equity strategies. Furthermore, the long-term returns offered by the U.S. equity market have historically outperformed alternative asset classes in the majority of multi-year periods. The aim of most institutional investors (even those that do not hold core investments per se) is to capture, or outdo, this equity return premium.

The core equity market can be broken down into subsets that comprise stocks with similar price behaviors — large-cap growth, large-cap value, and small-cap stocks. In Exhibit 1, the wedges circling the core represent these style subsets. The aggregate of the stocks forming the subsets equals the overall core market.

---

[1] See also Bruce I. Jacobs and Kenneth N. Levy, "How to Build a Better Equity Portfolio," *Pension Management* (June 1996), pp. 36-39.

Exhibit 2: Small-Cap Stocks May Outperform Large-Cap in Some Periods and Underperform in Others

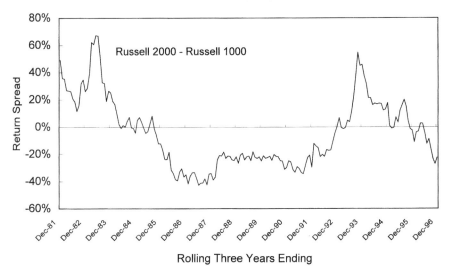

One advantage of viewing the market as a collection of subsets is the ability it confers upon the investor to "mix and match." Instead of holding a core portfolio, for example, the investor can hold market subsets in market-like weights and receive returns and incur risks commensurate with those of the core. Alternatively, the investor can depart from core weights to pursue returns in excess of the core market return (at the expense, of course, of incremental risk). Investors who believe that small-cap stocks offer a higher return than the average market return, for example, can overweight that subset and underweight large-cap value and growth stocks.

Over time, different style subsets can offer differing relative payoffs as economic conditions change. As Exhibit 2 shows, small-cap stocks outperformed large-cap stocks by 60 percentage points or more in the rolling 3-year periods ending in mid-1983 and by 45 to 55 percentage points in late 1993. But small cap underperformed by 20 to 40 percentage points in the rolling 3-year periods between early 1986 and December 1991.[2] Exhibit 3 shows that large-cap growth stocks outperformed large-cap value stocks by 30 to 40 percentage points in the rolling 3-year periods from mid-1991 to mid-1992 but underperformed by 20 to 35 percentage points in every rolling 3-year period from mid-1983 through 1986.[3]

---

[2] Exhibit 2 uses the Frank Russell 1000 (the largest stocks in the Russell 3000) as the large-cap index and the Russell 2000 (the smallest stocks in the Russell 3000) as the small-cap index.

[3] Exhibit 3 uses the Russell 1000 Growth and the Russell 1000 Value as the growth and value indexes; these indexes roughly divide the market capitalization of the Russell 1000. Results are similar using other indexes, such as the Wilshire and S&P 500/BARRA style indexes.

Exhibit 3: Large-Cap Growth Stocks Outperform Large-Cap Value in Some Periods and Underperform in Others

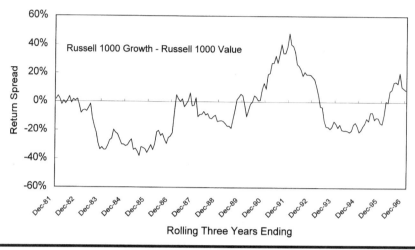

Just as some investors attempt to time the market by buying into and selling out of equities in line with their expectations of overall market trends, investors can attempt to exploit the dynamism of style subsets by rotating their investments across different styles over time, in pursuit of profit opportunities offered by one or another subset as market and economic conditions change.[4] The curved lines connecting the style wedges in Exhibit 1 represent this dynamic nature of the market.

The equity core and its constituent style subsets constitute the basic building blocks — the equity selection universes — from which investors can construct their portfolios. Another important choice facing the investor, however, is the investment approach or approaches to apply to the selection universe. Exhibit 4 categorizes possible approaches into three groups — traditional, passive, and engineered. Each of these approaches can be characterized by an underlying investment philosophy and, very generally, by a level of risk relative to the underlying selection universe.

TRADITIONAL ACTIVE MANAGEMENT

Traditional investment managers focus on "stock picking." In short, they hunt for individual securities that will perform well over the investment horizon. The search includes in-depth examinations of companies' financial statements and investigations of companies' managements, product lines, facilities, etc. Based on the findings of these inquiries, traditional managers determine whether a particular firm is a good "buy" or a better "sell."

[4] See Bruce I. Jacobs and Kenneth N. Levy, "High-Definition Style Rotation," *Journal of Investing* (Fall 1996), pp. 14-23.

Exhibit 4: Equity Investment Approaches

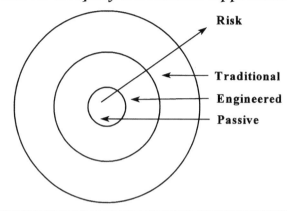

The search area for traditional investing may be wide — the equivalent of the equity core — and may include market timing that exploits the dynamism of the overall market. Because in-depth analyses of large numbers of securities are just not practical for any one manager, however, traditional managers tend to focus on subsets of the equity market. Some may hunt for above-average earnings growth (growth stocks), while others look to buy future earnings streams cheaply (value stocks); still others beat the grasses off the trodden paths, in search of overlooked growth and/or value stocks (small-cap stocks). Traditional managers have thus fallen into the pursuit of growth, value, or small-cap styles.

Traditional managers often screen an initial universe of stocks based on some financial criteria, thereby selecting a relatively small list of stocks to be followed closely. Focusing on such a narrow list reduces the complexity of the analytical problem to human (i.e., traditional) dimensions. Unfortunately, it may also introduce significant barriers to superior performance.

Exhibit 5 plots the combinations of breadth and depth of insights necessary to achieve a given investment return/risk level.[5] Here the breadth of insights may be understood as the number of independent insights — i.e., the number of investment ideas or the number of stocks. The depth, or goodness, of insights is measured as the *information coefficient* — the correlation between the return forecasts made for stocks and their actual returns. Note that the goodness of the insights needed to produce the given return/risk ratio starts to increase dramatically as the number of insights falls below 100; the slope gets particularly steep as breadth falls below 50.

---

[5] The plot reflects the relationship:

$$IR = IC \times \sqrt{BR}$$

where *IC* is the information coefficient (the correlation between predicted and actual returns), *BR* the number of independent insights, and IR (in this case set equal to one) the ratio of annualized excess return to annualized residual risk. See Richard C. Grinold and Ronald N. Kahn, *Active Portfolio Management* (Chicago, IL: Probus Publishing, 1995), Chapter 6.

Exhibit 5: Combination of Breadth (Number) of Insights and Depth, or "Goodness," of Insights Needed to Produce a Given Investment Return/Risk Ratio

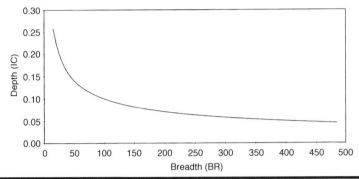

Traditional investing in effect relies on the ability of in-depth research to supply information coefficients that are high enough to overcome the lack of breadth imposed by the approach's fairly severe limitations on the number of securities that can be followed. As Exhibit 5 shows, however, the level of information coefficients required at such constricted breadth levels constitutes a considerable hurdle to superior performance. The insights from traditional management must be very, very good to overcome the commensurate lack of breadth.[6]

Furthermore, lack of breadth may also have detrimental effects on the depth of traditional insights. While reducing the range of inquiry makes tractable the problem of stock selection via the labor-intensive methods of traditional active management, it is also bound to result in potentially relevant (and profitable) information being left out. Surely, for example, the behavior of the growth stocks not followed by traditional growth managers — even the behavior of value stocks outside the growth subset — may contain information relevant to the pricing of those stocks that do constitute the reduced traditional universe.

Another inherent weakness of traditional investment approaches is their heavy reliance on subjective human judgments. An ever-growing body of research suggests that stock prices, as well as being moved by fundamental information, are influenced by the psychology of investors. In particular, investors often appear to be under the influence of cognitive biases that cause them to err systematically in making investment decisions.[7]

---

[6] Market timing strategies are particularly lacking in breadth, as an insight into the market's direction provides only one investment decision. Quarterly timing would produce four "bets" a year — a level of diversification few investors would find acceptable. Furthermore, unless timing is done on a daily basis or the timer is prodigiously skilled, it would take a lifetime to determine whether the results of timing reflect genuine skill or mere chance.

[7] See, for example, Daniel Kahneman and Amos Tversky, "Prospect Theory: An Analysis of Decision Under Risk," *Econometrica* (Number 2, 1979), pp. 263-292, and Richard H. Thaler (ed.), *Advances in Behavioral Finance* (New York, NY: Russell Sage Foundation, 1993).

Kenneth Arrow, for example, finds that investors tend to overemphasize new information if it appears to be representative of a possible future event; thus, if investors perceive a firm's management to be "good," and the firm has recently enjoyed high earnings, they will tend to place more reliance on the higher than the lower earnings estimates provided by analysts.[8] Robert Shiller finds that investors are as susceptible as any other consumers to fads and fashions — bidding up prices of "hot" stocks and ignoring out-of-favor issues.[9] We describe below four common cognitive errors that investors may fall prey to.

Cognitive Errors
Loss Aversion (The "Better Not Take the Chance/ What the Heck" Paradox)
Investors exhibit risk-averse behavior with respect to potential gains: faced with a choice between (1) a sure gain of $3,000 and (2) an 80% chance of gaining $4,000 or a 20% chance of gaining nothing, most people choose the sure thing, even though the $3,000 is less than the expected value of the gamble, which is $3,200 (80% of $4,000). But investors are generally risk-seeking when it comes to avoiding certain loss: faced with a choice between (1) a sure loss of $3,000 and (2) an 80% chance of losing $4,000 or a 20% chance of losing nothing, most people will opt to take a chance. It's only human nature that the pain of loss exceed the glee of gain, but putting human nature in charge of investment decision-making may lead to suboptimal results. Shirking risk leads to forgone gains. Pursuing risk in avoidance of loss may have even direr consequences ("digging a deeper hole"), as recent episodes at Barings and Daiwa have demonstrated.

Endowment Effect (The "Pride in Ownership" Syndrome)
The price people are willing to pay to acquire an object or service is often less than the price they would be willing to sell the identical object or service for if they owned it. Say you bought a stock last year and it's quadrupled in price. If you won't buy more because "it's too expensive now," you should sell it. If you won't sell it because you were so brilliant when you bought it, you're sacrificing returns for pride in ownership.

The Gambler's Fallacy ("Hot Streaks, Empty Wallets")
Is it more likely that six tosses of a coin will come up HTTHTH or HHHTTT? Most people think the former sequence is more typical than the latter, but in truth both are equally likely products of randomness. In either case, the probability of the next flip of the coin turning up heads, or tails, is 50%. Market prices, too, will display patterns. It's easy to interpret such patterns as persistent trends, and tempt-

[8] Kenneth J. Arrow, "Risk Perception in Psychology and Economics," *Economic Inquiry* (Number 1, 1982), pp. 1-8.
[9] Robert J. Shiller, "Stock Prices and Social Dynamics," *Brookings Papers on Economic Activity* (Number 2, 1984), pp. 457-510.

ing to trade on them. But if the latest "hot streak" is merely a mirage thrown up by random price movements, it will prove an unreliable guide to future performance.

Confirmation Bias ("Don't Confuse Me with the Facts")

People search for and place more reliance upon evidence that confirms their pre-conceived notions, ignoring or devaluing evidence that refutes them. Four cards lie on a table, showing A, B, 2, and 3: What is the fewest number of cards you can turn over to confirm or refute that every card with a vowel on one side has an even number on the other side? Most people choose A, then 2. An odd number or a let-ter on the reverse of A would refute the conjecture. The 2, however, can merely confirm, not refute; the presence of a vowel on the reverse would confirm, but any-thing else would simply be immaterial. The correct choice is to turn A, 3, and B. A vowel on the reverse of 3 can refute, as can a vowel on the reverse of B. Invest-ment approaches that do not have a method of systematically searching through all available evidence without prejudice, in order to find the exceptions that disprove their rules, may leave portfolios open to blindsiding and torpedo effects.

Investors susceptible to these biases will tend to take too little (or too much) risk; to hold on to an investment for too long; to see long-term trends where none exist; and to place too much reliance on information that confirms existing beliefs. As a result, the performances of their portfolios are likely to suffer.

The reliance of traditional investment management on the judgments of individual human minds makes for idiosyncrasies of habit that work to the detri-ment of investment discipline, and this is true at the level of the investment firm as well as the individual at the firm. It may be difficult to coordinate the individual mindsets of all analysts, economists, investment officers, technicians, and traders, and this coordination is even harder to achieve when subjective standards for security analysis differ from individual to individual.

Constructing Portfolios

The qualitative nature of the outcome of the security evaluation process, together with the absence of a unifying framework, can give rise to problems when indi-vidual insights into securities' performances are combined to construct a portfo-lio. However on target an analyst's buy or sell recommendations may be, they are difficult to translate into guidelines for portfolio construction. Portfolio optimiza-tion procedures require quantitative estimates of relevant parameters — not mere recommendations to buy, hold, or sell.

The traditional manager's focus on stock picking and the resulting ad hoc nature of portfolio construction can lead to portfolios that are poorly defined in regard to their underlying selection universes. While any particular manager's portfo-lio return may be measured against the return on an index representative of an under-lying equity core or style subset, that index does not serve as a "benchmark" in the sense of providing a guideline for portfolio risk. Traditional portfolios' risk-return profiles may thus vary greatly relative to those of the underlying selection universe.

As a result, portfolios do not necessarily fit into the market's architecture. A traditional value manager, for example, may be averse to holding certain sectors, such as utilities. Not only will the portfolio's returns suffer when utilities perform well, but the portfolio will suffer from a lack of "integrity" — of wholeness. Such a portfolio will not be representative of the whole value subset. Nor could it be combined with growth and small-cap portfolios to create a core-like holding.

Because the relationship between the overall equity market and traditional managers' style portfolios may be ambiguous, "value" and "growth," "small-cap" and "large-cap" may not be mutually exclusive. Value portfolios may hold some growth stocks, or growth portfolios some value stocks. There is no assurance that a combination of style portfolios can offer a market-like or above-market return at market-like risk levels.

Because of their heavy reliance on human mind power and subjective judgment, traditional approaches to investment management tend to suffer from a lack of breadth, a lack of discipline, and a resulting lack of portfolio integrity. Traditional management, while it may serve as well as any other approach for picking individual stocks, suffers from severe limitations when it comes to constructing portfolios of stocks. Perhaps it is for this reason that traditionally managed portfolios have often failed to live up to expectations.

PASSIVE MANAGEMENT

The generally poor performance of traditional investment management approaches helped to motivate the development, in the late 1960s and the 1970s, of new theories of stock price behavior. The efficient market hypothesis and random walk theory — the products of much research — offered a reason for the meager returns reaped by traditional investment managers: stock prices effectively reflect all information in an "efficient" manner, rendering stock price movements random and unpredictable. Efficiency and randomness provided the motivation for passive investment management; advances in computing power provided the means.

Passive management aims to construct portfolios that will match the risk/return profiles of underlying market benchmarks. The benchmark may be core equity (as proxied by the S&P 500 or other broad index) or a style subset (as proxied by a large-cap growth, large-cap value, or small-cap index). Given the quantitative tools at its disposal, passive management can fine-tune the stock selection and portfolio construction problems in order to deliver portfolios that mimic very closely both the returns and risks of their chosen benchmarks.

Passive portfolios, unlike traditional portfolios, are disciplined. Any tendencies for passive managers to succumb to cognitive biases will be held in check by the exigencies of their stated goals — tracking the performances of their underlying benchmarks. Their success in this endeavor also means that the resulting portfolios will have integrity. A passive value portfolio will behave like its underlying selection universe, and a combination of passive style portfolios in market-like weights can be expected to offer a return close to the market's return at a risk level close to the market's.

As the trading required to keep portfolios in line with underlying indexes is generally less than that required to "beat" the indexes, transaction costs for passive management are generally lower than those incurred by active investment approaches. As much of the stock selection and portfolio construction problem can be relegated to fast-acting computers, the management fees for passive management are also modest. For the same reason, the number of securities that can be covered by any given passive manager is virtually unlimited; all the stocks in the selection universe can be considered for portfolio inclusion.

Unlike traditional management, then, passive management offers great breadth. Breadth in this case doesn't count for much, however, because passive management is essentially insightless. Built on the premise that markets are efficient, hence market prices are random and unpredictable, passive management does not attempt to pursue or offer any return over the return on the relevant benchmark. Rather, its appeal lies in its ability to deliver the asset class return or to deliver the return of a style subset of the asset class. In practice, of course, trading costs and management fees, however modest, subtract from this performance.

An investor in pursuit of above-market returns may nevertheless be able to exploit passive management approaches via style subset selection and style rotation. That is, an investor who believes value stocks will outperform the overall market can choose to overweight a passive value portfolio in expectation of earning above-market (but not above-benchmark) returns. An investor with foresight into style performance can choose to rotate investments across different passive style portfolios as underlying economic and market conditions change.

ENGINEERED MANAGEMENT

Engineered management recognizes that markets are reasonably efficient in digesting information and that stock price movements in response to unanticipated news are largely random. It also recognizes, however, that significant, measurable pricing inefficiencies do exist, and it seeks to deliver incremental returns by modeling and exploiting these inefficiencies. In this endeavor, it applies to the same company fundamental and economic data used by traditional active management many of the tools that fostered the development of passive management, including modern computing power, finance theory, and statistical techniques — instruments that can extend the reaches (and discipline the vagaries) of the human mind.

Engineered approaches use quantitative methods to select stocks and construct portfolios that will have risk/return profiles similar to those of underlying equity benchmarks but offer incremental returns relative to those benchmarks, at appropriate incremental risk levels. The quantitative methods used may range from fairly straightforward to immensely intricate. In selecting stocks, for example, an engineered approach may use something as simple as a dividend discount model. Or it may employ complex multivariate models that aim to capture the complexities of the equity market.[10]

The engineered selection process can deal with and benefit from as wide a selection universe as passive management. It can thus approach the investment problem with an unbiased philosophy, unhampered, as is traditional management, by the need to reduce the equity universe to a tractable subset. At the same time, depending upon the level of sophistication of the tools it chooses to use, engineered management can benefit from great depth of analysis — a depth similar to that of traditional approaches. Multivariate modeling, for example, can take into account the intricacies of stock price behavior, including variations in price responses across stocks of different industries, economic sectors, and styles.

Because engineered management affords both breadth and depth, the manager can choose a focal point from which to frame the equity market, without loss of important "framing" information. Analysis of a particular style subset, for example, can take advantage of information gleaned from the whole universe of securities, not just stocks of that particular style (or a subset of that style, as in traditional management). The increased breadth of inquiry should lead to improvements in portfolio performance vis-a-vis traditional style portfolios.

Engineering Portfolios

Engineered management utilizes all the information found relevant from an objective examination of the broad equity universe to arrive at numerical estimates for the expected returns and anticipated risks of the stocks in that universe. Unlike the subjective outcomes of traditional management, such numerical estimates are eminently suitable for portfolio construction via optimization techniques.[11]

The goal of optimization is to maximize portfolio return while tying portfolio risk to that of the underlying benchmark. The portfolio's systematic risk should match the risk of the benchmark. The portfolio's residual risk should be no more than is justified by the expected incremental return. Risk control can be further refined by tailoring the optimization model so that it is consistent with the variables in the return estimation process.

The quantitative nature of the stock selection and portfolio construction processes imposes discipline on engineered portfolios. With individual stocks defined by expected performance parameters, and portfolios optimized along those parameters to provide desired patterns of expected risk and return, engineered portfolios can be defined in terms of preset performance goals. Engineered managers have little leeway to stray from these performance mandates, hence are less likely

---

[10] See Bruce I. Jacobs and Kenneth N. Levy, "Investment Analysis: Profiting from a Complex Equity Market," Chapter 2 in this book.

[11] See also Bruce I. Jacobs and Kenneth N. Levy, "Engineering Portfolios: A Unified Approach," *Journal of Investing* (Winter 1995).

than traditional managers to fall under the sway of cognitive errors. In fact, engineered strategies may be designed to exploit such biases as investor overreaction (leading to price reversals) or investor herding (leading to price trends).

The discipline of engineered management also helps to ensure portfolio integrity. The style subset portfolios of a given firm, for example, should be non-overlapping, and the style subset benchmarks should in the aggregate be inclusive of all stocks in the investor's universe. Value portfolios should contain no growth stocks, nor growth portfolios any value stocks. The underlying benchmarks for value and growth portfolios, or large and small-cap portfolios, should aggregate to the equity core.

Engineering should reduce, relative to traditional management, portfolio return deviations from the underlying core or subset benchmark, while increasing expected returns relative to those available from passive approaches. While judicious stock selection can provide excess portfolio return over a passive benchmark, optimized portfolio construction offers control of portfolio risk.

Exhibit 6 compares the relative merits of traditional, passive, and engineered approaches to portfolio management. Traditional management offers depth, but strikes out with lack of breadth, susceptibility to cognitive errors, and lack of portfolio integrity. Passive management offers breadth, freedom from cognitive error, and portfolio integrity, but no depth whatsoever. Only engineered management has the ability to construct portfolios that benefit from both breadth and depth of analysis, are free of cognitive errors, and have structural integrity.

MEETING CLIENT NEEDS

A broad-based, engineered approach offers investment managers the means to tailor portfolios for a wide variety of client needs. Consider, for example, a client that has no opinion about style subset performance, but believes that the equity market will continue to offer its average historical premium over alternative cash and bond investments. This client may choose to hold the market in the form of an engineered core portfolio that can deliver the all-important equity market premium (at the market's risk level), plus the potential for some incremental return consistent with the residual risk incurred.

Exhibit 6: Comparison of Equity Investment Approaches

	Traditional	Passive	Engineered
Depth of Analysis	Yes	No	Simple — No Complex — Yes
Breadth of Analysis	No	Yes	Yes
Free of Cognitive Error	No	Yes	Yes
Portfolio Integrity	No	Yes	Yes

Alternatively, the client with a strong belief that value stocks will outperform can choose from among several engineered solutions. An engineered portfolio can be designed to deliver a value-benchmark-like return at a comparable risk level or to offer, at the cost of incremental risk, a return increment above the value benchmark. Traditional value portfolios cannot be designed to offer the same level of assurance of meeting these goals.

With engineered portfolios, the client also has the ability to fine-tune bets. For example, the client can weight a portfolio toward value stocks while retaining exposure to the overall market by placing some portion of the portfolio in core equity and the remainder in a value portfolio, or by placing some percentage in a growth portfolio and a larger percentage in a value portfolio. Exposures to the market and to its various subsets can be engineered. Again, traditional management can offer no assurance that a combination of style portfolios will offer the desired risk-return profile.

Expanding Opportunities

The advantages of an engineered approach are perhaps best exploited by strategies that are not constrained to deliver a benchmark-like performance. An engineered style rotation strategy, for example, seeks to deliver returns in excess of the market's by forecasting style subset performance. Shifting investment weights aggressively among various style subsets as market and economic conditions evolve, style rotation takes advantage of the historical tendency of any given style to outperform the overall market in some periods and to underperform it in others. Such a strategy uses the entire selection universe and offers potentially high returns at commensurate risk levels.

Allowing short sales as an adjunct to an engineered strategy — whether that strategy utilizes core equity, a style subset, or style rotation — can further enhance return opportunities. While traditional management focuses on stock picking — the selection of "winning" securities — the breadth of engineered management allows for the consideration of "losers" as well as "winners." With an engineered portfolio that allows shorting of losers, the manager can pursue potential mispricings without constraint, going long underpriced stocks and selling short overpriced stocks.

In markets in which short selling is not widespread, there are reasons to believe that shorting stocks can offer more opportunity than buying stocks. This is because restrictions on short selling do not permit investor pessimism to be as fully represented in prices as investor optimism. In such a market, the potential candidates for short sale may be less efficiently priced, hence offer greater return potential, than the potential candidates for purchase.[12]

Even if all stocks are efficiently priced, however, shorting can enhance performance by eliminating constraints on the implementation of investment

---

[12] See, for example, Bruce I. Jacobs and Kenneth N. Levy, "20 Myths About Long-Short," *Financial Analysts Journal* (September/October 1996).

insights. Consider, for example, that a security with a median market capitalization has a weighting of approximately 0.01% of the market's capitalization. A manager that cannot short can underweight such a security by, at most, 0.01% relative to the market; this is achieved by not holding the security at all. Those who do not consider this unduly restrictive should consider that placing a like constraint on the maximum portfolio overweight would be equivalent to saying the manager could hold, at most, a 0.02% position in the stock, no matter how appetizing its expected return. Shorting allows the manager free rein in translating the insights gained from the stock selection process into portfolio performance.

Long-Short Portfolios

If security returns are symmetrically distributed about the underlying market return, there will be fully as many unattractive securities for short sale as there are attractive securities for purchase. Using optimization techniques, the manager can construct a portfolio that balances equal dollar amounts and equal systematic risks long and short. Such a long-short balance neutralizes the risk (and return) of the underlying market. The portfolio's return — which can be measured as the spread between the long and short returns — is solely reflective of the manager's skill at stock selection.[13]

Not only does such a long-short portfolio neutralize underlying market risk, it offers improved control of residual risk relative even to an engineered long-only portfolio. For example, the long-only portfolio can control risk relative to the underlying benchmark only by converging toward the weightings of the benchmark's stocks; these weights constrain portfolio composition. Balancing securities' sensitivities long and short, however, eliminates risk relative to the underlying benchmark; benchmark weights are thus not constraining. Furthermore, the long-short portfolio can use offsetting long and short positions to fine-tune the portfolio's residual risk.

In addition to enhanced return and improved risk control, an engineered long-short approach also offers clients added flexibility in asset allocation. A simple long-short portfolio, for example, offers a return from security selection on top of a cash return (the interest received on the proceeds from the short sales). However, the long-short manager can also offer, or the client initiate, a long-short portfolio combined with a position in derivatives such as stock index futures. Such an "equitized" portfolio will offer the long-short portfolio's security selection return on top of the equity market return provided by the futures position; choice of other available derivatives can provide the return from security selection in combination with exposure to other asset classes. The transportability of the long-short portfolio's return offers clients the ability to take advantage of a manager's security selection skills while determining independently the plan's asset allocation mix.

---

[13] See Bruce I. Jacobs and Kenneth N. Levy, "The Long and Short on Long-Short," *Journal of Investing* (Spring 1997), pp. 73-86.

THE RISK-RETURN CONTINUUM

The various approaches to investment management — as well as the selection universes that are the targets of such approaches — can be characterized generally by distinct risk-return profiles. For example, in Exhibit 1, risk levels tend to increase as one moves from the core outward toward the dynamic view of the market; expected returns should also increase. Similarly, in Exhibit 4, risk can be perceived as increasing as one moves from passive investment management out toward traditional active management; expected returns should also increase.

Where should the investor be along this continuum? The answer depends in part on the investor's aversion to risk. The more risk-averse the investor, the closer to core/passive the portfolio should be, and the lower its risk and expected return. Investors who are totally averse to incurring residual risk (that is, departing from benchmark holdings and weights) should stick with passive approaches. They will thus be assured of receiving an equity market return at a market risk level. They will never "beat" the market.

Less risk-averse investors can make more use of style subsets (static or dynamic) and active (engineered or traditional) approaches. With the use of such subsets and such approaches, however, portfolio weights will shift away from overall equity market weights. The difference provides the opportunity for excess return, but it also creates residual risk. In this regard, engineered portfolios, which control risk relative to underlying benchmarks, have definite advantages over traditional portfolios.

The optimal level of residual risk for an investor will depend not only on the investor's level of aversion to residual risk, but also on the manager's skill. Skill can be measured as the manager's information ratio, or *IR* — the ratio of annualized excess return to annualized residual risk. For example, a manager that beats the benchmark by 2% per year, with 4% residual risk, has an *IR* of 2%/4%, or 0.5.

Grinold and Kahn formulate the argument as follows:[14]

$$\omega^* = \frac{IR}{2\lambda}$$

where ω^* equals the optimal level of portfolio residual risk given the manager's information ratio and the investor's level of risk aversion, λ. Increases in the manager's *IR* will increase the investor's optimal level of residual risk and increases in the investor's risk-aversion level will reduce it.

Exhibit 7 illustrates some of the trade-offs between residual risk and excess return for three levels of investor aversion to residual risk and two levels of manager skill. Here the straight lines represent the hypothetical continuum of portfolios (defined by their residual risks and excess returns) that could be offered

[14] Grinold and Kahn, *op. cit.*

by a highly skilled manager with an *IR* of 1.0 and a good manager with an *IR* of 0.5.[15] The points H, M, and L represent the optimal portfolios for investors with high, medium, and low aversions to residual risk. The point at the origin, P, with zero excess return and zero residual risk, may be taken to be a passive strategy offering a return and a risk level identical to the benchmark's.

Several important observations can be made from Exhibit 7. First, it is apparent that greater tolerance for risk (a lower risk aversion level) allows the investor to choose a portfolio with a higher risk level that can offer a higher expected return. Second, the more highly skilled the manager, the higher the optimal level of portfolio residual risk, and the higher the portfolio's expected excess return, whatever the investor's risk-aversion level. In short, higher excess returns accrue to higher-risk portfolios and to higher-*IR* managers.

Exhibit 7: Risk and Return Change with Investor Risk and Manager Skill

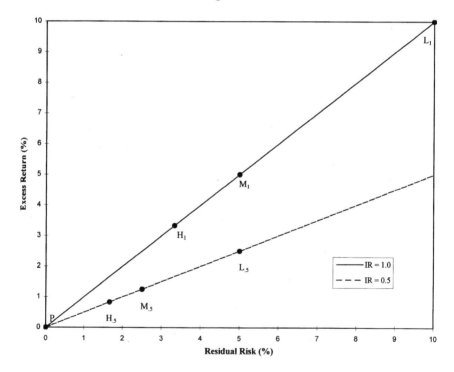

---

[15] In reality, no manager will offer a strategy for each possible risk/return combination. Furthermore, although *IR* is a linear function of residual risk when liquidity is unlimited and short selling unrestricted, in the real world *IR* will begin to decline at high levels of residual risk.

Exhibit 8: Sacrifice in Return from Overestimating Investor Risk Aversion

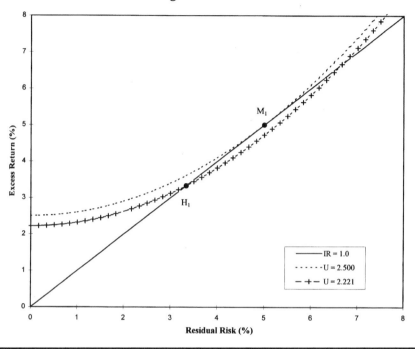

Within this framework, an investor who takes less than the optimal level of residual risk or who selects less than the best manager will sacrifice return.[16] Exhibit 8, for example, shows the decrease in return and utility (U) that results when an investor overestimates risk aversion. Here, an investor with a highly skilled manager, who actually has a medium level of risk aversion (M_1), chooses a portfolio suitable for an investor with a high level of risk aversion (H_1). The investor give-up in return can be measured as the vertical distance between M_1 and H_1. In somewhat more sophisticated terms, the higher-risk portfolio corresponds to a certainty-equivalent return of 2.500% and the less risky portfolio to a certainty-equivalent return of 2.221%, so the investor who overestimates his or her level of risk aversion and therefore chooses a suboptimal portfolio sacrifices 0.279 percentage points.

Exhibit 9 illustrates the return give-up that results when an investor with medium risk aversion uses a less skilled manager (*IR* of 0.5) rather than a higher-skill manager (*IR* of 1.0). Here the give-up in certainty-equivalent return between portfolio M_1 and portfolio $M_{.5}$ amounts to 1.875 percentage points. Choice of manager can significantly affect portfolio return.

---

[16] See also Bruce I. Jacobs and Kenneth N. Levy, "Residual Risk: How Much is Too Much?" *Journal of Portfolio Management* (Spring 1996).

Exhibit 9: Sacrifice in Return from
Using Less Skillful Manager

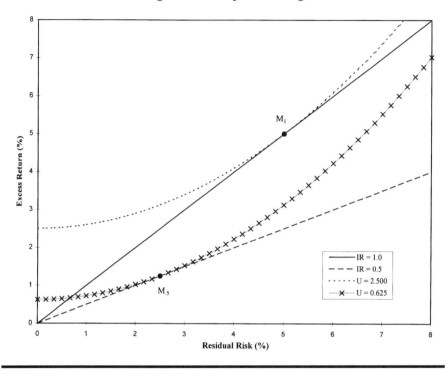

Suppose an investor finds a highly skilled manager (IR = 1), but that manager does not offer a portfolio with a risk level low enough to suit the investor's high level of risk aversion. A less skilled (IR = 0.5) manager, however, offers portfolios $H_{.5}$ and $M_{.5}$, which do provide about the right level of residual risk for this investor.

The investor might try to convince the IR = 1 manager to offer a lower-risk portfolio. If that fails, however, is the investor constrained to go with the less skilled manager? No. The investor can instead combine the highly skilled manager's H_1 portfolio with an investment in the passive benchmark portfolio P, reducing risk and return along the IR = 1 manager frontier. Such combination portfolios will offer a higher return than the portfolios of the less skilled manager, at a level of residual risk the investor can live with.

Finally, the manager's investment approach may affect the investor's optimal level of portfolio risk. Because engineered strategies control portfolio systematic and residual risk relative to the benchmark and take only compensated risks, they offer more assurance than traditional active strategies of achieving a return commensurate with the risk taken. Investors may feel more comfortable taking more risk with engineered portfolios, where risk and expected return are rigorously and explicitly assessed, than with traditional active portfolios.

THE ULTIMATE OBJECTIVE

The ultimate objective of investment management, of course, is to establish an investment structure that will, in the aggregate and over time, provide a return that compensates for the risk incurred, where the risk incurred is consistent with the investor's risk tolerance. The objective may be the equity market's return at the market's risk level or the market return plus incremental returns commensurate with incremental risks incurred.

This may be accomplished by focusing on the core universe and a passive representation or by mixing universes (core and static subsets, for example) and approaches (e.g., passive with traditional active or engineered). Whatever the selection universe and investment approach chosen, success is more likely when investors start off knowing their risk-tolerance levels and their potential managers' skill levels. The goal is to take no more risk than is compensated by expected return, but to take as much risk as risk-aversion level and manager skill allow.

Success is also more likely when equity market architecture is taken into account. Without explicit ties between portfolios and the underlying market or market subsets (and thus between market subsets and the overall market), managers may be tempted to stray from their "fold" (core, value, or growth investing, say) in search of return. If value stocks are being punished, for example, an undisciplined value manager may be tempted to "poach" return from growth stock territory. An investor utilizing this manager cannot expect performance consistent with value stocks in general, nor can the investor combine this manager's "value" portfolio with a growth portfolio in the hopes of achieving an overall market return; the portfolio will instead be overweighted in growth stocks, and susceptible to the risk of growth stocks falling out of favor. The investor can mitigate the problem by balancing non-benchmark-constrained, traditional portfolios with engineered or passive portfolios that offer benchmark-accountability.

When investors set goals in terms of return only, with no regard to equity architecture, similar problems can arise. Consider an investor who hires active managers and instructs them to "make money," with no regard to market sector or investment approach. Manager holdings may overlap to an extent that the overall portfolio becomes overdiversified and individual manager efforts are diluted. The investor may end up paying active fees and active transaction costs for essentially passive results.

Equity architecture provides a basic blueprint for relating equity investment choices to their potential rewards and their risks. It can help investors construct portfolios that will meet their needs. First, however, the investor must determine what those needs are in terms of desire for return and tolerance for risk.

Then the investor can choose managers whose investment approaches and market focuses offer, overall, the greatest assurance of fulfilling those needs.

We believe that engineered management can provide the best match between client risk-return goals and investment results. An engineered approach that combines range with depth of inquiry can increase both the number and goodness of investment insights. As a result, engineered management offers better control of risk exposure than traditional active management and incremental returns relative to passive management, whether the selection universe is core equity, static style subsets, or dynamic style subsets.

Chapter 2

Investment Analysis: Profiting from a Complex Equity Market

Bruce I. Jacobs, Ph.D.
Principal
Jacobs Levy Equity Management

Kenneth N. Levy, CFA
Principal
Jacobs Levy Equity Management

INTRODUCTION

Scientists classify systems into three types — ordered, random, and complex. Ordered systems, such as the structure of diamond crystals or the dynamics of pendulums, are definable and predictable by relatively simple rules and can be modeled using a relatively small number of variables. Random systems like the Brownian motion of gas molecules or white noise (static) are unordered; they are the product of a large number of variables. Their behavior cannot be modeled and is inherently unpredictable.

Complex systems like the weather and the workings of DNA fall somewhere between the domains of order and randomness. Their behavior can be at least partly comprehended and modeled, but only with great difficulty. The number of variables that must be modeled, and their interactions, are beyond the capacity of the human mind alone. Only with the aid of advanced computational science can the mysteries of complex systems be unraveled.[1]

The stock market is a complex system.[2] Stock prices are not completely random, as the efficient market hypothesis and random walk theory would have it.

---

[1] See, for example, Heinz Pagels, *The Dreams of Reason: The Computer and the Rise of the Sciences of Complexity* (New York, NY: Simon and Schuster, 1988).

[2] See, for example, Bruce I. Jacobs and Kenneth N. Levy, "The Complexity of the Stock Market," *Journal of Portfolio Management* (Fall 1989).

The authors thank Judith Kimball for her editorial assistance.

Some price movements can be predicted, and with some consistency. But nor is stock price behavior ordered. It cannot be successfully modeled by simple rules or screens such as low price/earnings ratios or even elegant theories such as the Capital Asset Pricing Model or Arbitrage Pricing Theory. Rather, stock price behavior is permeated by a complex web of interrelated return effects. A model of the market that is complex enough to disentangle these effects provides opportunities for modeling price behavior and predicting returns.

This chapter describes one such model, and its application to the stock selection, portfolio construction, and performance evaluation problems. We begin with the very basic question of how one should approach the equity market. Should one attempt to cover the broadest possible range of stocks, or can greater analytical insights be garnered by focusing on a particular subset of the market or a limited number of stocks? As we will see, each approach has its advantages and disadvantages. Combining the two, however, may offer the best promise of finding the key to market complexity and unlocking investment opportunity.

AN INTEGRATED APPROACH TO A SEGMENTED MARKET

While one might think that U.S. equity markets are fluid and fully integrated, in reality there exist barriers to the free flow of capital. Some of these barriers are self-imposed by investors. Others are imposed by regulatory and tax authorities or by client guidelines.

Some funds, for example, are prohibited by regulation or internal policy guidelines from buying certain types of stock — non-dividend-paying stock, or stock below a given capitalization level. Tax laws, too, may effectively lock investors into positions they would otherwise trade. Such barriers to the free flow of capital foster market segmentation.

Other barriers are self-imposed. Traditionally, for example, managers have focused (whether by design or default) on distinct approaches to stock selection. Value managers have concentrated on buying stocks selling at prices perceived to be low relative to the company's assets or earnings. Growth managers have sought stocks with above-average earnings growth not fully reflected in price. Small-capitalization managers have searched for opportunity in stocks that have been overlooked by most investors. The stocks that constitute the natural selection pools for these managers tend to group into distinct market segments.

Client preferences encourage this Balkanization of the market. Some investors, for example, prefer to buy value stocks, while others seek growth stocks; some invest in both, but hire separate managers for each segment. Both institutional and individual investors generally demonstrate a reluctance to upset the apple cart by changing allocations to previously selected "style" managers. Several periods of underperformance, however, may undermine this loyalty and motivate a flow of capital from one segment of the market to another (often just as the out-of-favor segment begins to benefit from a reversion of returns back up to their historical mean).

In the past few decades, a market segmented into style groupings has been formalized by the actions of investment consultants. Consultants have designed style indexes that define the constituent stocks of these segments and have defined managers in terms of their proclivity for one segment or another. As a manager's performance is measured against the given style index, managers who stray too far from index territory are taking on extra risk. Consequently, managers tend to stick close to their style "homes," reinforcing market segmentation.

An investment approach that focuses on individual market segments can have its advantages. Such an approach recognizes, for example, that the U.S. equity market is neither entirely homogeneous nor entirely heterogeneous. All stocks do not react alike to a given impetus, but nor does each stock exhibit its own, totally idiosyncratic price behavior. Rather, stocks within a given style, or sector, or industry tend to behave similarly to each other and somewhat differently from stocks outside their group.

An approach to stock selection that specializes in one market segment can optimize the application of talent and maximize the potential for outperformance. This is most likely true for traditional, fundamental analysis. The in-depth, labor-intensive research undertaken by traditional analysts can become positively ungainly without some focusing lens.

An investment approach that focuses on the individual segments of the market, however, presents some severe theoretical and practical problems. Such an approach may be especially disadvantaged when it ignores the many forces that work to integrate, rather than segment, the market.

Many managers, for example, do not specialize in a particular market segment but are free to choose the most attractive securities from a broad universe of stocks. Others, such as style rotators, may focus on a particular type of stock, given current economic conditions, but be poised to change their focus should conditions change. Such managers make for capital flows and price arbitrage across the boundaries of particular segments.

Furthermore, all stocks can be defined by the same fundamental parameters — by market capitalization, price/earnings ratio, dividend discount model ranking, and so on. All stocks can be found at some level on the continuum of values for each parameter. Thus growth and value stocks inhabit the opposite ends of the continuums of P/E and dividend yield, and small and large stocks the opposite ends of the continuums of firm capitalization and analyst coverage.

As the values of the parameters for any individual stock change, so too does the stock's position on the continuum. An out-of-favor growth stock may slip into value territory. A small-cap company may grow into the large-cap range.

Finally, while the values of these parameters vary across stocks belonging to different market segments — different styles, sectors, and industries — and while investors may favor certain values — low P/E, say, in preference to high P/E — arbitrage tends to counterbalance too pronounced a predilection on the part of investors for any one set of values. In equilibrium, all stocks must be owned. If too many investors want low P/E, low-P/E stocks will be bid up to higher P/E levels, and some investors will step in to sell them and buy other stocks deserving of higher P/Es. Arbitrage works toward market integration and a single pricing mechanism.

A market that is neither completely segmented nor completely integrated is a complex market. A complex market calls for an investment approach that is 180 degrees removed from the narrow, segment-oriented focus of traditional management. It requires a complex, unified approach that takes into account the behavior of stocks across the broadest possible selection universe, without losing sight of the significant differences in price behavior that distinguish particular market segments.

Such an approach offers three major advantages. First, it provides a coherent evaluation framework. Second, it can benefit from all the insights to be garnered from a wide and diverse range of securities. Third, because it has both breadth of coverage and depth of analysis, it is poised to take advantage of more profit opportunities than a more narrowly defined, segmented approach proffers.[3]

A COHERENT FRAMEWORK

To the extent that the market is integrated, an investment approach that models each industry or style segment as if it were a universe unto itself is not the best approach. Consider, for example, a firm that offers both core and value strategies. Suppose the firm runs a model on its total universe of, say, 3000 stocks. It then runs the same model or a different, segment-specific model on a 500-stock subset of large-cap value stocks.

If different models are used for each strategy, the results will differ. Even if the same model is estimated separately for each strategy, its results will differ because the model coefficients are bound to differ between the broader universe and the narrower segment. What if the core model predicts GM will outperform Ford, while the value model shows the reverse? Should the investor start the day with multiple estimates of one stock's alpha? This would violate what we call the "Law of One Alpha."[4]

Of course, the firm could ensure coherence by using separate models for each market segment — growth, value, small-cap — and linking the results via a single, overarching model that relates all the subsets. But the firm then runs into a second problem with segmented investment approaches: To the extent that the market is integrated, the pricing of securities in one segment may contain information relevant to pricing in other segments.

For example, within a generally well integrated national economy, labor market conditions in the U.S. differ region by region. An economist attempting to

---

[3] See, for example, Bruce I. Jacobs and Kenneth N. Levy, "Engineering Portfolios: A Unified Approach," *Journal of Investing* (Winter 1995).

[4] See Bruce I. Jacobs and Kenneth N. Levy, "The Law of One Alpha," *Journal of Portfolio Management* (Summer 1995).

model employment in the Northeast would probably consider economic expansion in the Southeast. Similarly, the investor who wants to model growth stocks should not ignore value stocks. The effects of inflation, say, on value stocks may have repercussions for growth stocks; after all, the two segments represent opposite ends of the same P/E continuum.

An investment approach that concentrates on a single market segment does not make use of all available information. A complex, unified approach considers all the stocks in the universe — value and growth, large and small. It thus benefits from all the information to be gleaned from a broad range of stock price behavior.

Of course, an increase in breadth of inquiry will not benefit the investor if it comes at the sacrifice of depth of inquiry. A complex approach does not ignore the significant differences across different types of stock, differences exploitable by specialized investing. What's more, in examining similarities and differences across market segments, it considers numerous variables that may be considered to be defining.

For value, say, a complex approach does not confine itself to a dividend discount model measure of value, but examines also earnings, cash flow, sales, and yield value, among other attributes. Growth measurements to be considered include historical, expected, and sustainable growth, as well as the momentum and stability of earnings. Share price, volatility, and analyst coverage are among the elements to be considered along with market capitalization as measures of size.[5]

These variables are often closely correlated with each other. Small-cap stocks, for example, tend to have low P/Es; low P/E is correlated with high yield; both low P/E and high yield are correlated with DDM estimates of value. Furthermore, they may be correlated with a stock's industry affiliation. A simple low-P/E screen, for example, will tend to select a large number of bank and utility stocks. Such correlations can distort naive attempts to relate returns to potentially relevant variables. A true picture of the variable-return relationship emerges only after "disentangling" the variables.

DISENTANGLING

The effects of different sources of stock return can overlap. In Exhibit 1, the lines represent connections documented by academic studies; they may appear like a ball of yarn after the cat got to it. To unravel the connections between variables and return, it is necessary to examine all the variables simultaneously.

---

[5] At a deeper level of complexity, one must also consider alternative ways of specifying such fundamental variables as earnings or cash flow. Over what period does one measure earnings, for example? If using analyst earnings expectations, which measure provides the best estimate of future real earnings? The consensus of all available estimates made over the past six months? Only the very latest earnings estimates? Are some analysts more accurate or more influential? What if a recent estimate is not available for a given company? See Bruce I. Jacobs, Kenneth N. Levy, and Mitchell C. Krask, "Earnings Estimates, Predictor Specification, and Measurement Error," *Journal of Investing* (Summer 1997), pp. 29-46.

Exhibit 1: Return Effects Form a Tangled Web

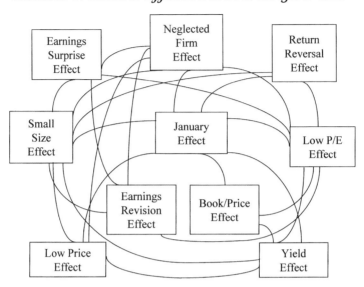

For instance, the low-P/E effect is widely recognized, as is the small-size effect. But stocks with low P/Es also tend to be of small size. Are P/E and size merely two ways of looking at the same effect? Or does each variable matter? Perhaps the excess returns to small-cap stocks are merely a January effect, reflecting the tendency of taxable investors to sell depressed stocks at year-end. Answering these questions requires disentangling return effects via multivariate regression.[6]

Common methods of measuring return effects (such as quintiling or univariate — single-variable — regression) are "naive" because they assume, naively, that prices are responding only to the single variable under consideration — low P/E, say. But a number of related variables may be affecting returns. As we have noted, small-cap stocks and banking and utility industry stocks tend to have low P/Es. A univariate regression of return on low P/E will capture, along with the effect of P/E, a great deal of "noise" related to firm size, industry affiliation and other variables.

Simultaneous analysis of all relevant variables via multivariate regression takes into account and adjusts for such interrelationships. The result is the return to each variable separately, controlling for all related variables. A multivariate analysis for low P/E, for example, will provide a measure of the excess return to a portfolio that is market-like in all respects except for having a lower-than-average P/E ratio. Disentangled returns are "pure" returns.

[6] See Bruce I. Jacobs and Kenneth N. Levy, "Disentangling Equity Return Regularities: New Insights and Investment Opportunities," *Financial Analysts Journal* (May/June 1988).

Exhibit 2: Naive and Pure Returns to High Book-to-Price Ratio

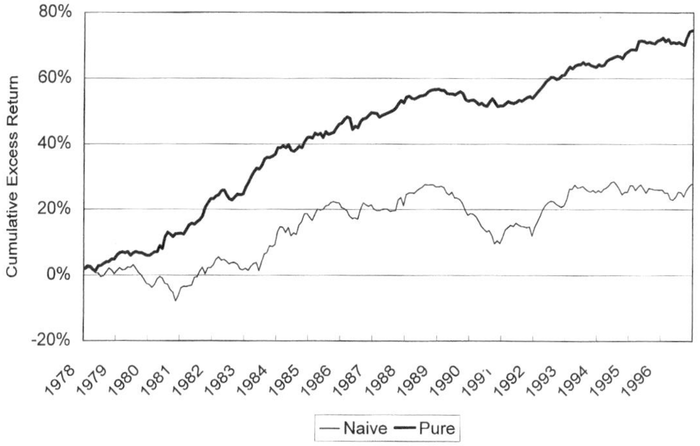

Noise Reduction

Exhibit 2 plots naive and pure cumulative excess (relative to a 3,000-stock universe) returns to high book-to-price ratio.[7] The naive returns show a great deal of volatility; the pure returns, by contrast, follow a much smoother path. There is a lot of noise in the naive returns. What causes it?

Notice the divergence between the naive and pure return series for the 12 months starting in March 1979. This date coincides with the crisis at Three Mile Island nuclear power plant. Utilities such as GPU, operator of the Three Mile Island power plant, tend to have high-B/Ps, and naive B/P measures will reflect the performance of these utilities along with the performance of other high-B/P stocks. Electric utility prices plummeted 24% after the Three Mile Island crisis. The naive B/P measure reflects this decline.

But industry-related events such as Three Mile Island have no necessary bearing on the book/price variable. An investor could, for example, hold a high-B/P portfolio that does not overweight utilities, and such a portfolio would not have experienced the decline reflected in the naive B/P measure in Exhibit 2. The naive returns to B/P reflect noise from the inclusion of a utility industry effect. A pure B/P measure is not contaminated by such irrelevant variables.

Disentangling distinguishes real effects from mere proxies and thereby distinguishes between real and spurious investment opportunities. As it separates high B/P and industry affiliation, for example, it can also separate the effects of firm size from the effects of related variables. Disentangling shows that returns to small firms in January are not abnormal; the apparent January seasonal merely proxies for

---

[7] In particular, naive and pure returns are provided by a portfolio having a book-to-price ratio that is one standard deviation above the universe mean book-to-price ratio. For pure returns, the portfolio is also constrained to have universe-average exposures to all the other variables in the model, including fundamental characteristics and industry affiliations.

year-end tax-loss selling.[8] Not all small firms will benefit from a January rebound; indiscriminately buying small firms at the turn of the year is not an optimal investment strategy. Ascertaining true causation leads to more profitable strategies.

Return Revelation

Disentangling can reveal hidden opportunities. Exhibit 3 plots the naively measured cumulative excess returns (relative to the 3,000-stock universe) to portfolios that rank lower than normal in market capitalization and price per share and higher than normal in terms of analyst neglect.[9] These results derive from monthly univariate regressions. The "small-cap" line thus represents the cumulative excess returns to a portfolio of stocks naively chosen on the basis of their size, with no attempt made to control for other variables.

 All three return series move together. The similarity between the small-cap and neglect series is particularly striking. This is confirmed by the correlation coefficients in the first column of Exhibit 4. Furthermore, all series show a great deal of volatility within a broader up, down, up pattern.

Exhibit 3: Naive Returns Can Hide Opportunities: Three Size-Related Variables

Exhibit 4: Correlations between Monthly Returns to Size-Related Variables*

Variable	Naive	Pure
Small Cap/Low Price	0.82	−0.12
Small Cap/Neglect	0.87	−0.22
Neglect/Low Price	0.66	−0.11

* A coefficient of 0.14 is significant at the 5% level.

[8] See Bruce I. Jacobs and Kenneth N. Levy, "Calendar Anomalies: Abnormal Returns at Calendar Turning Points," *Financial Analysts Journal* (November/December 1988).
[9] Again, portfolios with values of these parameters that are, on average, one standard deviation away from the universe mean.

Exhibit 5: Pure Returns Can Reveal Opportunities: Three Size-Related Variables

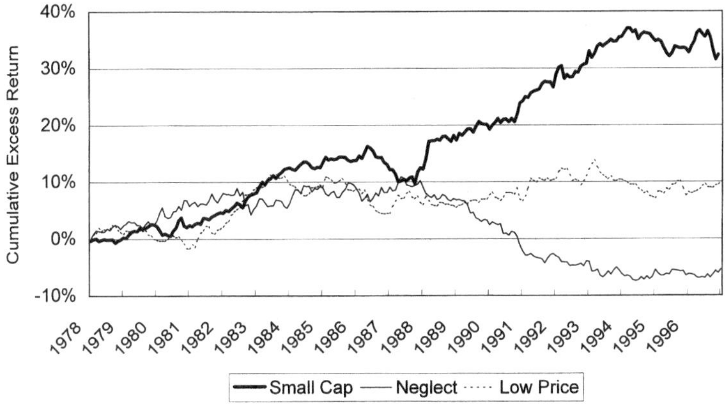

Exhibit 5 shows the pure cumulative excess returns to each size-related attribute over the period. These disentangled returns adjust for correlations not only between the three size variables, but also between each size variable and industry affiliations and each variable and growth and value characteristics. Two findings are immediately apparent from Exhibit 5.

First, pure returns to the size variables do not appear to be nearly as closely correlated as the naive returns displayed in Exhibit 3. In fact, over the second half of the period, the three return series diverge substantially. This is confirmed by the correlation coefficients in the second column of Exhibit 4.

In particular, pure returns to small capitalization accumulate quite a gain over the period; they are up 30%, versus an only 20% gain for the naive returns to small cap. Purifying returns reveals a profit opportunity not apparent in the naive returns. Furthermore, pure returns to analyst neglect amount to a substantial loss over the period. Because disentangling controls for proxy effects, and thereby avoids redundancies, these pure return effects are additive. A portfolio could have aimed for superior returns by selecting small-cap stocks with a higher-than-average analyst following (i.e., a negative exposure to analyst neglect).

Second, the pure returns appear to be much less volatile than the naive returns. The naive returns in Exhibit 3 display much month-to-month volatility within their more general trends. By contrast, the pure series in Exhibit 5 are much smoother and more consistent. This is confirmed by the standard deviations given in Exhibit 6.

The pure returns in Exhibit 5 are smoother and more consistent than the naive return responses in Exhibit 3 because the pure returns capture more "signal" and less noise. And because they are smoother and more consistent than naive returns, pure returns are also more predictable.

Exhibit 6: Pure Returns are Less Volatile, More Predictable: Standard Deviations of Monthly Returns to Size-Related Variables*

Variable	Naive	Pure
Small Cap	0.87	0.60
Neglect	0.87	0.67
Low Price	1.03	0.58

* All differences between naive and pure return standard deviations are significant at the 1% level.

Exhibit 7: Market Sensitivities of Monthly Returns to Value-Related Variables

Variable	Naive	(t-stat.)	Pure	(t-stat.)
DDM	0.06	(5.4)	0.04	(5.6)
B/P	−0.10	(−6.2)	−0.01	(−0.8)
Yield	−0.08	(−7.4)	−0.03	(−3.5)

Predictability

Disentangling improves return predictability by providing a clearer picture of the relationship between stock price behavior, fundamental variables, and macroeconomic conditions. For example, investors often prefer value stocks in bearish market environments, because growth stocks are priced more on the basis of high expectations, which get dashed in more pessimistic eras. But the success of such a strategy will depend on the variables one has chosen to define value.

Exhibit 7 displays the results of regressing both naive and pure returns to various value-related variables on market (S&P 500) returns over the 1978-1996 period. The results indicate that DDM value is a poor indicator of a stock's ability to withstand a tide of receding market prices. The regression coefficient in the first column indicates that a portfolio with a one-standard-deviation exposure to DDM value will tend to outperform by 0.06% when the market rises by 1.00% and to underperform by a similar margin when the market falls by 1.00%. The coefficient for pure returns to DDM is similar. Whether their returns are measured in pure or naive form, stocks with high DDM values tend to behave procyclically.

High book-to-price ratio appears to be a better indicator of a defensive stock. It has a regression coefficient of −0.10 in naive form. In pure form, however, B/P is virtually uncorrelated with market movements; pure B/P signals neither an aggressive nor a defensive stock. B/P as naively measured apparently picks up the effects of truly defensive variables — such as high yield.

The value investor in search of a defensive posture in uncertain market climates should consider moving toward high yield. The regression coefficients for both naive and pure returns to high yield indicate significant negative market sensitivities. Stocks with high yields may be expected to lag in up markets but to hold up relatively well during general market declines.

Exhibit 8: Forecast Response of Small Size to Macroeconomic Shocks

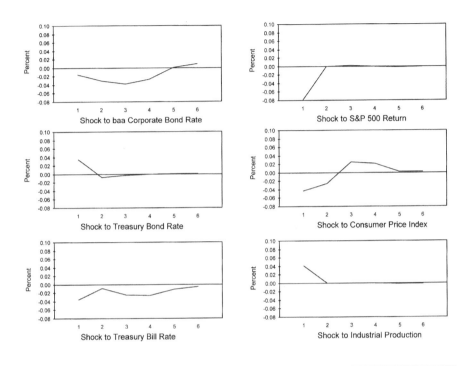

These results make broad intuitive sense. DDM is forward-looking, relying on estimates of future earnings. In bull markets, investors take a long-term outlook, so DDM explains security pricing behavior. In bear markets, however, investors become myopic; they prefer today's tangible income to tomorrow's promise. Current yield is rewarded.[10]

Pure returns respond in intuitively satisfying ways to macroeconomic events. Exhibit 8 illustrates, as an example, the estimated effects of changes in various macroeconomic variables on the pure returns to small size (as measured by market capitalization). Consistent with the capital constraints on small firms and their relatively greater sensitivity to the economy, pure returns to small size may be expected to be negative in the first four months following an unexpected increase in the BAA corporate rate and positive in the first month following an unexpected increase in industrial production.[11] Investors can exploit such predict-

[10] See also Bruce I. Jacobs and Kenneth N. Levy, "On the Value of 'Value'," *Financial Analysts Journal* (July/August 1988).
[11] See Bruce I. Jacobs and Kenneth N. Levy, "Forecasting the Size Effect," *Financial Analysts Journal* (May/June 1989).

able behavior by moving into and out of the small-cap market segment as economic conditions evolve.[12]

These examples serve to illustrate that the use of numerous, finely defined fundamental variables can provide a rich representation of the complexity of security pricing. The model can be even more finely tuned, however, by including variables that capture such subtleties as the effects of investor psychology, possible nonlinearities in variable-return relationships, and security transaction costs.

Additional Complexities

In considering possible variables for inclusion in a model of stock price behavior, the investor should recognize that pure stock returns are driven by a combination of economic fundamentals and investor psychology. That is, economic fundamentals such as interest rates, industrial production, and inflation can explain much, but by no means all, of the systematic variation in returns. Psychology, including investors' tendency to overreact, their desire to seek safety in numbers, and their selective memories, also plays a role in security pricing.

What's more, the modeler should realize that the effects of different variables, fundamental and otherwise, can differ across different types of stocks. The value sector, for example, includes more financial stocks than the growth sector. Investors may thus expect value stocks in general to be more sensitive than growth stocks to changes in interest rate spreads.

Psychologically based variables such as short-term overreaction and price correction also seem to have a stronger effect on value than on growth stocks. Earnings surprises and earnings estimate revisions, by contrast, appear to be more important for growth than for value stocks. Thus Intel shares can take a nose dive when earnings come in a penny under expectations, whereas Ford shares remain unmoved even by fairly substantial departures of actual earnings from expectations.

The relationship between stock returns and relevant variables may not be linear. The effects of positive earnings surprises, for instance, tend to be arbitraged away quickly; thus positive earnings surprises offer less opportunity for the investor. The effects of negative earnings surprises, however, appear to be more long-lasting. This nonlinearity may reflect the fact that sales of stock are limited to those investors who already own the stock (and to a relatively small number of short-sellers).[13]

Risk-variable relationships may also differ across different types of stock. In particular, small-cap stocks generally have more idiosyncratic risk than large-cap stocks. Diversification is thus more important for small-stock than for large-stock portfolios.

---

[12] See, for example, Bruce I. Jacobs and Kenneth N. Levy, "High-Definition Style Rotation," *Journal of Investing* (Fall 1996), pp. 14-23.

[13] See Bruce I. Jacobs and Kenneth N. Levy, "Long/Short Equity Investing," *Journal of Portfolio Management* (Fall 1993).

Return-variable relationships can also change over time. Recall the difference between DDM and yield value measures: high-DDM stocks tend to have high returns in bull markets and low returns in bear markets; high-yield stocks experience the reverse. For consistency of performance, return modeling must consider the effects of market dynamics — the changing nature of the overall market.

The investor may also want to decipher the informational signals generated by "informed agents." Corporate decisions to issue or buy back shares, split stock, or initiate or suspend dividends, for example, may contain valuable information about company prospects. So, too, may insiders' (legal) trading in their own firms' shares.

Finally, a complex model containing multiple variables is likely to turn up a number of promising return-variable relationships. But are these perceived profit opportunities translatable into real economic opportunities? Are some too ephemeral? Too small to survive frictions such as trading costs? Estimates of expected returns must be combined with estimates of the costs of trading to arrive at realistic returns net of trading costs.

CONSTRUCTING, TRADING, AND EVALUATING PORTFOLIOS

To maximize implementation of the model's insights, the portfolio construction process should consider exactly the same dimensions found relevant by the stock selection model. Failure to do so can lead to mismatches between model insights and portfolio exposures.

Consider a commercially available portfolio optimizer that recognizes only a subset of the variables in the valuation model. Risk reduction using such an optimizer will reduce the portfolio's exposures only along the dimensions the optimizer recognizes. As a result, the portfolio is likely to wind up more exposed to those variables recognized by the model — but not the optimizer — and less exposed to those variables common to both the model and the optimizer.

Imagine an investor who seeks low-P/E stocks that analysts are recommending for purchase, but who uses a commercial optimizer that incorporates a P/E factor but not analyst recommendations. The investor is likely to wind up with a portfolio that has a less than optimal level of exposure to low P/E and a greater than optimal level of exposure to analyst purchase recommendations. Optimization using all relevant variables ensures a portfolio whose risk and return opportunities are balanced in accordance with the model's insights. Furthermore, the use of more numerous variables allows portfolio risk to be more finely tuned.

Insofar as the investment process — both stock selection and portfolio construction — is model-driven, it is more adaptable to electronic trading venues. This should benefit the investor in several ways. First, electronic trading is generally less costly, with lower commissions, market impact, and opportunity costs.

Second, it allows real-time monitoring, which can further reduce trading costs. Third, an automated trading system can take account of more factors, including the urgency of a particular trade and market conditions, than individual traders can be expected to bear in mind.

Finally, the performance attribution process should be congruent with the dimensions of the selection model (and portfolio optimizer). Insofar as performance attribution identifies sources of return, a process that considers all the sources identified by the selection model will be more insightful than a commercial performance attribution system applied in a "one-size-fits-all" manner. Our investor who has sought exposure to low P/E and positive analyst recommendations, for example, will want to know how each of these factors has paid off and will be less interested in the returns to factors that are not a part of the stock selection process.

A performance evaluation process tailored to the model also functions as a monitor of the model's reliability. Has portfolio performance supported the model's insights? Should some be reexamined? Equally important, does the model's reliability hold up over time? A model that performs well in today's economic and market environments may not necessarily perform well in the future. A feedback loop between the evaluation and the research/modeling processes can help ensure that the model retains robustness over time.

PROFITING FROM COMPLEXITY

It has been said that: "For every complex problem, there is a simple solution, and it is almost always wrong."[14] For complex problems more often than not require complex solutions.

A complex approach to stock selection, portfolio construction, and performance evaluation is needed to capture the complexities of the stock market. Such an approach combines the breadth of coverage and the depth of analysis needed to maximize investment opportunity and potential reward.

Grinold and Kahn present a formula that identifies the relationships between the depth and breadth of investment insights and investment performance:

$$IR = IC \times \sqrt{BR}$$

IR is the manager's information ratio, a measure of the success of the investment process. *IR* equals annualized excess return over annualized residual risk (e.g., 2% excess return with 4% tracking error provides 0.5 *IR*). *IC*, the information coefficient, or correlation between predicted and actual results, measures the goodness of the manager's insights, or the manager's skill. *BR* is the breadth of

---

[14] Attributed to H.L. Mencken.

the strategy, measurable as the number of independent insights upon which investment decisions are made.[15]

One can increase *IR* by increasing *IC* or *BR*. Increasing *IC* means coming up with some means of improving predictive accuracy. Increasing *BR* means coming up with more "investable" insights. A casino analogy may be apt (if anathema to prudent investors).

A gambler can seek to increase *IC* by card-counting in blackjack or by building a computer model to predict probable roulette outcomes. Similarly, some investors seek to outperform by concentrating their research efforts on a few stocks: by learning all there is to know about Microsoft, for example, one may be able to outperform all the other investors who follow this stock. But a strategy that makes a few concentrated stock bets is likely to produce consistent performance only if it is based on a very high level of skill, or if it benefits from extraordinary luck.

Alternatively, an investor can place a larger number of smaller stock bets and settle for more modest returns from a greater number of investment decisions. That is, rather than behaving like a gambler in a casino, the investor can behave like the casino. A casino has only a slight edge on any spin of the roulette wheel or roll of the dice, but many spins of many roulette wheels can result in a very consistent profit for the house. Over time, the odds will strongly favor the casino over the gambler.

A complex approach to the equity market, one that has both breadth of inquiry and depth of focus, can enhance the number and the goodness of investment insights. A complex approach to the equity market requires more time, effort, and ability, but it will be better positioned to capture the complexities of security pricing. The rewards are worth the effort.

---

[15] Richard C. Grinold and Ronald N. Kahn, *Active Portfolio Management* (Chicago, IL: Probus, 1995).

Chapter 3

The Active versus Passive Debate: Perspectives of an Active Quant

Robert C. Jones, CFA
Managing Director
Goldman Sachs Asset Management

INTRODUCTION

Active or passive? Passive or active? The debate rages on. Proponents of indexing cite theory and mountains of evidence: the average active manager has simply not outperformed the S&P 500 on a consistent basis. Still the vast majority of equity assets are managed actively: investors seem to believe that they, or at least their chosen agents, can earn risk-adjusted excess returns. This chapter examines both sides of the issue. We use behavioral analysis and empirical evidence to argue that the theoretical basis for indexing is weak, yet the performance of active managers is weaker still. We end up with something of a paradox: investor behavior argues against *both* market efficiency *and* active management. Our solution to this dilemma is to follow an objective, disciplined and risk-controlled approach to active management.

We begin by presenting the case for passive investing, which is based on both financial theory and the historical performance of active managers. We then lay out the case against efficient markets (and, by implication, passive investing), using theoretical, behavioral and empirical arguments. We also discuss the failure of active managers to add value, and try to reconcile this failure with the case against market efficiency. This leads to some natural implications for ways to improve the active management process in the face of known behavioral tendencies and market inefficiencies. The chapter ends with a summary and some concluding remarks.

This chapter benefited from insightful comments from (and discussions with) Cliff Asness, Peter Bernstein, Kent Clark, Bob Krail, John Liew, and Diane Misra, among others. I would also like to thank Kent Clark, Jacques Friedman, Vinti Khanna, and Jason Segal for supplying much of the statistical analysis contained herein.

THE CASE FOR INDEXING

The case for indexing is based on both theory and empirical evidence. First we will discuss theory.

The Theoretical Case

The theoretical case for indexing boils down to this: Because markets are efficient, prices immediately, fully and correctly reflect all commonly-known information. Thus, the only way for active managers to add value is to use inside information, which is illegal. Since active managers can't beat the market, yet they charge fees and incur transactions costs, investors are better served by passive management (i.e., indexing). Below we outline the formal theory behind indexing in a bit more detail.

Assume the following: (1) investors are perfectly rationale (i.e., they develop expectations using Bayesian strategies), utility-maximizing agents with a shared set of homogeneous expectations; and (2) markets are "frictionless," meaning primarily that taxes and trading costs are inconsequential. In such a world, prices and expected returns will remain stable until new value-relevant information reaches the market, at which point investors will immediately alter their expectations to reflect this information, and prices will adjust accordingly. Thus, prices will only change in response to new, *unexpected* information. Since the arrival of unexpected information is essentially random, prices will follow a random walk, and returns will be normally distributed (i.e., the entire return distribution can be described by its mean and its standard deviation).

More than 40 years ago, Harry Markowitz[1] described how rational investors should create portfolios, given a set of return expectations, volatilities, and cross correlations. Markowitz showed that we can calculate an expected return and volatility measure for every possible portfolio, given the expected returns, volatilities, and cross correlations of the component stocks. His genius was in seeing that a stock's risk should be evaluated not in isolation, but in terms of its contribution to the risk of a diversified portfolio. From this, he derived the concept of an efficient frontier, which is depicted graphically in Exhibit 1. The efficient frontier is the set of portfolios that has the highest expected return at each level of risk — or, conversely, the lowest risk at each level of expected return. If investors are rational utility maximizers, and utility is defined in terms of risk and return, then all investors will hold portfolios along the efficient frontier depicted in Exhibit 1.

In the 1960s, Sharpe[2] and Lintner,[3] extended the original work of Markowitz and developed the Capital Asset Pricing Model (CAPM). If we assume

---

[1] Harry Markowitz, "Portfolio Selection," *Journal of Finance* (March 1952), pp. 77-91.
[2] William F. Sharpe, "Capital Asset Prices: A Theory of Market Equilibrium Under Conditions of Risk," *Journal of Finance* (September 1964), pp. 425-442.
[3] John Lintner, "The Valuation of Risk Assets and the Selection of Risky Investments in Stock Portfolios and Capital Bedgets," *Review of Economics and Statistics* (February 1965), pp. 13-37.

a risk-free asset (R_f), and costless borrowing and lending, then some combination of R_f and the tangency efficient portfolio (or TEP,[4] see Exhibit 2) will offer a better risk/reward trade-off, at every level of risk, than other points on the Markowitz efficient frontier. The straight line from R_f through TEP will therefore define a new efficient frontier, and all rational investors will hold some portfolio on that line (i.e., some combination of R_f and TEP). Since there is only one risky portfolio (namely, TEP) that is held by all rational investors, that portfolio must be "the market." Therefore, all rational investors will hold some combination of R_f and the market. This, in a nutshell, is the theoretical case for indexing.

Exhibit 1: The Markowitz Efficient Frontier

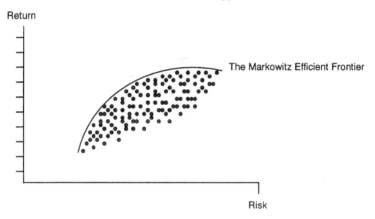

Exhibit 2: The CAPM Efficient Frontier

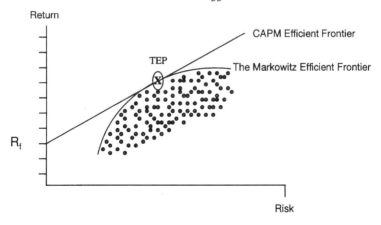

---

[4] The TEP concept was originally presented in James Tobin, "Liquidity Preference as Behavior Towards Risk," *Review of Economic Studies* (February 1958), pp. 65-86.

Exhibit 3: Median Large-Cap Fund versus the S&P 500 Index

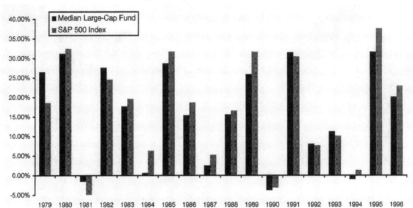

Exhibit 4: Actively Managed Mutual Funds versus the S&P 500 Index

	1979-1984	1985-1990	1991-1996	1979-1996
Percent of Funds that Outperformed	54.7%	12.3%	31.3%	30.9%
Median Fund Return	16.0%	13.6%	16.4%	15.4%
S&P 500 Return	15.4%	16.4%	17.6%	16.4%

The Empirical Evidence

Active managers themselves provide perhaps the most persuasive case for passive investing. Dozens of studies[5] have examined the performance of mutual funds and other professionally-managed assets, and virtually all of them have concluded that, on average, active managers underperform passive benchmarks. Exhibit 3 shows annual returns, from 1979 through 1996, for the median fund in the Lipper large-cap fund universe[6] and for the S&P 500 Index. The median active fund underperformed the passive index in 12 out of 18 years. Exhibit 4 show the percentage of funds that outperformed the S&P 500 over various time periods. Note that these returns are net of fees and expenses, but before taxes. Comparing after-tax returns would make the case for indexing even more compelling.[7] The bottom line is that, over most periods, the majority of mutual fund investors would have been better off investing in an S&P 500 Index fund.

---

[5] For a particularly thorough example, see Burton G. Malkiel, "Returns from Investing in Equity Mutual Funds, 1971 to 1991," *Journal of Finance* (June 1995), pp. 549-572.

[6] These include all funds in the Lipper "Growth" and "Growth and Income" categories.

[7] Since index funds follow a buy-and-hold strategy, realized capital gains are minimal compared to those of actively managed funds.

THE CASE AGAINST INDEXING

The case against indexing is based on (1) theoretical arguments; (2) empirical arguments; and, (3) behavioral arguments. We'll begin with theory.

Theoretical Arguments

The efficient market hypothesis (EMH) is based on a set of simplifying and unrealistic assumptions. Below we discuss how relaxing two of these assumption would impact the case for passive investing.

Assumptions

No Taxes or Trading Costs Assumption In the real world, taxes and trading costs are significant and variable, both through time and across investors. If one group of investors (e.g., pension funds) pays no taxes, while another group of investors (e.g., individuals) pays high taxes, they will have very different optimal portfolios. Individuals will avoid high-yielding stocks, and will delay realizing capital gains. Because of tax consequences, they may not trade even if new information produces a reasonably large change in (pretax) expected returns. Similarly, if one group of investors (e.g., dealers) has lower transactions costs, while another group (e.g., investors) has higher costs, they will respond differently to a small change in value-relevant information. If the change in expected return exceeds the dealers' trading costs, but is less than the investors' trading costs, then the former will trade while the latter will not. Note that all of the above observations will be true even if all four groups (i.e., pension funds, individuals, dealers, and investors) share the same expectations for nominal pre-tax risks and returns. Because of their varying circumstances, they will hold different optimal portfolios even if they share the same expectations. Thus, there is no single "market" portfolio that is optimal for all investors.

Of course passive investing may still be appropriate, even if there is no single optimal portfolio. Perhaps there is enough similarity among members of different groups, that each group could have its own optimal index, and all members of the group could passively hold the "group-optimal" portfolio. Ignoring the fact that no one has developed a set of indices targeted at different investor groups,[8] we believe that, in most cases, individual circumstances are so different that such a solution is impractical. The most obvious exception is tax-exempt pension funds, which is also the investor group that has been most receptive to passive investing.[9]

Homogenous Expectations Assumption In the EMH world, risk is defined by the uncertainty of events. But while events may be uncertain, *probabilities* are assumed to be known and agreed on by all investors. Thus, all investors share the same expectations for risk and return. In such a world, almost by tautology, prices

---

[8] We will return later to the inability of the EMH to describe how investors actually invest and behave.

[9] Of course, behaviorists would argue that pension funds embrace indexing to avoid the pain of "regret" that comes form picking a manager who underperforms the index.

will quickly and accurately reflect investors' shared expectations. But what if investors don't agree on the basic probabilities? What if investors who share the same information, but different models of how the world works, arrive at very different probabilities for the same outcome?

In the real world, heterogeneity rules. For example, although they share essentially the same information, different economic schools have radically different assessments for the likelihood that inflation will increase over the coming year. Keynesians see strong growth and low unemployment as signs that inflation is likely to increase. Monetarists and supply-siders see increasing production and stable money supply (i.e., more goods chased by the same number of dollars) as signs that inflation will remain stable or decline. Similarly, despite years of debate and numerous empirical studies (i.e., shared information), financial economists still can't agree on whether the market is efficient or not. Who is right? Nobody. All theories are imperfect models of reality that are wrong in ways that are both unknown and unknowable. The more important question is: who is "less wrong?" Those will be the investors whose forecasts will prove most accurate and profitable.

Even in a world of heterogeneous expectations, however, the "consensus" view can, on average, be more correct (or less wrong) than the various views of most investors. In such a world, passive investing (or accepting the consensus) may still be the best solution for *most* investors. But this does not mean that passive investing is optimal for *all* investors. Investors with a comparative advantage — e.g., better technology, better information, better analytic capabilities, and/or a better model of how the world works — should be able to outperform a passive benchmark. Of course, these investors need to be pretty darned sure that their information, technology, analysis, and/or models are actually better. If not, they will underperform the benchmark. This is the risk in active management.

Efficient Markets: A Catch-22?[10]

Our final theoretical argument against passive investing concerns the "catch-22 of market efficiency." In a perfectly efficient market, prices always equal fair values. There will be no profit opportunities from estimating fair values, and hence no incentive to gather and evaluate information. But if no one bothers to gather and evaluate information, how will prices come to reflect fair values? Trading will cease and markets will collapse. Therefore, there must be sufficient profit opportunities (i.e., market inefficiencies), net of trading costs, to encourage market participants to gather information and estimate fair values. Efficiency, then, is a relative characteristic of markets: markets can be more efficient or less efficient, but perfect efficiency is an unattainable and undesirable goal.

In quasi-efficient markets, the return to gathering and evaluating information can be thought of as an economic rent that is proportional to the risks and marginal costs involved. But who pays the rent? If all investors are passive and share

---

[10] The gist of this argument was originally presented in Sanford Grossman and Joseph Stiglitz, "On the Impossibility of Informationally Efficient Markets," *American Economic Review* (1980), pp. 393-408.

homogenous expectations, then the information gatherers will have no one to trade with, and markets will again collapse. Thus, for markets to exist at all, we need a sufficiently large group of active managers, with enough variation in expectations and information, to ensure continued trading activity. Now who pays the rent? Active managers whose information gathering and processing skills are below average.[11] Of course, if these managers realized their skills were sub-par, they would become passive investors. Thus, for unskilled managers to remain in the game, either: (1) they must be naive enough to think that their sub-par results are actually above average; or, more likely, (2) there is enough random noise in the system that many unskilled managers earn above-average returns purely by chance, but they attribute their good fortune to skill. Either condition violates the assumption of investor rationality — which we will discuss in more detail in a later section.

Empirical Arguments

Many researchers have offered empirical results that seem to contradict market efficiency, damaging the case for passive investing. We think the most persuasive and influential results are related to: (1) the failure of CAPM beta to explain returns; (2) the "excess" volatility in market prices; and, (3) a variety of "anomalies" whereby publicly-available information can apparently be used to generate risk-adjusted excess returns.

Beta and Returns

From the Black, Jensen and Scholes[12] study in 1972 through the oft-cited Fama and French[13] study in 1992, researchers have consistently been unable to demonstrate a significant positive relationship between CAPM beta and realized stock returns. Since sensitivity to market movements (or beta) is the sole determinant of expected stock returns in the CAPM world, this failure means either (1) the market is inefficient, in the sense that expected returns consistently differ from realized returns; or (2) the market is efficient, but investors don't base their expectations on the CAPM (or, perhaps, that their "true" beta estimates are not equal to the historical beta estimates used in these studies). Since both explanations are consistent with the evidence, we can't reach a final conclusion. This so-called "joint hypothesis" problem pervades all tests of asset-pricing models and market efficiency. Because all market efficiency tests assume an implicit asset-pricing model, we can *never* determine if an apparent inefficiency is real, or the result of a mis-specified model. Still, at the very least, the failure of CAPM beta to explain returns implies that no *single* index is optimal for all investors.

---

[11] Since prices will reflect the opinions of both skilled and unskilled managers, passive investors will also pay *some* of the rent, but less than that paid by unskilled managers.

[12] See Fischer Black, Michael C. Jenson, and Myron Scholes, "The Capital Asset Pricing Model: Some Empirical Tests," in M. Jenson (ed.), *Studies in the Theory of Capital Markets* (1972).

[13] Eugene F. Fama and Kenneth R. French, "The Cross-Section of Expected Stock Returns," *Journal of Finance* (June 1992), pp. 427-466.

Excess Volatility

If prices "fully reflect all available information," then they will only respond to new information. Furthermore, price volatility should be roughly similar to the volatility in underlying fundamentals (i.e., interest rates and cash flows). Many studies have compared stock price volatility to the volatility of pricing fundamentals.[14] Most conclude that prices are just too volatile to be justified by the less volatile changes in interest rates and cash flows. Other studies have attempted to tie major price moves to the arrival of new information, usually concluding that many large price swings occur in an information vacuum. Essentially, price moves are just too large, and too capricious, to be consistent with a market where prices fully reflect all available information. Instead, it seems that prices often change simply because investors reassess their interpretation of existing information. Such behavior, although inconsistent with perfect market efficiency, is perfectly consistent with the notion of a quasi-efficient market, where investors have heterogeneous, quasi-rational expectations, and earn economic rents from information gathering and analysis.

Anomalies

The anomaly literature consists of dozens (or even hundreds) of studies showing how investors can apparently earn positive risk-adjusted returns using publicly-available information. An anomaly is a regular and predictable return pattern that is widely known, yet continues to exist. Examples include: the "January effect;" the "turn-of-the-month effect;" the "size effect;" the "low-P/E effect;" "post earnings announcement drift;" and a host of others. Although the joint hypothesis problem makes it impossible to refute market efficiency based solely on anomalies — EMH proponents will argue that these variables are surrogates for unknown risk factors, or that the excess returns disappear after trading costs — we believe it is a bit of a stretch to derive a risk story that can explain all these varied relationships. As we will explain in the next section, however, most anomalies are perfectly consistent with the known cognitive errors that influence human decisions.

Exhibit 5 shows the results of some of our tests on global anomalies. In each test, we regressed monthly stock returns against beginning-of-month factor values (properly lagged, where necessary) and calculated the average monthly regression coefficient and t-statistic for the series.[15] We ran these tests on two separate groups: (1) stocks in the Russell 1000 Index (large-cap domestic stocks); and (2) stocks in the MSCI-EAFE Index (large-cap stocks from 20 developed markets). All excess returns and factor values were standardized relative to the

---

[14] For example, see Robert Shiller, "Do Stock Prices Move Too Much To Be Justified By Subsequent Changes in Dividends," *American Economic Review* (1981), pp. 421-436.

[15] These are called "Fama-MacBeth regressions" and are described in Eugene F. Fama and James D. Mac-Beth, "Risk, Return, and Equilibrium: Empirical Tests," *Journal of Political Economy* (May-June 1973), pp. 607-636.

local-market mean (i.e., the coefficients measure stock-selection ability, not country-selection ability). Finally, we also report the number of countries (out of 21 considered) where the local-market regression produces the same sign as the global regression, and the number of countries where the local results are statistically significant.[16]

Because of data limitations, our non-U.S. results only go back to 1989, but they are remarkably similar to the longer-term U.S. results that begin in 1979. In both tests, the coefficients have the same sign and similar levels of statistical significance. Furthermore, the regressions produce the same signs in most countries. The fact that the results are not statistically significant in many countries is primarily due to the lack of observations in those countries — both in time and (for most markets) number of companies. When we test whether the local regression coefficient is significantly different from the global coefficient, we get results that are consistent with the power of the test — i.e., 17 of the 210 comparisons[17] (8.1%) are statistically significant at the 95% confidence level, with only 10 comparisons (4.8%) in the "wrong" tail. Our conclusion is that these anomalies are significant and pervasive, on both the local and global level.

Exhibit 5: Global Anomalies

	U.S. Results (1979-1996)		Int'l. Results (1989-1996)		Number of Countries	
	Coeff.	t-Stat	Coeff.	t-Stat	Same Sign	Significant
Value Factors						
Book/market	0.24	2.96	0.18	3.04	17	4
Earnings/price	0.40	5.46	0.16	2.95	15	4
Sales/price	0.28	4.25	0.10	1.75	12	3
Cash flow/price	0.38	5.28	0.14	3.38	17	4
Momentum Factors						
Estimate revisions	0.56	13.22	0.27	4.99	19	12
Revisions ratio	0.55	14.72	0.29	6.80	20	8
Price momentum	0.61	7.17	0.21	2.44	19	13
Risk Factors						
CAPM beta	−0.17	−1.83	−0.09	−0.88	14	3
Residual risk	−0.42	−4.05	−0.22	−2.38	17	5
Estimate uncertainty	−0.33	−6.39	−0.16	−2.33	18	9

---

[16] Further details on these tests are available on request.

[17] Comparisons to the global mean are made for 21 countries (including the United States) across 10 variables.

EMH supporters might argue that, because these relationships are so universal, they are probably proxies for unidentified risk factors rather than true market anomalies. If so, they need to identify the risks. We categorized these anomalies/risk factors according to their underlying investment themes: (1) value; (2) momentum; and (3) low-risk. Some would argue that the excess return to value investing is really compensation for accepting distress risk,[18] but they fail to demonstrate that a diversified portfolio of value stocks has above-average risk of actual distress (e.g., bankruptcy, default or dividend omission). The momentum effect is even more difficult to explain using unidentified risks. But perhaps the most perplexing results for EMH-adherents are those for the risk variables. How is it rational for investors to price stocks in such a way that those with the *least* amount of uncertainty have the *highest* expected returns? In the next section we will show how all three results have a perfectly logical and consistent behavioral explanation.

Behavioral Arguments

People aren't perfectly rational. Behavioral psychologists have demonstrated that people frequently make systematic errors in judgment and probability assessment.[19] These departures from perfect rationality are quite common, and can be both large and economically relevant. Although there are a whole litany of systematic cognitive errors — which go by such terms "selective perception," "illusory correlation," "wishful thinking," "availability," "illusion of control," and "hindsight bias" — one of the most pervasive and damaging is "overconfidence." Psychologists have found that people are far more confident in their abilities and predictions than they have any right to be. Studies show that when people are asked to place a 95% confidence band around their predictions, the band includes the actual observation roughly 50% of the time. Similarly, surveys show that most people consider themselves to be better-than-average automobile drivers, and more than 90% of American males describe themselves as having above-average athletic ability. We suspect that most, if not all, active managers believe that they can generate above-average investment returns.

We also believe that overconfidence alone can explain all of the anomalies discussed in the previous section,[20] although other cognitive errors also play a part. If investors make overconfident predictions based on limited information, then they will either overreact and underreact to new information based on whether it supports or contradicts their prior beliefs. That is, if investors are bull-

---

[18] See Eugene F. Fama and Kenneth R. French, "Multifactor Explanations of Asset Pricing Anomalies," *Journal of Finance* (March 1996), pp. 55-84.

[19] For a more complete discussion, see Daniel Kahneman, Paul Slovic, and Amos Tversky, *Judgment Under Uncertainty: Heuristics and Biases* (New York, NY: Cambridge University Press, 1982).

[20] For a developed theory of how overconfidence affects market return patterns, see Kent Daniel, David Hirshleifer, and Avanidhar Subrahmanyam, "A Theory of Overconfidence, Self-Attribution, and Security Market Under- and Over-reactions," University of Michigan Working Paper #9605-26-R (February 1997).

ish on a company's prospects, and new information arrives that seems to support that outlook, they will overreact to the information, become increasingly bullish and overconfident, and push prices to excessive levels. The opposite holds when investors are bearish. This overreaction to confirming information largely explains the value effect. Conversely, if new information challenges the original bullish outlook, it will usually be discounted or "explained away." Investors will underreact to the information, become only marginally less bullish and overconfident, and fail to adjust prices appropriately. This underreaction to conflicting information — along with the related phenomenon of continuing overreaction — largely explains the momentum effect.

But what about the low-risk effect? If there is no prevailing consensus (that is, uncertainty reigns), then there will be both over-confident pessimists and over-confident optimists. In the idealized academic world, the two competing groups will cancel each other out and prices will reflect fair values. In the real world, however, optimists will usually set prices. Why? Because short selling is rare,[21] leaving only pessimistic owners to sell. Furthermore, because of "regret aversion," few owners are likely to be pessimists — i.e., they won't want to admit that their original purchase decision was wrong. Thus, on balance, over-confident optimists will set prices for risky stocks, which means they will usually be over-valued.[22] Therefore, the low-risk effect should be related to the value effect, since they both rely on investor overreaction. Our analysis confirms this: in the United States, the average correlation between the monthly returns to value anomalies and low-risk anomalies has been 0.55.

The final behavioral argument against efficient markets and passive investing is the most obvious: no one actually behaves the way theory says they should. For example: most investors don't use optimizers to build risk-return efficient portfolios; they don't hold some combination of risk-free securities and the optimal risky portfolio; they don't measure a security's risk in terms of its contribution to the risk of a diversified portfolio;[23] and, most important, *they don't forego active management*. If investors don't behave as if the market is efficient, then they must not believe it is. If the market really is efficient, but investors don't believe it, then this itself implies inefficiencies (i.e., irrational behavior). Conversely, if investors are right, then the market must not be efficient. We are back to the catch-22 of efficient markets: if the market really is efficient, then investors

---

[21] Short selling is probably rare because: (1) it is too complicated for most investors; (2) fiduciaries view it as "imprudent" due to the potential for unlimited loss; and/or (3) Americans are naturally optimistic (i.e., shorting is "un-American").

[22] Similarly, lottery tickets are overpriced because of overconfident optimists (i.e., the rest of us can't short lottery tickets).

[23] For example, most investors view individual low price-to-book (or value) stocks as being quite risky, without realizing that a diversified portfolio of value stocks is actually less volatile than a similar portfolio of growth stocks — i.e., even after 45 years, most investors still haven't accepted Markowitz's basic lesson that the only risks that matter are those which can't be diversified away.

must behave as if it is (i.e., become passive); but if investors quit gathering and evaluating information, markets prices will no longer fully reflect available information.

THE VERDICT

This is not a criminal trial in which we must decide the ultimate fate of the EMH. Rather, it is more like a civil trial where we must decide whether the EMH paradigm is now clouding our understanding of the way markets work. Thus, our decision criterion should be the "preponderance of evidence" rather than "beyond a reasonable doubt." We believe that theoretical inconsistencies, empirical evidence, behavioral analysis, and the catch-22 of efficient markets, all point to a world where active management must (and does) exist and *can* add value. In fact, there really is no such thing as purely passive management, since selecting a benchmark is itself an active decision.[24] We believe the important question is not whether the markets are efficient or not, or whether active management can add value, but rather, how do investors form expectations, and how do those expectations impact market prices. Behavioral psychologists have shown that investors, like all people, make systematic errors when forming expectations and making probability assessments.[25] Of course, it is *possible* that a collection of irrational and overconfident investors can still come together to create an efficient market — it just seems a bit unlikely. (The burden should be on EMH proponents to explain exactly how this would occur.) Thus, we believe that active managers who can minimize their behavioral biases, and develop more realistic expectations and probability assessments, can and will add value.

WHY DO ACTIVE MANAGERS UNDERPERFORM?

Active management *can* add value, but on balance it hasn't. The evidence presented earlier indicates that, over the past 18 years, most active large-cap domestic mutual funds underperformed the S&P 500 Index. Why have most active managers lagged the market? We believe the culprits are: (1) poor investment decisions; (2) poor risk control; and (3) high fees and expense.

---

[24] Even for a nominally "passive" investor, choosing among the S&P 500, the Wilshire 5000, and the MSCI-World Indices (GDP-weighted or cap-weighted) will have a significant impact on terminal wealth.

[25] For a concrete example of how errors in expectations cause return regularities (anomalies), see Rafeal La Porta, "Expectations and the Cross-Section of Stock Returns," *Journal of Finance* (December 1996), pp. 1715-1741. La Porta demonstrates that security analysts' growth expectations are too extreme, and that these extreme forecasts largely explain the value effect. La Porta also shows that a contrarian strategy of buying the slowest expected growers and shorting the fastest expected growers produces 20% annualized hedged returns (before trading costs).

Poor Investment Decisions

Like all people, most active managers are overconfident, form irrational expectations, and make unrealistic probability assessments. They equate good companies
with good investments; they overreact to confirming information, pushing valuation levels to extremes; they underreact to information that doesn't fit their prior
beliefs; and so forth. Accordingly, most investors would be better off investing in
a buy-and-hold passive vehicle than in active funds managed by faulty decision
makers — i.e., when it comes to investing, it is better to make no decisions than to
make bad ones. Thus, we are left with something of a paradox: behavioral arguments both support and reject active management. We believe that a solution to
this dilemma can be found in an objective, disciplined and quantitative approach
to active management — which we will discuss in more detail later.

Poor Risk Control

Exhibits 3 and 4 compared the average large-cap mutual fund to the S&P 500
Index. But is this a fair comparison? The average mutual fund may have different
risk parameters that make a simple direct comparison inappropriate. We analyzed
the performance of the average mutual fund using a three-factor model similar to
the one proposed by Fama and French.[26] The dependent variable (ACTIVE) is the
average of the return on the Lipper Growth and the Lipper Growth and Income
Indices, less the return on the S&P 500.[27] The independent variables are: (1)
MARKET, which equals the difference between the S&P 500 return and the 90-
day Treasury rate; (2) VALUE, which equals the difference between the return on
the Russell 3000 Value Index and the Russell 3000 Growth Index; and (3) SIZE,
which equals the difference between the return on the Russell 1000 Index (large-
cap stocks) and the Russell 2000 Index (small-cap stocks). The regression was run
over 219 months from January 1979 through March 1997, with the results shown
in equation (1) (t-statistics in parentheses):

$$ACTIVE = -0.007 - 0.083 \times MARKET - 0.071 \times VALUE - 0.244 \times SIZE(1)$$
$$(-0.192)\ (-8.771) \qquad\qquad (-3.628) \qquad\qquad (-17.380)$$

Thus, relative to the S&P 500, the average large-cap mutual fund makes
statistically significant bets against the market, against value, and against size.
Together, these bets explain 63% of the variation in the average mutual fund's
active returns (i.e., the adjusted r-squared of the regression is 0.63). Furthermore,
after controlling for risk (i.e., net of these bets), the average active return is indis-
tinguishable from zero (−0.7 basis points). Thus, since the Lipper Index returns

---

[26] See Eugene F. Fama and Kenneth R. French, "Multifactor Explanations of Asset Pricing Anomalies,"
Journal of Finance (March 1996), pp. 55-84.
[27] Using the Lipper Indices eliminates survivorship bias, since they are defined as the average return on the
largest 30 funds in each category at that time. Tests using the median fund (not shown) produced very similar results.

are net of fees and expenses, the average mutual funds covers its costs on a risk-adjusted basis.

Although this is a more intellectually-satisfying conclusion, we hardly think it provides a ringing endorsement for actively-managed funds. Why? Because we believe that all three "bets" reflect poor risk control, rather than well-conceived and intentional decisions. Of the three "bets," only that against SIZE has any sort of empirical or theoretical justification — and that is tenuous at best.[28] Over any extended period, stocks should and usually do outperform cash, so it would be silly for active *equity* managers to consistently bet against the MARKET. Instead, we believe this "bet" reflects the tendency of active mutual-fund managers to hold cash for reasons unrelated to risk management or market timing — e.g., to meet redemptions, fund future purchases, or avoid accidental leverage (outspending available cash). Similarly, we believe the bet against SIZE results from the common practice of holding equally-weighted positions — thereby giving proportionately more weight to smaller stocks relative to a cap-weighted index — rather than a conscious decision to exploit the small-cap effect. Finally, the bet against VALUE is empirically misguided, but is easily explained by overreaction and the other cognitive errors discussed earlier.

High Fees and Expenses

All mutual fund returns, including those in the Lipper Indices, are net of fees and expenses. Thus, high fees and expenses could also account for the average manager's underperformance. The average large-cap mutual fund has an expense ratio of approximately 100 basis points. To this we add 45 basis points, reflecting the average fund's annual turnover (roughly 90%) and the average round-trip trading costs on large-cap stocks (estimated at 50 basis points). Therefore, we estimate that the average mutual fund needs to outperform the S&P 500 Index by roughly 145 basis points before fees and expenses just to break even. In the last section we saw that the average mutual fund had a risk-adjusted net excess return of −8.4 basis points per year (−0.7 times 12) after statistically eliminating "bets" against the market, value, and size. This means that, before fees and expenses, the average active manager must have some real stock selection skill, amounting to approximately 135-140 basis points per year. Hence, the $64,000 question: How can investors access these skills without also being trapped by the pitfalls of active management?

QUANTITATIVE SOLUTIONS

This section describes how active managers can use quantitative techniques to maximize the value of their insights and minimize potential underperformance.

---

[28] We believe the so-called "size effect" has little theoretical basis, is extremely inconsistent through time, and is generally overrated.

Specifically we will discuss (1) risk control; (2) process discipline; and, (3) portable alpha strategies.[29] Essentially our advice is to "be the House" — e.g., only invest when the odds are in your favor, and makes lots of small, diversified bets.

Risk Control

Perhaps the easiest way for active managers to improve their relative comparisons to the S&P 500 (or any relevant benchmark) is to eliminate any misguided and/or unintentional bets. Exhibit 6 is from a study by RogersCasey[30] that compares the relative performance of different types of institutional managers in their PIPER database. Managers are first placed into one of three style categories: (1) large-cap value; (2) large-cap growth; and (3) risk-controlled (or "enhanced index"). The study then compares the 5-year (June 1991 through June 1996) average excess returns (versus the S&P 500) and t-statistics for managers at various percentile breakpoints within their style categories. Note that at the higher percentiles, value and growth managers outperformed risk-controlled managers, but the volatility of their excess returns were higher as well. Thus, except for the very best growth managers, t-tests find it hard to reject the hypothesis that these excess returns are due to luck, and that the true excess returns are zero. Conversely, risk-controlled managers have lower excess returns at the higher percentiles, but also much lower volatility. The t-tests indicate that these risk-controlled managers very probably have true excess returns that exceed zero. In fact, even at the median it would be reasonable to conclude that risk-controlled managers can add value (the one-tailed p-value is 95.4%).

Exhibit 6: Comparisons of Active Management Styles (June 1991 - June 1996)

Percentile	Large-Cap Growth		Large-Cap Value		Risk-Controlled	
	Excess Return	t-Statistic	Excess Return	t-Statistic	Excess Return	t-Statistic
95th	5.8%	2.01	3.5%	1.30	1.7%	3.78
75th	3.9%	0.74	0.9%	0.49	1.4%	3.02
50th	0.4%	0.16	−0.2%	−0.11	0.8%	1.72
25th	−1.2%	−0.51	−1.6%	−0.98	0.3%	0.27
5th	−3.4%	−1.36	−4.0%	−2.55	−0.3%	−0.13

Source: Drew D. DeMakis, "Active Management Effectiveness," RogersCasey, October, 1996.

---

[29] For an excellent tutorial on how to improve the active management with quantitative techniques, see Richard C. Grinold and Ronald N. Kahn, *Active Portfolio Management* (Chicago, IL: Richard D. Irwin Inc., 1995).

[30] Drew D. DeMakis, "Active Management Effectiveness," RogersCasey, October, 1996.

How exactly should active managers control risk? We suggest following the advise offered by Harry Markowitz back in 1952: use optimization technology to find the portfolio with the least amount of risk for a given level of expected return. Expected returns should reflect the investor's private insights, but should be statistically defensible (see the next section). Risks and covariances should be based on a relevant risk model that seems intellectually appealing (e.g., a historical covariance matrix, a factor model, or an industry- and syle-based model). Risk can be defined as either total risk (volatility), downside risk, active risk (tracking error), or some other measure that best reflects the portfolio's objectives. In order to avoid over-trading to achieve small improvements in expected return, the optimization algorithm should explicitly include trading costs in its objective function.

Finally, when first using optimization technology, it is important to "play around" with the various inputs until the optimizer produces a portfolio that fits the manager's style and intuition. Some educational assistance is usually needed to help most active managers understand why optimizers pick some stocks over others, but once they understand the process, it is easier to accept the result. Conversely, understanding the process also helps managers learn how to massage the input parameters to reach a more acceptable portfolio. Even if the ultimate portfolio is not too different from what it would have been without an optimizer, this exercise will at least help managers understand the tradeoffs involved.

Process Discipline

If return regularities (anomalies) are caused by irrational investor behavior, over-confidence, and poor probability assessments, then a second "fix" for active managers is to minimize these cognitive errors by following a well-conceived and disciplined investment process. Managers should design stock-selection systems that reflect their investment philosophies, *and then test those systems on historical data to determine their statistical probability of success*. If a preferred system has no statistical correlation with stock returns, the manager should consider whether s/he has unfounded confidence in the system. We believe the best systems will be those that explicitly attempt to exploit the return regularities that arise from the cognitive shortcomings of other investors. In particular, managers should look for stocks that sell at reasonable valuations, have strong momentum, and below-average risk.

Similarly, if the manager's process is based on private forecasts, the manager needs to consider whether these forecasts are realistic. Overconfidence in extreme forecasts is the bane of active management. All active managers should maintain a history of their prior forecasts to determine their statistical accuracy, and to derive appropriate confidence intervals for future forecasts. This can prove to be a valuable lesson in humility that can minimize overconfidence in future decisions — and the resultant underperformance that often comes with it.

Finally, once a manager has designed a strategy that seems sound and has some statistical validity, s/he should stick with it even when things seem uncomfortable. Situations that seem risky in isolation often disappear in a diversified portfolio. If the manager still decides to override the system, it is particularly important to maintain a record of that decision and its ultimate resolution. Again, this exercise in humility can only improve the investment process: If statistics show that the history of overrides produces random results or worse, this will help managers avoid the temptation in the future.

Portable Alpha Strategies

Most of the dismal comparisons for active managers are for large-cap domestic managers versus the S&P 500 Index. Active managers have a much better record in the small-cap and international markets. For example, although only 23% of Lipper growth funds beat the S&P 500 for the 10-year period ending in May 1997, 79% of international funds beat the MSCI-EAFE Index (unhedged), and 77% of small-cap funds outperformed the Russell 2000 Index. Given the impossibility of perfectly efficient markets (i.e., the catch-22 discussed earlier), efficiency is a *relative* term rather than an absolute one. In fact, we can define a relatively efficient market as one where few active managers outperform, and where it requires a significant competitive advantage (skill) to add value. Conversely, a relatively inefficient market is one where more active managers add value, and less skill is required. A viable active strategy, then, is to seek alpha in less-efficient markets (using a risk-controlled and disciplined process) and use derivatives to get exposure to more-efficient ones.

For example, if a pension fund wants to get $100 million exposure to the highly-efficient large-cap domestic market, it could hire a superior small-cap manager, then short $100 million of Russell 2000 futures while simultaneously going long $100 million of S&P 500 futures. Assuming the futures are fairly priced, the net return on this position would be the S&P 500 return plus the small-cap manager's alpha relative to the Russell 2000. Similarly, the fund could hire a market-neutral (or long/short) manager and gain exposure to the large-cap market with S&P 500 futures. Here the fund would earn the S&P 500 return plus the return spread between the market-neutral manager's long and short portfolios. If futures don't exist (for example, if the active manager has an EAFE benchmark), the pension could transfer market exposures using the OTC swap market (i.e., swap EAFE returns for S&P 500 returns). Although a swap strategy will cost more than a futures strategy (reflecting the swap dealer's higher hedging costs in the cash market), the higher alpha should more than compensate for the higher cost. Thus, with portable alpha strategies, investors can separate the manager-selection decision from the market-selection decision — allowing them to pursue alpha in less-efficient markets, while maintaining their strategic exposure to more-efficient ones.

What About the Rest of Us?

Alpha transfer strategies work fine for large pension funds, but what about mutual fund investors? They are unlikely to be able to engage in the sophisticated types of futures and swaps transactions that such strategies require. Are retail investors doomed to a life without alpha? For mutual fund investors in the relatively efficient large-cap domestic market, an index fund may be the best solution — especially after considering the tax consequences of active management.[31] The alternative is to look for funds that: (1) stay fully invested; (2) don't make any bad bets against value or size;[32] (3) have modest fees and expenses; and, (4) follow a sound, disciplined, and *repeatable* investment process.

Unfortunately, the popular mutual fund rating services usually evaluate funds based on a combination of total return and return volatility, making it difficult to uncover effective managers. Our tests indicate that if investors use equation (1) to evaluate managers, they can get a better sense for both the fund's risks and its future ability to add value. That is, the coefficients on MARKET, VALUE, and SIZE will help define the manager's investment style so that investors can determine if they want the implied exposures. In addition, the alpha (or intercept) in equation (1) can tell investors whether the manager has added value above and beyond the fund's normal style exposures. Furthermore, as compared to looking only at prior excess returns, alpha is more predictive of future performance. For example, when we rank funds by their alphas from 1987 to 1991, and by their alphas from 1992 to 1996, the correlation between the two rankings is 0.16 (t-statistic = 2.72); the equivalent correlation using excess returns is −0.02 (−0.27). We think traditional pension fund consultants could provide a valuable service to retail investors by performing this type of risk-adjusted analysis on mutual funds.[33]

CONCLUSION

The efficient market hypothesis (EMH) and the capital asset pricing model (CAPM) fail miserably as descriptive theories, but guess what? They're pretty good proscriptive theories. They may do a lousy job of describing how investors and markets actually behave, but they are pretty good paradigms for how investors *should* behave. Most investors don't evaluate a security's risk in terms of its contribution to the risk of a diversified portfolio, but they *should*. They don't forego active management when they have no competitive advantage, but they *should*. They don't adjust their risk-reward posture by borrowing or lending against the optimal risky portfolio, but they *should*. They don't build portfolios

---

[31] A little-discussed tax disadvantage of index funds is their large unrealized gains. New (taxable) investors in an index fund will have to pay taxes on those gains, even though they didn't experience them, if the fund is ever forced to liquidate shares — as might happen, for instance, if there are net liquidations during a market correction.

[32] Investors who want to bet against the market, size, or value can do so directly using the appropriate vehicle.

[33] A good rating service would also evaluate the fund's current portfolio to detect style drift, and would also try to determine if the manager follows a sound, disciplined and repeatable investment process. Fortunately, consultants are already adept at such analysis from their work with institutional portfolios.

using optimizers that balance expected returns against portfolio risk, but they *should*. And finally, they don't form expectations using rational Bayesian decision rules, but they definitely *should*. (Unfortunately, they *shouldn't* have to pay taxes and transactions costs, but they most certainly do.)

Nonetheless, even though most investors *should* behave as proscribed by the EMH and the CAPM, we're glad they don't. If it weren't for the foibles and follies of active managers, the market would be even harder to beat than it already is. If it weren't for investor overconfidence and other cognitive errors, return regularities would disappear, and disciplined quantitative techniques would lose their competitive advantage. In short, if all investors were perfectly rational and shared homogenous expectations (and there were no taxes or transactions costs), the world would be a terribly boring place indeed: markets would be perfectly efficient; trading would cease; and most of the financial community would be unemployed. Although this might please many on Main Street, those of us on Wall Street should pray each day that the world continues to need active managers.

Chapter 4

Overview of Equity Style Management

Frank J. Fabozzi, Ph.D., CFA
Adjunct Professor of Finance
School of Management
Yale University

INTRODUCTION

In the early 1970s, several studies found that there were categories of stocks that had similar characteristics and performance patterns. Moreover, the returns of these stock categories performed differently than other categories of stocks. That is, the returns of stocks within a category were highly correlated and the returns between categories of stocks were relatively uncorrelated. The first such study was by James Farrell who called these categories of stocks "clusters."[1] He found that for stocks there were at least four such categories or clusters — growth, cyclical, stable, and energy. In the later half of the 1970s, there were studies that suggested even a simpler categorization by size (as measured by total capitalization) produced different performance patterns.

Practitioners began to view these categories or clusters of stocks with similar performance as a "style" of investing. Some managers, for example, held themselves out as "growth stock managers" and others as "cyclical stock managers." Using size as a basis for categorizing style, some managers became "large cap" investors while others were "small cap" investors. Moreover, there was a commonly held belief that a manager could shift "styles" to enhance performance return.

Today, the notion of an equity investment style is widely accepted in the investment community. The acceptance of equity style investing can also be seen from the proliferation of style indices published by several vendors and the introduction of futures and options contracts based on some of these style indices.

In this chapter, we will look at the practical aspects of style investing. First, we look at the popular style types and the difficulties of classifying stocks according to style. Second, we look at the empirical evidence on style management. Third, we discuss active style management and how it can be implemented.

---

[1] James L. Farrell, Jr. "Homogenous Stock Groupings: Implications for Portfolio Management," *Financial Analysts Journal* (May-June 1975), pp. 50-62.

TYPES OF EQUITY STYLES

Stocks can be classified by style in many ways. The most common is in terms of one or more measures of "growth" and "value." Within a growth and value style there is a sub-style based on some measure of size. The most plain vanilla classification of styles is as follows: (1) large value, (2) large growth, (3) small value, and (4) small growth.

The motivation for the value/growth style categories can be explained in terms of the most common measure for classifying stocks as growth or value — the price-to-book value per share (P/B) ratio.[2] Earnings growth will increase the book value per share. Assuming no change in the P/B ratio, a stock's price will increase if earnings grow. A manager who is growth oriented is concerned with earnings growth and seeks those stocks from a universe of stocks that have higher relative earnings growth. The growth manager's risks are that growth in earnings will not materialize and/or that the P/B ratio will decline.

For a value manager, concern is with the price component rather than with the future earnings growth. Stocks would be classified as value stocks within a universe of stocks if they are viewed as cheap in terms of their P/B ratio. By cheap it is meant that the P/B ratio is low relative to the universe of stocks. The expectation of the manager who follows a value style is that the P/B ratio will return to some normal level and thus even with book value per share constant, the price will rise. The risk is that the P/B ratio will not increase.

Each quarter the Mobius Group surveys institutional money managers and asks their style. In June 1996, there were 1,526 domestic equity money managers in the survey who responded that they follow an active strategy. Of these survey participants, 503 indicated that growth was an "accurate" or a "very accurate" description of their style. Moreover, these managers indicated that it was wrong to classify them as value managers. There were 460 managers of the 1,526 surveyed that responded that value was an "accurate" or a "very accurate" description of their style and that it would be wrong to classify them as growth managers.

Within the value and growth categories there are sub-styles. As mentioned above, one sub-style is based on size. The sub-styles discussed below are based on other classifications of the stocks selected.

Sub-Styles of Value Category

In the value category, there are three sub-styles: low price-to-earnings (P/E) ratio, contrarian, and yield.[3] The *low-P/E manager* concentrates on companies trading at

---

[2] Support for the use of this measure is provided in the following study: Eugene F. Fama and Kenneth R. French, "Common Risk Factors on Stocks and Bonds," *Journal of Financial Economics* (February 1993), pp. 3-56.

[3] Jon A. Christopherson and C. Nola Williams, "Equity Style: What it is and Why it Matters," Chapter 1 in T. Daniel Coggin, Frank J. Fabozzi, and Robert D. Arnott (eds.), *The Handbook of Equity Style Management: Second Edition* (New Hope, PA: Frank J. Fabozzi Associates, 1997).

low prices relative to their P/E ratio.[4] The P/E ratio can be defined as the current P/E, a normalized P/E, or a discounted future earnings. The *contrarian manager* looks at the book value of a company and focuses on those companies that are selling at low valuation relative to book value. The companies that fall into this category are typically depressed cyclical stocks or companies that have little or no current earnings or dividend yields. The expectation is that the stock is on a cyclical rebound or that the company's earnings will turn around. Both these occurrences are expected to lead to substantial price appreciation. The most conservative value managers are those that look at companies with above average dividend yields that are expected to be capable of increasing, or at least maintaining, those yields. This style is followed by a manager who is referred to as a *yield manager.*

Sub-Styles of Growth Category

Growth managers seek companies with above average growth prospects. In the growth manager style category, there tends to be two major sub-styles.[5] The first is a growth manager who focuses on high-quality companies with consistent growth. A manager who follows this sub-style is referred to as a *consistent growth manager.* The second growth sub-style is followed by an *earnings momentum growth manager.* In contrast to a growth manager, an earnings momentum growth manager prefers companies with more volatile, above-average growth. Such a manager seeks to buy companies in expectation of an acceleration of earnings.

Hybrid Styles: Value-Growth Managers

There are some managers who follow both a growth and value investing style but have a bias (or tilt) in favor of one of the styles. The bias is not sufficiently identifiable to categorize the manager as growth or value managers. Most managers who fall into this hybrid style are described as *growth at a price managers* or *growth at a reasonable price managers.* These managers look for companies that are forecasted to have above-average growth potential selling at a reasonable value.

As noted above, the Mobius Group surveys institutional money managers quarterly and asks them to classify their style. In the June 1996 survey, 503 indicated they were growth managers and 460 value managers. There were 252 managers who indicated that both value and growth styles were an "accurate" or "very accurate" description of their styles. Most of these managers probably fell into the category of growth at a price managers.

STYLE CLASSIFICATION SYSTEMS

Now that we have a general idea of the two main style categories, growth and value, and the further refinement by size, let's see how a manager goes about clas-

---

[4] For a discussion of an approach based on low price-earnings, see Gary G. Schlarbaum, "Value-Based Equity Strategies," Chapter 7 in *The Handbook of Equity Style Management.*
[5] Christopherson and Williams, "Equity Style."

sifying stocks that fall into the categories. We call the methodology for classifying stocks into style categories as a *style classification system*. Vendors of style indices have provided direction for developing a style classification system. However, managers will develop their own system.

Developing such a system is not a simple task. To see why, let's take a simple style classification system where we just categorize stocks into value and growth using one measure, the price-to-book value ratio. The lower the P/B ratio the more the stock looks like a value stock. The style classification system would then be as follows:

> *Step 1:* Select a universe of stocks.
> *Step 2:* Calculate the total market capitalization of all the stocks in the universe.
> *Step 3:* Calculate the P/B ratio for each stock in the universe.
> *Step 4:* Sort the stocks from the lowest P/B ratio to the highest P/B ratio.
> *Step 5:* Calculate the accumulated market capitalization starting from the lowest P/B ratio stock to the highest P/B ratio stock.
> *Step 6:* Select the lowest P/B stocks up to the point where one-half the total market capitalization computed in Step 2 is found.
> *Step 7:* Classify the stocks found in Step 6 as value stocks.
> *Step 8:* Classify the remaining stocks from the universe as growth stocks.

While this style classification system is simple, it has both theoretical and practical problems. First, from a theoretical point of view, in terms of the P/B ratio there is very little distinguishing the last stock on the list that is classified as value and the first stock on the list classified as growth. From a practical point of view, the transaction costs are higher for implementing a style using this classification system. The reason is that the classification is at a given point in time based on the prevailing P/B ratio and market capitalizations. At a future date, P/B ratios and market capitalizations will change, resulting in a different classification of some of the stocks. This is often the case for those stocks on the border between value and growth that could jump over to the other category. This is sometimes called "style jitter." As a result, the manager will have to rebalance the portfolio to sell off stocks that are not within the style classification sought.

Refinements to the Basic Style Classification System

There are two refinements that have been made to style classification systems in an attempt to overcome these two problems. First, more than one categorization variable has been used in a style classification system. Two types of categorization variables have been used: deterministic and expectational. Deterministic variables are those derived from historical data. These variables include dividend/price ratio (i.e., dividend yield), cash flow/price ratio (i.e., cash flow yield), return on equity, and earnings variability. Expectational variables are those based on expectations or forecasts. Examples are earnings growth estimates or variables which rely on some stock valuation model (such as a the dividend discount model or a factor model).

As examples of this refinement, consider the style classification system developed by one vendor of style indices, Frank Russell, and one developed by a broker/dealer, Salomon Brothers Inc. For the Frank Russell style indices, the universe of stocks (either 1,000 for the Russell 1000 index or 2,000 for the Russell 2000 index) were classified as part of their value index or growth index using two categorization variables. The two variables are the B/P ratio (a deterministic variable) and a long-term growth forecast (an expectational variable).[6] The latter variable is obtained from the Institutional Brokerage Estimates Survey (IBES). Salomon Brothers uses more than two variables. The variables included are P/B ratio, earnings growth, P/E ratio, dividend yields, and historical returns.[7]

When using several variables in the style classification system, a score is developed for each stock. The classification is then done as follows:

> *Step 1:* Select a universe of stocks.
> *Step 2:* Calculate the total market capitalization of all the stocks in the universe.
> *Step 3:* Using the variables for classification, develop a score for each stock, with the highest score being value.
> *Step 4:* Sort the stocks from the highest score to the lowest score.
> *Step 5:* Calculate the capitalization-weighted median of the scores.
> *Step 6:* Select the stocks with a score above the capitalization-weighted median found in Step 5 and classify them as value stocks.
> *Step 7:* Classify the remaining stocks in the universe as growth stocks.

With this system, half of the market capitalization is in each group.

The second refinement has been to develop better procedures for making the cut between growth and value. This involves not classifying every stock into one category or the other. Instead, stocks may be classified into three groups: "pure value," "pure growth," and "middle-of-the-road" stocks. The three groups would be such that they each had one third of the total market capitalization. The two extreme groups, pure value and pure growth, are not likely to face any significant style jitter. The middle-of-the road stocks are assigned a probability of being value or growth. This style classification system is used by Frank Russell and Salomon Brothers Inc.

We will illustrate this approach using the Salomon Brothers model, called the *Growth/Value* (GV) *Model* for distinguishing between growth and value stocks.[8] The model uses a statistical technique called discriminant analysis to

---

[6] "Russell Equity Indices: Index Construction and Methodology," Frank Russell Company, July 8, 1994 and September 6, 1995.

[7] Sergio Bienstock and Eric H. Sorensen, "Segregating Growth from Value: It's Not Always Either/Or," Salomon Brothers Inc., Quantitative Equities Strategy, July 1992.

[8] Bienstock and Sorensen, "Segregating Growth from Value: It's Not Always Either/Or."

"discriminate" between growth and value stocks. Discriminant analysis gives a score, called the "discriminant score," and it is this score that is used to make the cut-off between growth and value. The bottom line output of the model is a ranking of a universe of stocks based on the probability that any particular stock will be a growth stock. This probability is called the "growth stock probability" and its complement, 1 minus the growth stock probability, is the "value stock probability." When the growth stock probability of a particular stock approaches 1, then it is concluded that that particular stock is a growth stock. Similarly, when the value stock probability of a particular stock approaches 1, then it is concluded that that particular stock is a value stock. Stocks that do not clearly fall into the growth or value categories are identified by the model based on these probabilities.

The product of the model is illustrated in Exhibit 1. The results of the GV model shown in the figure are the result of an application to the largest 3,000 capitalization stocks in 1991. The horizontal axis shows the discriminant score. The vertical axis shows the growth-stock probability. As the discriminant score increases, the growth-stock probability increases. The dots in Exhibit 1 are specific stocks from the 3,000 analyzed with the GV model. Because most of the stocks analyzed fall near the middle, it looks like a solid curve in that area. There are five vertical lines in the figure. These lines indicate the percentage of the 3,000 stocks that fall below the line. Specifically, moving from left to right, the first line represents 10%, the second 25%, the third 50%, the fourth 75%, and the last 90%. This means that 10% of the 3,000 stocks fell below the first line and 10% were above the last line. Salomon Brothers views stocks that fall below the 10% line as being unambiguously value stocks (because they have a low growth stock probability) and those that are above the 90% line as being unambiguously growth stocks (because they have a high growth stock probability). The stocks that fall in between are unassigned.

Thus far our focus has been on style classification in terms of value and growth. As we noted earlier, sub-style classifications are possible in terms of size. Within a value and growth classification, there can be a model determining large value and small value stocks, and large growth and small growth stocks. The variable most used for classification of size is a company's market capitalization. To determine large and small, the total market capitalization of all the stocks in the universe considered is first calculated. The cutoff between large and small is the stock that will give an equal market capitalization.

This simple classification based on size with value and growth has been refined by creators of style indices. For example, Wilshire Associates creates broad-based style indices. The broadest based index is the Wilshire 5000. Wilshire's approach to size was to limit the stocks to the largest 2,500 because it was felt that they better represent stocks held by institutional investors. This index is called the Wilshire Top 2500. Studies of the performance profile of the stocks in this index by Wilshire's Institutional Services/Equity Division found that there was different performance between the 700th and 800th stocks. Wilshire selected the 750th largest stock as the cut-off for the large category. This is the Wilshire Top 750 stocks. Stocks 751 to 2,500 are included in the Wilshire Next 1750.

Exhibit 1: Product of Salomon Brothers Growth-Value Model for Probability Ranking of 3,000 Largest Capitalization Stocks in 1991

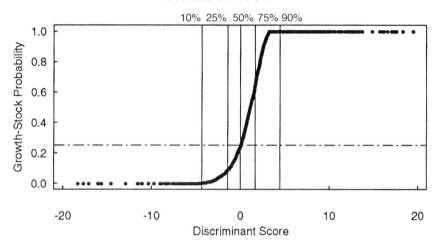

Source: Figure 2 in Sergio Bienstock and Eric H. Sorensen, "Segregating Growth from Value: It's Not Always Either/Or," Salomon Brothers Inc., Quantitative Equities Strategy, July 1992, p. 5.

RELATIVE PERFORMANCE OF VALUE AND GROWTH

Now that we understand the various style classification systems, we next look at the most important question associated with style management: is style management worth the effort and cost? To answer this question, we can look at the evidence on the relative performance of value and growth stocks.

Robert Arnott, David Leinweber, and Christopher Luck present evidence on this relative performance for the United States, Japan, United Kingdom, Canada, and Germany.[9] Using the simple measure of value and growth based on the P/B ratio, they calculated the growth of $1 invested in growth stocks and value stocks from January 1975 to June 1995. The results are reported in Exhibit 2. For the U.S. analysis, the universe of stocks included are those in the S&P 500. As can be seen from Exhibit 2 in every country, value outperformed growth based on the simple definition of growth and value. Exhibit 3 presents this superior performance over the entire time period in terms of the difference in the cumulative return between value stocks and growth stocks for the markets of the same five countries.

---

[9] David J. Leinweber, Robert D. Arnott, and Christopher G. Luck, "The Many Sides of Equity Style: Quantitative Management of Core, Value, and Growth Portfolios," Chapter 11 in *The Handbook of Equity Style Management*.

Exhibit 2: Growth of $1 Invested in Growth Stocks and Value Stocks Using Simple Price/Book Classification: January 1975 to June 1995

| | Growth of $1 invested in | | | Portion of monthly |
Country	Value Stocks	Growth Stocks	Best of Value-or-Growth	returns where Growth exceeded Value
U.S.	$23	$14	$42	45%
U.K.	42	24	82	44
Japan	37	10	89	39
Canada	12	5	31	39
Germany	14	9	30	45

Source: Exhibit 10 in David J. Leinweber, Robert D. Arnott, and Christopher G. Luck, "The Many Sides of Equity Style: Quantitative Management of Core, Value, and Growth Portfolios," Chapter 11 in T. Daniel Coggin, Frank J. Fabozzi, and Robert D. Arnott (eds.), *The Handbook of Equity Style Management: Second Edition* (New Hope, PA: Frank J. Fabozzi Associates, 1997), p. 188.

While the results are informative, they are based on raw returns. That is, they make no adjustment for differences in risk that might exist between growth and value stocks. A comprehensive analysis that addresses this issue was performed by Richard Roll.[10] He addressed the following three questions:

1. Are the observed differences in the performance between equity styles just statistical aberrations and therefore not likely to be repeated?
2. Are the observed differences in performance between equity styles simply a reflection of the compensation for the differences in the risks associated with each equity style?
3. Are the observed differences in performance between equity style truly an investment opportunity that can generate an enhanced return without incurring any additional exposure to loss?

To empirically address these questions, Roll used the following three categorization variables: (1) large or small size; (2) high or low earnings per share/price (E/P) ratio; and, (3) high or low book equity/market equity (B/M) ratio. A low relative P/E ratio is viewed as an indicator of value, therefore a high relative E/P ratio is a measure of value. A low relative P/B ratio is an indicator of value. It has the same meaning when expressed in terms of the B/M ratio (i.e., a low relative B/M ratio is an indicator of value); therefore a high relative B/M ratio is an indicator of value.

Only U.S. stocks were included in Roll's study. The universe of stocks included all listed NYSE and AMEX stocks available from the CRSP database. The period covered was April 1984 to March 1994. The number of stocks in the universe varied each month.

[10] Richard Roll, "Style Return Differentials: Illustrations, Risk Premiums, or Investment Opportunities," Chapter 5 in *The Handbook of Equity Style Management*.

Exhibit 3: Cumulative Returns of Value Minus Growth Stocks by Country: January 1975 to June 1997

A: U.S. S&P500 Value – Growth

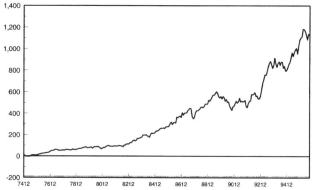

B: Japan Value – Growth

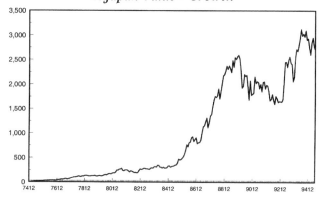

C: U.K. Value – Growth

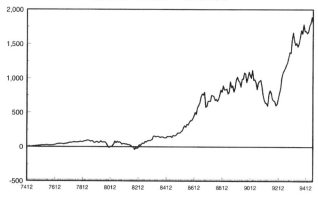

Exhibit 3 (Continued)
D: Canada Value – Growth

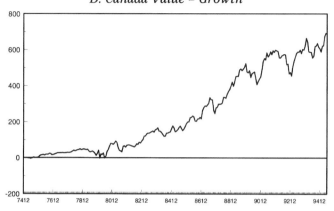

E: Germany Value – Growth

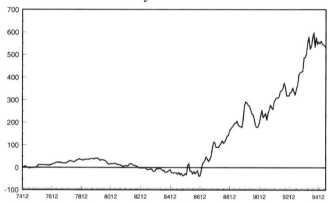

Source: Exhibit 5, 6, 7, 8, and 9 in David J. Leinweber, Robert D. Arnott, and Christopher G. Luck, "The Many Sides of Equity Style: Quantitative Management of Core, Value, and Growth Portfolios," Chapter 11 in T. Daniel Coggin, Frank J. Fabozzi, and Robert D. Arnott (eds.), *The Handbook of Equity Style Management: Second Edition* (New Hope, PA: Frank J. Fabozzi Associates, 1997), pp. 185- 187.

Each month the stocks in the universe were classified into one of eight portfolios. This was done as follows. The stocks were ranked separately from low to high based on a given style categorization variable. Then a stock was assigned to one of eight style portfolios as follows. Each portfolio was designated by three letters. Each letter represented the stock assignment within a style classification variable as either "low" denoted by "L" or "high" denoted by "H." The first letter for a portfolio indicated size, the second letter E/P ratio, and the third letter B/M ratio. For example, a portfolio designated LHL meant the stocks in this portfolio were the smallest capitalization stocks with the highest E/P ratio, and the lowest

B/M ratio. Each month the stocks in the style portfolio changed based on their classification according to the style categorization variable.

For each of the eight style portfolios, a value-weighted monthly total return was calculated. The total return included price change, dividends, and reinvestment of dividends. Exhibit 4 shows the growth of $1 invested in each style portfolio over the period and ranks the performance of the style portfolios. The best performing style portfolio was "LHH." This is a small capitalization portfolio that has a high E/P and a high B/M. This is clearly a value portfolio and the findings are therefore consistent with the results presented in Exhibit 2 of the superior performance of value stocks based on raw returns. The worst performing style portfolio was "LLL." The low E/P and low B/M indicate that this style portfolio is biased in the direction of growth. In terms of return performance, the best performing style portfolio outperformed the worst performing style portfolio by more than 15% annually.

Roll then statistically tested whether the monthly excess returns on the style portfolios (i.e., the difference between the return on a style portfolio and the risk-free rate) was significantly different. Using an elaborate statistical test, Roll found that they were statistically significant.

The results in Exhibit 4 (as well as those in Exhibit 2) are based on raw returns. No adjustment was made in the results reported to account for the risks associated with each portfolio style. Roll takes this into account by analyzing the risk-adjusted returns for the style portfolios. He used two risks models: the capital asset pricing model and a factor model. Roll does not find that accounting for risk can explain the difference in performance of the style portfolios. That is, he found that there were still differences in return performance after adjusting for risk. This suggests that equity style provided extra return without incurring additional risk.

Exhibit 4: Growth of $1 Invested and Performance of Style Portfolios from March 31, 1985 to March 31, 1994

Rank	Growth of $1	Style Size	Earnings/Price	Book/Market
1	$6.85	Low	High	High
2	5.34	High	High	High
3	5.15	Low	High	Low
S&P 500	3.96	—	—	—
4	3.49	High	High	Low
5	3.05	High	Low	Low
6	2.76	High	Low	High
7	2.02	Low	Low	High
8	1.64	Low	Low	Low

Source: Richard Roll, "Style Return Differentials: Illustrations, Risk Premiums, or Investment Opportunities," Chapter 5 in T. Daniel Coggin, Frank J. Fabozzi, and Robert D. Arnott (eds.), *The Handbook of Equity Style Management: Second Edition* (New Hope, PA: Frank J. Fabozzi Associates, 1997), p. 102.

Why Have Value Stocks Outperformed Growth Stocks?

There is considerable debate as to why it has been empirically observed that value stocks have outperformed growth stocks over extended periods. The results may merely be the result of data mining. There are other explanations that have been proffered.

The first explanation is that there are one or more risks that are not being recognized in the analysis.[11] If there are risks that are not identified, then it is possible that the premium realized by value stocks over growth stocks is a risk premium to compensate for such risks. While one can never be sure of capturing all the risks, the study by Roll described above uses the latest technology in asset pricing modeling and still finds differential performance. The second explanation is that there are systematic errors in forecasts that cause the difference in performance.[12]

A partial explanation for the difference in performance of growth and value stocks where the criteria for classification is the price-earnings ratio has been suggested by Scott Bauman and Robert Miller.[13] They looked at the earnings forecast and found that earnings were consistently underestimated for the lowest price-earnings stocks and consistently overestimated for the highest price-earnings stocks. The low price-earnings stocks are value stocks. An underestimate of future earnings means that such stocks will perform better than expected. In the case of growth stocks, which are the high price-earnings stocks, an overestimate of earnings will result in worse performance than expected. Why does this bias exist? Bauman and Miller argue that it is the result of too much reliance by analysts on recent past earnings trends in formulating forecasted earnings.

ACTIVE STYLE MANAGEMENT

The results of the studies by Arnott-Leinweber-Luck and Roll suggest that a value style outperforms a growth style. The outperformance of value over growth, however, did not occur for every time period studied. Even though the cumulative return differential favored value stocks, there were dips in the curves shown in Exhibit 5 (a) through (e). A dip means that there were periods where growth stocks outperformed value stocks. The last column in Exhibit 2 shows the percentage of months over the January 1975 to June 1995 period in which growth stocks outperformed value stocks.

The implication of this is that there are opportunities to switch styles based on expectations of what will be the best performing style. This portfolio strategy is called *active style management* or *tactical style management*. (Selecting one style

[11] Eugene F. Fama and Kenneth R. French, "The Cross-Section of Expected Returns," *Journal of Finance* (June 1992), pp. 427-465.

[12] This explanation has been suggested in the following studies: Josef Lakonishok, Andrei Shleifer, and Robert Vishny, "Contrarian Investment, Extrapolation, and Risk," *Journal of Finance* (December 1994), pp. 1541-1578; and, Robert A. Haugen, *The New Finance: The Case Against Efficient Markets* (Englewood Cliffs, NJ: Prentice Hall, 1995).

[13] W. Scott Bauman and Robert E. Miller, "Investment Styles, Stock Market Cycles, Investor Expectations, and Portfolio Performance," Chapter 8 in *The Handbook of Equity Style Management*.

and sticking with it is referred to as *passive style management*.)[14] The potential for enhanced performance by pursuing such a strategy can be seen by looking at what a style switching strategy would have done in terms of the growth of $1 if a manager could *perfectly predict* the better performing of the two styles each month and invested in that style. This is shown in the fourth column of Exhibit 2. For example, in the United States a perfect foresight style switching strategy would have generated a growth of $1 equal to $42 at the end of 20 years compared to $23 for value stocks.

Now we know that with perfect foresight a style switching strategy which ignores transaction costs would have produced a significantly enhanced return compared to a passive style management. The question is how to implement a real-world style switching strategy to enhance returns. To do so, it is necessary to accurately forecast returns to style. Moreover, any realistic style switching strategy must recognize the costs of trading large positions in one style into a large position of another style.

Implementing a Style Switching Strategy

Typically, the costs of implementation of style switching do not make it economic to pursue a style switching strategy over short time periods. There are more effective ways to implement a style switching strategy.[15] Rather than a style switching strategy from value to growth or growth to value, a policy of tilting a portfolio toward a style can be employed. For example, a style switching strategy means that at a given time either (1) 100% is allocated to a value portfolio and 0% to a growth portfolio or (2) 0% is allocated to a value portfolio and 100% to a growth portfolio. In a style tilting strategy, there is some allocation to each style, the percentage allocation based on the expected relative performance of the two styles. In addition to reducing transaction costs, style tilting reduces the size of the bet made on a style.

There are two additional ways to effectively implement an active style management strategy. First, as noted earlier, a probabilistic style classification system can be used so as to focus only on the strongest value stocks or growth stocks. This increases the probability that the manager is achieving the target style exposure and reduces transaction costs from stocks at the border crossing over. Second, a style switching or style tilting strategy should occur only based on longer-term forecasted better return performance of a style. The reason is that transaction costs associated with the frequent shifting of the portfolio between styles for short periods will more than likely eat up the potential enhanced return.

Transaction costs are critical in a strategy. Futures contracts provide a cost effective means for altering an exposure to an asset. Because of the increased interest in style investing, futures on style indices have been developed and are currently trading. Futures on style indices provide a means for reducing the transaction costs associated with active style management.[16]

---

[14] See Bruce I. Jacobs and Kenneth N. Levy, Chapter 1 of this book, for more on style and active equity management.

[15] Leinweber, Arnott, and Luck, "The Many Sides of Equity Style."

[16] See, Joanne M. Hill and Maria E. Tsu, "Value and Growth Index Derivatives," Chapter 19 in *The Handbook of Equity Style Management.*

SUMMARY

Studies suggest that there are categories of stocks that have had similar characteristics and performance patterns, and that the returns of these stock categories performed differently than other categories of stocks. Practitioners view these categories of stocks with similar performance as a "style" of investing. The notion of an equity investment style is widely accepted in the investment community. While stocks can be classified by style in many ways, the most common classification is in terms of "growth" and "value". The measure most commonly used to classify growth and value stocks is the price-to-book value per share.

Within a growth and value style there are sub-styles based on some measure of size. The most plain vanilla classification of styles is as follows: (1) large value, (2) large growth, (3) small value, and (4) small growth. In the value category, there are three sub-styles: low price-to-earnings ratio, contrarian, and yield. In the growth manager style category, the two major sub-styles are consistent growth and earnings momentum growth. A common hybrid style is growth-at-a-price.

A style classification system is a methodology for classifying stocks into style categories. Developing such a system is not a simple task. A major concern in designing a style classification system is style jitter — the frequent jumping of stocks from one style category into the other. The two major refinements that have been made to style classification systems are (1) the use of more than one categorization variable and (2) development of better procedures for making the cut between growth and value stocks (probabilistic approach).

The empirical evidence appears to support the superior performance of value stocks over growth stocks, even after adjusting for risk factors. There is evidence that this superior performance is also the case in several non-U.S. equity markets. There are several major criticisms of these findings. First, the results may be due to data mining. Second, all risk factors may not be captured in the studies and therefore it is possible that the results reflect a risk premium required for investing in value stocks. The study by Roll, however, does not support this view. Finally, there may be systematic errors in forecasts that cause the difference in performance.

While the results of studies suggest that a value style has outperformed a growth style, the better performance did not occur for every period of time. This suggests that there are opportunities to switch styles based on expectations of what will be the best performing style. This is called active style management or tactical style management. The costs of implementation of style switching do not make it economic to pursue a short-term style switching strategy. More effective ways to implement a style switching strategy involve a policy of tilting a portfolio toward a style that is expected to perform best.

Chapter 5

Factor-Based Approach to Equity Portfolio Management

Frank J. Fabozzi, Ph.D., CFA
Adjunct Professor of Finance
School of Management
Yale University

INTRODUCTION

The theory of asset pricing in terms of factors is well developed in the academic literature and is explained in every textbook on investment management. In this chapter, we will show how factor models can be used to construct equity portfolios and control portfolio risk

TYPES OF FACTOR MODELS

There are three types of factor models being used today to manage equity portfolios: statistical factor models, macroeconomic factor models, and fundamental factor models.[1] We describe these three factor models below.

Statistical Factor Models

In a *statistical factor model,* historical and cross-sectional data on stock returns are tossed into a statistical model. The statistical model used is *principal components analysis* which is a special case of a statistical technique called *factor analysis.* The goal of the statistical model is to best explain the observed stock returns with "factors" that are linear return combinations and uncorrelated with each other.

For example, suppose that monthly returns for 1,500 companies for ten years are computed. The goal of principal components analysis is to produce "factors" that best explain the observed stock returns. Let's suppose that there are six "factors" that do this. These "factors" are statistical artifacts. The objective in a

---

[1] Gregory Connor, "The Three Types of Factor Models: A Comparison of Their Explanatory Power," *Financial Analysts Journal* (May-June 1995), pp. 42-57.

I wish to thank Bruce Jacobs and Kenneth Levy of Jacobs Levy for their helpful comments on an earlier draft of this chapter.

statistical factor model then becomes to determine the economic meaning of each of these statistically derived factors.

Because of the problem of interpretation, it is difficult to use the factors from a statistical factor model for valuation and risk control. Instead, practitioners prefer the two other models described below, which allow them to prespecify meaningful factors, and thus produce a more intuitive model.

Macroeconomic Factor Models

In a *macroeconomic factor model*, the inputs to the model are historical stock returns and observable macroeconomic variables. That is, the raw descriptors are macroeconomic variables. The goal is to determine which macroeconomic variables are pervasive in explaining historical stock returns. Those variables that are pervasive in explaining the returns are then the factors and included in the model. The responsiveness of a stock to these factors is estimated using historical time series data.

Two examples of proprietary macroeconomic factor models are the Burmeister, Ibbotson, Roll, and Ross (BIRR) model[2] and the Salomon Brothers model.[3] Salomon Brothers refers to its model as the "Risk Attribute Model" or RAM. A RAM is built for the United States and other countries

In the BIRR model, there are five macroeconomic factors that reflect unanticipated changes in the following macroeconomic variables:

- Investor confidence (confidence risk)
- Interest rates (time horizon risk)
- Inflation (inflation risk)
- Real business activity (business cycle risk)
- A market index (market timing risk)

Exhibit 1 explains each of these macroeconomic factor risks

In the U.S. version of the Salomon Brothers RAM model, the following six macroeconomic factors have been found to best describe the financial environment and are therefore the factors used:

- change in expected long-run economic growth
- short-run business cycle risk
- long-term bond yield changes
- short-term Treasury bill changes
- inflation shock
- dollar changes versus trading partner currencies

---

[2] Edwin Burmeister, Roger Ibbotson, Richard Roll, and Stephen A. Ross, "Using Macroeconomic Factors to Control Portfolio Risk," unpublished paper. The information used in this chapter regarding the BIRR model is obtained from various pages of the BIRR website (*www.birr.com*).

[3] This model is described in Eric H. Sorensen, Joseph J. Mezrich, and Chee Thum, *The Salomon Brothers U.S. Risk Attribute Model, Salomon Brothers*, Quantitative Strategy, October 1989, and Joseph J. Mezrich, Mark O'Donnell, and Vele Samak, *U.S. RAM Model: Model Update*, Salomon Brothers, Equity Portfolio Analysis, April 8, 1997.

Exhibit 1: Macroeconomic Factor Risks in the BIRR Factor Model

Confidence Risk

Confidence Risk exposure reflects a stock's sensitivity to unexpected changes in investor confidence. Investors always demand a higher return for making relatively riskier investments. When their confidence is high, they are willing to accept a smaller reward than when their confidence is low. Most assets have a positive exposure to Confidence Risk. An unexpected increase in investor confidence will put more investors in the market for these stocks, increasing their price and producing a positive return for those who already held them. Similarly, a drop in investor confidence leads to a drop in the value of these investments. Some stocks have a negative exposure to the Confidence Risk factor, however, suggesting that investors tend to treat them as "safe haven" when their confidence is shaken.

Time Horizon Risk

Time Horizon Risk exposure reflects a stock's sensitivity to unexpected changes in investors' willingness to invest for the long term. An increase in time horizon tends to benefit growth stocks, while a decrease tends to benefit income stocks. Exposures can be positive or negative, but growth stocks as a rule have a higher (more positive) exposure than income stocks.

Inflation Risk

Inflation Risk exposure reflects a stock's sensitivity to unexpected changes in the inflation rate. Unexpected increases in the inflation rate put a downward pressure on stock prices, so most stocks have a negative exposure to Inflation Risk. Consumer demand for luxuries declines when real income is eroded by inflation. Thus, retailer, eating places, hotels, resorts, and other "luxuries" are harmed by inflation, and their stocks therefore tend to be more sensitive to inflation surprises and, as a result, have a more negative exposure to Inflation Risk. Conversely, providers of necessary goods and services (agricultural products, tire and rubber goods, etc.) are relatively less harmed by inflation surprises, and their stocks have a smaller (less negative) exposure. A few stocks attract investors in times of inflation surprise and have a positive Inflation Risk exposure.

Market Timing Risk

Market Timing Risk exposure reflects a stock's sensitivity to moves in the stock market as a whole that cannot be attributed to the other factors. Sensitivity to this factor provides information similar to that of the CAPM Beta about how a stock tends to respond to changes in the broad market. It differs in that the Market Timing factor reflects only those surprises that are not explained by the other four factors.

Business Cycle Risk

Business Cycle Risk exposure reflects a stock's sensitivity to unexpected changes in the growth rate of business activity. Stocks of companies such as retail stores that do well in times of economic growth have a higher exposure to Business Cycle Risk than those that are less affected by the business cycle, such as utilities or government contractors. Stocks can have a negative exposure to this factor if investors tend to shift their funds toward those stocks when news about the growth rate for the economy is not good.

Source: Reproduced from pages of the BIRR website (*www.birr.com*).

Exhibit 2: Macroeconomic Factors in the Salomon Brothers U.S. Risk Attribute Model

Economic Growth[a]
Monthly change in industrial production as measured concurrently with stock returns.

Business Cycle[b]
The change in the spread between the yield on 20-year investment-grade corporate bonds and 20-year Treasury bonds is used as a proxy for the shorter-term cyclical behavior of the economy. Changes in the spread capture the risk of default resulting from the interaction of earnings cyclicality and existing debt structure.

Long-Term Interest Rates[b]
The change in interest rates is measured by the change in the 10-year Treasury yield. Changes in this yield alters the relative attractiveness of financial assets and therefore induces a change in the portfolio mix.

Short-Term Interest Rates[b]
The change in short-term interest rates is measured by changes in the 1-month Treasury bill rate.

Inflation Shock[a]
Inflation is measured by the Consumer Price Index. The inflation shock component is found by subtracting expected inflation from realized inflation. Expected inflation is measured using a proprietary econometric model.

U.S. Dollar[b]
The impact of currency fluctuations on the market is measured by changes in the basket of currencies. Specifically, a 15-country, trade-weighted basket of currencies is used.

a. Adapted from Joseph J. Mezrich, Mark O'Donnell, and Vele Samak, *U.S. RAM Model: Model Update*, Salomon Brothers, Equity Portfolio Analysis, April 8, 1997, p. 1.
b. Adapted from the discussion on page 4 of Eric H. Sorensen, Joseph J. Mezrich, and Chee Thum, *The Salomon Brothers U.S. Risk Attribute Model*, Salomon Brothers, Quantitative Strategy, October 1989.

In addition, there is another factor called "residual market beta" which is included to capture macroeconomic factors after controlling for the other six macroeconomic factors. Exhibit 2 provides a brief description of each macroeconomic factor.

We'll use the RAM model to explain the procedure for estimating the parameters of the model. For each stock in the universe used by Salomon Brothers (about 3,500) a multiple regression is estimated. The dependent variable is the stock's monthly return. The independent variables are the six macroeconomic factors, the residual market factor, and other market factors. The size and statistical significance of the regression coefficients of each of the macroeconomic factors is examined. Then for all stocks in the universe the regression coefficient for each of the macroeconomic factors is standardized. The purpose of standardizing the estimated regression coefficients is that it makes a comparison of the relative sensitivity of a stock to each macroeconomic factor easier.

The standardization methodology is as follows. For a given macroeconomic factor, the average value and standard deviation of the estimated regression coefficient from all the stocks in the universe are computed. The standardized regression coefficient for a stock with respect to a given macroeconomic factor is then found by calculating the difference between the estimated regression coefficient and the average value and then dividing this value by the standard deviation. The standardized regression coefficient is restricted to a value between −5 and +5.

A stock's standardized regression coefficient for a given macroeconomic factor is then the measure of the sensitivity of that stock to that risk factor. The standardized regression coefficient is therefore the factor sensitivity. If a stock has a factor sensitivity for a specific macroeconomic factor of zero, this means that it has average response to that macroeconomic factor. The more the factor sensitivity deviates from zero, the more responsive the stock is to that risk factor. For example, consider the economic growth factor. A positive value for this macroeconomic factor means that if all other factors are unchanged, a company is likely to outperform market returns if the economy improves. A negative value for the economic growth factor means that if all other factors are unchanged, a company is likely to underperform market returns if the economy improves.

The sensitivity for the factors are estimated so that they are statistically independent. This means that there will be no double counting the influence of a factor.

Fundamental Factor Models

Fundamental factor models use company and industry attributes and market data as raw descriptors. Examples are price/earnings ratios, book/price ratios, estimated economic growth, and trading activity. The inputs into a fundamental factor model are stock returns and the raw descriptors about a company. Those fundamental variables about a company that are pervasive in explaining stock returns are then the raw descriptors retained in the model. Using cross-sectional analysis the sensitivity of a stock's return to a raw descriptor is estimated.

As determined by Jacobs and Levy,[4] many of these descriptors are highly correlated. Adding highly correlated factors to a model neither enhances returns nor lowers risk. Factors that by themselves seem to be important may be unimportant when combined with other factors; factors that by themselves seem not to be important may be important when combined with other factors. A manager must be able to untangle these relationships.

Two commercially available fundamental factor models are the BARRA and the Wilshire models. The BARRA E2 model begins with raw descriptors.[5] It then combines raw descriptors to obtain risk indexes to capture related company attributes. For example, raw descriptors such as debt-to-asset ratio, debt-to-equity ratio, and fixed-rate coverage are measures that capture a company's financial leverage. These measures would be combined to obtain a risk index for financial leverage.

---

[4] Bruce I. Jacobs and Kenneth N. Levy, "Disentangling Equity Return Regularities: New Insights and Investment Opportunities," *Financial Analyst Journal* (May-June 1988), pp. 18-43.

[5] The BARRA E2 model is BARRA's second generation U.S. equity model. In 1997, BARRA released its third generation U.S. equity model (BARRA E3). The discussion in this chapter and the information provided in Exhibits 3 and 4 are based on the BARRA E2 model. The E3 model closely resembles the E2 model in structure, but with improved industry and risk index definitions.

   The BARRA E2 fundamental factor model has 13 risk indexes and 55 industry groups. For 12 of the risk indexes and the 55 industry groups, the model is estimated for BARRA's HICAP universe (1,000 of the largest-capitalization companies plus selected slightly smaller companies to fill underrepresented industry groups) using statistical techniques. The universe has varied from 1,170 to 1,300 companies.

   Exhibit 3 reproduces the information about the 13 risk indexes as published by BARRA. Also shown in the exhibit are the raw descriptors used to construct each risk index. For example, the earnings-to-price ratio is a combination of the following raw descriptors: current earnings-to-price ratio, earnings-to-price ratio for the past five years, and IBES earnings-to-price ratio projection. Before each raw descriptor in Exhibit 3 is a plus or minus sign. The sign indicates how the raw descriptor influences a risk index. The 55 industry classifications are shown in Exhibit 4.

Exhibit 3: BARRA E2 Model Risk Index Definitions*

1. Variability In Markets (VIM)

This risk index is a predictor of the volatility of a stock based on its behavior and the behavior of its options in the capital markets. Unlike beta, which measures only the response of a stock to the market, Variability in Markets measures a stock's overall volatility, including its response to the market. A high beta stock will necessarily have a high Variability in Markets exposure. However, a high exposure will not necessarily imply a high beta; the stock may be responding to factors other than changes in the market.

   This index uses measures such as the cumulative trading range and daily stock price standard deviation to identify stocks with highly variable prices. BARRA uses different formulas for three categories of stocks.

   a. Optioned stocks — all stocks having listed options.
   b. Listed stocks — all stocks in the HICAP universe that are listed on an exchange but do not have listed options.
   c. Thin stocks — all stocks that are traded over the counter or are outside the HICAP universe, except those with listed options.

   Optioned stocks are distinct for several reasons. First, the option price provides an implicit forecast of the total standard deviation of the stock itself. Second, optioned stocks tend to be those with greatest investor interest and with the most effective trading volume. Stock trading volume descriptors understate the effective volume because they omit option volume.

   Thin stocks, about ten percent of the basic sample, are broken out because they tend to trade differently from other stocks. Over-the-counter stocks and other thinly traded securities show price behavior inconsistent with efficient and timely prices. Thin stocks are less synchronized with market movements, and exhibit frequent periods in which no meaningful price changes occur as well as occasional outlying price changes that are promptly reversed. These influences cause some indicators of stock price variability to be biased.

   In calculating this index, BARRA standardizes the formulas for the three stock categories relative to one another to provide one index for the total population.

   A. Optioned Stock Descriptors
      + Cumulative Range, 12 months
      + Beta * Sigma
      + Option Standard Deviation
      + Daily Standard Deviation

Exhibit 3 (Continued)

B. Listed Stock Descriptors
  + Beta * Sigma
  + Cumulative Range, 12 months
  + Daily Standard Deviation
  + Trading Volume to Variance
  − Log of Common Stock Price
  + Serial Dependence
  − Annual Share Turnover
C. Thin Stock Descriptors
  + Beta * Sigma
  + Cumulative Range, 12 months
  + Annual Share Turnover
  − Log of Common Stock Price
  − Serial Dependence

2. Success (SCS)
The Success index identifies recently successful stocks using price behavior in the market (measured by historical alpha and relative strength) and, to a lesser degree, earnings growth information. The relative strength of a stock is significant in explaining its volatility.

  + Relative Strength
  + Historical Alpha
  + Recent Earnings Change
  + IBES Earnings Growth
  − Dividend Cuts, 5 years
  + Growth in Earnings per Share

3. Size (SIZ)
The Size index values total assets and market capitalization to differentiate large stocks from small stocks. This index has been a major determinant of performance over the years as well as an important source of risk.

  + Log of Capitalization
  + Log of Total Assets
  + Indicator of Earnings History

4. Trading Activity (TRA)
Trading activity measures the relative activity of a firm's shares in the market, or the "institutional popularity" of a company. The most important descriptors are the share turnover variables. In addition, this index includes the ratio of trading volume to price variability, the logarithm of price, and the number of analysts following the stock, as reported in the IBES database. The stocks with more rapid share turnover, lower price, and signs of greater trading activity are generally the higher risk stocks.

  + Annual Share Turnover
  + Quarterly Share Turnover
  + Share Turnover, 5 years
  + Log of Common Stock Price
  + IBES Number of Analysts
  + Trading Volume to Variance

Exhibit 3 (Continued)

5. Growth (GRO)

The Growth index is primarily a predictor of a company's future growth but also reflects its historical growth. BARRA estimates earnings growth for the next five years using regression techniques on a comprehensive collection of descriptors, all of which are distinct elements of the growth concept. The Growth index includes descriptors of payout, asset growth and historical growth in earnings, the level of earnings to price, and variability in capital structure.

- − Payout, 5 years
- − Earnings to Price Ratio, 5 years
- + Earnings Growth
- + Capital Structure Change
- − Normalized Earnings to Price Ratio
- + Recent Earnings Change
- − Dividend Yield, 5 years
- + IBES Earnings Change
- − Yield Forecast
- + Indicator of Zero Yield
- − Earnings to Price Ratio
- − IBES Earnings to Price Ratio
- + Growth in Total Assets

6. Earnings to Price Ratio (EPR)

The Earnings to Price Ratio measures the relationship between company earnings and market valuation. To compute the Earnings to Price Ratio, BARRA combines measures of past, current, and estimated future earnings.

- + Current Earnings to Price Ratio
- + Earnings to Price Ratio, 5 years
- + IBES Earnings to Price Ratio Projection

7. Book to Price Ratio (BPR)

This index is simply the book value of common equity divided by the market capitalization of a firm.

8. Earnings Variability (EVR)

The Earnings Variability index measures a company's historical earnings variability and cash flow fluctuations. In addition to variance in earnings over five years, it includes the relative variability of earnings forecasts taken from the IBES database, and the industry concentration of a firm's activities.

- + Variance in Earnings
- + IBES Standard Deviation to Price Ratio
- + Earnings Covariability
- + Concentration
- + Variance of Cash Flow
- + Extraordinary Items

9. Financial Leverage (FLV)

The Financial Leverage index captures the financial structure of a firm as well as its sensitivity to interest rates using the debt to assets ratio, the leverage at book value, and the probability of fixed charges not being covered. Bond market sensitivity is included only for financial companies.

Exhibit 3 (Continued)

– Bond Market Sensitivity
+ Debt to Assets Ratio
+ Leverage at Book (Debt to Equity)
+ Uncovered Fixed Charges

10. Foreign Income (FOR)
This index reflects the fraction of operating income earned outside the United States. It is a measure of sensitivity to currency exchange rate changes.

11. Labor Intensity (LBI)
This index estimates the importance of labor, relative to capital, in the operations of a firm. It is based on ratios of labor expense to assets, fixed plant and equipment to equity, and depreciated plant value to total plant cost. A higher exposure to Labor Intensity indicates a larger ratio of labor expense to capital costs and can be a gauge of sensitivity to cost-push inflation.

+ Labor Share
– Inflation-adjusted Plant to Equity Ratio
– Net Plant to Gross Plant

12.Yield (YLD)
The Yield index is simply a relative measure of the company's annual dividend yield.

1 3. LOCAP
The LOCAP characteristic indicates those companies that are not in the HICAP universe. It permits the factors in the model to be applied across a broader universe of assets than that used to estimate the model. The LOCAP factor is, in part, an extension of the Size index, allowing the returns of approximately 4500 smaller companies to deviate from an exact linear relationship with ιe Size index.

*In 1997, BARRA released its E3 model which closely resembles the E2 model but with improved risk index definitions.
Source: *United States Equity Model Handbook* (Berkeley, CA: BARRA, 1996), pp. 19-23.

Exhibit 4: BARRA E2 Model Industry Classifications*

The industry classifications in the U.S. Model are:			
1. Aluminum	15. Liquor	29. Photographic, Optical	43. Retail (All Other)
2. Iron & Steel	16. Tobacco	30. Consumer Durables	44. Telephone, Telegraph
3. Precious Metals	17. Construction	31. Motor Vehicles	45. Electric Utilities
4. Misc. Mining, Metals	18. Chemicals	32. Leisure, Luxury	46. Gas Utilities
5. Coal & Uranium	19. Tires & Rubber	33. Health Care (Non-drug)	47. Banks
6. International Oil	20. Containers	34. Drugs, Medicine	48. Thrift Institutions
7. Dom. Petroleum Reserves	21. Producer Goods	35. Publishing	49. Miscellaneous Finance
8. For. Petroleum Reserves	22. Pollution Control	36. Media	50. Life Insurance
9. Oil Refining, Distribution	23. Electronics	37. Hotels, Restaurants	51. Other Insurance
10. Oil Service	24. Aerospace	38. Trucking, Freight	52. Real Property
11. Forest Products	25. Business Machines	39. Railroads, Transit	53. Mortgage Financing
12. Paper	26. Soaps, Housewares	40. Air Transport	54. Services
13. Agriculture, Food	27. Cosmetics	41. Transport by Water	55. Miscellaneous
14. Beverages	28. Apparel, Textiles	42. Retail (Food)	

* In 1997, BARRA released its E3 model which has improved industry classifications.
Source: *United States Equity Model Handbook* (Berkeley, CA: BARRA, 1996), pp. 32.

Exhibit 5: Fundamental Factors and Market Sensitive Factor Definitions for Wilshire Atlas Factor Model

1.Earnings/price ratio	Sum of the most recent four quarters' earnings per share divided by the closing price.
2. Book value/price ratio	Book value divided by common equity shares outstanding.
3. Market capitalization	The natural logarithm of the product of a security's price multiplied by the number of shares outstanding.
4. Net earnings revision	Analysts momentum measure: Net earnings revision, based on I/B/E/S data, measures analysts' optimism of earnings. Net earnings revision is the percentage of analysts who are feeling more optimistic about earnings in the next period. The higher the net earnings revision number, the more optimistic analysts are about an increase in that company's earnings.
5. Reversal	Price momentum measure: Reversal captures the mean reversion tendencies of stocks. It is a measure of the difference between a security's actual return in the last period and the expected return with respect to its beta. If a stock has a positive reversal this means that it had a higher than expected return in the last period given its beta. Thus, this security is expected to have a lower than expected return in the next period so that the returns for this security will conform to the norm expectations over the long run.
6. Earnings torpedo	Earnings momentum measure: Earnings torpedo, based on I/B/E/S data, is a measure of the estimated growth in earnings for a security relative to historical earnings. Earnings torpedo is based on the ratio of next years estimated earnings per share versus its historical earnings per share. The securities in the universe are then ranked by the estimate and given an earnings torpedo score. A security with a high earnings torpedo score is considered to be vulnerable to a large drop in price if earnings do not meet the higher earnings estimates forecasted by analysts in the next period.
7. Historical beta	Classic measure of security volatility. Measured for each security by regressing the past 60 months worth of excess returns against the S&P500. A minimum of 38 months are required for the data to be valid.

Source: Adapted from *U.S. Equity Risk Model* (Santa Monica, CA: Wilshire Associates, July 1997 draft).

As with the macroeconomic factor model, the raw descriptors are standardized or normalized. The risk indices are in turn standardized. The sensitivity of each company to each risk index is standardized.

The Wilshire Atlas model uses six fundamental factors, one market factor sensitivity, and 39 industry factors to explain stock returns. The six fundamental factors and the market factor sensitivity are listed in Exhibit 5, along with their definitions.

The BARRA and Wilshire factor models are commercially available. Now we'll look at a proprietary model developed by a firm for its own use in managing client equity portfolios — Goldman Sachs Asset Management (GSAM). This firm is the investment management subsidiary of Goldman Sachs & Co., a broker/dealer firm. There are nine descriptors used in the GSAM factor model. These descriptors which are the factors in the model are described in Exhibit 6. The factors fall into three categories: (1) value measures, (2) growth and momentum measures, and (3) risk measures.

Exhibit 6: Factor Definitions for the Goldman Sachs Asset Management Factor Model

Factor	Definition
Book/Price	Common equity per share divided by price
Retained EPS/Price	Year-ahead consensus EPS forecast less indicated annual dividend divided by price. One-year forecast EPS is a weighted average of the forecasts for the current and next fiscal years.
EBITD/Enterprise Value	Earnings before interest, taxes and depreciation divided by total capital. Total capital is equity at market plus long-term debt at book.
Estimate Revisions	The number of estimates raised in the past three months, less the number lowered, divided by the total number of estimates.
Price Momentum	Total return over the last 12 months, less the return for the latest month (to adjust for short-term reversals).
Sustainable Growth	The consensus long-term growth forecast.
Beta	The regression coefficient from a 60-month regression of the stock's excess returns (above the T-bill rate) against the market's excess returns.
Residual Risk	The "unexplained" variation from the above regression; the standard error of the regression.
Disappointment Risk	The risk that actual earnings will not meet projections. Stocks with high expected one-year earnings growth have high disappointment potential; stocks with low expectations have less disappointment risk.

Source: Table 4 in *Select Equity Investment Strategy*, Goldman Sachs Asset Management, February 1997, p. 4.

THE OUTPUT AND INPUTS OF A FACTOR MODEL

Now that we have identified the types of factor models, let's look at the output of the model and the inputs to the model after the estimation has taken place. The output of a factor model is found by first multiplying a factor sensitivity by the assumed value for the factor measure (assumed risk factor).[6] This gives the contribution to the model's output from a given risk factor exposure. Summing up over all risk factors gives the output. For a *K*-factor model this is expressed mathematically as follows:

$$\text{Output} = \text{Beta}_1 \times (\text{Factor}_1 \text{ measure}) + \text{Beta}_2 \times (\text{Factor}_2 \text{ measure}) + \dots$$
$$+ \text{Beta}_K \times (\text{Factor}_K \text{ measure})$$

Let's look first at the Beta's. These are the factor sensitivities and are estimated statistically. As explained earlier, they are commonly standardized or normalized.

The output varies by model. For example, in the BIRR macroeconomic factor model, the output is the *expected excess return* given the estimated factor sensitivities and the assumed values for the factor measures. The expected excess return is the expected return above the risk-free rate. In contrast, in the Salomon

---

[6] For an example of quantitative estimation of returns to the size factor using economic variables, see Bruce I. Jacobs and Kenneth N. Levy, "Forecasting the Size Effect," *Financial Analysts Journal* (May-June 1989), pp.61-78.

Brothers RAM factor model, the output is a score that is used to rank the outcome given the estimated factor sensitivities and assumed values for the factor measures.

The factor measures vary by model. In the BIRR macroeconomic factor model, for example, a factor measure is the estimated market price of the risk factor expressed in percent per year. For the Salomon Brothers RAM factor model, a factor measure is the normalized value for the factor.

Let's use the two macroeconomic models described earlier to show how the output is obtained. First, the BIRR model. The estimated risk exposure profile for Reebok International Limited and the assumed values for the risk factors (expressed in percent per year) are shown below:

Risk factor	Estimated factor sensitivity	Estimated market price of risk (%)
Confidence risk	0.73	2.59
Time horizon risk	0.77	−0.66
Inflation risk	−0.48	−4.32
Business cycle risk	4.59	1.49
Market timing risk	1.50	3.61

The expected excess return is then found as follows:

Expected excess return for Reebok = 0.73 (2.59) + 0.77 (−0.66)
+ (−0.48) (−4.32) + 4.59 (1.49) + 1.50 (3.61) = 15.71%

To obtain the expected return, the risk-free rate must be added. For example, if the risk-free rate is 5%, then the expected return is 20.71% (15.71% plus 5%).

In the Salomon Brothers RAM model, the set of forecasts for the factor measures are called *scenario factors*. Based on scenario factors, the sensitivity of a stock to each factor can be calculated. Adding up the sensitivity of a stock to each factor gives a stock's *scenario score*. Recall that in this factor model there are six macroeconomic factors (described in Exhibit 2) and the residual beta. Each factor is expressed in normalized or standardized form. For Pepsico (in October 1989) the factor betas and a factor scenario for a weakening economy are given below:[7]

Risk factor	Estimated factor sensitivity	Factor scenario (Weakening economy)
Economic growth	−1.8	−1.0
Business cycle	−0.9	−0.5
Long rate	0.0	0.5
Short rate	0.1	0.3
Inflation rate	−0.3	0.1
U.S. dollar	0.1	0.3
Residual beta	−1.1	−0.5

[7] Sorensen, Mezrich, and Thum, "The Salomon Brothers U.S. Stock Risk Attribute Model," p. 6.

The scenario score for Pepsico is then:

Pepsico scenario score = −1.8 (−1.0) + (−0.9) (−0.5) + 0 (0.5) + 0.1 (0.3)
+ (−0.3) (0.1) + 0.1 (0.3) + (−1.1) (−0.5) = 1.7

This scenario score is then compared to the scenario score of other stocks in the universe of purchase or short-sale candidates of a portfolio manager.

PORTFOLIO CONSTRUCTION WITH FACTOR MODELS

Now let's see how factor models are used in portfolio construction. Specifically, based on expectations about the future outcomes of the factors, an active equity manager can construct a portfolio to add value relative to some benchmark should those outcomes be realized.

Portfolio Expected Excess Returns and Risk Exposure Profiles

In factor models in which the output is an expected excess return for a stock, the expected excess return for a portfolio can be easily computed. This is the weighted average of the expected excess return for each stock in the portfolio. The weights are the percentage of a stock value in the portfolio relative to the market value of the portfolio. Similarly, a portfolio's sensitivity to a given factor risk is a weighted average of the factor sensitivity of the stocks in the portfolio. The set of factor sensitivities is then the portfolio's risk exposure profile. Consequently, the expected excess return and the risk exposure profile can be obtained from the stocks comprising the portfolio.

Since a stock market index is nothing more than a portfolio that includes the universe of stocks making up the index, an expected excess return and risk exposure profile can be determined for an index. This allows a manager to compare the expected excess return and the risk profile of a stock and/or a portfolio to that of a stock market index whose performance the portfolio manager is measured against. For example, in the BIRR model, the risk exposure profile for the S&P 500 is shown below, as well as that of Reebok for comparative purposes:

Risk factor	Estimated factor sensitivity for	
	S&P 500	Reebok
Confidence risk	0.27	0.73
Time horizon risk	0.56	0.77
Inflation risk	−0.37	−0.48
Business cycle risk	1.71	4.59
Market timing risk	1.00	1.50

By comparing the risk exposure profile of Reebok to the S&P 500, a portfolio manager can see the relative risk exposure. Using the same assumed values for the risk factors as used earlier for Reebok, the expected excess return for the S&P 500 is 8.09% compared to 15.71% for Reebok.

Exhibit 7: Portfolio Holdings for Manager X

BARRA Microcomputer Products:		Interactive PORCH					Page 1
Portfolio: SAMPLE		Market: SAP500				Pricing Date: 07-31-90	

IDENT	NAME	SHARES	PRICE	%WGT	BETA	%YLD	IND
1 FDX	FEDERAL EXPRESS CORP	80700	41.625	3.00	1.15	0.00	AIR
2 NEM	NEWMONT MNG CORP	67500	49.500	2.98	0.76	1.21	GOLD
3 I	FIRST INTST BANCORP	167700	33.000	4.94	1.32	9.09	BANKS
4 HWP	HEWLETT PACKARD CO	126900	43.125	4.89	1.15	0.97	BUS MN
5 IBM	INTERNATIONAL BUS MACH	141400	111.500	14.08	1.01	4.34	BUS MN
6 F	FORD MTR CO DEL	273100	41.500	10.12	0.98	7.17	MOT VH
7 HCSG	HEALTHCARE SVCS GRP IN	93000	24.250	2.01	1.29	0.28	SERVCS
8 TXN	TEXAS INSTRS INC	81500	32.000	2.33	1.41	2.25	ELCTRN
9 S	SEARS ROEBUCK & CO	342900	33.625	10.30	1.09	5.94	RET OT
10 AXP	AMERICAN EXPRESS CO	291900	29.125	7.59	1.20	3.15	FINANC
11 JNJ	JOHNSON & JOHNSON	205800	70.625	12.98	1.02	1.92	HEALTH
12 EK	EASTMAN KODAK CO	324800	38.125	11.06	1.10	5.24	PHOTOG
13 WMX	WASTE MGMT INC	185900	41.375	6.87	1.24	0.86	POLL C
14 PCI	PARAMOUNT COMMUNICATIO	118900	39.500	4.20	1.14	1.77	PUBLSH
15 TAN	TANDY CORP	79800	36.750	2.62	1.26	1.63	RET OT

Source: The information in this exhibit is adapted from Figure VI-1 of *United States Equity Model Handbook* (Berkeley, CA: BARRA, 1996), p. 40.

In factor models such as the Salomon Brothers RAM model where the output is a *scenario score*, the risk exposure profile of a portfolio and market index is calculated in the same manner as when the model's output is the expected excess return. However, in scenario score models the portfolio's and market index's output is a ranking.

The power of a factor model regardless of the type of output is that given the risk factors and the factor sensitivities, a portfolio's risk exposure profile can be quantified and controlled. The examples below show how this can be done with a fundamental factor model. This allows managers to avoid making unintended bets.

Assessing the Exposure of a Portfolio

A fundamental factor model can be used to assess whether the current portfolio is consistent with a manager's strengths. In this application of factor models and the one that follows, we will use the BARRA factor model.[8] Exhibit 7 is a list of the holdings of manager X as of July 31, 1990.[9] There are 15 stocks held with a total market value of $111.9 million.

Exhibit 8 assesses the risk exposure of manager X's portfolio relative to the risk exposure of the S&P 500. The boxes in the second column of the exhibit indicate the significant differences in the exposure of manager X's portfolio relative to the S&P 500. There are two risk indices boxed — success and foreign

---

[8] The illustrations are adapted from Chapter VI of *United States Equity Model Handbook* (Berkeley, CA: BARRA, 1996).
[9] This was an actual portfolio of a BARRA client.

income — and two industry groupings boxed — business machines and miscellaneous finance. Exhibit 3 describes the risk indices. The -0.45 exposure to the success risk index reveals that manager X's portfolio exhibits low relative strength as measured by stock price and earnings momentum — a style characteristic. Consequently, the success risk index indicates an exposure to style. Thus, we can see that manager X is making a style bet. The 0.62 exposure to the foreign income risk index tells manager X that the companies in the portfolio tend to earn a significant portion of their operating income abroad. Consequently, manager X is making an international bet. In terms of industry exposure, manager X is extremely more aggressive in his or her holdings of business machine stocks and miscellaneous finance stocks.

Notice in this example how the manager is able to identify where the bets are made. Manager X has made a style bet, an international bet, and a bet on two industries. If the manager did not intend to make these bets, the portfolio can be rebalanced to eliminate any unintended bets.

Tilting a Portfolio

Now let's look at how an active manager can construct a portfolio to make intentional bets. Suppose that manager Y seeks to construct a portfolio that generates superior returns relative to the S&P 500 by tilting it toward high-success stocks. At the same time, the manager does not want to increase tracking error risk significantly. An obvious approach may seem to be to identify all the stocks in the universe that have a higher than average success risk index. The problem with this approach is that it introduces unintentional bets with respect to the other risk indices.

Instead, an optimization method combined with a factor model can be used to construct the desired portfolio. The input to this process is the tilt exposure sought, the benchmark stock market index, and the number of stocks to be included in the portfolio. The BARRA optimization model also requires a specification of the excess return sought. In our illustration, the tilt exposure sought is high success stocks, the benchmark is the S&P 500, and the number of stocks to be included in the portfolio is 50. While we do not report the holdings of the optimal portfolio here, Exhibit 9 provides an analysis of that portfolio by comparing the risk exposure of the 50-stock optimal portfolio to that of the S&P 500.

Fundamental Factor Models and Equity Style Management

In Chapter 4, we covered equity style management. Notice that the factors used in fundamental factor models such as the BARRA factor model (Exhibit 3), Wilshire factor model (Exhibit 5), and the GSAM factor model (Exhibit 6) are the same characteristics used in style management. Since the factors can be used to add value and control risk, this suggests that factor models can be used in style management for the same purposes.

Exhibit 8: Analysis of Manager X Portfolio's Exposure Relative to the S&P 500

```
Comparison Summary Report                          Date: 07-31-90

Portfolio            SAMPLE
Comparison Port.     SAP500
Market               SAP500

Number of Assets           15
Port. Value    111,940,087.50
Predicted Yield          3.78
Alpha                    0.00
Utility                 -0.36
Tracking Error           7.25
```

FACTORS	SAMPLE	SAP500	DIFF	MCTE
VARIABILITY IN MARKETS	0.02	-0.06	0.09	0.010
SUCCESS	-0.45	0.01	-0.47	-0.021
SIZE	0.54	0.29	0.26	0.004
TRADING ACTIVITY	0.22	0.00	0.22	-0.002
GROWTH	-0.12	-0.05	-0.07	0.016
EARNINGS/PRICE	0.08	0.01	0.08	0.007
BOOK/PRICE	0.18	-0.02	0.20	0.001
EARNINGS VARIATION	0.00	-0.05	0.05	0.003
FINANCIAL LEVERAGE	0.28	0.03	0.25	-0.001
FOREIGN INCOME	0.62	0.12	0.51	-0.001
LABOR INTENSITY	0.30	0.01	0.29	-0.003
YIELD	0.16	0.02	0.14	0.007
LOCAP	0.02	0.00	0.02	-0.005
ALUMINUM	0.00	0.60	-0.60	0.099
IRON AND STEEL	0.00	0.30	-0.30	0.081
PRECIOUS METALS	1.25	0.42	0.83	0.071
MISC. MINING, METALS	0.54	0.61	-0.07	0.073
COAL AND URANIUM	0.00	0.40	-0.40	0.013
INTERNATIONAL OIL	0.00	4.49	-4.49	-0.033
DOM PETROLEUM RESERVES	0.51	3.46	-2.96	-0.047
FOR PETROLEUM RESERVES	0.69	2.25	-1.56	-0.037
OIL REFINING, DISTRIBUTN	0.00	1.29	-1.29	-0.011
OIL SERVICE	0.00	1.02	-1.02	-0.017
FOREST PRODUCTS	0.00	0.30	-0.30	0.120
PAPER	0.00	2.06	-2.06	0.082
AGRICULTURE, FOOD	0.00	4.99	-4.99	0.047
BEVERAGES	0.00	1.41	-1.41	0.066
LIQUOR	0.00	1.05	-1.05	0.050
TOBACCO	0.00	1.38	-1.38	0.067
CONSTRUCTION	0.00	0.88	-0.88	0.098
CHEMICALS	1.99	3.44	-1.45	0.083
TIRE & RUBBER	0.00	0.10	-0.10	0.101
CONTAINERS	0.00	0.17	-0.17	0.069
PRODUCERS GOODS	0.02	4.49	-4.47	0.086
POLLUTION CONTROL	6.87	1.13	5.75	0.124
ELECTRONICS	2.21	2.39	-0.18	0.126
AEROSPACE	0.00	2.47	-2.47	0.089
BUSINESS MACHINES	19.07	4.80	14.26	0.130
SOAPS, HOUSEWARE	0.00	1.99	-1.99	0.084
COSMETICS	4.54	0.94	3.60	0.096
APPAREL, TEXTILES	0.00	0.77	-0.77	0.080
PHOTOGRAPHIC, OPTICAL	6.75	0.55	6.20	0.114
CONSUMER DURABLES	0.00	0.99	-0.99	0.104
MOTOR VEHICLES	8.91	2.42	6.49	0.114
LEISURE, LUXURY	0.00	0.18	-0.18	0.096
HEALTH CARE (NON-DRUG)	5.06	1.85	3.21	0.070
DRUGS, MEDICINE	5.70	6.81	-1.12	0.066
PUBLISHING	2.10	1.48	0.62	0.090
MEDIA	2.10	1.67	0.43	0.079
HOTELS, RESTAURANTS	0.00	1.75	-1.75	0.094
TRUCKING, FREIGHT	0.00	0.13	-0.13	0.098
RAILROADS, TRANSIT	0.00	0.92	-0.92	0.046
AIR TRANSPORT	3.00	0.59	2.41	0.139
TRANSPORT BY WATER	0.00	0.03	-0.03	0.039
RETAIL (FOOD)	0.00	0.85	-0.85	0.062
RETAIL (ALL OTHER)	6.12	5.19	0.93	0.098
TELEPHONE, TELEGRAPH	0.00	8.26	-8.26	0.036
ELECTRIC UTILITIES	0.00	4.37	-4.37	0.024
GAS UTILITIES	0.00	1.17	-1.17	0.019
BANKS	6.49	2.93	3.56	0.063
THRIFT INSTITUTIONS	0.00	0.28	-0.28	0.073
MISC. FINANCE	10.87	2.20	8.67	0.094
LIFE INSURANCE	0.00	0.92	-0.92	0.061
OTHER INSURANCE	2.37	2.24	0.13	0.059
REAL PROPERTY	0.82	0.19	0.63	0.107
MORTGAGE FINANCING	0.00	0.00	-0.00	0.068
SERVICES	2.01	1.89	0.12	0.070
MISCELLANEOUS	0.00	0.56	-0.56	0.053

Source: The information in this exhibit is adapted from Figure VI-3 of *United States Equity Model Handbook* (Berkeley, CA: BARRA, 1996), p. 42.

Exhibit 9: Analysis of a 50-Stock Portfolio Constructed to be Tilted Toward High Success Stocks

Comparison Summary Report		Date: 07-31-90
Portfolio	SUCCESS	
Comparison Port.	SAP500	
Market	SAP500	
Number of Assets	50	
Port. Value	99,999,723.50	
Predicted Yield	3.04	
Alpha	0.31	
Utility	0.18	
Tracking Error	4.19	

FACTORS	US50	SAP500	DIFF
VARIABILITY IN MARKETS	0.10	-0.06	0.16
SUCCESS	0.77	0.01	0.76
SIZE	0.24	0.29	-0.05
TRADING ACTIVITY	-0.06	0.00	-0.07
GROWTH	0.10	-0.05	0.15
EARNINGS/PRICE	-0.00	0.01	-0.01
BOOK/PRICE	-0.16	-0.02	-0.14
EARNINGS VARIATION	0.00	-0.05	0.05
FINANCIAL LEVERAGE	-0.16	0.03	-0.19
FOREIGN INCOME	-0.10	0.12	-0.21
LABOR INTENSITY	-0.04	0.01	-0.05
YIELD	-0.11	0.02	-0.13
LOCAP	0.00	0.00	-0.00
ALUMINUM	1.98	0.60	1.38
IRON AND STEEL	0.00	0.30	-0.30
PRECIOUS METALS	0.50	0.42	0.07
MISC. MINING, METALS	0.47	0.61	-0.14
COAL AND URANIUM	0.42	0.40	0.02
INTERNATIONAL OIL	4.36	4.49	-0.13
DOM PETROLEUM RESERVES	2.45	3.46	-1.01
FOR PETROLEUM RESERVES	3.19	2.25	0.94
OIL REFINING, DISTRIBUTN	1.44	1.29	0.15
OIL SERVICE	1.79	1.02	0.77
FOREST PRODUCTS	0.03	0.30	-0.27
PAPER	1.07	2.06	-0.99
AGRICULTURE, FOOD	5.29	4.99	0.30
BEVERAGES	0.00	1.41	-1.41
LIQUOR	0.37	1.05	-0.68
TOBACCO	3.13	1.38	1.75
CONSTRUCTION	2.27	0.88	1.39
CHEMICALS	3.39	3.44	-0.05
TIRE & RUBBER	0.00	0.10	-0.10
CONTAINERS	0.00	0.17	-0.17
PRODUCERS GOODS	4.36	4.49	-0.14
POLLUTION CONTROL	2.38	1.13	1.25
ELECTRONICS	4.24	2.39	1.84
AEROSPACE	3.11	2.47	0.64
BUSINESS MACHINES	1.39	4.80	-3.42
SOAPS, HOUSEWARE	4.79	1.99	2.80
COSMETICS	0.29	0.94	-0.66
APPAREL, TEXTILES	0.98	0.77	0.21
PHOTOGRAPHIC, OPTICAL	0.00	0.55	-0.55
CONSUMER DURABLES	0.73	0.99	-0.27
MOTOR VEHICLES	4.35	2.42	1.94
LEISURE, LUXURY	0.00	0.18	-0.18
HEALTH CARE (NON-DRUG)	2.10	1.85	0.25
DRUGS, MEDICINE	4.60	6.81	-2.21
PUBLISHING	0.00	1.48	-1.48
MEDIA	0.16	1.67	-1.51
HOTELS, RESTAURANTS	0.59	1.75	-1.16
TRUCKING, FREIGHT	0.00	0.13	-0.13
RAILROADS, TRANSIT	0.00	0.92	-0.92
AIR TRANSPORT	0.00	0.59	-0.59
TRANSPORT BY WATER	0.00	0.03	-0.03
RETAIL (FOOD)	4.78	0.85	3.93
RETAIL (ALL OTHER)	9.80	5.19	4.62
TELEPHONE, TELEGRAPH	0.00	8.26	-8.26
ELECTRIC UTILITIES	12.31	4.37	7.95
GAS UTILITIES	1.03	1.17	-0.14
BANKS	0.00	2.93	-2.93
THRIFT INSTITUTIONS	0.00	0.28	-0.28
MISC. FINANCE	2.10	2.20	-0.10
LIFE INSURANCE	1.67	0.92	0.75
OTHER INSURANCE	1.55	2.24	-0.69
REAL PROPERTY	0.23	0.19	0.04
MORTGAGE FINANCING	0.00	0.00	-0.00
SERVICES	0.19	1.89	-1.70
MISCELLANEOUS	0.15	0.56	-0.42

Source: The information in this exhibit is adapted from Figure VI-7 of *United States Equity Model Handbook* (Berkeley, CA: BARRA, 1996), p. 47.

Exhibit 10: Summary of Perfect Foresight Tests Two
Strategies Using Factor Models: 12-Month Rolling Value
Added (%) from January 1987 to July 1995

Country	Long Stock Strategy			Market Neutral Strategy		
	High	Low	Average	High	Low	Average
United States	82%	39%	55%	195%	75%	138%
United Kingdom	131	52	82	326	50	155
Japan	106	56	74	236	66	121
Canada	91	63	77	—	—	—

Source: Table 15 from David J. Leinweber, Robert D. Arnott, and Christopher G. Luck, "The Many Sides of Equity Style," Chapter 11 in T. Daniel Coggin, Frank J. Fabozzi, and Robert D. Arnott (eds.), *The Handbook of Equity Style Management* (New Hope, PA: Frank J. Fabozzi Associates, 1997).

RETURN PERFORMANCE POTENTIAL OF FACTOR MODELS

It is interesting to see how well a portfolio constructed using a factor model would have performed with perfect foresight. For example, suppose we are examining monthly returns. We look at the actual factor return for the month and use that as our expectation at the beginning of the month. Given the forecasts an optimization model can be used to design the optimal portfolio.

Leinweber, Arnott, and Luck performed this experiment for several countries using the BARRA factor model for those countries — United States, United Kingdom, Japan, and Canada — for the period January 1987 to July 1995.[10] Transaction costs for rebalancing a portfolio each month were incorporated. A 12-month rolling value added return was calculated. A value added return is the return above a broad-based stock index for the country.

Two strategies were followed. One was simply a long position in the stocks. The second was a market neutral long-short strategy.[11] Exhibit 10 reports the results of the perfect foresight tests. With perfect foresight, the BARRA factor model would have added significant value for each country stock portfolio. For example, in the United States even in the worst 12-month rolling period the factor-based model added 39% for the long stock strategy and 75% for the market neutral long-short strategy.

Eric Sorensen, Joseph Mezrich, and Chee Thum performed two backtests of the Salomon Brothers RAM (a macroeconomic factor model) to assess the model. The tests were basically event studies.[12] In the first backtest, these

[10] David J. Leinweber, Robert D. Arnott, and Christopher G. Luck, "The Many Sides of Equity Style," Chapter 11 in T. Daniel Coggin, Frank J. Fabozzi, and Robert D. Arnott (eds.), *The Handbook of Equity Style Management* (New Hope, PA: Frank J. Fabozzi, 1997).
[11] See Bruce I. Jacobs and Kenneth N. Levy, "The Long and Short on Long-Short," *Journal of Investing* (Spring 1997), pp. 73-86.
[12] Sorensen, Mezrich, and Thum, *The Salomon Brothers U.S. Risk Attribute Model.*

researchers looked at daily returns following an unexpected announcement regarding an inflation measure. Specifically, on July 14, 1989 the Producer Price Index that was announced was sharply less than anticipated. As a result, the yield on Treasury bills with one month to maturity fell on that day from 8.6% to 8.4%. An optimized portfolio that had a high sensitivity to inflation was constructed. The inflation sensitive tilted portfolio outperformed the S&P 500 by 46 basis points from the day prior to the event (July 13, 1989) through the day after the event (July 15, 1989). This result supports the position that the factor model was an important tool for constructing a portfolio based on expectations.

The second backtest was based on a longer period of time. The event in this case was the movement of the U.S. dollar during the spring of 1989. Specifically, there was an unexpected strengthening (i.e., appreciation) of the U.S. dollar relative to the German mark from May 12 to June 2, 1989. An optimized portfolio was constructed that was tilted towards stocks that benefited from a stronger U.S. dollar. The RAM-based portfolio tilted with this bias outperformed the S&P 500 by 62 basis points.

DIVIDEND DISCOUNT MODELS VERSUS FACTOR MODELS

Another approach used to value common stock is a dividend discount model (DDM). Based on certain assumptions, a DDM gives the expected return for a stock. As explained in this chapter, a factor model also gives the expected return for a stock. Thus both a factor model and a DDM are valuation models. The DDM can be either a stand-alone model or one of several inputs to a factor model.

A study by Bruce Jacobs and Kenneth Levy suggests that simple factor models can outperform a traditional dividend discount model.[13] Specifically, when they compared the contribution of a simple factor model with a traditional dividend discount model they found that less than one-half of 1% of the quarterly average actual returns is explained by the DDM. In contrast, about 43% of the average actual returns is explained by a factor model which includes the DDM and other factors. Thus, in their study the factor model outperformed the DDM hands down.

SUMMARY

There are three types of factor models: statistical factor models, macroeconomic factor models, and fundamental factor models. Statistical factor models use a statistical technique called principal components analysis to identify which raw descriptors best explain stock returns. The resulting factors are statistical artifacts

---

[13] Jacobs and Levy, "On the Value of 'Value'," *Financial Analysts Journal* (July/August 1988).

and are therefore difficult to interpret. Consequently, a statistical factor model is rarely used in practice. The more common factor models are the macroeconomic factor model and the fundamental factor model.

In a factor model, the sensitivity of a stock to a factor is estimated. The risk exposure profile of a stock is identified by a set of factor sensitivities. The risk exposure profile of a portfolio is the weighted average of the risk exposure profile of the stocks in the portfolio. Similarly, the risk exposure profile of a market index can be obtained.

The output of a factor model can be either the expected excess return or a scenario score. The expected excess return of a stock is found by multiplying each factor sensitivity by the assumed value for the risk factor and summing over all risk factors. The expected return is the expected excess return plus the risk-free rate. The expected excess return for a portfolio and a market index is just the weighted average of the expected excess return of the stocks comprising the portfolio or the market index.

The power of a factor model is that given the risk factors and the factor sensitivities, a portfolio's risk exposure profile can be quantified and controlled. Applications of factor models include the ability to assess whether or not the current portfolio is consistent with a manager's strengths and to construct a portfolio with a specific tilt without making unintentional bets. Since many factors in a fundamental model are the same characteristics used in style management, factor models can be used in controlling risk in a style management strategy.

Both dividend discount models and factor models can be used to value common stock. The output of a dividend discount model can be used as a factor in a factor model. One study suggests that factor models have significantly outperformed dividend discount models.

Chapter 6

Normal Portfolios: Construction of Customized Benchmarks

Jon A. Christopherson, Ph.D.
Research Fellow
Investment Policy and Research Group
Frank Russell Company

INTRODUCTION

It is axiomatic that investment manager portfolios returns should be compared against benchmarks composed of securities in the same asset class from which the portfolio was selected. Investment managers, though, will often specialize in subsets of a universe of securities, rather than consider the entire universe. This has come to be widely recognized, and the institutional investing industry has moved away from judging all equity managers against the S&P 500 index and toward the use of more manager-specific benchmarks. The choice of proper benchmarks to evaluate manager performance is a continuing problem for fund managers. One of the better known types of specialized benchmark (or index) for a specific manager is the normal portfolio.

Our purpose in this chapter is to discuss not only how to create normal portfolios but how to use them. We will show how to identify one that is well-constructed and how to properly apply it to fund management. The virtues and limitations of different methods will not be explored in great detail; however, we will address some of those virtues and limitations. The examples that follow are taken primarily from U.S. equities; however, the framework for developing normal portfolios presented here is applicable to other asset classes or to funds of different classes.

DEFINITION OF A NORMAL PORTFOLIO

The notion of a normal portfolio was first introduced by Barr Rosenberg and the BARRA organization. The choice of the word "normal" to describe a portfolio is intended to capture the idea that for each money manager there exists a habitat of securities whose composition is very similar to the manager's average portfolio over time. In this sense, the normal portfolio is long-term "typical" or "average."[1] But average or typical of what? It is not clear that there should be a unique or single normal portfolio for a manager. There is more than one reasonable average in which we might be interested; hence, there might be more than one normal portfolio we could construct. One useful definition of "normal portfolio" is:

> A normal portfolio is a set of securities that contains all of the securities from which a manager normally chooses, weighted as the manager would weight them in a portfolio. As such, a normal portfolio is a specialized index.

To get an idea of how we can approach the construction of normal portfolios, let us identify two basic dimensions of "desirability" in constructing normal portfolios. Benchmarks can be designed that are desirable in terms of closely matching the actual portfolio holdings of a manager. Alternatively, benchmarks can be designed that are desirable in terms of closely matching the available factors of return and risk in the marketplace to which the manager's portfolios are exposed. And more recently, benchmarks have been created from weighted combinations of asset class component indexes which themselves are composed of factors of return and risk. Each approach to creating benchmarks will produce portfolios and return series against which a manager's portfolio and performance can be evaluated.

The object of using a normal portfolio as a benchmark is to improve one's understanding of a manager's investment activities. This is accomplished by comparing the manager's performance against a passive investment alternative (such as a portfolio of securities from which the manager actually selects) that approximately matches the manager's investment activity. The aggregate of the normal portfolios for a mix of managers can be used to manage the total risk exposure of a fund. It is simple to identify over or underexposed sectors or risks by comparing such a combination of normal portfolios to a target asset class benchmark. Thus, a properly constructed normal portfolio may be used as a performance measurement benchmark and as a tool for constructing manager mixes. Let us examine each of these purposes in turn.

NORMAL PORTFOLIOS AS
MANAGER PERFORMANCE BENCHMARKS

The normal portfolio is normal or neutral because it includes all of the securities in the manager's investment habitat or the manager's opportunity set. Although the

---

[1] See Mark Kritzman, "How to Build a Normal Portfolio in Three Easy Steps," *Journal of Portfolio Management* (Summer 1987), pp. 21-23. The BARRA methodology is discussed in *The Normbook* (Berkeley, CA: BARRA, September 1988). For a discussion of more philosophical issues see Arjun Divecha and Richard Grinold, *Normal Portfolios: Issues for Sponsors, Managers, and Consultants* (Berkeley, CA: BARRA, February 1989).

Russell 3000 index or the S&P 500 could be a manager's normal portfolio, often this is not the case. Managers tend to specialize in different segments of the market, and broad market indicators are not generally useful for evaluating their stock selection and sector allocation skill. Broad market indexes are also inadequate as benchmarks for most managers because they contain many stocks managers would normally not even consider, much less choose. They also contain stocks in proportions managers would normally not hold. As a result, the average equity characteristics of many managers' portfolios can be quite different from a broad market index.

In fact, as Richard Roll pointed out, inappropriate use of broad market indexes can cause us to make incorrect judgments regarding a manager's riskiness and skill.[2] For example, a manager who specializes in defensive stocks will often outperform a broad market index during bear markets and underperform it during bull markets. In other words, when a manager's style is in favor he appears to be skillful, and when the style is out of favor his returns indicate a lack of skill. Without an adequate normal, it is difficult to determine if the manager has skill.

Therefore, to produce useful performance benchmarks, we must create a portfolio whose characteristics can be used to determine a manager's stock selection capability and, if appropriate, sector allocation skill. Presumably, the manager adds value by selecting the better performing stocks and/or the better performing sectors of his normal universe. If his portfolio return is worse than his normal universe return, then the manager made mistakes in choosing stocks, in departing from his normal weighting scheme, in choosing sectors, or all three.

The normal portfolio will also be useful not only if it is representative of the universe of securities that constitute the manager's "normal habitat," but if it holds these in proportions the manager normally holds. Furthermore, the normal portfolio's equity characteristics should closely resemble the manager's typical equity characteristics over time. Note however, that a manager's observed portfolio may vary considerably at any point in time — deviations from the normal are not unusual. This latter point is a constant source of difficulty because we are never really quite sure whether the observed current portfolio's deviation from the normal portfolio is merely the result of short-term tactical bets or a sign of a major shift in investment philosophy and style.

HOW TO CREATE A NORMAL PORTFOLIO

Approaches to Normal Portfolio Construction

There are several methods for creating normal portfolios. The most easily created is a list of stocks derived from an analysis of the manager's past behavior and is the approach most commonly used. A second approach is to base the list of stocks on factor risk exposures. A third approach, taking advantage of the advent of

---

[2] Richard Roll, "A Critique of the Asset Pricing Theory's Tests," *Journal of Financial Economics* (March 1977), pp. 129-176.

equity style indexes, is to create a simple weighted combination of indexes to match the manager portfolio. The first two approaches are the same in that they require reducing a broad universe of securities, such as the Russell 3000 index list of stocks, based on some characteristic(s) of the securities (e.g., price/earnings ratio or factor exposure) to obtain a subset of the broad universe. The resulting list of stocks is then weighted to produce a normal portfolio. The two approaches differ in the manner in which they derive screening and weighting rules. The third approach sacrifices portfolio membership accuracy but is easy to do. These benchmarks can all be used for performance and other portfolio comparisons.

If our interest is whether or not a manager picks the best stocks out of his "normal universe of stocks," where "normal universe" means the subset of all stocks that the manager actually considers for investment, then we can create a *manager-specific stock-matching benchmark*. In the approach advocated by Russell, the screening rules are determined by obtaining the proper screen criteria from the manager directly or from his written materials as augmented by an examination of his equity profiles over time. The resulting normal portfolio is used as a benchmark to determine performance attribution using the Russell standard analytic tools.

If our interest is to isolate macroeconomic sources of return and risk, we can create a *manager-specific factor benchmark*. A normal portfolio in this conception reflects the prominent financial characteristics the manager's portfolio would exhibit in the absence of active investment judgment. Given a credible factor model of stock returns and risks, our task is to create a portfolio of stocks similar to the manager's choice set and with factor exposures similar to the manager's average exposures. Such a benchmark allows us to evaluate how efficiently the manager chooses stocks given the exposures the manager undertakes.

In a factor model approach, the screening criteria are derived by examining the risk factor exposures over time.[3] The factor model approach analyzes the manager's average exposure to the various risk indexes of the BARRA risk model and assigns typical or average risk index exposures for the manager. Then the manager's performance is subsequently compared to the return that would have been generated by the hypothetical portfolio with the risk exposure of the normal.

If our interest is whether or not a manager can outperform a combination of readily available style indexes, then we can create a *manager-specific conditional style weighted benchmark*. There are two competing methods for obtaining the style weights. One is called "effective mix" and is based on the convariance of manager returns with style index returns.[4] The other method is called "portfolio characteristics analysis" and is based on the conditional evaluation of manager

---

[3] A procedure for factor normals is outlined in BARRA, *The Normbook* and Divecha and Grinold, *Normal Portfolios: Issues for Sponsors, Managers, and Consultants*.

[4] William F. Sharpe, "Determining a Funds Effective Asset Mix," *Investment Management Review* (December 1988), pp. 59-69 and William F. Sharpe, "Asset Allocation: Management Style and Performance Measurement," *Journal of Portfolio Management* (Winter 1992), pp. 7-19.

market relative equity characteristics.[5] The resulting normal portfolio is used as a benchmark just like the other two normal portfolio creation methods.

All three approaches provide useful, if somewhat different, information and all can be used profitably. However, the manager-specific stock-matching benchmark approach is somewhat easier to understand, implement, and provides the least ambiguous results. This approach will be the primary focus of this chapter.

MANAGER-SPECIFIC STOCK-MATCHING BENCHMARK

The Beginning Universe of Securities

In the manager-specific stock-matching benchmark the central goal is to capture stocks from which the manager normally chooses and on which one can obtain information reliably and readily. One could begin with all possible U.S. equities, which number over 6,000. The difficulty with this strategy is that sufficient data are often not available for many of the small capitalization stocks in this group. Furthermore, few investors in the United States actively trade the very small stocks which make up the tail end of the equity market.

There are a number of ways of isolating the beginning universe. Choosing subsets on the basis of capitalization is an easy first cut. A practical starting list would include the stocks in the Russell 3000. Using the Russell 3000 index list of stocks will provide coverage of nearly all U.S. stocks with capitalization above $20 million. One could also choose the list of stocks of the S&P 500 or some other major index; however, most of these are subsets of the Russell 3000.

Choosing the Securities for the Normal

Assuming the chosen universe contains all or most of the stocks from which the manager is likely to select, the next step is to reduce the list of stocks to those from which the manager actually does select. This is usually accomplished by subsetting the universe using screening criteria consistent with the manager's stock selection habit patterns. Decision rules are required for this process (i.e., it is necessary to have a numeric basis for deciding whether or not a stock belongs in the normal). Exhibit 1 is an example of the kind of information one needs to know in order to build a normal portfolio. This example comes from materials distributed by a well-known money management firm with a growth orientation. Note that these screens may not be used in any order. Sometimes the sequence of decision screens can make a great deal of difference.

The screens (as shown in Section A of Exhibit 1) must accurately capture the sub-universe of stocks from which the manager actually chooses. These

---

[5] Jon A. Christopherson and Dennis J. Trittin, "Equity Style Classification System," Chapter 4 in T. Daniel Coggin and Frank J. Fabozzi (eds.), *The Handbook of Equity Style Management,* (Frank J. Fabozzi Associates, New Hope, PA; 1995) pp. 69-98.

screens may be determined through communication with the manager or developed independently based on the fund manager's assessment of the manager's key selection criteria. In either case, the content of the screens is critical. Since, in our example, the manager will choose among large rather than small capitalization stocks, we would choose the broad, large capitalization market as the beginning universe (i.e., the Russell 1000). We would then subdivide or screen the universe on such criteria as those listed in Section A of Exhibit 1.

Exhibit 1: Example of Normal Portfolio Specification

Section A: Screening Procedure
Choose all stocks that meet the following criteria:

1. Capitalization	$\geq$	$350,000,000 *(i.e., large capitalization)*
2. Yield	$\leq$	5.00%
3. Book Price	$\leq$	0.5 Std. Deviation *(translates to Price/Book Ratio 1.00)*
4. Dividend Payout Ratio	$\leq$	Market *(translates to less than or equal to the mean of the distribution)*
5. Historical Beta	$\geq$	0.85
6. Earnings Variability	$\geq$	(0.5) Std. Deviation *(translates to one-half standard deviation below the mean of the distribution)*

Section B: Weight Scheme
Equal Weight Within the Following Parameters

	% of Portfolio
$350 Million - $1 Billion	15%
$1 Billion - $3 Billion	30%
$3 Billion - $6 Billion	35%
$6 Billion and up	15%
IBM	5%

Section C: Rebalancing Scheme
Prior to 1989, the manager ran the screens semiannually and rebalanced position sizes monthly. After 1989, they do not rebalance monthly, rather they let the positions run for the full six months.

Of course, "average" can mean either the mean or median of the distribution, depending on the skewness of the underlying distribution. The equity portfolio statistics of the Russell 1000 or 3000 are useful market mean values since they are capitalization-weighted means. One could divide the universe in half by using the median, since the distributions of many characteristics are skewed, but there is the problem of whether to use weighted or unweighted medians. Where possible, the breakpoints should be set on the basis of the manager's behavior, either as described by the manager or as it has been observed. If the manager's decision criteria are not known, it may be desirable to try several screening values and examine how representative the resulting sub-universes are.

There are no unambiguous rules about setting screening values. The only good check is the reasonableness of the resulting sub-universe given the manager's style of investing. Two ways to judge the reasonableness of a sub-universe are (1) by evaluating how well the manager's return patterns fit the normal and (2) by evaluating how well the normal fits the manager's portfolio characteristics. If we had to choose between the two criteria, we should be more concerned with the portfolio characteristics than with similarity of performance because of the role of noise in stock returns. However, we would expect to find, on average, significantly higher correlations between the manager's performance and the normal than with the broad market and also a lower residual variance relative to the normal than to other indexes. The size of these differences is a function of the differences between the normal universe and the broad market as well as the noise introduced by the size of the bets the manager makes relative to his normal.

Conditional Decision Making and Manager Universe Misfit

If stock characteristics used in screens are independent (i.e., they are not correlated or causally related), then the sequence in which the variables are taken does not matter. However, the variables many managers use to choose stocks for their normal universe are not independent, and the sequence in which the screens are applied often makes a great deal of difference. For example, in screening the Russell 1000 stocks, the top 10% (of stocks based on return on equity) of the bottom 10% (based on price/earnings) is not likely to be the same set of stocks as the bottom 10% (based on price/earnings) of the top 10% (based on return on equity).

Most people do not stop to think that linear models, such as factor models, simultaneously evaluate all variables in the model at any given point in time. For example, in a factor model equation, each factor is a potential contributor to security returns. A factor exposure cannot be conditionally included in an equation; that is, included only if some condition is met as in our example above.[6] Optimizing on key portfolio characteristics cannot effectively portray a manager's selection process when conditional decision making matters. Ignoring conditional

---

[6] One can approach this through reformulation and imaginative use of dummy variables.

decision making can lead to choosing stocks for the normal portfolio that are not considered by the manager, and universe misfit will be the result.[7]

Weighting the Securities

Once the normal sub-universe of stocks has been specified, the critical problem of how to combine them into an index remains (i.e., the weights that should be applied to each stock). Broad market indexes such as the Russell indexes and the S&P 500 are capitalization-weighted indexes. Managers, on the other hand often do not capitalization-weight their portfolios. An example will demonstrate the importance of choosing a correct weighting scheme when creating normal portfolios.

Let us assume we have screened our universe in such a way that we end up with the same four stocks held in the manager's portfolio and the normal portfolio. Assume also that we choose to weight the normal portfolio on a capitalization basis even though our manager chooses an equal-weighted basis. Finally, let us assume that at the end of the quarter, the security return numbers shown in Exhibit 2 emerge. As can be seen, the normal portfolio has a much higher return than the manager's portfolio even though their holdings are identical. This example highlights the importance of the choice of weighting scheme. It always makes a significant difference in total performance. Generally, the normal portfolio and the manager's current portfolio will not include exactly the same stocks, so the weighting scheme can easily become a source of confusion and/or contention.

Bear in mind that while one wants to choose a weighting scheme that fairly reflects the manager's behavior, the fund manager also needs to evaluate other aspects of the manager's behavior that can affect overall performance, such as sector weighting and other bets. Note that when a manager equal-weights his portfolio there is an implicit bias against large capitalization stocks and toward smaller capitalization stocks.

Exhibit 2: Example of the Importance of Choosing a Correct Weighting Scheme when Creating Normal Portfolios

Stock	Cap Weight	Security Return	Stock Impact on Return	Manager Security		Stock Impact on Return
A	50%	15%	7.50%	25%	15%	3.75%
B	30	10	3.00	25	10	2.50
C	15	5	0.75	25	5	1.25
D	5	5	0.25	25	5	1.25
Total Returns			11.50%			8.75%

[7] See Jon A. Christopherson, "Selecting an Appropriate Benchmark: Problems with Normal Portfolios and Their Uses," *Russell Research Commentary* (April 1993, Frank Russell Company, Tacoma WA), pp. 4-6.

Weighting Alternatives

One can choose from a variety of weighting schemes. Here are three examples of weighting schemes based on capitalization:

1. *Equal weighting:* the same portfolio percentage for each stock regardless of stock capitalization
2. *Capitalization weighting:* each stock weighted according to its percentage of the total market value of the portfolio
3. *Capitalization weighting with break points:* each stock weighted according to its percentage of the total market value of the portfolio, down to a certain capitalization size; below the breakpoint each stock is equal-weighted (e.g., equal weight below $1 billion in market capitalization)

Other weighting schemes are feasible, such as the complex scheme shown in Section B of Exhibit 1. One might assign percentage weightings based on the logarithm of capitalization to compensate for the high degree of skewness in the distribution of capitalization (i.e., to give the smaller companies a larger percentage of the portfolio).

Of course, one is not confined to assigning portfolio percentages on the basis of capitalization. Weighting could be a function of other data. The treatment of such stocks as IBM often causes membership and weighting problems for normal portfolios. No "maybes" are usually allowed in portfolio membership — a stock is either in or out — but partial weighting can be obtained through controlling weights of classes of stocks. For example, value managers will often restrict the percentage of the portfolio that can be in utilities.

Advantages and Disadvantages of Capitalization Weighting

When choosing a weighting scheme for normal portfolios, one should be aware that capitalization weighting has certain advantages and disadvantages. Unlike an equal-weighted normal portfolio, a capitalization-weighted normal portfolio need not be rebalanced because of fluctuations in the price of the stocks in the portfolio. Also, since one is purchasing a percentage of each company in a capitalization-weighted portfolio, liquidity problems tend to be minimized. This makes them easier to passively replicate, if desired. Capitalization weighting also makes a buy-and-hold strategy easier to pursue.

The disadvantages of capitalization weighting are not inconsequential. As mentioned earlier, managers tend to not capitalization-weight their portfolios for a variety of reasons. The most often cited reason is related to the manager's aversion to putting too much money in any one basket (such as IBM) — they want stock name diversification. When compared against a capitalization-weighted portfolio, this aversion can be seen as a bet against certain sectors and stocks.

Finally, capitalization weighting tends to weight some sectors of the market more than would the average institutional money manager. In our experience, capitalization weighting will cause differences between the average characteristics of the manager's portfolio and his normal portfolio, as well as differences in performance.

Note, however, that weighting other than by capitalization is fraught with theoretical difficulties. For example, not every investor can purchase equal-weighted portfolios. Second, these types of benchmarks make passive management difficult. Furthermore, if one creates a noncap-weighted normal portfolio, a cap-weighted portfolio will also have to be created so that the user can understand the performance effect of underweighting large capitalization stocks. This is not a moot point. In the latter part of 1996 and early 1997, the large cap stocks performed much better than the overall market; managers who did not cap-weight their portfolios were negatively affected by their capitalization bets. It seems reasonable that the fund manager would want to know the extent of this bet against large cap stocks. As a general rule, for simplicity of passive management and to retain all market opportunities available to investors, capitalization weighting for normal portfolios is desirable.

Style-Weighted Normal Portfolio

A relatively new approach to creating normal portfolios takes advantage of readily available style indexes for segments of asset markets and newly developed methods that portray manager portfolios as weighted combinations of style indexes. For example, a value manager that has tight sector controls so that his portfolio has market-like sector exposures might have weights of 60% value and 40% growth, which can be described as market oriented with a value tilt.

As previously mentioned, there are two methods currently used to determine style weights — return pattern analysis and portfolio characteristics analysis. When an analysis of style is performed on a manager's portfolio using the methods described in the appendix for a given time period, a set of weights are obtained that represent the manager's style as of the end of that time period. A return that an investor can obtain over the next quarter (or month) as an alternative to purchasing the manager portfolio under investigation is a portfolio formed by purchasing passive style indexes in proportion to the weights suggested by the style analysis. The portfolio called the *style weighted normal portfolio* or *poor man's normal portfolio* is a realistic alternative because the investor could have purchased this portfolio rather than the portfolio under investigation. The argument is that the manager portfolio ought to be able to outperform this basic normal portfolio.

The style weighted normal portfolio is computed as follows:

$$R_{Nt} = w_{1t\text{-}1}\, S_{1t} + w_{3t\text{-}1}\, S_{2t} + \ldots + w_{nt\text{-}1}\, S_{nt} + \varepsilon_{nt}$$

where

R_{Nt} = style weighted normal portfolio return at time t

$w_{nt\text{-}1}$ = style weight of style index n at the beginning of the time interval or at the end of the last time period

S_{nt} = style index n return at time t or over the interval from t-1 to t
ε_{nt} = residual return not correlated with the n style indexes
n = the number of style indexes in the analysis

The portfolio R_{Nt} can be used as any other benchmark for performance evaluation and fund management purposes as discussed herein. Note that any alpha the manager may have is confounded in the error term e_t with any specific risk. If return pattern analysis methods are used to compute the style weights, the alpha may be embedded in the weights assigned to the style indexes. Any return that is not captured in the style indexes is forced into the error term; hence these methods are inherently inferior to the manger-specific stock list method of creating normals.

ISSUES TO CONSIDER WHEN CREATING NORMAL PORTFOLIOS

Limitations of the Stock List Model

There are certain implicit assumptions about normal portfolios that one should bear in mind when creating and using normals. For example, the assumption inherent in the methodology described above is that the universe of securities from which a manager chooses can be determined by the fundamental stock characteristics used in screens. Hence, some styles of management such as market timing behavior would represent bets against a normal portfolio. If the manager has the discretion to move funds out of equities and into cash or other assets, this cannot be captured in a normal portfolio of equities only. A normal portfolio for market timers must also have a "normal" weight in the type of securities which the manager uses in market timing (e.g., cash).

Limitations of Factor Model Approach

There are several potential fit problems for factor-model normals when managers choose stocks on a basis other than the factors in the factor model. First, when a manager's key decision characteristics for each stock are not found in the multifactor model, the missing characteristics are matched by the factor model through a weighted combination of factors the model does have. Second, since the starting point is past portfolios, a persistent incidental and unintentional bet on factors could be misinterpreted as a normal bet (e.g., the sometimes high P/E of contrarian managers' portfolios that typically results from low earnings due to distress). Third, if a manager seeks exposure to a particular factor, stocks that have large exposures to that factor can easily be preferred by an optimizer. Hence, the optimizer might select an issue that "helps out" in optimizing several factor exposures.[8]

---

[8] For a discussion of normal portfolios and the problems managers and sponsors have tended to have with factor-based normals, see Christopherson, "Selecting an Appropriate Benchmark," pp. 8-15.

Limitations of Weighted Style Index Approach

There are several logical problems for weighted style index normals. First, style indexes by their nature are generally more broad lists of securities than the other two types of normal portfolios. If a manager is 90% large value and 10% large growth, then 100% of the security names, their weights and their equity characteristics are included in the benchmark. This will obviously lead to misfit between the manager's portfolio and the benchmark. This, in turn, means that evaluating the sector bets the manager takes is inherently more difficult. Because the stock lists of the normal and the manager do not match, explaining the inevitable difference in performance becomes problematical. These faults exist for either effective mix or portfolio characteristics methods of style determination. Although, the portfolio characteristics method is less likely to suffer less from these problems than return pattern analysis due to the nature of their methodology. The primary utility of the weighted style index approach to normal creation is the relative ease in creating these benchmarks and their concomitant low cost.

Communication Prior to Measurement

It is important to choose a normal portfolio in advance of the performance measurement period so that the manager and the sponsor both know the investment objective. The manager may be unclear concerning his most appropriate equity style. One should negotiate or otherwise determine before the performance period what characteristics the manager feels are a "fair" description of his universe. Such an *a priori* agreement can go a long way toward avoiding the "it doesn't fit me" argument.

NORMAL PORTFOLIOS AS INVESTMENT STRATEGY TOOLS

So far we have examined how to create and use normals for the purpose of manager performance measurement. We will now turn to the second purpose of normals — the use of normals as investment strategy tools.

Normal Portfolios and the Policy Portfolio

The aggregate of the normal portfolios can be used to show the total equity exposure of the fund — the "policy portfolio." For example, a comparison of total exposure in the normal portfolios to a market benchmark such as the Russell 3000 will help identify over- or under-exposed sectors or factors. Passively managed "completeness" funds can be created to fill the gaps in exposure if needed. Of course, each of the multiple normal portfolios can be matched against one or more managers to help effectively mix multiple managers. Note also that normal portfolios can be seen as policy portfolios at the manager level.

Difficult Management Questions

While combining normals to achieve a policy portfolio appears simple on the surface, the decision to use normals presupposes the answers to several difficult, interrelated management questions.

Why Do We Create Normal Portfolios?

We create normals to provide an *ideal benchmark* against which to measure individual manager performance. In other words, we want to see how well he picks stocks within the group from which he normally chooses. We also want to see how well he allocates funds across industrial sectors and company sizes, and perhaps how well he covers a portion of the market.

Another, equally valid answer is to provide a tool for fund management. The sum of our normal portfolios across a fund can tell us what portion of the market has been covered. The sum of the normals plus a completeness fund can tell us how close we are to our policy portfolio or target portfolio. In this way normal portfolios can be used to guide our selection of managers and control the fund's exposure to market risks (i.e., to manage the fund).

These two answers are in conflict in certain ways. For example, in creating an ideal benchmark we would weight stocks in the normal portfolio exactly the way the manager does, but in using normals to manage a fund, capitalization weighting is desirable to minimize fund complexity and to determine the effects of capitalization bets. Also, we may capitalization weight the normal because we may like to think of it as an investable alternative, in which case capitalization weighting is essential. So the sponsor's purpose in creating normal portfolios is crucial to how they are constructed.

As for "ideal benchmarks," highly customized normal portfolios may provide much less useful tools for measuring performance than generic normals. It may very well be that the manager's returns correlate with a generic style index as highly or more highly than with a customized normal. In such a case the question naturally arises about whether the expense and effort of creating individual normal portfolios are worthwhile.

For What Should a Manager Be Given Credit?

The second question is related to the first. If, for example, a manager through intuition or research arrives at the contrarian investment strategy in which he buys only out-of-favor or undervalued stocks, then how much value added over a broad market benchmark should the manager be accorded — all of the contrarian style performance above or below the benchmark or only that portion not explained by a contrarian normal portfolio? This question, of course, moves the previous question of why we hire active managers in the first place. Presumably, we do so because we think managers can add value over a passive alternative. To the extent that active managers do not add excess return above their normal portfolios, the fund manager "could" or "should" create a passive portfolio of the securities in the normal portfolio and save a portion of the active management fees. Is this fair? Managers, want the credit for the wisdom of their style of investing. If we capture most of the manager's alpha by creating and subsequently passively investing in a normal portfolio, what is our moral obligation to the manager? Are we stealing the manager's alpha?

How Close to the Manager's Ideal Portfolio Do We Wish to Come?

Does the sponsor want a customized normal portfolio which matches the manager's style as closely as possible or a more generic normal which captures the manager's general style of management? The virtue of a close match is that it allows us to know more precisely where the manager added value (i.e., how well he chose securities). The virtue of the more generic normal is that we can judge how well the manager's variation on a theme — his skill in security weighting, sector allocation, and security selection — added value. A more generic normal portfolio also makes it possible to judge the skill of other managers of a similar style. The broader the normal portfolio, the more useful it will be for measuring opportunity costs, i.e., answering the question of how much better off would the sponsor be with Manager A rather than Manager B (given that the generic normal portfolio fairly accurately captures the investment style of both). The answer to this third question falls out of the answer to the first two, but it might very well be the first issue a fund manager decides.

How Much Cooperation is Necessary from the Manager?

The fourth question is more of a personnel management issue. Does the fund manager need and want the cooperation of the portfolio manager in creating the normal portfolio? If we know the securities from which a manager tends to choose and we do not care much whether or not the manager likes being compared to a normal which we feel represents his universe and/or strategy, then we can proceed without the manager's cooperation. The virtue of this approach is that it allows greater flexibility in fund management. The sponsor can define a set of "target" normals that come close to a policy portfolio and hold managers accountable for doing or not doing their part. In this context, normals may be seen as analogous to management by objective.

On the other hand, developing a customized normal for performance measurement usually requires the close cooperation of the manager to obtain the correct subset of securities for the normal and the correct weighting rules; hence, the closer we want to fit the normal to the manager's investment behavior, the more cooperation from the manager is required. Furthermore, a manager must know the basis of his evaluation, and to force a normal portfolio down a manager's throat can be seen as an arrogant, presumptive, and unfriendly act.

The resolution of this question has implications for all the other questions. If we decide the generic normal is close enough for our fund management purposes, then the manager's cooperation is less critical. This decision in turn is related to the question of giving credit for a manager's style. The more credit the sponsor wants to give the manager for his style and active management within his style, the less closely the normal will fit the manager's portfolio and the more closely it will fit the broad market. And, of course, the further away the normal is from the manager's typical portfolio, the less useful it is as a benchmark to measure manager skills within his universe — bringing us back to the question of what purpose the sponsor has in mind.

In summary, how the fund manager intends to use normal portfolios in fund management has much to do with the critical decisions the sponsor must make about the nature of each normal portfolio. Making any one decision has implications for all the other decisions, and the cumulation of them determines the overall usefulness of the normal portfolios.

CONCLUDING REMARKS

As we have seen, normal portfolios provide useful tools for fund managers to evaluate their money managers' performance and behavior as it relates to the overall fund structure. Some users of normal portfolios advocate producing normal portfolios that mirror as closely as possible the average portfolios of their managers. While this is a perfectly legitimate purpose for normal portfolios, we should also consider the merits of using normal portfolios to manage the fund structure. This provides a better basis for creating a set of normal portfolios. In other words, in addition to providing a close benchmark for performance measurement, the normal should also be created with opportunity costs in mind. This decision means that strict cooperation will not be required from the manager, and that the manager will be given credit for the nuances of his implementation of the investment style. It also recognizes that so long as it is reasonably close, the normal will be an effective benchmark for measuring not only security selection, but also sector allocation and capitalization bets.

While one could create normals that model a management firm so precisely they can pick up the differences between portfolio managers within one firm, it is more realistic to create normal portfolios that reflect the average portfolios of managers one could have chosen instead of the manager selected. In this way, the fund manager can evaluate the opportunity cost of hiring this manager rather than another or buying a passively managed alternative. At the same time, the sponsor can create a flexible instrument for fund management purposes.

APPENDIX

Return Pattern Analysis of Style

The object of return pattern analysis is to find a set of weights which, when applied to the indexes selected, minimizes the residual squared errors or differences between the optimal weighted set and the input portfolio's return series. In the least squares sense, this problem is similar to standard multiple regression but differs (and becomes non-linear) because the weights cannot be less than zero or greater than one and must sum to one. The method was first proposed by Sharpe.[9]

The number of optimizations depends on the length of the window used to set up the inputs for the optimization. The recommended choice is 60 months or 5 years of data. The first 60 months of index and manager data are analyzed and the means, variances, and covariances (correlations) are passed to the optimizer to find the optimal set of weights. The 61st month is then added to the data set and the first month is dropped, essentially rolling the window one month ahead, and the optimization is repeated. This rolling of the window and analyzing the data sets continues until the last time point in the data set is reached. The number of optimizations or analyses that can be obtained is equal to the number of time points (of complete data sets) minus the length of the rolling window, plus one. For example a data set covering 75 time points or months, using a rolling window of 60 months, will yield 16 analyses or optimizations ($75 - 60 + 1 = 16$). The choice of indexes is critical to the results obtained. Adding or dropping an index such as Treasury bill returns can dramatically effect the results. Changing the window length can also dramatically effect the weights.[10]

Portfolio Characteristics Analysis of Style

The object in portfolio characteristics analysis is to find a weighted set of indexes that has the same equity characteristics as the portfolio being analyzed. No optimization to match portfolio returns is attempted. The returns are the returns to a portfolio with a blended set of equity characteristics. The interest in portfolio characteristics flows from the expectation that portfolios with certain key equity characteristics will tend to earn a certain pattern of returns in the marketplace. The RSC system used by Russell Manager Research conditionally evaluates manager portfolio characteristics using non-linear probability of style membership functions to build a style assessment. The logic behind this system was developed by Christopherson and Trittin.[11]

The market relative equity characteristics analyzed are (1) price/book, (2) dividend yield, (3) price/earnings, and (4) return on equity (5 years). The portfolio characteristics that are judged in absolute terms are (1) sector deviation and (2) percent of capitalization in the small segment of market capitalization. The characteristics are analyzed sequentially, or more precisely, conditionally, so that the assessment earlier in the chain of logic is refined using subsequent information. In this sense it is an artificial intelligence system.

---

[9] Sharpe, "Determining a Funds Effective Asset Mix," and "Asset Allocation."

[10] For a review of the issues one should bear in mind when using return pattern analysis see, Jon A. Christopherson, "Equity Style Classification: Adventures in Return Pattern Analysis," *Journal of Portfolio Management* (Spring 1995), pp. 32-43.

[11] Christopherson and Trittin, "Equity Style Classification System."

Chapter 7

Quantitative Tools for Equity Style Management

David J. Leinweber, Ph.D.
Managing Director
First Quadrant, L.P.

David Krider
Associate
First Quadrant, L.P.

Peter Swank, Ph.D.
Associate Director
First Quadrant, L.P.

INTRODUCTION

A quantitative approach to equity style management has been successfully used for both long and market neutral portfolios in the United States and internationally.[1] In this chapter we discuss topics relating to the role of advanced quantitative techniques and information technology in developing, operating, and efficiently implementing these strategies. In the course of developing and running these strategies, and in the ongoing R&D process associated with them, we have written a number of special purpose software tools, for data collection and quality assurance, for model development, and for monitoring and controlling the cost of implementation. We briefly describe these in this chapter.

These systems can appear complex. In discussing them we have tried to follow the advice of J. Robert Oppenheimer, the physicist who led the development of the atomic bomb at Los Alamos in the 1940s. He maintained that any scientist who could not explain work to a six year-old child was a charlatan. This standard should apply to quantitative investment managers. The mathematical ideas and computer tools behind these strategies should be explicable without

---

[1] David J. Leinweber, Robert D. Arnott, and Christopher G. Luck, "The Many Sides of Equity Style: Quantitative Management of Core, Value, and Growth Portfolios," Chapter 11 in T. Daniel Coggin, Frank J. Fabozzi, and Robert D. Arnott (eds.), *The Handbook of Equity Style Management* (New Hope, PA: Frank J. Fabozzi Associates, 1997).

invoking the Greek alphabet or technical jargon. We have tried to follow Oppenheimer's advice and make these ideas accessible to the general reader.

In other publications we have focused our attention on the financial aspects of a quantitative approach to equity style management and how these portfolios can be used by institutional investors.[2] For many readers, this is all they need or want to know. This chapter is for managers who want to know more about the details of the quantitative and technological aspects of the research, operations, and trading underlying the process.

We describe a specialized system for designing the forecasting models used in these strategies, and elaborate on the methods of building and evaluating style management models. We discuss the data management issues which must be addressed in developing and using these models.

Implementation is a key aspect of any equity strategy. Real trading costs for equities, including market impact as well as commissions, can be large enough to overwhelm the potential value added.[3] There are variety of strategies available to avoid this, by avoiding trades whose costs are likely to exceed their contribution to value added, and by actively monitoring and controlling the cost of trades that are made. We have developed a number of trade analysis and support systems, which, when used by skilled traders, can be effective tools in reducing the costs of implementation, which translates into real value added. The technology being applied to these issues is described here.

There is reason to believe that this aggressive approach to transaction cost control is a fruitful activity. In a 1996 survey comparing the execution costs for a large sample of equity managers, the trading performance for the style management process we have described ranked in the 97th percentile.

ARTIFICIAL INTELLIGENCE IN
QUANTITATIVE STYLE MANAGEMENT

In both the modeling and trading areas, we discuss the use of techniques that are based on artificial intelligence, the genetic algorithm for modeling, and real-time expert systems for trading. *Artificial intelligence* (AI) is a term that is often over-hyped and misused. The lofty goals of AI researchers often sound like science fiction. They are a long way off from coming anywhere close to creating an artificial human mind. But there are many, admittedly more modest, successes which have come out the AI laboratories. One was the idea of "visual programming." In the 1970s, it was an esoteric MIT Artificial Intelligence Lab research project to build systems which could allow non-programmers to set up an example solution to a problem, and have the computer produce a program that would solve all similar

---

[2] David J. Leinweber, Christopher G. Luck, and Peter Swank, "Structuring Returns from Global Market Neutral Strategies," Chapter 12 in *The Handbook of Equity Style Management*.

[3] See Chapter 11 by Wayne Wagner and Mark Edwards for a discussion of trading costs.

examples. By the 1980s, it was out of the lab renamed Visicalc, and later Lotus 1-2-3. It made programmers out of millions of people so painlessly they hardly knew it was happening.

Other AI ideas have become increasingly common, such voice recognition, and sophisticated diagnostic systems for everything from automobiles to global telecommunications networks. There are specific, focused application areas where AI techniques can substantially expand on the scope and power of more traditional solutions. Two examples are our use of the genetic algorithm to improve model design, and in the use of rule based real-time trading analytics to help reduce implementation costs.[4] Both of these applications are described here.

Developing and Maintaining Quantitative Models

A multi-billion dollar global quantitative investment process requires solutions to unique information gathering and analysis problems. Data from many sources needs to be brought in on a timely basis and verified before going in to the forecasting models used to make investment decisions.

The development of these models is the most challenging aspect of quantitative investing. The technology underlying these models pushes the boundary of the state-of-the-art and practice in quantitative forecasting. The unprecedented growth in the computational resources that can be brought to bear on these problems[5] opens up a world of possibilities which were inaccessible in the recent past. In recent years we have seen major breakthroughs in mathematics, biology, physics and engineering brought about by the intelligent application of advanced computer technology. Investing is also transformed by this technological revolution.

The Model Engineering System (MES) is a framework we have developed to apply new computational tools in the development of investment models. The MES greatly improves the quantitative research effort and development, making it more accurate and productive. It achieves this result by streamlining all steps in the model development process, integrating them into a single program with an intuitive and flexible user interface. Developed in-house from the ground up, the MES provides a means to improve performance in all quantitative investment strategies.

A Philosophical MES

Modern econometric theory has achieved much but it has not accomplished everything. Lacking from the theory is a solid basis upon which to evaluate the predictive power of models. Several "information criteria" have been proposed that emphasize the importance of parsimony (i.e., simplicity) and stability (i.e., the model parameters are steady over time) but the debate continues on. The guiding

[4] David J. Leinweber and Yossi Beinart, "A Little Artificial Intelligence Goes a Long Way on Wall Street," *Journal of Portfolio Management* (Winter 1996).
[5] Robert D. Arnott and David J. Leinweber, "Quantitative and Computational Innovation in Investment Management," *Journal of Portfolio Management* (Winter 1995).

idea behind the MES is that econometric model building is an *art* as well as a *science*. As such, the artist/scientist needs to be provided with tools that serve as an extension of his thought process. The problems of data collection and parameter estimation should be secondary to the more important ones of model specification and evaluation. The MES achieves this by abstracting the data and estimating steps from the user, bringing specification and evaluation to the forefront of the process where once they played an equal or lesser role.

The Quantitative Research Process

To appreciate the impact of the MES upon research, it is important to understand the research process itself. There are four essential steps: data gathering, model specification, parameter estimation and performance evaluation.

Data Gathering

The models developed for quantitative investment management are predictive in nature. Nearly all data are time series data. Time series data are ordered by time, an example of which would be quarterly GNP for the United States from 1970 to 1996. Conversely, cross sectional data would be the GNP for a given quarter across all countries.

Data come from various sources: commercial services, government agencies and academia. They can be delivered via tape, the Internet, modem, published material, fax or over the telephone. They also come in various formats: text files, spreadsheets, and databases. The first step in the research process is to gather the necessary data from the various sources and convert them to a common format for use by the statistical analysis package of choice. Additionally, it may be required to adjust the data if they are sampled at different times. Data sampled at the beginning of the month should be treated differently from that taken in the middle or at the end of the month.

Model Specification

Model specification is the art of selecting the data which are useful in forecasting returns and how they should be combined and transformed to use in the model. Specification is the process of determining which data are of interest, the transformations that should be performed thereon, and the structure of the model itself. For example, to predict monthly returns to the broad stock market (SPR) or a style index we could have available the following data: unemployment rate (UMP), consumer price index (CPI), bond risk premium (BRP), and butter production in Bangladesh.

The first step in specification would be to decide that butter production in Bangladesh is not applicable. The second step would be to transform the CPI data so that we use percent changes (CPIR) in modeling returns instead of the raw levels. The last is to decide to use a linear model such as:

Exhibit 1: Expanding Window Estimation

January	February	March	April	May	June	July	August	September	October
In-Sample							Out		
In-Sample								Out	
In-Sample									Out

$$SPR_{t+1} = \beta_0 + \beta_1 \cdot UMP_t + \beta_2 \cdot CPIR_t + \beta_3 \cdot BRP_t + \varepsilon$$

The β_i coefficients are the influences that each datum has in predicting the return to the stock market in the following month. Estimating these coefficients is termed *parameter estimation*.

Parameter Estimation

The parameters of a model are estimated in such a way that their values are the most probable given the data. For the linear model described previously, we could use ordinary least squares (OLS) which selects β_i such that the sum of the squared errors (ε) is as small as possible. There are other estimation procedures as well, such as: generalized least squares (GLS), kernel estimation, neural networks, and genetic programming. Each of these differs both in the structure of the model (linear or nonlinear) and in the criteria used to determine which parameters are optimal for a given set of data.

Data that are used to estimate parameters are referred to as *in-sample data*. The estimated parameters may then be used to predict observations beyond the time frame of the data. Data that are used to predict are called *out-of-sample data*. To evaluate the performance of a model it is common to estimate parameters over the in-sample data and then use the model to predict results in the following time period. The in-sample period is then expanded to include the following month and the month after that is then predicted. This process is referred to as *expanding window estimation*[6] and is illustrated in Exhibit 1.

Here the in-sample period extends from January through July. The parameters are estimated for these data and then this model is used to predict the observation corresponding to August. The in-sample period is increased, the out-of-sample period is moved one month ahead, and the model parameters are re-estimated.

Two features are the hallmark of a well specified and estimated model: stable parameters over the several in-sample estimations and a strong correlation between the predicted and actual observations in the out-of-sample period. This forms one aspect of *model evaluation*.

---

[6] *Moving window estimation* is identical except that the size of the in-sample period remains constant by shifting the first observation one month ahead at each step.

Exhibit 2: Selecting a Model and Data with the MES

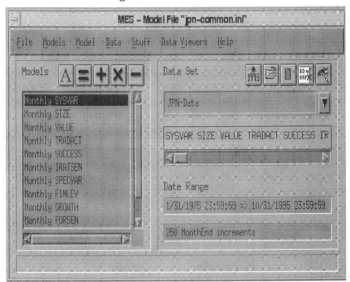

Model Evaluation

Clever programming and modern statistical tools easily automate data collection and parameter estimation. However, the skill of the model builder is requisite to interpret the results of these processes and recommend changes to the model specification. Model evaluation comprises the observation and interpretation of diagnostic statistics generated through the parameter estimation process. These diagnostic statistics consist of the accuracy in magnitude and direction of the forecasts, the stability of the coefficients, as well as others beyond the scope of this chapter. The Modeling Engineering System generates these statistics as well as providing a uniform and intuitive manner to view and act upon them.

The Model Engineering System

The MES is a program that integrates the aforementioned steps into an intuitive framework that speeds the model development process while enhancing the accuracy of the models created. It does this by abstracting from the user the chores of gathering data and estimating parameters while enhancing the facilities for model specification and evaluation.

The MES employs a graphical user interface to enhance the process of model specification. Exhibit 2 is the main window around which all model development occurs. On the left-hand side are listed the factor models and on the right hand side is information on the data currently being used. "Test," and the current dataset is called "JPN-Data." The data is sampled on a monthly basis. The first step in developing a model (or set of models) is to select an appropriate dataset and the variables of interest.

Data Gathering

The modeling system needs to have a means to access the various data available for use in building the forecasting models. As mentioned earlier, these data exist in a wide variety of formats. In the MES, a data management program called *DataMan* provides a means to bring these sources into the models uniformly. In this uniform view, all time series data are simply time-value pairs with a descriptive name attached. Whereas in reality, time series data are found in a myriad of formats all throughout the file system. DataMan brings reality to the schematic by dynamically converting the various formats into one that is uniform as well as flexible.

In addition, DataMan gives the flexibility of combining data found in several distinct formats into one virtual data set. Often there are variables whose values are a function of other variables. A derived series calculating returns from stock market index levels would be an example. DataMan can be configured to calculate these dynamically so that storage is reduced and only one series need be maintained instead of several. This is all accomplished transparently to the user, who simply selects a dataset and those variables of interest, using a graphic interface which displays two lists of variables. UK-Data is a virtual dataset that combines all data from the other UK datasets. The list on the left has all of the unselected variables while that on the right are the variables that could potentially form the model. Once the list is correct, a push of the button will invoke DataMan which will then perform the task of retrieving the data for the given time span at the desired sampling rate.

From a retrieval standpoint, DataMan frees the modeler from any concern with the location and format of the data. However, from a maintenance standpoint, it is of great importance to keep the data in as centralized a format as possible. For this reason all operational data should be stored on a centralized relational database server. This facilitates the storage, validation updating, and backup of all critical data.

Data Transformation and Model Specification

Transformations are important because they make sense out of data. Intuitively, knowing only the last value of a variable (like unemployment or interest rate) isn't as important as knowing where it is now relative to where its been over time and whether its rising, falling, or drifting. This is how people interpret financial and economic data and it is also how this same data is incorporated in most forecasting models. The number, kind, and transformations of the raw data are again manipulated through the graphical interface of the MES.

A unique transformation language has been created that has been optimized for time series data. Through this language, any modification of the data may be effected that will bring it in line with the requirements of the model. For example, trending data should be corrected by using the difference between successive observations instead. More powerful transformations may also be performed such as using the difference between an observation and straight line fit to a set of prior observations. In this way "surprises" may be captured in a trending series. Transformations may take on an unlimited number of forms, the nature of which depends upon the application.

As the number and complexity of transformations increase so does the number of their associated storage parameters. For this reason, the MES has powerful facilities for searching through the large number of combinations of plausible storage values. This search may be both exhaustive and through the genetic algorithm.[7] When run under the UNIX operating system, the MES will automatically distribute the computation of the models over the network, greatly speeding the process.[8] These searching tools must be given a set of potential transforms over which to search, the rest is automatic.

In addition to setting the transformations and their associated parameter values, the forecasting method for the model as well as the estimation engine may be specified. The MES is flexible enough to allow a wide variety of estimation engines as the need arises such as ordinarily least square, generalized least squares, kalman filtering, neural networks, genetic programming, and kernel estimation. Once the transformations are specified, the storage parameter values given, and an engine selected, the step of parameter estimation ensues.

Parameter Estimation

From a user's perspective, parameter estimation is the simplest of all chores performed by the MES. It is performed either by pressing the estimation button (the hard way) or by having the parameters *automatically* estimated whenever a transformation or storage parameter is changed. This automatic estimation is an extremely powerful tool in the model evaluation phase as changes in the model are immediately reflected in the diagnostic statistics.

Model Evaluation

The MES generates a wide range of diagnostic statistics as a result of the parameter estimation process. These statistics are both *model-related* and *variable-related*. Model-related statistics are those that pertain to the model as a whole; variable-related statistics that pertain to each transformed variable that enters the model.

A view data window is created with a grid containing the statistics for model evaluation. From this grid may be derived any number of graphs and charts; however, a line chart is most appropriate for these data. Exhibit 3 illustrates this for the case of the OLS variable-related statistic, coefficient. These are the β_i coefficients estimated for the model at each stage in the expanding window regression. It is now apparent that the coefficients are not very stable and even

---

[7] The genetic algorithm (GA) is described in more detail later in this chapter.

[8] A network of a dozen moderately powerful workstations will outpace a conventional serial supercomputer, for a highly parallelizable application like the GA. A parallel supercomputer, such as a Connection Machine or the IBM SP2, can greatly speed up the GA, and allow exploration of a much larger set of alternative modeling techniques.

change sign halfway through the estimation. This could be indicative of a poor model specification so different data or transformations should be investigated. A similar analysis could be made on such model-related statistics as R^2 or RMSE (root mean squared error), but they will be omitted for the sake of brevity.

Any number of graphs and charts may be derived from a single grid. Exhibit 4 illustrates this for a plot of the model's predictions against the actual observations. At the top left is a two-dimension plot and at the top right is a three-dimensional plot of the same data. The plots are fully interactive. Clicking on a point will bring up the date associated with it. By grabbing a corner on the cube and moving the mouse, the plot will rotate to follow it.

Raw data in a grid may also be transformed into a more interesting format using one of the various analysis tools: Transpose, Correlation, Descriptive, Frequency, and Transformation. Transpose will transpose the grid, exchanging rows for columns and vice versa. This is useful if the user desires to view data in cross section instead of in time series. Correlation will calculate a correlation matrix for the data in the grid. Descriptive calculates descriptive statistics such as mean, standard deviation, median, etc. Frequency calculates a two dimensional frequency plot of the data. This tool is illustrated in Exhibit 5 along with a three-dimensional bar chart illustrating where the data are concentrated.

Exhibit 3: A MES Data View Window

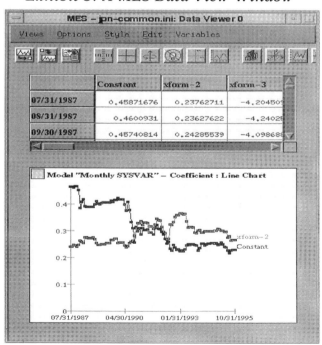

Exhibit 4: MES — Multiple Graphic Views of a Single Grid

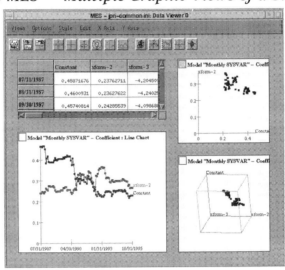

Exhibit 5: MES — Data Analysis Tools: Frequency Histogram

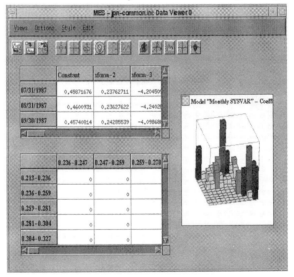

MES Summary

The model development process begins with the collection of data which is followed by the crucial phase of model specification. Once model parameters are calculated, they may be evaluated and the information gleaned if fed back into the model specification. When done correctly, improvements are found at each pass through this loop. The Model Engineering System greatly reduces the time to traverse this loop and improves upon the process itself. In addition, by explicitly allowing the in-sample and out-of-sample data sets to be controlled, the risk of data mining is also reduced. These tools are a central element of the ongoing model development and refinement process which underlies all of our quantitative style management strategies.

Data Quality and Timeliness

We have described a very data intensive process. This is true for the development of the models, as well as their operation for portfolio management. Clean, timely, and accurate data are critical for quantitative investing. The DataMan data management system provides a uniform interface for operational systems as well as for researchers using the MES to design better models. But an equally important side of data management is the one that looks outward, to the external world. The outside world of data isn't always pretty. There are tapes, disks, and communications line protocols in a profusion of changing and incompatible formats. The data on the them are often wrong and sometimes missing entirely. This is another area in which we have used information technology aggressively. Here are some examples.

- *Use of the Internet to replace overnight shipments.* We used to receive much of our data on tapes or CD-ROMs that were shipped using an overnight delivery service. This introduced a one day delay from the time the data were available to the time we could use them. Occasionally, the tapes were unreadable or unusable, and another day would pass before a replacement arrived. We worked with the data providers to build an automated system on their end which sends an e-mail message to DataMan telling it that the data are ready. DataMan then initiates an Internet file transfer to move the data over in a few minutes. The former 24 hour delay is reduced to something less than 24 minutes.

- *Automated data validation, verification and correction.* There are several means of detecting and correcting errors, all of which would be extremely tedious for humans.

- *Plausibility checking and correction.* An option priced at an eighth can easily move up 400% to one half in a single day. A similar move by a stock would be suspect. Detectors of unusual changes need to have a sense of what they are looking at, not just a list of numbers. Many of the errors which are caught in this way are easily corrected, since they arise from common data entry mistakes. Anyone can spot and correct the errors in this sequence of prices: 57.25, 57.5, 58.0, 57.75, 575, 58.0, 7.75, 57.25. It is just as easy for the machine to do it, every time a new data item arrives, and critical when the data are being used by other machines instead of people who will spot the errors.

Exhibit 6: A Simple Way to View the GA

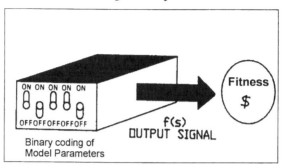

Source: Figure 1.6 in D. Goldberg, *Genetic Algorithms in Search, Optimization, and Machine Learning,*
copyright 1989 Addison-Wesley Publishing Company.
Reprinted by permission of Addison-Wesley Longman Inc.

- *Internal consistency checks.* Many data items have structural relationships that allow another level of error detection. For example, the market capitalization of a company should be the share price multiplied by the number of shares outstanding, if it isn't something is wrong. This type of check, like the plausibility screen, needs to be applied every time the data are updated.

- *Multiple source cross checks.* It is truly remarkable how different data sources report widely different values for identical data items. Comparison and correction of multiple values that should be the same, or very close, is aided by both the plausibility and consistency checks, and by having at least two and preferably three sources for each data item.

All of this requires a substantial commitment of resources: a central server computer to gather, verify, and when possible, correct data from multiple sources, a central database kept current by the data server to fill the needs of research and portfolio management processes, and people to keep it all running and current as new data sources are added.

GENETIC ALGORITHM

The *genetic algorithm* (GA) is a powerful "artificially intelligent" search tool that has enhanced model performance considerably. The sort of problem solved by the GA can be viewed in a simple way by looking at Exhibit 6. The problem is to find the parameters (represented by the switch settings in the exhibit) that maximize some payoff (represented by a dollar sign). This is simple when only a few parameters are involved: You just try all possible combinations. If the problem is "well-behaved," and corresponds to an established solution technique, then it is only slightly more

difficult. It is much more difficult when there are a huge number of possible variations, and the function relating them is not well-behaved, or when the problem and
its constraints and parameters do not lend themselves to traditional tools.

Parallel Search and Evolving Populations

The GA solves problems by following the principle of survival of the fittest. It
mimics simplified versions of biological evolutionary processes to produce successive generations of problem solutions that combine the best features of their
ancestors. This use of an evolving population of solutions (rather than taking
steps based on a single current best solution) creates a parallel search through a
very large space of possible solutions. This is illustrated in Exhibit 7. The GA has
been used successfully in many fields, ranging from jet engine design through
image processing to currency trading. We use it to solve the problem of constructing high-performance financial forecasting models.

Chromosomes for Forecasting Models

The first step in applying the GA in any context is to design a "chromosome" to represent a candidate solution. A simple way of thinking about the chromosome is as a list
of parameters that describe the solution. A narrowly constructed chromosome could
consist of a few numerical parameters (such as the type and gauge of steel used in a
fixed type of bridge design). A more elaborate chromosome includes structural
parameters, which set the nature of the solution (for example, whether the bridge is
suspended from cables or supported from below). There are many possibilities in
designing a chromosome for forecasting models. The chromosome codings encom-
pass both the "what" and "how" aspects of forecasting. What data items are used, how
they are measured, and what technique will be used to turn them into models.

Exhibit 7: Genetic Algorithm Schematic

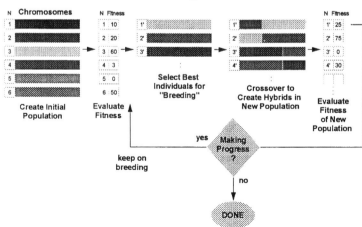

Exhibit 8: Different Ways to Window Data

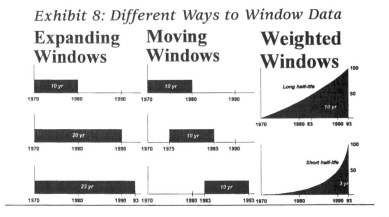

Our goal is to maximize predictability of factor returns, and our possible designs vary in their inputs and methods. Inputs are the data going into our forecasting models. Of the vast amount of market and macroeconomic data available, which indicators are most useful, and in what contexts and combinations? Are the variables useful as reported? Or do we extract more predictive power by measuring their value relative to their recent history, or by examining their changes or rates of change? Should they be considered in comparison to other variables? Will mathematical transforms, such as logs, squares, or square roots, increase their predictive value?

Techniques are the methods we use to do the forecasts. The simplest method is ordinary least squares regression. More elaborate techniques include robust regressions, kernel estimations, and neural networks. In each case, there are further structural decisions to be made regarding the type of window applied in calculating the model parameters.

The window choices are expanding, moving, or weighted, all depicted graphically in Exhibit 8. An expanding window uses all the data, but gives less weight to each new observation as time progresses. An expanding window cannot capture non-stationarity in the model data. A moving window of a fixed length does capture the effects of these changes over time, but in a coarse way. If moving windows are used, how long should they be?

There are some conceptual problems as well. Consider a 10-year moving window. If the current month is January 1995, January 1985 is included in the data used with the same weight as the current observation. However, in the next month, February 1995, the data for January 1985 have "fallen off the edge," and do not count at all. There is something unappealing about this. A more satisfying approach is to use a weighted window, which uses all the data, but reduces the weights for older observations. The issue here is how quickly the weights should fall for older observations.

Exhibit 9: GA Optimized versus Unoptimized Portfolio Full Sample

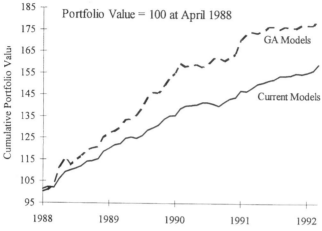

Genetic Model Optimization

An appropriate set of parameters is encoded on the chromosome used to represent the models for the various factor returns. An initial population is generated, which includes the conventionally developed set of models. A fitness function is designed that captures desirable features in a model: greater predictive power, improved returns, and lower volatility of returns. The fitness function determines which of the chromosomes are fit enough to survive. As expected, the fitness rises with the number of generations. By allowing the highest-performance individual to survive across generations, we ensure a nondecreasing maximum fitness.

Genetical Algorithm Sample Results

The value of genetic optimization is clearly seen in Exhibit 9, which shows the cumulative return to a Japanese style portfolio using the conventionally developed and GA optimized style process. In simulation the GA consistently adds about 3.7% per year over six years (in-sample performance). The more telling results are for the out-of-sample period, the data that the GA does not use in its model specification search. The performance over this period alone is shown in Exhibit 10. The GA adds over 4.7% per year during this 24-month period.

The Genetic Algorithm Warning Label

As a technology becomes more powerful, more skill is required to apply it correctly. Given enough time, many people could walk from Los Angeles to San Diego — but it is faster to drive, and it is much faster to fly. In each case, more skill is required to arrive safely. Quantitative modeling technology is now more like an airplane than a walking shoe, so we need to understand the danger this entails.

Exhibit 10: GA Optimized versus Unoptimized Portfolio Out-of-Sample Period Only

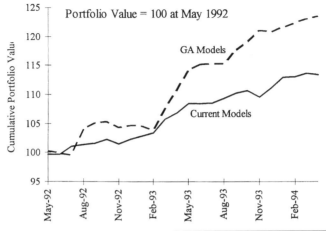

The danger in using the GA (and many other techniques) is that you may fall deep into the data mine. Recall that if you look at 100 statistical relationships that are significant at the 5% level, five of them are there only by chance. If you look at a million relationships, then 50,000 are significant only by chance. Early in our use of the GA technology, a chromosome evolved encoding for a variable based on a 15-month average lagged 7 months minus a 7-month average lagged 15 months. It had a nice symmetry to it. It had high statistical significance. It makes no sense whatsoever, and was ignominiously retired to the bit bucket.

With the GA, we know we can dig down to the deepest region of the data mine to produce models with ever better statistics and ever wackier variables. It is easy to generate models with perfect predictive power and coefficients significant at the 1% level on randomly generated data. It is important to be careful not to fool ourselves. Here are some of the ways we achieve this.

- *Wetware before software.* *Wetware* is the gray matter between your ears. The brain needs to be engaged before the GA is put into gear. The starting population always includes models developed using established econometric and quantitative methods. They make sense economically. Often, the result of the GA is only a slight refinement or adjustment of the initial solution. Immortality for the stars: the best few solutions in each generation survive unchanged into the next. This is also called elitism. It keeps good results from being submerged by random events.

- *Keep nonsensical variables out of the population from the start.* We design our own genetic code. It does not include the vocabulary for the type of nonsense variable described above, or for many other equally specious varieties.

- *Good fitness functions.* Predictive ability measured by information coefficient is just one part of fitness. Total squared error, consistency and correctness of direction, and stability are also important measures of model quality that are incorporated in our fitness measures.

- *Judicious use of out-of-sample periods.* To be absolutely, 100%, not guilty of any data-mining sins, each financial researcher would be allowed only one look at the out-of-sample period, and be foreclosed from reading any material on the subject. Ideally, all researchers would not have seen the *Wall Street Journal* (or each other) for the last five years. These people are hard to find, as we all have lived through the out-of-sample period. The next best thing is to be extremely careful about human looks into the out-of-sample period, and never to let the GA look it at all.

- *Cross-country validations.* It is easier to have faith in similar models that produce similar results in different countries than in those that do not travel well across borders. This is more applicable to asset class models than to factor models, since factors differ from country to country.

- *Calibrate new and improved tools carefully.* If a new process can produce seemingly great results using random inputs, there is something wrong with the process. If it seems too good to be true, it is.

Genetical Algorithm Summary

Quantitative investment strategies are based on the exploitation of empirically quantifiable market inefficiencies. They must make economic and financial sense. Within this framework, there are innovative means to leverage additional performance from the fundamentally sound underlying concepts. This is the role of the genetic algorithm in our research. It is driven by the strong forces of an artificial evolutionary process. Like natural evolution, it can produce undesirable outcomes. We have described the multi-faceted approach we use to avoid them. The end results are better strategies, evolved from good strategies.

TURNOVER, TRANSACTIONS COSTS, AND LIQUIDITY

Implementation is a crucial element of any investment strategy, and equity style management is no exception. High transaction costs can erode or eliminate the potential value added of any investment idea.[9,10]

---

[9] Robert D. Arnott and Wayne Wagner, "The Measurement and Control of Trading Costs," *Financial Analysts Journal* (November-December 1990).

[10] David P. Leinweber, "Using Information from Trading in Trading and Portfolio Management," *Journal of Investing* (Summer 1995).

Trading Cost Control

One important way to counter the drag on performance caused by high cost trades is not to make them at all. Screening the investment universe before making trading decisions is important in restricting the size of positions held and trades below the levels where anticipated trading costs exceed the alpha. For most stocks, this means deciding on upper bounds for trades and holdings; for the least liquid names, it means deciding not to hold them at all.

There are a variety of measures we have taken to aid in controlling these costs. They are applied before, during and after the actual trade. This takes the form of restricting the investable universe and the size of the portfolio, monitoring trades in progress, and analyzing completed trades effectively.

Maintaining a Liquid Investable Universe

Liquidity (or the lack of it), can't be measured directly in any one way. Tracking the actual cost of your trades is a good way to measure liquidity. This is the most expensive and scarcest form of liquidity data and not available if you haven't traded a particular security in the past. A fair amount of analysis may be needed to forecast future costs from past trading, and there is no guarantee in the accuracy of the forecasts.

A variety of surrogate measurements derived from market data are indicative of liquidity. The raw indicators are trade prices and sizes, and quoted spreads and sizes on each side of the quote. Many liquidity measurements can be derived from this market data: liquidity ratios, resilience measurements, indications of buyer or seller initiation. This is a rich area for analysis; there are many variations and elaborations on all of these analytic tools. These measurements are useful in trading, in analyzing past trades, and before trading in screening a potential investment universe for liquidity.

Here, a series of plots graphed together as in Exhibit 11, show an example of this type of multidimensional liquidity data using a 2-D and 3-D graphic visualization tool. This is a good way to sort through this kind of data. All the plots in the exhibit use data provided by the Quality of Markets Division at the London Stock Exchange. The full dataset contains market value, average spreads, and average quote size data, total trade volume, dealer volume and customer volume, for all stocks in the FT All Share index. It is updated quarterly. We have restricted these views to show only the FTSE 350, and we look only at customer volume.

The axis labels used in Exhibit 11 are: Market Value: MKTVAL, Modal (most frequent) Large Quote Size: AVGLQT, Average Spread: AVGBBO, and Daily Customer Volume: DAYVOLPD The first plot, Exhibit 11a, shows the average spread on the vertical axis and market value horizontally. As one would expect, the largest stock by market value, British Telecomm, also has one of the smallest spreads. The smallest market value stock, Body Shop, has a much larger average spread, but smaller than some larger stocks. Exhibit 11b plots market value against trading volume. Both of our sample stocks show up where we expect to find them, at the extreme ends. Exhibit 11c plots market value against the most common quote size. This one is a little different. Since quote sizes are discontinuous, the points don't scatter over the range as seen previously, and interestingly, British Telecomm does not show up in the top tier of liquidity by this measure, at least in this period. We can put the previous two dimensional plots together in a three dimensional view as shown in Exhibit 11d.

Exhibit 11: Visualization Tools Applied to
UK Stock Market Liquidity Data
A: Average Spread versus Market Value

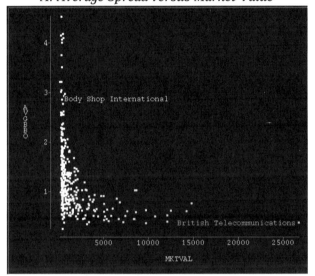

B: Average Daily Trading Volume versus Market Value

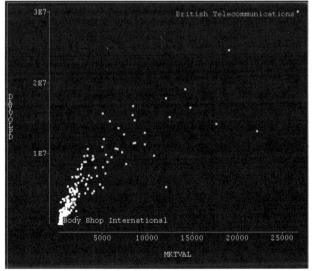

Exhibit 11 (Continued)
C: Most Common Quoted Size versus Market Value

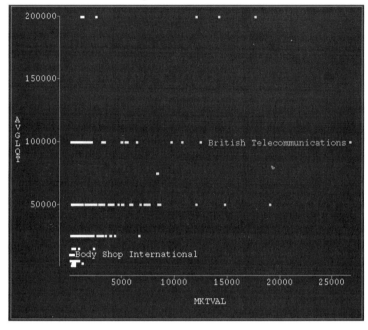

D: Average Spread, Most Common Quote, and Average Daily Volume

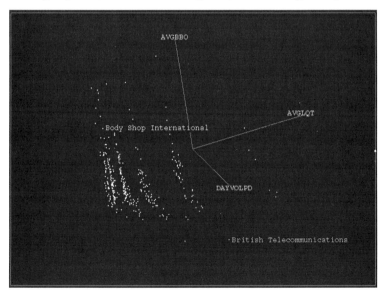

Geometrically speaking, the previous plots were projections of this 3-D cloud of points onto the axis planes. In this plot, the spread axis heads off toward the top of the page, the volume axis comes out toward the viewer, and the quote size axis goes from left to right. We can clearly see the discrete character of the quote size data in the four major layers of points, each of which corresponds to a scatter plot of spread against volume. When this type of plot is viewed on the computer screen, it is interactive. Any view can be selected by rotating the image, any of the axes can be switched to show market value, or other data. Any point can be selected to determine which stock it refers to, and display all the rest of the data associated with it.

In the 1950s, the famous statistician, Tukey, advocated a graphical approach to exploratory data analysis, and even wrote an entire book with that title showing how to do this efficiently using pencil and paper. The visualization tools readily available today make this whole process infinitely easier, and are particularly useful in exploring the information such as this liquidity data.

It is noteworthy that the obvious correlations between these various liquidity indicators are present, but perhaps not as strongly as one would expect. Stocks which are most (or least) liquid by one measure are often found not be so when evaluated along a different dimension, so these multiple measurements are not simply surrogates for each other. As in model building, liquidity analysis is part art and part science.

Monitoring Changes in Liquidity

Liquidity varies over time, on multiple time scales. A decision implemented in January to hold five days volume of a stock may be found to be a position equivalent to ten days volume in March. A stock that is easy to buy in quantity in the morning may be much harder to come by in the afternoon.

On the longer time scales, on-going monitoring of changes in estimated liquidity, automated as agent-based computations, which trigger messages warning of liquidity changes that indicate that a position might be much more costly to trade out of than it was to get in, and that a gradual reduction might be in order.

Controlling Costs During the Trade

On shorter, intraday time scales liquidity can be monitored using real time trading analytics. The details are described elsewhere,[11] but the basic idea is to combine real time calculations with rule-based systems to sort out the events of interest from the mass of data that always results when a whole set of indications are calculated for a long list of names.

This is another example of an application of artificial intelligence technology. The same sorts of raw market data as we discussed in the section on choosing an liquid investable universe are used, but the calculations are typically made over minutes and hours instead of days and months. A real time expert system sorts out the important events, and as seen in Exhibit 12a, lets the names with potentially significant liquidity problems float to the top of an "alarm window."

---

[11] Leinweber and Beinart, "A Little Artificial Intelligence Goes a Long Way on Wall Street."

Exhibit 12a: Multiple Alarm Windows

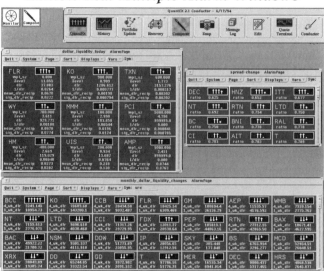

Exhibit 12b: "No GUI, No Glory," Marketmind's Hierarchical Graphical User Interface

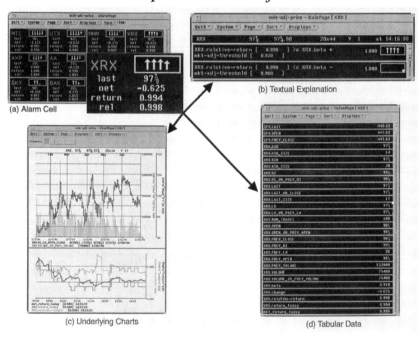

(a) Alarm Cell

(b) Textual Explanation

(c) Underlying Charts

(d) Tabular Data

Exhibit 12c: "Conductor" Control Panel and Composer

In the Quantex system, shown in these exhibits, all the details underlying a liquidity warning are a mouse click away, as seen in Exhibit 12b. But most importantly, the system is able to continuously apply order setting rules to calculate the best order type, size, and price (if limit orders are used) to minimize expected transaction costs. The results of these order calculations are shown in an electronic execution pad (shown in Exhibit 12c) where they can be accepted, modified or rejected by the trader, and routed directly to an exchange, brokerage desk, or alternate market system for execution.

Timely Post-Trade Analysis

All this technology and pre-trade screening is great, it helps avoid costly trades, and it helps traders make the many "when, where, and how to trade" decisions they are faced with every day. It is important to measure how this process is working, and this information is useful on multiple time scales. Annual reviews indicate which brokers are doing a better job. A two cent per share commission may not be such a bargain if it comes packaged with fifty cents of market impact. Similarly, the overall low cost of a seemingly high commission trade may make it a better decision than would appear.

There are a number of trade analysis services which provide this information on a quarterly or annual schedule. These are useful for the broker review decisions which are made on these time scales, and they include valuable comparisons to other managers which are not available elsewhere. We use these services, but recognize their limitations, i.e., they are only vaguely useful for day-to-day trading decisions. We have developed a system to remedy this situation. It provides a graphical window into up-to-date trade information at the trading desk.

Exhibit 13: Trade Database at the Trading Desk
a: Basic View

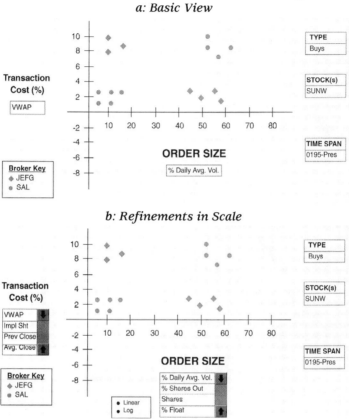

b: Refinements in Scale

The basic idea is seen in Exhibit 13a. A trader faced with an order to fill types in the symbol and a buy/sell selection. The graphic displays the previous trades, with size, scaled by percentage of daily volume on the horizontal axis, and trading cost, measured by implementation shortfall, on the vertical axis. Each broker's trades are shown with a colored symbol which identifies the broker. In this (admittedly contrived) example it is obvious that one broker has done consistently well on smaller trades, and another on larger ones. The selection would be easy. Real life is not always so neat. Perhaps the stock has not been traded very much, or at all. As shown in Exhibit 13b, the scope of the analysis can be expanded to include both buys and sells, and the range of names included can expand to include similar stocks, or an entire industry group. Finally, acknowledging that there are many ways to look at trading costs, and many scales that may be used to gauge order size, the trader can refine the scales used for both axes on the graph, as illustrated in Exhibit 13c. To borrow a phrase from the ubiquitous Microsoft advertisements, it puts "information at your fingertips" for daily trading decisions.

Exhibit 13 (Continued)
c: Refinements in Scope

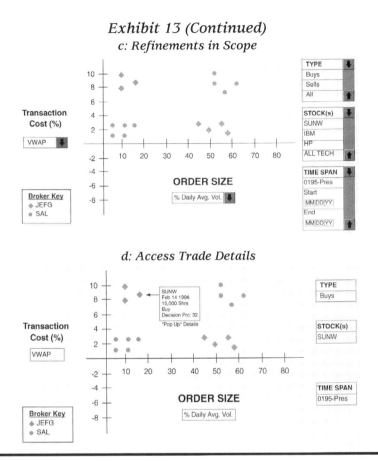

d: Access Trade Details

SUMMARY

We examined the role of specialized model building tools for equity style management, and for any quantitative forecast-based strategy. The machine learning technique called the genetic algorithm has proven to be a valuable amplifier for more traditional modeling techniques in these applications. We discussed the importance of data management and quality control, and the use the Internet and other technologies in maintaining a high-quality, timely data supply for quantitative investing.

Finally, we reviewed several techniques and technologies for controlling the transaction costs which have the potential to erode alpha. These are applicable before trading, in restricting the investable universe; during a trade, in timing, sizing, and directing orders; and, after a trade in analyzing the information it produced to illuminate future trading decisions. We combine these techniques for modeling, analysis, and implementation of modern information intensive equity strategies.

Chapter 8

Managing the Small Cap Cycle

Eric H. Sorensen, Ph.D.
Managing Director
Salomon Brothers Inc.

Joseph J. Mezrich, Ph.D.
Director
Salomon Brothers Inc.

Keith L. Miller
Director
Salomon Brothers Inc.

INTRODUCTION

Many academic studies have concluded that investment style (e.g., growth or value) and capitalization explain 90% of the price variability in certain institutional portfolios.[1] We have conducted extensive research on classifying/defining investment style and on forecasting the cycle of relative style performance.[2] In this chapter, we will explore returns to size/capitalization in the United States and Japanese equity markets. More specifically, we will examine the small-cap cycle and attempt to identify factors which are important in assessing prospective returns to size.

In Exhibit 1, we summarize our findings in these two markets. Under various scenarios (e.g., high economic growth or strong currency), we identify whether small caps or large caps displayed a higher probability of significant outperformance. The results are economically sensible. Moreover, there appears to be a measure of commonality in the determinants of returns to capitalization in Japan and the United States.

---

[1] See William F. Sharpe, "Asset Allocation: Management Style and Performance Measurement," *Journal of Portfolio Management* (Winter 1992).

[2] See Sergio Bienstock and Eric H. Sorensen, *Segregating Growth From Value: It's Not Always Either/Or*, Salomon Brothers Inc. (July 1992). For a detailed discussion of forecasting style returns, see Eric H. Sorensen, and Craig J. Lazzara, "Equity Style Management: The Case of Growth and Value," in Robert A. Klein and Jess Lederman (eds.), *Equity Style Management* (Burr Ridge, IL: Irwin Professional Publishing, 1995).

Exhibit 1: Gauging the Size Effect Under Different Scenarios — Which Wins

Scenario	United States	Japan
Strong Growth	Small-cap	Small-cap
Weak Growth	Large-cap	Large-cap
Strong Currency	Small-cap	Small-cap
Weak Currency	Large-cap	NM
Rising Volatility	Large-cap	Large-cap
Declining Volatility	Small-cap	Small-cap
Rising Short Rates	NM	Small-cap
Declining Short Rates	NM	Large-cap
Rising Long Rates	Small-cap	Small-cap
Declining Long Rates	NM	NM

NM = Not Meaningful

Source: Salomon Brothers Inc.

Exhibit 2: Relative Performance: Ibbotson Small-Cap Index/S&P 500, 1960-1995

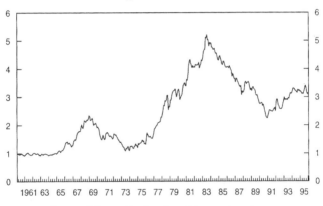

Source: Salomon Brothers Inc., Ibbotson Associates.

UNITED STATES: THE SMALL-CAP CYCLE

The long-term history of small-cap/large-cap relative performance in the United States is marked by extended periods (i.e., 4 to 7 years) of under- and outperformance (see Exhibit 2). Many observers have cited currency trends, the economic cycle, and changes in the tax code as explanations for the small-cap performance cycle. Clearly, the persistence of returns to size highlights the importance of understanding the small-cap cycle.

Given the relatively risky nature of small caps, one would expect a small-cap premium to compensate investors for additional risk. In Exhibit 3, we plot the probability distribution of rolling 6-month small-cap premia (defined as the total return of the lowest quintile of capitalization of the U.S. stock market less the total return of the S&P 500) over the last 35 years.[3] The horizontal axis in Exhibit 3 is the magnitude of the 6-month return differential. The vertical axis is the frequency of the return differential. When we sum over specific intervals along the horizontal axis, we determine the historical probability that the differential return lies within the specific interval.

For example, since 1960, the median 6-month return differential has been 0.8% — with a standard deviation of approximately 9.0%. The shaded areas represent return differentials of more than one standard deviation. (Since the median of the distribution is approximately 1.0%, a 9% standard deviation means that the shaded areas correspond to small-cap return differentials of less than −8% or more than 10%.) We will use these one-sigma thresholds as our definition of *significant* small- or large-cap outperformance. The historical probability that small-cap issues outperform large caps by 10% over six months is 22%; whereas the likelihood that small caps underperform by 8% is 15%. It will be important to use these unconditional probabilities as points of reference as we examine how various factors (such as fluctuations in economic growth or currencies) shift these probabilities. (For reference, Exhibit 7 summarizes the probabilities discussed throughout this section.)

Exhibit 3: Historical Probability Distribution of 6-Month Small-Cap Premia, 1960-1995

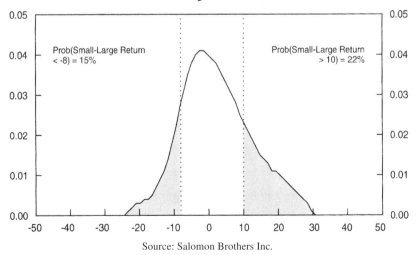

Source: Salomon Brothers Inc.

---

[3] More specifically, small-cap premium is defined as the total return of the lowest quintile of the NYSE and stocks on the AMEX and OTC that fall into the same capitalization range less the total return of the S&P 500. The source of small-cap premia in the United States is Ibbotson Associates.

Exhibit 4: Probability Distribution of 6-Month Small-Cap Premia Conditioned on Highest and Lowest Quartiles of 6-Month Change in Leading Indicators

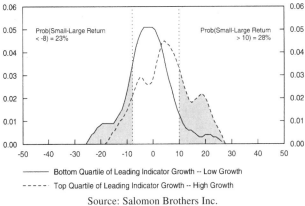

Bottom Quartile of Leading Indicator Growth -- Low Growth
Top Quartile of Leading Indicator Growth -- High Growth

Source: Salomon Brothers Inc.

Small-Cap Premia — Conditioned on Economic Growth

This perspective allows us to explore conditional probability distributions of small-cap premia. One way to assess a factor's importance in explaining the relative performance of small and large cap stocks is to compare the likelihood of a large return differential in the conditional distribution versus the unconditional distribution. In each figure, we shade in the portion of the curve above 10% and below −8%. The area of the shaded regions represent the probability of significant small-cap outperformance (greater than 10%) or significant large-cap outperformance (less than −8%).

In Exhibit 4, we present two probability distributions — one conditioned on a high-growth environment and one conditioned on a low-growth environment. If economic growth is influential in determining relative performance between large and small caps, then we should observe a difference between these distributions. The measure of economic growth that we use is the 6-month percentage change in the index of leading economic indicators. By quartile-ranking these changes, we are able to categorize each period into low, medium, and high growth regimes. We then generate contemporaneous probability distributions of the 6-month small-cap premia in these two environments.

In comparison to the unconditional probability distribution, the distribution of small-cap premia shifts to the right (i.e., favors small-caps) in a high-growth environment (i.e., the highest quartile of leading indicator change). More specifically, when high economic growth prevails, small caps outperform large caps 69% of the time (versus an unconditional probability of 55%). The probability that small-cap outperformance exceeds the one-sigma threshold rises to 28% (versus 22% unconditionally). Conversely, in a low-growth period, the probability of small-cap outperformance shrinks to 41%, and the probability of significant underperformance rises to 23%.

Exhibit 5: Probability Distribution of 6-Month Small-Cap Premia Conditioned on the Highest and Lowest Quartiles of 6-Month Change in Trade-Weighted Dollar, 1974-1996

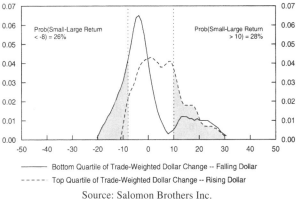

Source: Salomon Brothers Inc.

Small-Cap Premia Conditioned on the U.S. Dollar

We have found that currency trends are closely associated with the small-large cap relative performance cycle. Typically, a falling dollar provides large-cap multinational firms with favorable pricing and currency translation from operations abroad. A stronger dollar might reduce the relative earnings growth of multinationals vis-a-vis small caps, and therefore reduce the attraction of large caps. By definition, many small firms sell products largely in their own economy, where relative product demand is not subject to the vagaries of currency fluctuations. To the extent that small firms import some of their production inputs, relative costs decline when the dollar strengthens. As with economic growth, we quartile-rank currency trends. Specifically, we employ the 6-month percentage change in the trade-weighted dollar as our proxy of currency performance.

In Exhibit 5, we present the small-cap premia probability distributions conditioned on a strong dollar (i.e., the highest quartile of dollar performance) and a weak dollar (i.e., the lowest quartile of dollar performance). This analysis confirms the linkage between currency movements and the relative performance of small-cap stocks. For example, when the dollar is weak, small-caps underperform 71% of the time — while the odds are 26% of *significant* underperformance. Conversely, when the dollar is strong, the odds of small-cap outperformance are 68% — with a 28% chance that small caps beat large caps by 10% versus only a 5% chance that large caps will beat small caps by 8%.

Small-Cap Premia Conditioned on Volatility Trends

Volatility trends appear to exhibit a strong influence on small-cap premia. In Exhibit 6, we present the conditional probability distributions of the 6-month return differential between small and large cap stocks based on the 6-month change in our GARCH estimate of S&P 500 volatility. Typically, when the change in volatility is in the highest quartile, there is a stronger probability of small-cap underperformance.[4] The leverage effect describes the inverse relationship between changes in volatility and the price of an asset. Therefore, given that spikes in volatility are often associated with stock market declines and small-cap underperformance (due to their lower liquidity and higher beta), a view on future volatility could be valuable in assessing prospective relative performance.

In particular, when volatility is declining (i.e., in the lowest quartile of change), small caps outperform large caps 68% of the time. The probability of dramatic small-cap outperformance is 30% — or more than four times the probability of large-cap outperformance. However, these odds radically shift in favor of large-caps when volatility is rising.

In Exhibit 7, we present a table of probabilities of small- and large-cap outperformance under the various conditions discussed above. In addition, we include conditional probabilities based on other factors, such as inflation and interest rates, which did not prove to be particularly compelling. We also provide bivariate conditional probabilities — in which we examine outperformance probabilities based on a combination of scenarios (e.g., strong economic growth and rising volatility). In each case, we provide the probability of small-cap outperformance, as well as the probability of significant out- or underperformance (i.e., return differentials exceeding one standard deviation from the median). In Exhibit 8, we graph the small-cap premia, and the 6-month changes in the factors previously discussed over the last 35 years.

Exhibit 6: Probability Distribution of 6-Month Small-Cap Premia Conditioned on the Highest and Lowest Quartiles of 6-Month Change in Stock Market Volatility

Source: Salomon Brothers Inc.

---

[4] This finding is consistent with the leverage effect that we have identified in previous analysis. See Eric Sorensen, et al., *The Derivative Portfolio Matrix — Combining Market Direction with Market Volatility*, Salomon Brothers Inc. (November 1994).

Exhibit 7: United States: Probabilities of Small-Cap Performance Differentials, 1960-1995

Scenario	Small-Cap Outperformance	Small-Cap Exceeding Positive	Outperformance 1 Std. Dev. Negative
Unconditional	*0.55*	*0.22*	*0.15*
Leading Indicator Growth — Below Median	0.47	0.16	0.17
Leading Indicator Growth — Above Median	0.61	0.26	0.11
Leading Indicator Growth — Lowest Quartile	0.41	0.07	0.23
Leading Indicator Growth — Highest Quartile	0.69	0.28	0.11
Currency Change — Below Median	0.40	0.20	0.23
Currency Change — Above Median	0.62	0.27	0.06
Currency Change — Lowest Quartile	0.29	0.19	0.26
Currency Change — Highest Quartile	0.68	0.28	0.05
Volatility Change — Below Median	0.63	0.28	0.07
Volatility Change — Above Median	0.45	0.15	0.21
Volatility Change — Lowest Quartile	0.68	0.30	0.07
Volatility Change — Highest Quartile	0.38	0.11	0.28
Inflation — Below Median	0.58	0.16	0.10
Inflation — Above Median	0.51	0.25	0.18
Inflation — Lowest Quartile	0.65	0.13	0.03
Inflation — Highest Quartile	0.58	0.30	0.14
Short Rate Change — Below Median	0.53	0.19	0.16
Short Rate Change — Above Median	0.54	0.24	0.16
Short Rate Change — Lowest Quartile	0.56	0.20	0.16
Short Rate Change — Highest Quartile	0.50	0.23	0.18
Long Rate Change — Below Median	0.53	0.18	0.14
Long Rate Change — Above Median	0.51	0.23	0.18
Long Rate Change — Lowest Quartile	0.52	0.15	0.13
Long Rate Change — Highest Quartile	0.55	0.30	0.16
Highest Quartile of Growth and			
Below Median Inflation	0.70	0.24	0.12
Above Median Inflation	0.68	0.35	0.06
Below Median Exchange Rate Change (Weak)	0.50	0.26	0.07
Above Median Exchange Rate Change (Strong)	0.79	0.36	0.01
Below Median Volatility Change	0.71	0.32	0.08
Above Median Volatility Change	0.62	0.15	0.18
Lowest Quartile of Growth and			
Below Median Inflation	0.44	0.04	0.10
Above Median Inflation	0.39	0.09	0.28
Below Median Exchange Rate Change (Weak)	0.30	0.02	0.20
Above Median Exchange Rate Change (Strong)	0.42	0.22	0.16
Below Median Volatility Change	0.79	0.32	0.03
Above Median Volatility Change	0.27	0.01	0.26

Source: Salomon Brothers Inc.

Exhibit 8: History of U.S. Small-Cap Premium and Indicators, 1960-95

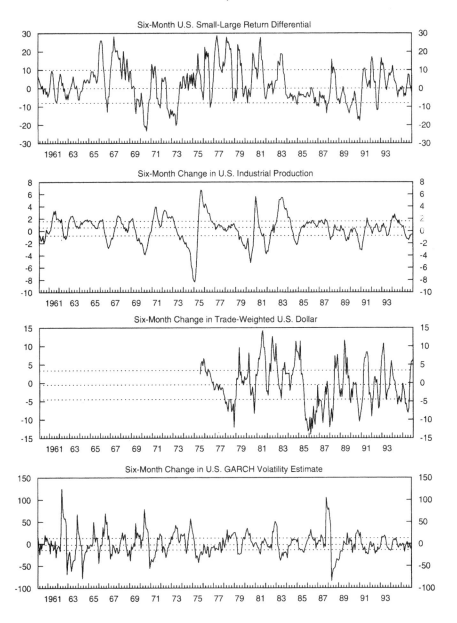

Exhibit 9: Relative Performance:
Ibbotson Small-Cap Index/TOPIX, 1974-1995

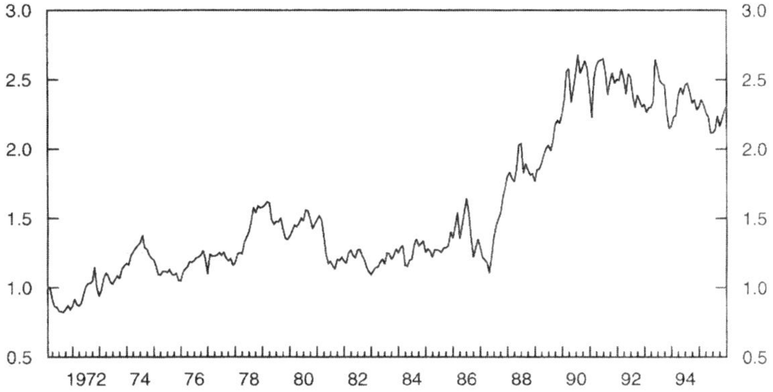

Source: Ibbotson Associates and Salomon Brothers Inc.

JAPAN: THE SMALL-CAP CYCLE

We have found a number of similarities in the sensitivities of small-cap premia in Japan to those in the United States. The Japanese small-cap premium is defined as the differential of the total return of the smallest quintile of capitalization in the Tokyo Stock Exchange First Section and total return of the Tokyo Stock Exchange First Section.[5] In Exhibit 9, we present the relative performance of small- and large-caps since 1974.

Since 1974, the median 6-month return differential has been 0.7% — with a standard deviation of approximately 10%. The shaded areas in Exhibit 10 represent the probabilities that small caps outperformed large caps by one standard deviation (roughly 11%) and small caps underperformed large caps by one standard deviation (roughly −9%). The historical/unconditional probability that small caps outperform large caps by 11% over six months is 21%; while the probability that large caps outperform by 9% is 16%. (For reference, Exhibit 15 summarizes the probabilities discussed in this section.)

Future Small-Cap Premia — Conditioned on Economic Growth
In Exhibit 11, we present small-cap premia distributions conditioned on economic growth in the highest quartile and economic growth in the lowest quartile. Economic growth is measured as the 6-month change in industrial production. As in the United States, small-cap premia appear to be largely influenced by the economic cycle. For example, when economic growth ascends to the highest quartile, the probability of small-cap outperformance rises to 71% (versus 50% uncondi-

---

[5] The source of small-cap premia in Japan is Ibbotson Associates.

tionally). The odds that small-cap outperformance exceeds the one-sigma threshold (i.e., 11%) increase to 35% — versus only a 5% chance of significant large-cap outperformance. Conversely, if growth is in the lowest quartile, large caps post superior performance 64% of the time.

Exhibit 10: Japan: Historical Probability Distribution of 6-Month Small-Cap Premia, 1974-1995

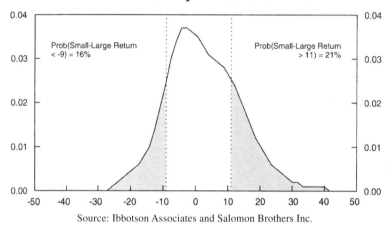

Source: Ibbotson Associates and Salomon Brothers Inc.

Exhibit 11: Probability Distribution of 6-Month Small-Cap Premia Conditioned on Highest and Lowest Quartiles of 6-Month Growth in Industrial Production

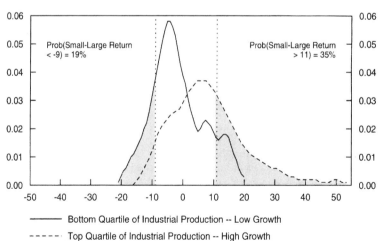

Source: Salomon Brothers Inc.

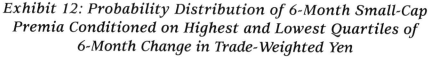

Exhibit 12: Probability Distribution of 6-Month Small-Cap Premia Conditioned on Highest and Lowest Quartiles of 6-Month Change in Trade-Weighted Yen

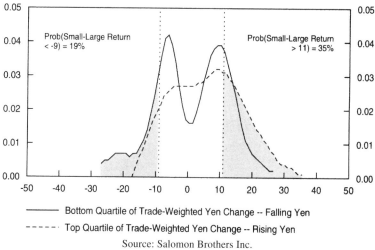

Source: Salomon Brothers Inc.

Japan Small-Cap Premia Conditioned on the Yen

In contrast to the United States, the effect of currency trends on relative performance is more ambiguous and asymmetric (see Exhibit 12). We chose the 6-month percentage change in the trade-weighted yen as our measure of currency trends. Conventional wisdom would suggest that a rising (falling) yen should be associated with superior large-cap (small-cap) performance. However, when the change in the yen is in the lowest quartile (i.e., a weak yen), the large caps actually underperform 51% of the time.

During periods of a rising yen (i.e., changes in the highest quartile), relative performance does conform to expectations as small caps outperform 67% of the time. Small caps also post significant outperformance in 35% of the cases or over 3 times the probability of large-cap significant outperformance.

Small-Cap Premia Conditioned on Interest Rates

In the United States, we were unable to find any strong relationship between contemporaneous changes in interest rates (long or short) and the relative performance of small and large stocks (see Exhibit 7). In contrast, changes in domestic interest rates had a more pronounced effect on small-cap premia in Japan. For example, during periods of rising short rates (above-median changes), small stocks outperformed 63% of the time. When in the highest quartile of short rate changes (rising rates), small-cap outperformance pierced the one-sigma threshold 31% of the time (see Exhibit 13). Similar results were found for movements in 10-year Japanese government bond yields (see Exhibit 15).

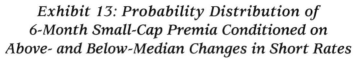

Exhibit 13: Probability Distribution of 6-Month Small-Cap Premia Conditioned on Above- and Below-Median Changes in Short Rates

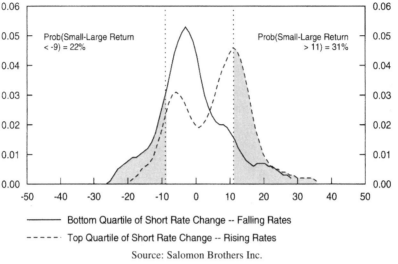

Prob(Small-Large Return < -9) = 22%

Prob(Small-Large Return > 11) = 31%

——— Bottom Quartile of Short Rate Change -- Falling Rates

------ Top Quartile of Short Rate Change -- Rising Rates

Source: Salomon Brothers Inc.

The interest rate sensitivity of small-cap premia in Japan is partly related to the sizable weighting of banks in the TOPIX. Given that financials represent nearly 30% of TOPIX and account for some of its largest constituents, it is not surprising that returns to size are influenced by the interest rate cycle.

Small-Cap Premia Conditioned on Stock Market Volatility

In Exhibit 14, we present the probability distributions of the 6-month small-cap premia conditioned on the 6-month change in our GARCH estimate of TOPIX volatility. As was the case in the United States, rising stock market volatility adversely affects small-cap performance relative to large-cap returns. Similarly, falling TOPIX volatility was associated with superior small-cap performance. For instance, during periods of falling volatility (i.e., volatility changes in the lowest quartile), small caps outperform large caps 67% of the time. In cases of rising volatility (i.e., volatility changes in the highest quartile), the odds of small-cap outperformance shrink to 40%.

In Exhibit 15, we present a table of probabilities of small- and large-cap outperformance under the various conditions discussed above. In each case, we provide the probability of small-cap outperformance, as well as the probability of significant out- or underperformance (i.e., return differentials exceeding one standard deviation from the median). In Exhibit 16, we graph the small-cap premia, and the 6-month changes in the factors previously discussed over the last 20 years.

Exhibit 14: Probability Distribution of 6-Month Small-Cap Premia Conditioned on the Highest and Lowest Quartiles of Changes in Stock Market Volatility

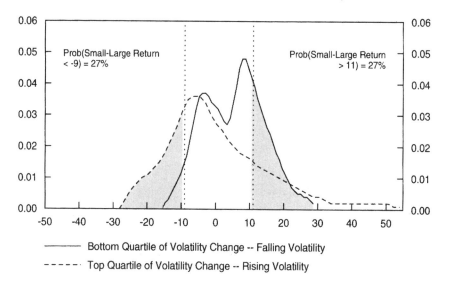

Prob(Small-Large Return < -9) = 27%

Prob(Small-Large Return > 11) = 27%

—————— Bottom Quartile of Volatility Change -- Falling Volatility

- - - - - Top Quartile of Volatility Change -- Rising Volatility

Source: Salomon Brothers Inc.

A Word on Accessing Small-Cap Exposure in Japan

There exist a number of ways to obtain small-cap exposure. For those investors who desire broad exposure to small caps, we believe that the appropriate benchmark is the Japanese component of the Salomon Brothers Extended Market Index (EMI). The EMI-Japan currently contains 1,170 companies representing the bottom 20% of the capitalization of all listed Japanese equities with a float greater than US$100 million.[6] Most of the companies in the EMI-Japan are traded in the First Section of the Tokyo Stock Exchange. The median total market capitalization of the EMI-Japan is approximately US$500 million (or approximately Yen 50 billion) — sufficiently large for institutional investors. Furthermore, each issue in the EMI-Japan is float-weighted thereby eliminating problems associated with cross-holding, large private holding, government owned shares, and shares cross-border investors cannot own.

---

[6] For a detailed discussion of the Extended Market Index, see Thomas S. Nadbielny, et al., *Introducing the Salomon Brothers World Equity Index*, Salomon Brothers Inc. (June 1994).

Exhibit 15: Japan: Probabilities of Small-Cap and Large-Cap Outperformance, 1974-1995

Scenario	Small-Cap Outperformance	Small-Cap Exceeding Positive	Outperformance 1 Std. Dev. Negative
Unconditional	*0.50*	*0.21*	*0.16*
Industrial Production Growth — Below Median	0.47	0.15	0.17
Industrial Production Growth — Above Median	0.57	0.27	0.11
Industrial Production Growth — Lowest Quartile	0.36	0.11	0.19
Industrial Production Growth — Highest Quartile	0.71	0.35	0.05
Currency Change — Below Median	0.48	0.18	0.16
Currency Change — Above Median	0.55	0.22	0.13
Currency Change — Lowest Quartile	0.51	0.18	0.19
Currency Change — Highest Quartile	0.67	0.35	0.11
Short Rate Change — Below Median	0.43	0.18	0.20
Short Rate Change — Above Median	0.63	0.24	0.10
Short Rate Change — Lowest Quartile	0.37	0.11	0.22
Short Rate Change — Highest Quartile	0.66	0.31	0.10
Long Rate Change — Below Median	0.46	0.15	0.14
Long Rate Change — Above Median	0.57	0.27	0.14
Long Rate Change — Lowest Quartile	0.45	0.13	0.13
Long Rate Change — Highest Quartile	0.61	0.31	0.13
Volatility Change — Below Median	0.61	0.20	0.05
Volatility Change — Above Median	0.42	0.18	0.23
Volatility Change — Lowest Quartile	0.67	0.27	0.04
Volatility Change — Highest Quartile	0.40	0.20	0.27
Inflation — Below Median	0.51	0.23	0.16
Inflation — Above Median	0.51	0.18	0.16
Inflation — Lowest Quartile	0.52	0.25	0.20
Inflation — Highest Quartile	0.53	0.22	0.15
Highest Quartile of Growth and			
Below Median Inflation	0.79	0.42	0.05
Above Median Inflation	0.68	0.26	0.04
Below Median Exchange Rate Change (Weak)	0.65	0.24	0.06
Above Median Exchange Rate Change (Strong)	0.81	0.42	0.03
Below Median Volatility Change	0.82	0.29	0.06
Above Median Volatility Change	0.68	0.37	0.04
Lowest Quartile of Growth and			
Below Median Inflation	0.29	0.09	0.19
Above Median Inflation	0.49	0.17	0.12
Below Median Exchange Rate Change (Weak)	0.34	0.05	0.25
Above Median Exchange Rate Change (Strong)	0.34	0.06	0.12
Below Median Volatility Change	0.49	0.14	0.06
Above Median Volatility Change	0.18	0.04	0.39

Source: Salomon Brothers Inc.

Exhibit 16: History of Japan Small-Cap Premium and Indicators, 1974-1995

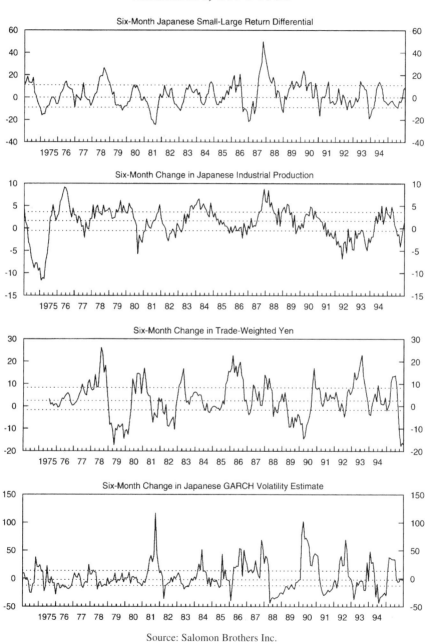

Source: Salomon Brothers Inc.

Chapter 9

Implications of Style in Foreign-Stock Investing

Paul M. Bagnoli
Senior Portfolio Manager
Director of International Product Development
Sanford C. Bernstein and Company, Inc.

INTRODUCTION

In 1988, foreign stocks accounted for $45 billion of U.S. pension assets. By 1996, the total had reached about $500 billion. This really isn't surprising, since foreign stocks represent an opportunity to invest in some of the best-run companies in the world — that just happen to be domiciled outside the United States. Equally important, foreign stocks are a high-expected-return asset that diversifies U.S. equities. Investors are aware of these facts and are globalizing their portfolios more and more. The rationale for expanding internationally is intuitive. But as the process unfolds, it raises the question of active management style. In the United States, management style is an integral part of the equity-allocation decision, and many investors purposely diversify between the two most common styles — value and growth — to try to reap the best of both worlds. Neither style wins all the time, and in fact, in the United States, there have been distinct cycles favoring one or the other approach.

Investors who choose to advocate an investment style must base this on certain essential propositions. We will assume three major propositions about value investing. First, it is efficacious. Buying earnings power, dividends, and assets for a price that is low compared with the standards of the day is very likely to produce a risk-adjusted return that is well above average. Second, value anomalies are outgrowths of behavioral, as opposed to financial, phenomena. Thus, the above-average returns produced by those anomalies will prove enduring, not because they are particularly difficult to identify or to capture, but because life in the value domain is fundamentally distasteful and will be avoided by many investors. Third, and most important, the value style in the United States applies equally well to all capital markets of the developed world and for precisely the same reasons. Despite cultural differences, the behavioral factors that drive the value style in the United States are manifest in each of the major foreign markets and in a global composite. We will develop two axioms that underlie these propositions and examine historical evidence that illustrate the axioms and make the case for an advantage to global value investing.

BIASES ABOUT WEALTH MANAGEMENT

Both introspection and focused observation suggest that some common biases are apparent in wealth management, and these biases work to the benefit of value investing.

The first bias is the overvaluation of certainty. People seem to have an overwhelming affection for things that are or appear to be certain. They like them so much that they consistently overbuy them and overpay for them. Household financial wealth, for example, is dominated by assets, such as money market funds that have very low or no perceived volatility-even when volatility should not make a difference, and at the sacrifice of considerable long-term return.

The second bias is the overreaction to big, unlikely, but consequential events. People are attracted to such events when the consequences of winning seem magnificent, even when they logically know the chances of winning are very small. This tendency explains the popularity of lotteries. In the financial markets, this behavioral bias fuels many financing and investing binges. Indeed, whole industries have been financed as a function of this behavioral bias; the most recent significant example is biotechnology.

The third bias is loss aversion. In people's minds, fear of losses looms considerably larger than expectation of gains. For most, the pain of a loss significantly exceeds the pleasure of an equivalent gain. Derived from real-world experiments performed by behavioral scientists Kahneman and Tversky,[1] Exhibit 1 depicts the value that people assign to perceived gains and losses. The asymmetry between pleasure and pain for an equivalent gain captures this result. The only thing investors dislike more than losing money is paying an investment manager to lose it for them.

---

[1] Amos Tversky and Daniel Kahneman, "Rational Choice and the Framing of Decisions," *Journal of Business* (1986).

Exhibit 1: Loss Aversion

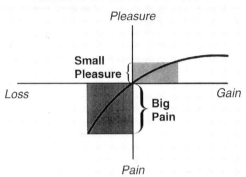

Source: Sanford C. Bernstein & Co., based on Amos Tversky and Daniel Kahneman, "Rational Choice and the Framing of Decisions," *Journal of Business*, No.4 (1986).

AXIOMS OF VALUE INVESTING

Axiom 1: Value Equals Anxiety

The aforementioned behavioral biases underlie the first of the two major axioms of value investing, namely, that *value equals anxiety*. That is, anxiety-producing capital assets — those framed in the domain of potential losses — will be priced to offer returns that are meaningfully higher than the returns justified by the actual risks taken. Assets in this domain typically do not achieve that status overnight; rather, they earn it by first persistently disappointing anyone who has been willing to invest in them. If the pattern of disappointment keeps up long enough, the reaction turns to disgust. If the pattern goes on still longer, if it attracts attention, if it becomes the subject of persistent negative media coverage, and in the extreme, if ownership carries serious risks to the owner's reputation, the disgust turns to despair and, ultimately, fear. Accordingly, value anomalies are almost always outgrowths of progressive discouragement, and given loss aversion, assets subject to this process should and do eventually provide disproportionately high returns. The behavioral basis for this phenomenon also suggests that these results should be observed in most, if not all, developed markets.

The impact on U.S. stock returns of changing investor expectations substantiates that value anomalies are generated by progressive discouragement and do produce above-average returns. Exhibit 2 plots the return impact on stocks in the S&P 500 index of changing expectations for near-term earnings — specifically, 12-month earnings forecasts — during the 20-year period ending in 1993. Changing expectations are reflected in either positive or negative earnings revisions, and the frequency bars indicate the number of incidences of both types of revisions, grouped by size. The leftward preponderance of frequency bars indicates more downward revisions than upward, which reflects the perennially optimistic positions that analysts take. The effects of the expectational shifts on relative returns are large, from +300 to −200 basis points (bps) versus the S&P 500, and take time to filter through to valuation. These performance premiums and penalties were measured for the period three months after the expectational shifts were observed. Stable expectations are neither rewarded nor penalized; no relative return is associated with the "no earnings revisions" frequency bar. But for upward and downward revisions, the relative performance response is basically monotonic. The larger the revisions, the larger the relative performance effect.

Significantly, the downward revisions are highly serially correlated. As Exhibit 3 reveals, the probability is very high that a stock that has already experienced one or more downward revisions will experience additional downward revision. These data reinforce something investment managers know from experience: people do not adjust to events all at once. Their first reactions to deterioration are almost always inadequate, so they are likely to generate additional downward revisions. This common behavioral bias is known as "anchoring."

Exhibit 2: Impact of Expectational Shifts

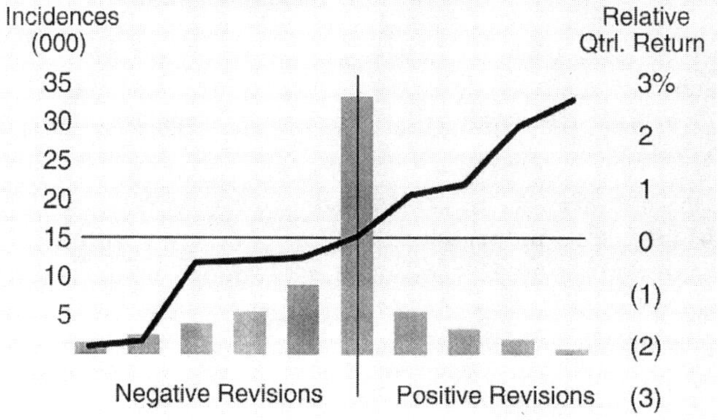

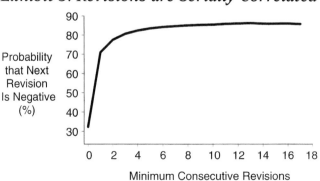

Source: Sanford C. Bernstein & Co., based on data from Institutional Broker's Estimate System (IBES).

Exhibit 3: Revisions are Serially Correlated

Source: Sanford C. Bernstein & Co.

Exhibit 4: Performance Impact of Negative Revisions

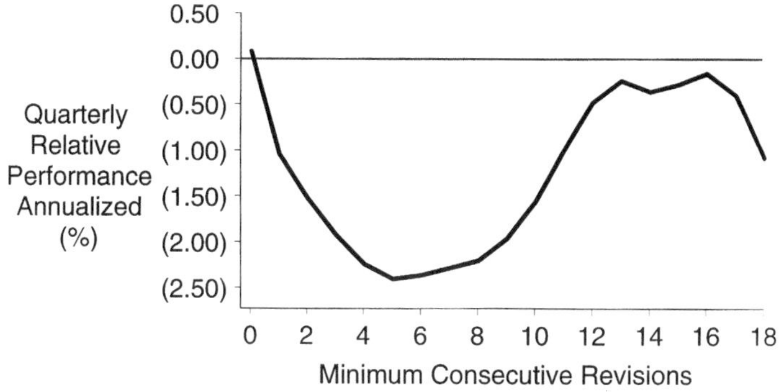

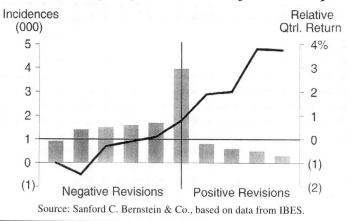

Source: Sanford C. Bernstein & Co.

Exhibit 5: Impact of Expectational Shifts — Cheap Stocks

Source: Sanford C. Bernstein & Co., based on data from IBES.

U.S. stock prices respond dramatically to progressive discouragement, as illustrated in Exhibit 4. Performance penalties increase as discouragement builds for the first six or seven of these revisions. After many such revisions, a curious phenomenon occurs: the incremental performance penalties begin to subside. Could a countervailing effect be surfacing? Perhaps value investors are beginning to find these stocks "cheap" and buy into the bad news, moderating its effects.

Exhibit 5 repeats the analysis shown in Exhibit 2 for a subset of stocks deemed cheap, as defined by traditional value investing metrics — price-to-book-value ratios, price-to-earnings ratios, and relative dividend yield. This subset is the domain of discouragement. Stocks in this subset are dominated by downward revisions. Of particular interest in this apparently gloomy environment is that the performance penalties associated with more disappointment diminish. Indeed, the returns in this group of stocks actually become positive (nearly 100 bps) in the mere presence of stability (no revisions) of expectations.

Exhibit 6: Impact of Expectational Shifts — Expensive Stocks

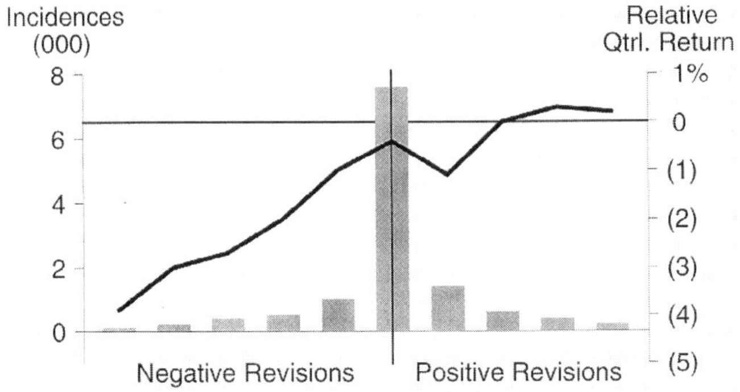

Source: Sanford C. Bernstein & Co., based on data from IBES.

Exhibit 5 depicts a high-return domain, but the selling of these stocks can be thought of as paying buyers to endure the stress of ownership that the sellers can no longer take. For example, consider buying housing stocks in 1982 with mortgage rates at 17%, or various auto and steel stocks in the Rust Belt years of the 1980s, oil stocks in 1986 when the price crashed from $25 to $10 a barrel, or financial stocks in the early 1990s — a value theme involving the most extreme form of ownership stress. This use of the seller's money is certainly fair, but it places the value investor, for all practical purposes, in a psychiatric role. The domain of discouragement is not for the timid, and value investors must be up to the challenge of pursuing what is uncomfortable. As a group, they often fail to beat benchmarks at the most critical times simply because life in this domain just before the moment of payoff can be extremely difficult to negotiate — in fact, so difficult that many investors cannot or will not stay the course.

The opposite kind of emotional state applies at the other end of the value spectrum — the subset of "expensive" stocks according to the value metrics. Exhibit 6 depicts the domain of presumed predictability, stability in earnings. People prize this stability. It makes them feel secure, and they are willing to pay to feel secure. In contrast to the no-return case in Exhibit 2 and the positive-return case in Exhibit 5, stable expectations in Exhibit 6 actually generate a negative return — roughly 50 bps. At the same time, the penalties for any disappointment are severe indeed — a drop in returns of as much as 400 bps. The benefits of positive revisions are surprisingly scant since the price is already very high.

The contrasts between Exhibits 2 and 6 and Exhibit 5 clearly demonstrate, for the United States, the validity of the first axiom: *pain and suffering are rewarded in the capital markets.*

Performing a similar analysis for the rest of the developed world is difficult because the available data are limited. The data that are available, however, are persuasive. Exhibit 7 compares the reactions in the United States with investor reactions to revisions of short-run expectations (revisions of 12-month earnings expectations measured three months after the fact) for ten developed countries: Australia, Canada,

France, Germany, Hong Kong, Italy, Japan, the Netherlands, Switzerland, and the United Kingdom. The index was a capitalization-weighted intersection of the Institutional Broker's Estimate System (IBES) and Morgan Stanley Capital International (MSCI) universes. The exhibit incorporates only seven years (1987-1993) of data for the international markets, but the lines show that investor response to changing expectations in these markets is remarkably similar to the U.S. experience, especially the absence of any return associated with stable expectations.

Exhibit 8 portrays investor response in the domain of cheap stocks from Exhibit 7, and Exhibit 9 presents the same analysis for expensive stocks, with the same value metrics applied to delineate the subsets. These exhibits carry the same message that held in the U.S. case: higher returns accrue when discouragement is high, and lower returns are associated with predictability. Although not conclusive, the data strongly suggest that non-U.S. investors are moved by short-run earnings disappointments in a manner analogous to the behavior of U.S. investors. If anything, the relative rewards and penalties are even more pronounced internationally.

Exhibit 7: Impact of Expectational Shifts — International

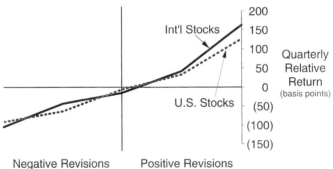

Source: Sanford C. Bernstein & Co., based on data from IBES and MSCI.

Exhibit 8: Impact of Expectational Shifts — International Cheap Stocks

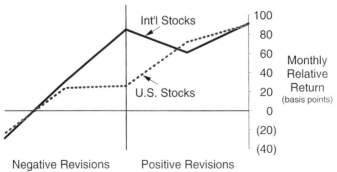

Source: Sanford C. Bernstein & Co., based on data from IBES and MSCI.

Exhibit 9: Impact of Expectational Shifts — International Expensive Stocks

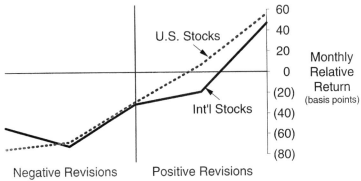

Source: Sanford C. Bernstein & Co., based on data from IBES and MSCI.

Exhibit 10: Return on Equity: U.S. Corporations Reversion to the Mean

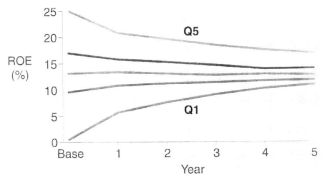

Source: Sanford C. Bernstein & Co., based on data from Compustat.

Axiom 2: Mean Reversion

The behavioral loop is not yet closed. Identifying the process by which value anomalies are generated — progressive discouragement — does not address how those anomalies are ultimately resolved. The second axiom of value investing addresses this issue and is popularly known as mean reversion: good things get worse; bad things get better.

Exhibit 10 shows quintiles ranked from highest to lowest based on corporate return on equity (ROE) for approximately 1,000 U.S. companies for the 1963-1993 period. The initial rankings reflect how well the companies were doing at the beginning of the period, not the prices of the stocks. The exhibit traces the quintile ROEs during the next five years. What the lines reveal is the strong tendency for ROEs to regress to the mean from both directions. Exhibit 11, for a subset of 800 companies in the MSCI universe from 1975 through 1993, suggests that mean reversion is a global phenomenon; the same tendency for ROEs to converge is evident in non-U.S. companies. Exhibit 12 provides market-specific evidence of mean reversion for four developed markets. That value-oriented strategies produce superior returns in these markets as well as in the U.S. market should be no surprise.

These results reflect another facet of human behavior: success has a strong tendency to attract emulators and, sometimes, to breed complacency and conservatism on the part of the successful. This phenomenon leaves the high-return companies vulnerable to erosion in profitability. Tough times cause the opposite kind of response; capital tends to flee, corporate managers rise to the occasion with initiative to turn the tied. If they do not, new managers will. In time, on average the tide does turn.

Exhibit 11: Return on Equity: International Corporations Reversion to the Mean

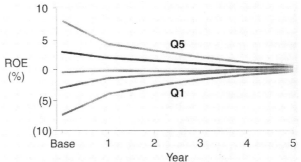

Source: Sanford C. Bernstein & Co., based on data from MSCI.

Exhibit 12: Return on Equity: Reversion to the Mean

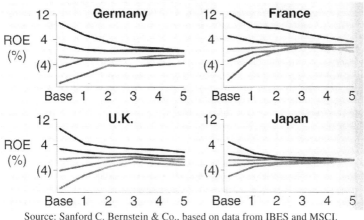

Source: Sanford C. Bernstein & Co., based on data from IBES and MSCI.

Exhibit 13: U.S. versus Japan Stock Performance

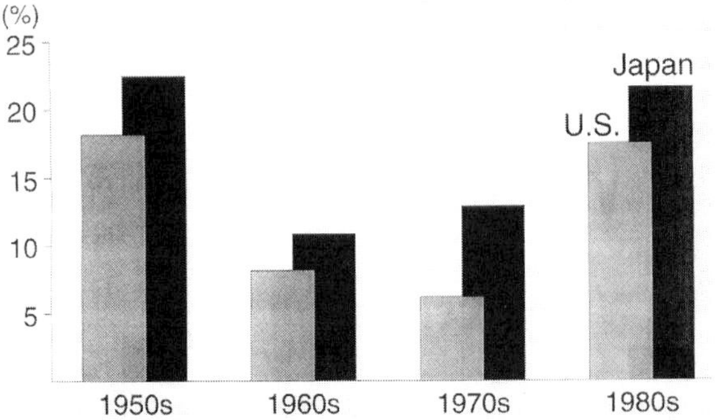

Source: Ibbotson Associates, MSCI, Goldman Sachs and Company, and Bernstein estimates.

A LOOK AT JAPAN

As an investor, the critical question becomes whether these behavioral biases are observed in equity valuations and, in turn, equity returns. Japan represents a country very different from the U.S. in customs, institutions, and social mores. Although there is little academic research on the issue, it would seem only logical that a country as different from ours in the sociopolitical sphere would also be different in the way its investors behave.

In many important ways, this is true. If we look at compound stock returns for the last four full decades, in local terms, Japanese equities have out-performed U.S. equities consistently — by margins ranging from three percentage points a year, in the 1960s, to seven points, in the 1970s (see Exhibit 13). It is important to note that in the 1990s, through the end of 1995, Japan was declining at about 8% per year and the United States appreciating by about 13% per year.

Looking at historical valuation, the story is equally extreme. The top of Exhibit 14 shows the price-to-book ratios of the Japanese and U.S. markets from 1975 through the middle of 1989, when the "bubble" in Japan was at its peak. These are the years that helped form our mindset on Japan, and gave credence to the notion that Japan was truly a domain apart. The gap between the two markets was impressive, and kept widening until Japanese stocks hit a high of five times book value. Even after the Japanese market collapse in 1990, the price-to-book ratio remained very high. We see the same pattern in P/Es (Exhibit 15), which went as high as 64. It's not easy to find a major U.S. company that trades at that multiple, let alone a market average.

A Closer Look

These observations do not bode well for the importance of investment style in Japan — and certainly not for the value approach. However, if the behavioral factors illustrated earlier hold within each country, anomalies should be available. The research turned out to be extremely provocative.

Exhibit 14: Historical Price/Book Ratios: 1975-89: 1H

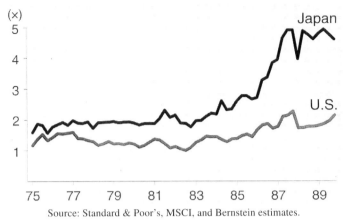

Source: Standard & Poor's, MSCI, and Bernstein estimates.

Exhibit 15: Historical Price/Book Ratios*: 1975-89: 1H

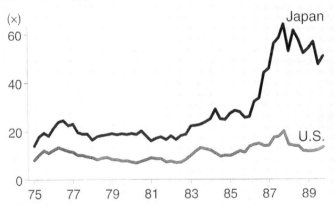

* Using trailing 12-month earnings.

Source: Standard & Poor's, MSCI, and Bernstein estimates.

Our research methodology (Exhibit 16) was highly systematic, and followed the models established in the United States. We went back to 1975, the earliest year for which reliable data are available, and, on a quarterly basis, we ranked the stocks in the Japanese market by their price-to-book ratios. We thought of the highest 20% of the market on this price-to-book measure as a proxy for growth stocks, and the lowest 20% as value stocks. We then built portfolios of growth stocks, and of value stocks, and measured their performance, in local-currency terms, going forward. (We applied the same methodology consistently across nine other major foreign markets in assessing worldwide value performance.)

Exhibit 16: Bernstein Research Methodology

- Universe = key foreign markets*
- Rank stocks by price-to-book ratios
- Highest 20% = "growth"
  Lowest 20% = "value"
- Construct value and growth portfolios
- Measure performance (in local currency) going forward

* Morgan Stanley Capital International coverage universe for each country

Exhibit 17: Japanese Price/Book Ratios: 1975-1995

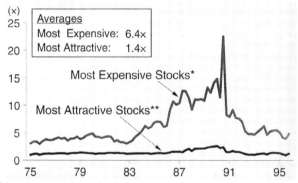

* Highest 20% of the market on price-to-book ratio
** Lowest 20% of the market on price-to-book ratio
Source: MSCI and Bernstein estimates.

Exhibit 17 shows the characteristics of the two subgroups of stocks: the top and bottom 20% of the Japanese market on this price-to-book basis from 1975 through 1995. The most expensive stocks show quite a pattern: their price-to-book averaged 6.4, and peaked at a phenomenal 22 times book. It is no surprise that numbers like these have colored investors' perceptions about the Japanese market. But in fact, they apply only to its growth subset. These stocks may represent a good chunk of the market on a capitalization basis, but they're only a small part of the total universe of opportunity in Japan. The bubble of the late 1980s, for example, was led by three industries: banking, insurance, and real estate.

But what about that least expensive 20% of Japanese stocks? There are three observations about this group. First, there's always been such a group — a "value" universe — in Japan. Second, its characteristics have been remarkably stable; its price-to-book ratio has never risen much higher than two, even when things were at their craziest in Japan, and it has stayed pretty consistently around its average of 1.4 — which would be attractive even by Western standards. Finally, the gap between what's cheap in Japan and what's expensive is remarkable.

Exhibit 18: Japanese Price/Earnings Ratios*: 1975-1995

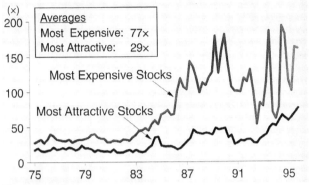

* Using trailing 12-month earnings.
Source: MSCI and Bernstein estimates.

Exhibit 19: Growth of ¥1: 1975-1995

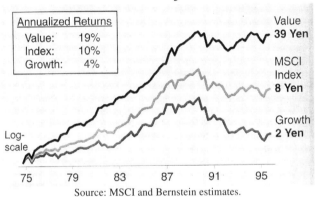

Source: MSCI and Bernstein estimates.

We see the same kind of picture in P/E ratios (see Exhibit 18). P/Es on expensive stocks have averaged 77 times and reached an outlandish 186 — versus a fairly consistent 25–50 for the value universe.

World's Best Market for Value

The question remains, do investors receive meaningfully higher returns for value stocks in Japan? The answer is, emphatically, yes. Between 1975 and 1995, Japanese value stocks compounded at 19% a year in yen terms, versus 10% for the market average, and 4% for growth stocks (see Exhibit 19). Looked at another way, it means that a yen invested in Japanese value stocks would have grown 39-fold over the period, versus eightfold for the benchmark, and two for growth stocks. Ironically enough, considering how unfriendly the Japanese environment looks for value, Japan has been the best market in the world for the approach. And value has achieved this outperformance with less volatility than growth stocks.

Exhibit 20: Composition of Returns: Japan
Annualized 1975-1995

	Batting Average (Frequency)		Slugging Percentage (Magnitude)	
	Winning	Losing	Win	Lose
Value	70%	30%	17 points	(10) points
Growth	33	67	8	(23)

Source: MSCI and Bernstein estimates

Extremes Create The Performance Edge

This level of performance has been fueled by the same extremes that at first glance appear so daunting. If you have a group of stocks selling for 70 times earnings, it suggests that price is no object: owning them becomes something you do without thinking. Other stocks — the ones facing short-term disappointments, or where earnings growth has been a little duller — just get crowded out. Investors are paying less attention and few have the patience to let cycles play out. With the discrepancy in Japan between the attention paid to expensive and cheap stocks, the value approach has flourished. If an investor believes that a company is under a temporary cloud and it's selling at a P/E of 35 when the market is at 70, the investor is likely to win big if right and the cloud lifts. Conversely, if an investor is looking at a fast-growing company that he bets is going to be able to sustain its growth, and the stock is trading at 185 times earnings, he better be right.

"Batting And Slugging" Averages

You can see the performance dynamic at work through one of our models that explains why value is efficacious: the so-called "batting average" and "slugging percentage." The batting average is the frequency of results: the percentage of the time that a group of stocks outperformed the market, versus the percentage of the time that it underperformed. The slugging percentage reflects the magnitude of outperformance when a style wins, or underperformance when it loses. Both have been very favorable for value in Japan (see Exhibit 20).

Between 1975 and 1995, Japanese value stocks, on average, outperformed the market 70% of the time, versus 33% for growth stocks. While that 70% clearly beats growth, it may not sound too impressive: it means that value stocks still underperformed 30% of the time. But here is where the slugging percentage comes in, because when value stocks won, they won by a lot — 17 percentage points over the market on average, versus eight for growth. And when they lost, it was by less. The combination of respectable batting and superior slugging has proved powerful for the value style in Japan. There's a Biblical precept that says, don't hide your candle under a bushel. That's what's happened with value in Japan. The "candle" of value tends to get lost under the bushel of P/Es of 180. As a result, many investors don't even look for it. Historically, it has been a sizable mistake.

Exhibit 21: Value Premium to Growth

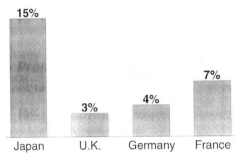

Source: MSCI and Bernstein estimates

Exhibit 22: Value versus Growth: Risk/Reward Profile
Annualized 1975-1995

	Return		Volatility	
	Value	Growth	Value	Growth
Japan	19%	4%	23%	24%
U.K.	25	22	21	23
Germany	15	11	19	21
France	21	14	26	22

Source: MSCI and Bernstein estimates

GLOBAL OUTPERFORMANCE — WITHOUT EXTRA RISK

Value also outperforms globally. The style has worked to varying degrees in the different countries, and it hasn't worked in every country every year. But, as shown in Exhibit 21 it has produced a meaningful long-term premium in key markets, with truly stand-out performance in Japan, where the style has extreme market characteristics in its favor. The absolute performance numbers behind these premiums are given in the left two columns of Exhibit 22. Risk, however, is just as important a consideration for plan sponsors, since excellent performance can mask unacceptable levels of volatility. It turns out that the risk of value investing is generally comparable to or lower than the risk of growth investing. Where value is modestly more risky, returns tend to be outsized. Look at France as an example.

An Additional Advantage

One reason the value style works so well is that at any time the efficacy of the approach tends to be different country to country. For example, when the value style is achieving sizable outperformance in the United Kingdom, it may be outperforming only modestly — or even underperforming — in Japan. So when you put value portfolios from the United Kingdom and Japan — or any other two countries — together, you get the benefit of an additional layer of risk reduction.

Exhibit 23: Value as a Diversifier

	Correlations of Value-Stock Relative Returns
U.K./Japan	0.14
Japan/Germany	0.05
U.K./France	0.36
France/Italy	0.11
U.K./Germany	0.22

Source: MSCI and Bernstein estimates

Exhibit 24: Value versus Market: Risk/Reward Profile
Annualized 1975-1995

	Return		Volatility	
	Value	Market	Value	Market
Japan	19%	10%	23%	24%
U.K.	25	23	21	22
Germany	15	11	19	19
France	21	16	26	24
Composite	17%	15%	18%	19%

Source: MSCI and Bernstein estimates

This can be quantified by showing the statistical correlation in relative performance between value stocks in several representative markets as shown in Exhibit 23. Performance hardly moves in lockstep. In fact, the correlation statistics have been extremely weak. The highest on the list, between the United Kingdom and France, is only 0.36 out of a possible 1.0, and in some pairings the relationship is essentially random (a zero correlation). In other words, how the value stocks of one country are doing relative to the market at any given time tells you very little about how the value stocks of another country are performing. The result is that the sharp ups and downs of short-term performance tend to be smoothed out when a systematic value approach is employed in each country. The investor achieves a more steady pattern of relative returns.

More Efficient Portfolios

To sum it up, Exhibit 24 compares returns and volatility for value stocks and the market benchmarks in the same four key countries since 1975. In Japan, value stocks have outperformed by nine percentage points a year on average, with an annualized volatility of 23% compared with a benchmark volatility of 24%. The pattern is similar for all the other countries: a meaningful performance premium with comparable — often modestly less — risk in most cases. It's a strong picture. The composite numbers are more provocative. Because the diversification effect smoothes the edges of country-by-country volatility, foreign value stocks in the aggregate compounded at two points higher than the composite benchmark without any incremental risk.[2] This is a classic case of finding a better risk and reward trade-off.

CONCLUSIONS

The conclusions are clear. First, despite the many differences between the U.S. and foreign markets, investment style is as key to performance abroad as it is in the United States. Second, value investing confers long-term benefits in all the major foreign markets. And third, when systematically employed on a global basis, value investing adds a further dimension of risk-reducing diversification. The need for style diversification is typically thought of as combining value and growth styles in a single geography to dampen the volatility of returns to active management. The data suggest that an equally efficacious, although not mutually exclusive, approach is to diversify the value style geographically.

As investors become more involved in the foreign markets, we believe they should pay careful attention to these concepts. The principal dynamics in the global capital markets revolve around a tug-of-war between feeling secure and making money. In the end, the feelings generally win out. A substantial amount of money can thus be made if an investor is willing to spend the bulk of his or her "investment" life feeling depressed, isolated, and afraid, waiting for the forces of mean reversion to relieve the stress. At which point the investor will sell those assets and use the proceeds to rebuild their anxiety level.

---

[2] Note that the composite return rounds down to 17% because of Germany, the six other countries in the analysis, and the fact that substantial transaction charges to rebalance across countries are assumed.

Chapter 10

Implementable Quantitative Research and Investment Strategies

Christopher K. Ma, Ph.D., CFA
KCM Asset Management Group, Inc.
and
Roland and Sarah George Chair of Applied Investments
Stetson University

James E. Mallett, Ph.D.
Director of George Investments Institute
Stetson University

INTRODUCTION

The easy accessibility of high-speed computing power and the dominant role of institutional trading in recent years result in the inevitable trend of implementing quantitative research and investment strategies. The gradual move of replacing traditional human judgments with machine calculations is based on the assumption that computers outperform most humans. Since a quantitative process is capabile of systematically handling a large amount of information quickly and consistently, ambiguity and unpredictability which are often associated with subjective choices during decision making can be kept to a minimum. David Leinweber provides an interesting comparison of this awesome implication — a high-speed workstation today exhibits a price/performance improvement factor of 400 million times that in 1960![1] For fact or fancy, most modern portfolio managers include some form of quantitative approach in their overall investment process.

However, the golden boy has not been born without growing pains. "Quants" are often too anxious and over zealous to prove their points. This attitude leads to several side effects which offset some of the advantages of quantitative analysis. First, cards can be unintentionally stacked toward locating some significant pattern which they are eager to show. Finding a way to do this is much easier

---

[1] David J. Leinweber, "Nerds on Wall Street," *Proceedings of Blending Quantitative and Traditional Equity Analysis* (Charlottesville, VA: Association for Investment Management and Research, 1994), pp. 17-24.

than conventional subjective reasoning, due to fast computing power which allows numerous trials and errors. Second, using the conventional criterion of significance at some statistical level, researchers who are superstitious of its power often quickly jump to the wrong conclusion. What they sometimes fail to realize is that statistical significance is neither a necessary nor sufficient condition for implementable economic profits. Third, humans have a tendency to only look at the unusual.[2] Do you notice an event because it is interesting or is it interesting because you notice it? The resulting bias is that theories are established or tests are performed more easily on extraordinary events, and seemingly correlations are easily mistaken for causalities. This bias is further reinforced by high-speed computing, since quantitative tools are very efficient in locating outliers and finding correlations.

A GENERAL FRAMEWORK

The common objective of a quantitative process is to identify any persistent pattern in the data and, in finance, convert it into implementable and profitable investment strategies. Given the relatively young life of its application to investment management, we find that there is a need to explore the general process of a quantitative procedure, and identify some of the commonly induced biases in this process. Specifically, in Exhibit 1 we outline the flowchart which demonstrates the process of how quantitative research is performed and converted into implementable trading strategies. Generally, it includes developing underlying economic theories, explaining actual returns, estimating expected returns, and formulating corresponding portfolios. We will discuss each step in the following sections.

Develop a Truly Ex Ante Economic Justification

Sound economic hypothesis is a necessary condition for the birth of an implementable and replicable investment strategy. True economics, however, can only be motivated with creative intuitions and scrutinized by strict logical reasoning, but it does not come from hindsight or prior experience. This requirement is critical since scientific conclusions can easily be contaminated by the process of data snooping, especially when a truly independent economic theory is not established first.

Data snooping (or data mining) is identifying seemingly significant but in fact spurious patterns in the data.[3] All empirical tests are at risk for this problem, especially if a large number of studies have been performed on the same data sets. Given enough time and trials, people who are convinced of the existence of a pattern will eventually manage to find that pattern, real or imagined. Furthermore, there is an identical life cycle of experience in data snooping. Researchers are

---

[2] See Stephen A. Ross, "Survivorship Bias in Performance Studies," and Andrew W. Lo, "Data-Snooping Biases in Financial Analysis," in *Proceedings of Blending Quantitative and Traditional Equity Analysis*, pp. 59-72.

[3] See Lo, "Data-Snooping Biases in Financial Analysis."

often confronted with the exact same issues and will have to make the same types of choices in the process.

The process of data snooping comes in several forms. At some basic but subtle level, an economic hypothesis is founded by the knowledge of past patterns in data. Researchers may establish their "prior" from their knowledge, learning, experience, or simply what others have said. A good example for a classic yet wrong way to model the excess return is "market capitalization should be included in the model because there is evidence of a size effect."

Exhibit 1: Process of Quantitative Research and Investment Strategy

Quantitative Research

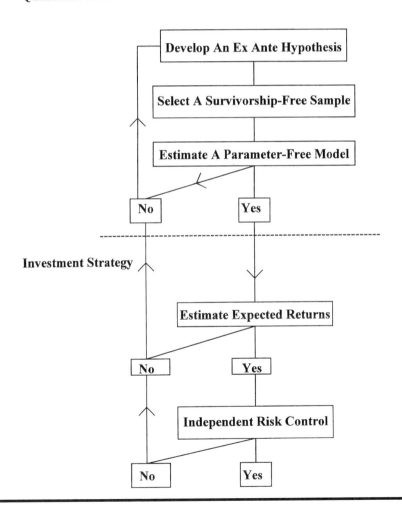

From then on, the problem can only get worse as long as there is more room for choices. A researcher may choose to design the same statistical tests because of what others have done using similar data.[4] The choices in these tests include the selection of explanatory variables, how to measure them, the functional form of the model, the length of the time period, the underlying probability distribution, and test statistics, etc. The difference in each of these artificial choices by itself may be small, but its resulting investment performance impact is often significant.

Ideally, there should be no need to make artificial selections since all of the tests should have been dictated by the underlying economic theories. However, even the best economic concept, being abstract and simplified, does not always fully specify its application in reality. There are ample opportunities that decision makers have to find proxies and instruments to complete the process.

If It Does Not Fit, You Must Acquit!

A common fallacy, however, is that researchers tend to go back to the most immediate prior step in searching for solutions when the result is not what they expect to see. Of course, this attitude reflects the general human tendency to overweigh the information in the most recent period in their decision making. This could easily lead to the mindless trial of numerous alternatives, which are most likely not justified.

Therefore, a direct way to control for data snooping at all levels is that the entire process will have to be reconstructed *right from the beginning* whenever the output at any step cannot pass the quality test. If the estimated model cannot explain the variation of excess returns to some satisfactory degree, the process needs to be stopped and abandoned. We need to go back to Step 1 and develop a new theory. If the predicted model does not produce acceptable excess returns, go back to Step 1. Finally, if the level of the actual risk-adjusted excess return found from following the strategy "does not cut the muster" — go back to Step 1. This "trial-and-error" process may correct for most, but not all, of the data snooping problem. As we throw away the obvious, "bad" models through testing, we learn from the experience of trial and error. This experience itself inevitably affects the seemingly "independent" creation of the economic intuition of next generation.

Of course, most of us would agree that there is almost no way to completely eliminate some form of data snooping since even the most rigorous scientific process is no more than a sequence of choices, subjective or not. As suggested by Lo, as in most forms of substance abuse, the first sign of recovery is the recognition of the problem.[5] The next step is to facilitate a research environment which avoids the temptations of making choices. (This reluctance is probably the single most important reason for the recently developed machine learning techniques.) What this conclusion also means is that researchers should be

---

[4] Fischer Black, "Estimating Expected Return," *Financial Analyst Journal* (September-October 1993), pp. 36-38.

[5] Lo, "Data-Snooping Biases in Financial Analysis."

extremely disciplined at every step of the process in making choices, with the explicit understanding of the problem and bias induced from data snooping.

SELECT A SAMPLE FREE FROM SURVIVORSHIP BIAS

Since all backtest research is performed on a data set which looks back in time, the entire history of an observation will not be available if it does not survive the present. The sample that researchers can work with is a set of observations which have been pre-selected through time by some common denominators. A sample of a sample should not pose a problem if the subset is selected randomly. But this is not the case for most samples which suffer from survivorship bias. The bias becomes relevant if the common bond to survive the observation is related to the pattern for which we are looking. A finding of a statistically significant pattern merely reflects the underlying common bond which was used to construct the testing sample.

One typical point of interest, which is severely affected by the survivorship bias, is performance comparison. By only looking at the portfolios currently outstanding, it is obvious that portfolios which did not survive through time due to poor performance are excluded from the sample. By design, the sample only contains good portfolios. How can the true factors which have caused the bad performance ever be identified?.

Commercial data vendors are not helping on this issue. Because of cost consideration, most data sets are only provided on a live basis. That is, for a currently non-existent sample observation, the common practice is to delete its entire history from the data set. To simulate the true historical situation, it is the researchers' responsibility to bring these observations back to the sample. The sample collection procedure should be reversed in time. Cases which existed at the beginning of the sample period should be included and tracked through time.

SELECT A METHODOLOGY TO ESTIMATE THE MODEL

The selection of a certain methodology should pass the same quality tests as developing economic theories and selecting samples. Without strong intuition, researchers should choose the methodology which needs the least amount of human inputs. A good example is the machine-learning method which uses computerized algorithms to discover the knowledge (pattern or rule) inherent in data.[6] Recent advances in modeling technology such as artificial intelligence, neural network, and genetic algorithms fit in this category. The beauty of this approach is its vast degree of freedom. There are none of the restrictions which are often explicitly specified in traditional, linear, stationary models.

---

[6] Gary Koehler, "Data Classification Algorithms," *Proceedings of Blending Quantitative and Traditional Equity Analysis*, pp. 51-58.

Of course, researchers should not rely excessively on the power of the method itself. Learning is impossible without knowledge. Even if you want to simply throw data into an algorithm and expect it to spit out the answer, you need to provide some background knowledge, such as the justification and types of input variables. There are still numerous occasions which require researchers to make justifiable decisions. For example, a typical way of modeling stock returns is using the following linear form,

$$ER_{it} = a + b_{1t}F1_{it-1} + b_{2t}F2_{it-1} + \ldots b_{nt}Fn_{it-1} \tag{1}$$

where

ER_{it} = excess return for the ith security in period t
Fj_{it-1} = jth factor value for the ith security at the beginning of period t
b_{kt} = the market-wide payoff for factor k in period t

Big Is Not Always Better!

Undoubtedly, in testing and estimating equation (1), the first task is to decide which and how many explanatory variables should be included. This decision should not be a question if the test is justified by a truly *ex ante* economic hypothesis. Economic theories, however, are often developed with abstract concepts which need to be measured by alternative proxies. The choice of proper proxies, while getting dangerously close to data snooping, makes the determination of both the type and the number of explanatory variables an art rather than a science. The choice of a particular proxy based on the rationale "because it works!" is not sufficient unless it is first backed up by the theory.

A Constant Tradeoff Between Better Estimations and Prediction Errors

One rule of thumb is to be parsimonious. A big model is not necessarily better, especially in the context of predictable risk-adjusted excess return. While the total power of explanation increases with the number of variables (size) in the model, the marginal increase of explanatory power drops quickly after some threshold. Whenever a new variable is introduced, what comes with the benefit of the additional description is the increase of estimation error of an additional parameter. In Exhibit 2, we demonstrate the explanatory power of a typical multi-factor model for stock returns by including one additional variable at a time. The second and the third columns clearly show that although by design the R-square increases with the number of the variables, the adjusted R-square, which also reflects the impact of the additional estimation error, levels off and starts decreasing after some point. This example suggests that in the process of estimation, there is an optimal number of explanatory variables in each model.

Exhibit 2: Marginal Contribution of
Additional Explanatory Variables

Additional Explanatory Variable	In-Sample		Out-of-Sample	
	Explanatory Power (R^2)	Explanatory Power (Adj. R^2)	Annualized Excess Return (%)	Annualized Standard Deviation (%)
1st	0.085	0.085	2.57	7.56
2nd	0.150	0.144	3.12	7.19
3rd	0.190	0.185	3.80	6.88
4th	0.220	0.210	4.04	6.45
5th	0.240	0.220	4.17	5.19
6th	0.275	0.243	4.11	5.21
7th	0.288	0.254	3.90	5.16
8th	0.310	0.239	3.88	5.71
9th	0.321	0.235	3.88	5.80
10th	0.323	0.221	3.67	6.31
11th	0.324	0.201	3.25	6.25
12th	0.330	0.188	3.01	7.01

Source: KCM Asset Management Group, Inc., 1996

The cost of estimation error is even compounded when new prediction is further extended into the forecast period. In Exhibit 2, we also perform out-of-sample prediction based on the estimated multi-factor model in each stage. Columns 4 and 5 show a more striking pattern that the risk-adjusted excess return, in the form of information ratio, deteriorates even more quickly when the model becomes large.

Animal Spirits

It is the exact same objectivity that quantitative analysts are proud of regarding their procedures that often leads to the question, "If everyone has the algorithms, will they not get the same answers?" The "over-mining" on the same data set using simple linear models almost eliminates the possibility of gaining economic profit.

Pessimism resulting from the competition of quantitative research also justifies the need to include some form of "animal spirit" in the decision process. Being able to do so is also probably the single most important advantage that traditional security analysis can claim over quantitative approach. Casual observations provide ample examples that investor behavior determining market pricing follows neither symmetric nor linear patterns: investors tend to react to bad news much differently than to good news;[7] information in more recent periods is over-

---

[7] K.C. Brown, W. V. Harlow, and S.M. Tinic., "Risk Aversion, Uncertain Information, and Market Efficiency," *Journal of Financial Economics* (1988), pp. 355-386.

weighed in the decision process;[8] investors ignore the probability of the event but emphasize the magnitude of the event;[9] stocks are purchased for their glamour but not for intrinsic value;[10] and, low PE stocks paying high returns do not imply that high PE stocks pay low returns.[11] We are not proposing that a quantitative model should include all these phenomenon, but the modeling methodology should be flexible enough to entertain such possibilities if they are warranted by the theory.

Statistical Significance Does Not Guarantee Economic Profits

As a result, staunch defenders of quantitative research argue that profitable strategies cannot be commercialized by quantitative analysis;[12] the production of excess returns will stay idiosyncratic and proprietary. Profits will originate in those proprietary algorithms that outperform commercially standardized packages for data analysis. In other words, researchers will have to learn to gain confidence even if there is no statistical significance, while statistical significance does not guarantee economic profit.

Since quantitative market strategists often start with the identification of a pattern which is defined by statistical standards, it is easy to assume economic profit from conventional statistical significance. To show that there is not necessarily a link, we perform a typical momentum trading strategy which is solely based on the predictability of future returns from past returns. A simplified version of the return-generating process under this framework follows:

$$E_{t-1}(R_t) = a + b_{t-1}R_{t-1}$$

where $E_{t-1}(R_t)$ is the expected return for the period t, estimated at point $t-1$, a is time-in variant return, and b_{t-1} is the momentum coefficient observed at time $t-1$. When b_{t-1} is (statistically) significantly positive, the time-series returns are said to exhibit persistence and positive momentum. To implement the trading strategy using the information in correlations, stocks with at least a certain level of correlation are included in portfolios at the beginning of each month, and their returns are tracked. The performance of these portfolios apparently reflects the statistical significance (or lack of) in correlation between successive returns. In Exhibit 3, we summarize the performance of some of the representative portfolios.

It is not surprising that higher excess returns are generally associated with higher correlation between successive returns. More importantly, higher risk seems to be related to lower statistical significance of the relationship (correla-

---

[8] W. F. DeBondt and Richard Thaler, "Does the Stock Market Overreact?" *Journal of Finance* (1985), pp. 793-805.

[9] K. C. Ma, "Preference Reversal in Futures Markets," Working paper, Texas Tech University, 1995.

[10] J. Lakonishok, A. Shleifer, and R. Vishny, "Contrarian Investment, Extrapolation, and Risk," *Journal of Finance* (1996), pp. 1541-1578.

[11] "How Many Factors Do You Need?" Research Paper # 96-4, KCM Asset Management Group, Inc., 1996.

[12] H. R Fogler, "Investment Analysis and New Quantitative Tools," *Journal of Portfolio Management* (Summer 1995), pp. 39-47.

tion). The bottom line is that an acceptable level of risk-adjusted excess return, in the form of information ratio (e.g., 1), cannot always be achieved by statistical significance alone. A more striking observation, however, is that, sometime without conventional statistical significance, the portfolio was able to deliver superior risk-adjusted economic profit. While the driving force may yet be known, evidence is provided for the disconnection between statistical significance and economic profit.

A Model to Estimate Expected Returns

The estimation for the model to explain past returns from Step 3, by itself, is not enough, since the objective of the process is to predict future returns. A good model for expected return is much harder to come by since we simply don't have enough data. As pointed out by Fischer Black, people are often confused between a model to explain average returns and a model to predict expected returns.[13] While the former can be tested on a large number of historical data points, the latter requires such a long time period (sometimes decades) to cover various conditions to predict the expected return. Since we do not have that time to wait, one common shortcut is to simply assume that the model to explain average returns will be the model to predict expected returns. Of course, such prediction is highly inaccurate, given the assumption of constant expected returns.

We can easily find evidence to show it is a bad assumption. For example, if one can look at the actual model which explains the cross-sections of short-term stock returns, even the most naive researcher can easily conclude that there is little resemblance between the models from one period to the next. This would in turn suggest, at least in the short term, the model to explain past returns cannot be used to predict expected returns.

Exhibit 3: Statistical Significance and Economic Profits

Correlation Coefficient*	T Value**	Annual Excess Return (%)	Annual Standard Deviation (%)
0.10	2.21*	0.48	4.07
0.25	4.22*	1.10	3.60
0.50	6.75*	3.27	2.15
0.15	1.34	0.61	4.10
0.35	2.86*	2.07	3.80
0.60	1.12	4.50	4.05

* Significant at the 1% level.
** T value is for the significance of correlation coefficient.

Source: KCM Asset Management Group, Inc., 1995

---

[13] Black, "Estimating Expected Return."

Exhibit 4: Potential Returns for Perfect Estimation and Prediction (The S&P 500 Stocks: 1975-1996)

	Annualized Excess Returns if Perfect Foresight for:			
	Best Model* for S&P 500		Actual** S&P 500 Quartiles	
	Top Quartile	Bottom Quartile	Top Quartile	Bottom Quartile
Monthly Period***	24.5%	−22.1%	144.5%	−85.5%
Quarterly Period	30.5	−28.7	106.2	−72.4
Annual Period	15.3	−12.3	54.6	−20.1

* The parameters of the actual model to explain S&P 500 performance is known beforehand.
** The performance of each stock, in terms of the actual quartile, is known beforehand.
*** The length of investment horizon for each portfolio is rebalanced based on the perfect information.
Source: KCM Asset Management Group, Inc., 1996

We are calling for brand new efforts to establish an *ex ante* expected return model. The process has to pass the same strict tests for quality which are required for any good modeling, as discussed earlier. These tests would include the independent formulation of the hypothesis for expected return and a methodology and sample period free from data snooping and survivorship bias. While they are not necessarily related, the process of developing hypotheses for conditional expected return models can greatly benefit from the insights from numerous models of past returns estimated over a long time period.

Largest Value Added

Apparently, the final risk-adjusted returns from a strategy can be attributed to the proper execution of each step described in Exhibit 1. The entire process can be generally described in a three-step procedure — economic hypothesis, model estimation, and prediction. It is only natural for researchers to ask how to allocate their efforts among the three steps to maximize the return contribution.

To answer this question, we examine the return contribution from model estimation and prediction. For this purpose, we use a typical multi-factor model to explain the return for all stocks in the Standard and Poor's 500 Index. Assume that at the beginning of each period, the best model actually describing the return in the period is known to the portfolio manager. Using this information, a portfolio consisting of the predicted top quartile is formed. The excess return from this portfolio generated with perfect information would suggest the extent of return contribution from model estimation. Accordingly, in Exhibit 4, the annual mean excess return of the top predicted quartile is between 15% to 31%, depending on the length of the investment horizon.

In contrast, the annual mean excess return of the actual top quartile in the S&P 500 Index is between 54% to 145%. The difference in excess return between the actual top quartile portfolio and the predicted top quartile portfolio, between 30% to 120%, would suggest the extent of the return contribution from model prediction. It is clear then that for all investment horizons, the return contribution from model prediction is on average 2 to 5 times the excess returns from model estimation.

Exhibit 5: The Sample Period

Estimation Period I	Testing Period I	Forecast Period I	Estimation Period II	Testing Period II	Forecast Period II	..... Now

Therefore, for all practical purposes, the step of identifying a predictable model is responsible for the largest potential value added in generating predictable excess returns. The implication is that resources allocated to research should be placed disproportionally toward the effort of out-of-sample prediction.

Test the Prediction Again!

Another safeguard against data snooping is to scrutinize the model once more through time. That is, the conditional model to estimate expected return needs to be tested again in a "fresh" data period. As it requires multiple time periods to observe the conditional model for expected returns, the prediction model derived under a single condition has to be confirmed again. In Exhibit 5, we specify the relationship in time periods among estimation, testing, and confirmation.

The sequential testing of the prediction model in the forecast period would affirm the condition that converts the model of actual returns to the model of expected returns still produces an acceptable level of performance. As the conditioning factor varies from one period to anther, the consistent performance of the three-period process suggests that it is not driven by a constant set of artificial rules introduced by data snooping.

RISK CONTROL

Even if the expected return is modeled properly at the individual stock level, the bottom line of implementable investment strategies is evaluated by an acceptable level of risk-adjusted *portfolio* excess returns. As most institutional portfolios are benchmarked, the goal is to minimize tracking error (standard deviation of excess returns), given some level of portfolio excess return. Consequently, risk control becomes technically much more complex than the conventional efficient portfolio concept. As shown by Richard Roll, an optimal portfolio which minimizes tracking error subject to a level of excess return is not a mean-variance efficient portfolio.[14] It should be noted that, due to the objective and competitive nature of the quantitative approach in its strong form, most models produce similar rankings in expected returns. The variation in performance among quantitative portfolios is mainly attributed to a superior risk control technology.

One commonly used, but less preferred, practice in risk management is often performed right at the stage of identifying the model for expected returns. It

---

[14] R. Roll, "A Mean/Variance Analysis of Tracking Error," *Journal of Portfolio Management*, (Summer 1992), pp. 13-23.

involves revising the estimates from the model to explain the actual return. The purpose is to control the risk by attempting to reduce the estimation error for the model of expected returns. This approach has several flaws. First, in most cases, the procedure of revising the parameter estimates (from the model of actual returns) so they can be used in the model of expected returns is often performed on an ad hoc basis, and vulnerable to data snooping. Second, in revising the parameter estimates, the task of building a relevant expected model with low prediction errors is mistaken for risk control on portfolio returns. Finally, there is a lesser degree of freedom in that estimates are made based on the estimates of previous steps. The "risk control" procedure becomes dependent to the process of estimating expected returns. Consequently, an independent risk control procedure, usually through an optimization process, should be performed as an overlay on the stock selections which are determined initially by the predicted expected returns.

For computing efficiency, the iterations can be significantly reduced if several other conditions are simultaneously imposed. For example, it has been shown that the largest source of tracking error is the deviation of portfolio sector weights from its benchmark sector weights.[15] Consequently, most optimal benchmarked portfolios are "sector neutral," i.e., portfolios do not make sector bets against the benchmark. This consideration would indicate the need to include a constraint which sets maximum acceptable deviations of portfolio sector weights from benchmark sector weights.

Along the same line, tracking error can be further controlled when the individual stock weight is constrained to conform to its corresponding weight in the benchmark. It is also accomplished by setting a maximum allowed deviation of stock weight in the portfolio from the weight in the benchmark.

Additional realistic portfolio constraints may be considered. Examples would include to specify (1) a minimum level of market liquidity for individual stocks, (2) a maximum absolute weight in which any stock is allowed to invest, (3) a minimum total number of stocks held, (4) a minimum number of stocks held in each sector, and (5) a maximum level of portfolio turnover allowed.

CONCLUSION

The technological advances in computing power have tempted investors to use machines to make investment decisions. In the process of doing so, it is easy to lose sight of the essence of human knowledge required in any good decision making process. We do not see that the development of quantitative process necessarily contradicts traditional analysis. The advantage of quantitative approach is in its objectivity, speed, and dependability, while subjective analysis provides great underlying intuitions, innovations, and, at times, imagination. In this chapter, we seek to reconcile the best of the two worlds and identify the concerns in the process of investment research and management.

---

[15] "Nonlinear Factor Payoffs?" Research Paper # 97-5, KCM Asset Management Group, Inc., 1995.

Chapter 11

Implementing Investment Strategies: The Art and Science of Investing

Wayne H. Wagner
President
Plexus Group

Mark Edwards
Director
Plexus Group

INTRODUCTION: THE IMPORTANCE OF THE IMPLEMENTATION PROCESS

"Success in investment management comes from picking good stocks. The rest is just plumbing." This quote from a well regarded money manager highlights one of the key reasons that active managers have failed to keep up with index funds over the past 10 years. Picking stocks is the Holy Grail, and the bulk of a manager's efforts and expenses goes to enhance their forecasting ability. To their credit, Plexus research suggests that active managers do pick stocks that outperform their respective market benchmarks over both a 6 week and a 52 week basis.[1] But, as the quote suggests, managers can become so attached to seeking winners that they become desensitized to the overall goal of maximizing returns.

Investment management can be viewed as a two part process: the information process and the implementation process. The *information process* is the core of stock selection, and is discussed at length throughout this book. The focus in this chapter is the implementation process, or executing investment ideas while preserving the underlying value. The combination of these actions — seeking valuable ideas and implementing them — is what we call the *investing* process. (See Exhibit 1.)

---

[1] W. Wagner, "Picking Good Stocks: Necessary, But Sufficient?" *Plexus Group Commentary #43* (January 1995) and "Decision Timeliness & Duration," *Plexus Group Commentary #46* (November 1995).

Exhibit 1: The Investing Process

Information Value	*less*	Implementation Cost	*equals*	Captured Value

The Vanguard S&P 500 fund has outperformed 80% of the active managers over the past decade.[2] But if managers are able to pick winning stocks, why are they losing? The bottom line is that there is more to the investing process than good stock selection. On average, the cost of getting ideas into portfolios exceeds the value of the research. Ironically, this does not have to be true. The problem is that implementation or trading costs have been understated and underestimated, leading to sub-par performance despite better than average ideas.

Industrial America has gone through a difficult process of self-examination that has led to dramatic improvements in productivity. The key to this process is TQM (Total Quality Management). The investment industry is now confronting the same issue. Managers need to look beyond the selection process to the implementation process — from invest*ment* to investi*ng*.

We will first discuss trading, the core of the implementation process. We will then look beyond trading to see how trading strategies fit within the manager's stock selection process.

WHY TRADING IS NOT LIKE PORTFOLIO MANAGEMENT

Equity trading is the action that results from portfolio management decisions. The portfolio manager's process is analytic and hypothetical; trading is in-the-trenches reality.

To the naive, trading can seem like a vending machine — an order to buy goes in, and a trade comes out. But vending machines purchases are expensive and inefficient compared to buying in bulk. To shift the analogy from the retail investor to the large institution, imagine trying to buy 10,000 cases of soda rather than one can. Even if the vending machine could supply that many sodas, the cost would be many times greater than buying wholesale. Similarly, trading strategies that work for the retail investor are inadequate to the task confronting institutional traders. Studies show that roughly two-thirds of institutional managers' orders are more than 50% of an average day's volume.[3] Executing these orders in a single trade can quickly overtax the market's liquidity. For these orders, a manufacturing process is a better analogy than a vending machine. Manufacturing liquidity means finding shares at a price that completes the trade at a price that preserves the value of the idea.

---

[2] Lipper Analytical Services. Ten-year comparison as of December 31, 1996. Comparisons include only managers with 10-year histories.

[3] M. Edwards and W. Wagner, "Best Execution," *Financial Analysts Journal* (January-February 1993).

Trading is fundamentally different from portfolio management in that selecting stocks does not require the cooperation of anyone else. The trader, however, needs somebody to trade with, and thus we move from a deductive exercise to a negotiation process. In a negotiation, one gives something in order to get something. In securities trading, one can trade for either liquidity or for information. Thus a trader is constantly concerned that value is received for value given. This is why large trades occur in successive pieces, each piece revealing only what is necessary to complete that step of the negotiation.

Trading can be thought of as the ongoing choice between trading now for a known price versus later for an unknown, and hopefully better, price. Effective trading requires a multi-step process:

1. Determine the motivation of the trade.
2. Assess market conditions and the liquidity of the stock.
3. Establish the initial trading strategy to assess supply and demand.
4. Probe for liquidity and information.
5. Adapt the strategy to changing market conditions.
6. Appraise the effectiveness when the trading is complete.

Trade Motivation

Jack Treynor[4] has identified three key trading motives: value, news/information, and cash flow. *Value* is represented by the familiar Graham and Dodd process, while information trading reflects the use of new information and changing expectations. *Cash flow* motivations arise from a desire to increase or decrease equity exposure, independent or even ignorant of the prospects for the stocks.

Information value is subject to rapid erosion, and information-based traders are always under pressure to complete trades before the information spreads across the market. This makes information traders time sensitive: their goal is to get the trades done quickly, even if this means paying up for liquidity.

In contrast, *value* trades are seldom timely. Value traders can use time to their advantage, stretching out the timeframe in an attempt to reduce the cost of trading. Value traders are more price sensitive than time sensitive.

Index traders and liquidity traders do not form opinions about the value of individual stocks. However, their buying and selling can exaggerate supply/demand imbalances.

Managers are quite consistent in their approach to investing. Their trade orders will reflect one of these styles for most — but not all — of their trading. The trader's job is to recognize which motivation applies to each trade, and to select a trading strategy that reflects the manager's here-and-now motivation.

---

[4] J. Treynor, "What Does it Take to Win the Trading Game?" *Financial Analysts Journal* (January-February 1981).

Assessing Market Conditions

The next step is to assess current market conditions to determine the expected cost of liquidity for the required size. An actively traded stock is like a supermarket with high turnover and low margins. But not all stocks trade in volume. The greater the desired percentage of the current trading volume, the greater the premium required to create liquidity. The liquidity cost must be added/subtracted from the decision price to determine the expected trading price.

In addition to how much stock typically trades, the trader also needs to consider how frequently the stock trades. Actively traded stocks require little broker intermediation, so there is little spread between the *bid* (the highest advertised buy price) and the *offer* (the lowest advertised selling price). As the frequency of trading drops, the broker is required to act as a middleman, carrying long and short inventories until buyers and sellers can be found. Holding stock creates a risk for the broker, resulting in higher spreads.

Diversity of opinion is another important characteristic of market condition. If everyone wants to sell and no one wants to buy, trading will be impossible. If buyers are now dominating the trading, buying will be difficult and costly, while selling will be easy and inexpensive. Trading tactics will be quite different depending on whether one is *supplying* or *demanding* liquidity.

The trader's first resource in assessing market conditions is the public information sources: ticker tape prints of recent trades and the display of bids and offers, either on the exchange or on the various proprietary trading and information networks.

This is not, however, the full story. All that can be seen here is that which someone else has chosen to reveal. Institutional traders frequently rely on block dealers to locate trading interest that has been quietly expressed but not publicly revealed.

Establish Initial Trading Strategy

At this point the buyside trader has two basic options: he can choose to buy stock directly from a broker (a principal trade), or slowly accumulate stock during the normal flow of the day (a working trade). Each approach carries some danger:

- The payment for immediate liquidity may exceed the value of the information motivating the trade.
- The patient trader risks share prices moving against him before the order is filled.

The art of trading is the balancing of these two risks, performed in the context of the manager's instructions and information.

Probing for Liquidity and Information

Trades occur only when a willing buyer meets a willing seller at a price acceptable to both. The seller may be a broker providing liquidity for a fee, or it may be a natural seller acting as though he believes the *opposite* of what the manager believes. Even though this negotiation may be conducted in private, the market is filled with prying eyes looking for a trading edge. Accumulating stock is a difficult activity to keep hidden in a closely watched market, and knowledge of unfilled trading interest is a most valuable commodity on Wall Street. Other traders try continuously to assess the potential size of the trade and the sagacity of the buyer, and will attempt to buy first and piggyback on likely future behavior. Seeking liquidity, therefore, creates additional risk — and potential cost.

Coaxing out a reluctant seller requires an elaborate give-and-take process to protect the value of the idea. Cagey traders will attempt to get as much information as possible while revealing as little as possible: What does she know that I don't? How big is her trading need? How much is she willing to pay? Everyone wants to be the last person to trade with a big contraparty — certainly not the first.

The buyer may start with *probing* trades to assess available liquidity and possible reactions. If liquidity is available, the buyer has time on his side. But probing may quickly give away the buyer's identity, so the buyer uses a broker to sniff out untapped sources of stock.

We learned in Economics 101 that price changes will attract more supply or demand. In the stock market, however, rising prices will not necessarily induce potential sellers to trade. Rather, rising prices may indicate previously unknown information that leads to a revised opinion, creating hoarding conditions that reduce the desire to sell.

Thus, while it may make sense to slowly trade a liquid stock motivated by a value decision, the same trade in an illiquid stock may trigger competition once other traders detect a short-term buying trend. In this case, the trader may be better served by using broker liquidity and letting the broker assume the time risk.

Adapting to Market Conditions

Every piece of information the trader receives has the potential to create a need for a mid-course correction in the trading strategy. When the assumptions underlying the initial strategy prove incorrect, the strategy must be changed — instantly. This implies that the trader needs a variety of skills to trade different stocks in different conditions — and the ability to switch quickly from one technique to another.

Assess Effectiveness

A critical component of TQM is an on-going process review. In the case of trading, what works when a firm is small may not work as the firm grows. Liquidity demands change, as does the tradable universe of stocks. In addition, the markets themselves are in constant state of change.

Every completed trade provides feedback to the trader, who in turn must constantly adapt to changing demands and changing market conditions. In a broader context, however, we can think of each trade as a manifestation of an ongoing process that involves the manager as well as the trader. The process itself is thus amenable to review and change in a wider context.

A FRAMEWORK FOR MEASURING IMPLEMENTATION

This section describes the process that Plexus clients use to assess the efficacy of their processes. By breaking down each step into definable and repeatable actions, the trader can see where actions add or lose value.

Trading costs are like an iceberg: the real danger comes from the portion that cannot be seen. Commissions are easily observed but represent only the tip of the iceberg. The remaining costs are far more significant, but because they cannot be easily observed, they have been too often ignored. Ignoring the real but hidden costs can compromise performance.

Andre Perold[5] developed a method to assess trading effectiveness in the context of the decisions being implemented. Simply stated, this *implementation short-fall*[6] approach compares the *information return* of the decision on a no-cost basis to the *realized return* on a fully-costed basis. For uncomplicated trades, this amounts to comparing the price at the time of the decision (strike price) with the average execution price. This puts the trading in context: what is the trader paying for liquidity, and does that payment square with the potential gain from executing the trade?

Further elaboration of the implementation shortfall approach allows a manager to disaggregate trading costs into components of commission, intraday impact, interday delay costs, and opportunity costs from abandoned trades. Furthermore, the computations can be made on subsets of the trading database to pinpoint whether problems are more prevalent in large trades, small cap trades, NASDAQ trades, etc.

Consider the following example:

What the ticker tape reveals:

• 30,000 NME bought @ $20.75.

What really happened:

• Manager wants to buy 50,000 shares of NME. The current price is $20.
• The trade desk parcels out an order to a broker to buy 40,000 NME. The price is $20.5.
• NME is bought at $20.75 plus a $.05 commission.
• Price jumps to $21.50, and the remainder of the order is canceled.
• 15 days later the price is $23.

---

[5] A. Perold, "The Implementation Shortfall: Paper versus Reality," *Journal of Portfolio Management* (Spring 1988).
[6] B. Collins and F. Fabozzi, "A Methodology for Measuring Transactions Costs," *Financial Analysts Journal* (March-April 1991).

An accurate assessment of the quality of trading requires knowledge of what really happened:

- What was the idea worth?
- How much did delay on the trade desk cost?
- What was the impact of the trade?
- How much was left on the table when the order was canceled?

Fortunately, modern paperless trading systems readily collect and organize data such as that above. The information provided shows (1) the portfolio manager's desires, (2) the strategies employed by the trade desk, and (3) the resulting executions. Thus we can observe the entire investing process and measure the parts.

THE COST COMPONENTS OF TRADING

Manager and trader actions can now be isolated and analyzed. We can define the actions and calculate the respective costs. When we observe a large number of trades, we can assess the costs within an organization. By gathering this data from many managers, we can assess the industry-wide components of the trading iceberg.

A *commission* is the explicit fee charged by the broker to handle and clear the trade. It is printed on the trade ticket, so it is readily available. In this example, the per share cost is $.05 — typical for an institutional trade.

Price impact is the price adjustment necessary to immediately purchase liquidity. We measure impact as the price difference between the time that the order is submitted to the broker and the actual trade. The broker received the order when the average price was $20.50, and the trade cost $20.75, resulting in a $0.25 per share impact.

Trader timing is the price move prior to contacting the broker. This can be thought of as the cost of seeking liquidity. We measure timing from the price when the order is submitted to the desk until it is released to the broker. The price was $20 when the order arrived on the desk, and the trader gave the order to the broker when the price was $20.50. Timing cost is $0.50 per share.

Opportunity cost is the cost of failing to complete the trade. What about the 20,000 shares that did not get traded? The idea generated a 15% return ($23/$20) over a 15-day period, but 40% of the order was never completed. On a dollar weighted basis, the manager "lost" 15% × 40%, or 6 percentage points of potential return. Good ideas are not always easy to come by, and it is as important to learn from what did not trade as it is to review what did trade.

THE ICEBERG OF TRADING COSTS

The example above simply illustrates what the costs are and how they are computed. Exhibit 2 represents nearly 700,000 trades by over 50 different management firms during the second half of 1996. This picture provides a realistic view of institutional trading costs.

Exhibit 2: The Iceberg of Trading Costs (in basis points)

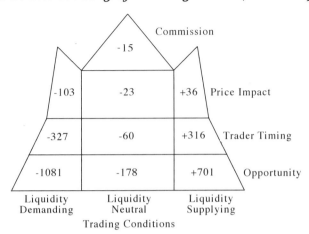

Commissions

Commissions have been under steady pressure since they were deregulated in May 1975. Despite this pressure, commissions have been relatively stable for the services rendered. Full service brokers charge an average of 6¢, while smaller brokers that provide exchange floor access will charge 3-5¢. Automated trades executed via DOT (Direct Order Transmission to the floor) or the Proprietary Trading Systems (Instinet, ITG, AZX, and the Crossing Network) charge 1-3¢. An increasing proportion of trading executed through these lower cost alternatives results in combined rates dropping to 4.5¢.

Price Impact

The next level of the iceberg is shrouded in fog, leaving the viewer aware of its presence but uncertain about its size. Like fog, these costs expand and contract, reflecting changes in available liquidity.

Impact reflects both the dealer spread plus any price movement required to attract additional liquidity to complete the trade. Actively traded stocks will typically be quoted in one eighth increments. As the frequency of trading activity drops, the dealer spread typically rises.

The average impact is 23 bp, or 9¢ per share. Exhibit 3 shows that the most important factor affecting impact is whether or not the trade *supplies* liquidity to the market, *demands* liquidity from the market, or is liquidity *neutral*. A buy order placed into a market where prices are falling will supply liquidity to the market, and should capture a concession. While Exhibit 3 shows the difference between liquidity-demanding and liquidity-supplying orders, it also shows an interesting skew that reflects a high cost when demanding liquidity versus a modest gain for supplying liquidity. This is a typical pattern: traders are willing to supply liquidity for much smaller concessions than they end up paying when put on the other side of the trade. The brokers capture the difference, often described as "vigorish."

Timing

The use of time as a trading tool for the buyside trader was previously discussed. By waiting for natural liquidity to appear at an acceptable price, the trader hopes to minimize direct price impact. This is why most large orders are broken up and worked in more easily digested pieces. Timing cost is the price change that occurs during this waiting period.

Timing is the counterpoint to impact. As time increases, impact should decrease. However, as time increases, so does the potential for adverse price moves. Because trading decisions usually reflect changes in publicly available information, short-term returns are likely to be positive. Consequently, delays to minimize impact leads to higher timing costs, as shown in Exhibit 4.

An information-sensitive trader who fails to find sufficient volume before prices move away will find the timing cost of delay to be very high. Conversely, a value-oriented trader providing liquidity may find that waiting leads to even greater gains than an immediate concession.

Opportunity

The final cost represents the base of the iceberg, never seen but possibly the most damaging to performance. This is the opportunity cost of uncompleted trades.

Money managers are like fishermen in their lament about the "one that got away." However, the manager's lament is legitimate: the most expensive trade is typically the one that never occurred. Exhibit 5 provides some insight into the average percentage of shares that are not completed by order type, as well as the 15-day opportunity effect.

Exhibit 3: Impact and Spread

Liquidity Demanding	Liquidity Neutral	Liquidity Supplying
−103 bp	−23 bp	+36 bp

Exhibit 4: Trader Timing

Liquidity Demanding	Liquidity Neutral	Liquidity Supplying
−327 bp	−60 bp	+316 bp

Exhibit 5: Opportunity Cost

	Foregone Return	% Not Completed
Liquidity Demanding	−1081 bp	13%
Liquidity Neutral	−71 bp	11%
Liquidity Supplying	+701 bp	10%

Exhibit 6: Definitions, Computations, and Experienced Cost

Cost	Definition	Measurement	Experienced Costs
Commission	Explicit fee charged by a broker for services.	Provided for listed trades.	−4.5¢
Impact	Cost of immediate execution.	The difference between the average execution price and the price at the time the order is revealed to the broker.	−8¢
Timing	Cost of seeking liquidity.	Price change between the time the order goes to the trade desk and when it is released to the broker.	−23¢
Opportunity	Cost of failing to find liquidity.	15 day return for unexecuted shares.	−71¢
Total	Difference between costless and fully costed returns	Weighted sum of the above	−38¢

There are two primary reasons for unexecuted orders. Either the trader cannot locate the shares to complete the trade, or the stock has moved out of the range that the manager is willing to pay. On a day to day basis, traders are quick to complete trades when the volume appears at an acceptable price — but as the timing costs show, they are not as willing to step up when a premium is required. Consequently, opportunity costs tend to be large. Exhibit 6 summarizes the definitions, computations, and cost experiences.

Conclusions about Trading Costs

Managing trading costs can be compared to squeezing a balloon: pushing in one side results in a distortion elsewhere. The commission, the most visible element of transactions costs, can be — and has been — driven down, but often at the cost of higher impact. Similarly, trade impact can be reduced by simply refusing to trade in high impact situations. In both cases, the trader diverts visible costs into less observable areas. This cannot be done without compromising investment performance. Thus the goal is to focus on total implementation costs, not simply trading costs.

This leads us to a functional definition of best execution: *best execution is that procedure most likely to capture the potential investment return.*

CASE STUDIES

In the remainder of this chapter we go beyond trading and explore the implications of different trading strategies within a manager's selection process. These are followed by some practical trading recommendations that we make to all desks.

Case Study #1: Momentum Manager Mismatched with Cautious Trader

Manager pattern: Manager reacts to news and price momentum to generate buying decisions. After the decision, the prices continue to appreciate.

Selectivity is excellent: decisions appreciate 6% over the six weeks after decision.

Trader pattern: Exhibit 7 shows the trader is sensitive to impact, and executes trades over several days. The table below reveals that although impact is low, timing costs run away as prices move while orders sit on the trade desk: when all costs are considered, the trader pays much more than other desks when faced with similar orders.

Recommendations: The trader's perspective focuses on creating zero impact with her trading. However, using a realistic cost benchmark of −115 bp rather than zero impact allows for more aggressive, and subsequently lower cost, trading.

Results: Within three quarters, timing costs had dropped to −65 bp while impact rose to −40 bp (Exhibit 8). Most importantly, total costs dropped from −190 bp to −117 bp. This case study perfectly illustrates the importance of controlling the total cost, instead of focusing on one component.

Case Study #2: Capturing an Insufficient Concession when Providing Liquidity

Manager pattern: Manager's buy decisions are deep value — almost contrarian. The more price drops relative to the fundamentals, the more likely this manager is to buy. Typical trade is very early, well in advance of the eventual price bottom.

Exhibit 7: Comparison of Cost Components — Minimizing Impact: Case Study #1

	Timing	Impact	Comm.	Total	Benchmark*
Trading G/L	−175 bp	−3 bp	−12 bp	−190 bp	−115 bp

* Benchmark costs are determined by averaging the costs for similar trades executed in the previous six months by all manager in the database. Over 700,000 trades are used to derive the benchmark equations.

Exhibit 8: Comparison of Cost Components — Minimizing Total Costs: Case Study #1

	Timing	Impact	Comm.	Total	Benchmark
Trading G/L	−65 bp	−40 bp	−12 bp	−117 bp	−115 bp
Change	+106 bp	−27 bp	—	−73 bp	—

Exhibit 9: Comparison of Cost Components — Capturing Available Opportunities: Case Study #2

	Timing	Impact	Comm.	Total	Benchmark
Trading G/L	+35 bp	+11 bp	-14 bp	+35 bp	+90 bp

Exhibit 10: Comparison of Cost Components — Taking More Time to Probe: Case Study #2

	Timing	Impact	Comm.	Total	Benchmark
Trading G/L	+112 bp	+11 bp	−11 bp	+115 bp	+90 bp
Change	+77 bp	—	+3 bp	+80 bp	—

Trader pattern: Exhibit 9 shows the trades are executed quickly, often at the best price of the day and at much better prices than the manager's decision price. However, there is no need to trade quickly given the repeating experience of subsequent weakness. Relative to other desks, this trader was providing a large concession to demanders of liquidity.

Recommendations: This case shows the opposite problem to the first case — fast trading in the face of weak returns. The trader should scale in gradually, letting the sellers come to him and making them pay for the privilege of liquidity. This is a case where probing trades to determine the level of buyer interest would be beneficial.

Results: Within three quarters, 95% completion was stretched out from 2 days to 5 days (see Exhibit 10). Timing gains rose to +112 bp while impact fell slightly. Total gains rose to +112 bp, slightly better than the benchmark.

Case Study #3: Over Reliance On Low Cost Brokers

Manager pattern: Manager used a quantitative model to generate lists of "alternate" trades. Model uses a timing overlay. Selectivity is good, with stocks rising 4% over six weeks.

Trader pattern: Trader believes strongly in using low cost proprietary trading systems to maintain anonymity and keep impact and commission costs to a minimum. (See Exhibit 11.) Trader takes pride in the low commission costs, avoiding the spread, and leaving no footprints in the market. Unfortunately, less than half the orders are completed, and there is evidence of strong adverse selection: stocks purchased appreciated 0.5%, while the untraded stocks went up 6.5%. The best model selections were left on the table. Performance suffers.

Exhibit 11: Comparison of Cost/Return Components — Low Cost, Low Return: Case Study #3

	Timing	Impact	Comm.	Total	Benchmark	Percent Traded	Net Returns Traded	Net Returns Unex.
Trading G/L	-91 bp	+27 bp	-4 bp	-68 bp	-62 bp	48%	55 bp	655 bp

Exhibit 12: Comparison of Cost/Return Components — Higher Costs, Higher Return: Case Study #3

	Timing	Impact	Comm.	Total	Benchmark	Percent Traded	Net Returns Traded	Net Returns Unex.
Trading G/L	−51 bp	−10 bp	−6 bp	−67 bp	−62 bp	76%	110 bp	73 bp
Change	+40 bp	−37 bp	−2 bp	−1 bp	—	+28%	+55 bp	+582bp

Recommendations: The problem with over-reliance on crossing networks is that there is no guarantee of finding the desired liquidity through these routes. As a result, trading stretches out over many days while prices moved upward. The manager's good selection and timing ability dissipates.

Results: This trader learned that passive trading is but an arrow in a quiver, and effective trading requires the use of all tools to find and capture liquidity at an acceptable price. (See Exhibit 12.) Expanding broker use and monitoring incompletes at the end of each day leads to better prioritizing of the next day's trading. Within three quarters, completion rates rise to 76%, trading costs are flat, and realized returns rise to +110 bp despite weaker underlying decisions. More costly trading leads to better capture of investment ideas.

FOUR PRACTICAL TRADING RECOMMENDATIONS

In each of the case studies, the trader and the manager firmly believed they were doing a good job. The truth is that they were! The problem is not how they did their job, but how they *defined* their job, and how they defined their objective. By focusing on a part of the process, they missed the big picture. Once they were able to see and accept the wider viewpoint, the solutions were straightforward and improvement was rapid.

In closing, we would like to present four general recommendations that come from the practical experience of working with institutional trade desks.

Recommendation #1 — One Trading Strategy does Not Fit All Situations

Case Study #3 shows the problem of over reliance on passive trading. No matter how consistent a manager is, occasional trades will not fit the normal pattern and require special treatment. Not all orders should be traded with the same sense of urgency. Many managers sell stocks to fund new purchases, and sell decisions often contain less short term value than do buy models. As a result, the sells will often move up with the buys. An effective desk needs to offset trading costs generated by liquidity demanding trades with trading gains when providing liquidity. *Know why the manager wants to trade, and plan accordingly.*

Recommendation #2 — Prioritize and Make Contingency Plans

The worst tactic is to trade the minimal costs trades first, and wait to work orders with little available liquidity or with higher levels of competition. Instead, the desk needs to rank orders by urgency based on both motive (information-based trades are more urgent than value-based trades) and on current levels of supply and demand (an imbalance will often signal short-run information that may not be publicly available). *Do the hard trades first.* In addition, the desk needs to have a process alert when stocks move into higher urgency categories.

Recommendation #3 — Build Expected Costs into Portfolio Decision Making

Identifying potential buys and sells is a critical part of the money manager's job, and manager stock picks do add value. The problem is the number of decisions where costs exceed the return. As assets continue to grow, the problem is compounded. Knowing the expected exit cost of each holding can help the manager determine both the desired size and desirability of trading. Knowing the cost of acquiring new positions puts the value of the decision in proper context. *Strive to capture return, not minimize costs.*

Recommendation #4 — Rationalize Broker Use

One of the first lessons in business is to make vendors and customers dependent on you while not becoming dependent upon them. The same holds true for the trade desk. By concentrating business with a few brokers, the trader becomes important enough to the broker to make a difference. The trade desks with the best consistent results are those that concentrate brokerage, and make sure their brokers know what is expected of them. *Trust, but verify.*

Not all brokers are equal in skill. All brokers can take a simple trade to the floor of the exchange for simple market or limit order execution. Trades that require significant size relative to the trading volume require a broker who has the skill, inventory, and integrity to handle the order and protect the customer's interests. *Use the commission to buy the needed trading services.*

CONCLUSION

Remember the Dali painting "Lincoln in Dalivision?" At first glance your eye sees a seemingly random pattern of color. When you step back, you see the likeness that was there all along. To effectively evaluate an investing process, you need to look at each component in detail, then step back to understand how each piece fits together into the big picture.

Searching for alpha within the investment management shop may be the most overlooked obvious idea in investment management since risk measurement. When managers widen their horizons beyond stock picking and analyze how their decisions thread into portfolios, they can capture risk-free, recurring returns. The secret to improving invest*ing* is to watch the handoffs and trade-offs.

Small improvements accumulate to make big differences in total performance. Since managers' track records are tightly bunched near the average, these improvements can raise a manager's ranking half a quartile or more. A good invest*ing* process is a crucial part of, and natural complement to, a good invest*ment* process.

Chapter 12

A New Technique for Tactical Asset Allocation

Eric H. Sorensen, Ph.D.
Managing Director
Salomon Brothers Inc.

Joseph J. Mezrich, Ph.D.
Director
Salomon Brothers Inc.

Keith L. Miller
Director
Salomon Brothers Inc.

INTRODUCTION

Asset allocation, by definition, is the most significant investment decision for investors that hold diversified portfolios. In its process, asset allocation decision making brings considerable complexity. The investor must consider risk preferences, the presence of existing liability streams, the formation of return expectations, and the estimation of asset correlations. Moreover, once decided, the investor must implement these criteria simultaneously and (in theory) continuously — a tall order.

Among these daunting tasks, forecasting future prices presents the most perplexing challenges. How *good* can we expect to be in modeling future returns of risky asset classes such as the stock market? What approach should we use to assign odds to the crystal ball of future equity market direction? By definition, asset diversification obviates some of the risk of forecasting any individual asset. However, in down markets diversification may fail us — when we need it the most.[1]

In this chapter we introduce the results of a new approach to modeling the relative performance of the equity market with respect to cash. The work of the model is to assign probabilities to three market categories — "outperform," "underperform," or "neutral." Our approach incorporates a sophisticated tree-structured data analysis technique that utilizes a set of "if-then" decision rules.

---

[1] Our research overwhelmingly indicates that when volatility and correlation rise, prices fall.

The approach effectively allows us to determine the most significant influences on the behavior of the market. We might ask: what is more important, the economy or the valuation of equities? Our model suggests that the relevance of valuation is subordinate to the economy. If the economy is strong, investors care less about market multiples.

By estimating the appropriate hierarchy of factors, we can associate the potential for market outperformance and underperformance with formal probabilities that depend on known market conditions at the time. On an *ex-ante* basis, this approach correctly identifies periods of extended equity market out- and underperformance.

If-then rules are a natural way to analyze complex problems under conditions of uncertainty. For example, when a patient is admitted to an emergency room, the attending physician determines the course of treatment by going through a set of hierarchical decisions. Some things are more important than others, and they are considered first. Questions of decreasing significance come later. For example, the attending physician cares more about the patient's pulse than about height and weight. The decision model for the physician is a decision tree, with an appropriate set of if-then rules.

Stock market performance is traditionally modeled not by if-then rules, but by utilizing regression analysis. One of the drawbacks of the regression framework is that it views the world from the perspective of averages; linear combinations of explanatory variables and regression coefficients which by design pick up an average effect. Besides, only considering an average effect, linear frameworks make it difficult to incorporate interactions among variables or to examine relationships on a conditional basis. In response to these shortcomings of traditional analysis, we use a technique know as classification and regression trees or CART[2] to model the U.S. equity market. CART provides a framework which allows us to explore non-linear behavior, capture variable interactions, and examine stock market performance on a conditional basis. We have pioneered the use of this technique in financial applications and have used it successfully in prior research.[3]

THE POWER OF CONDITIONING

The primary advantage of CART is that it enables us to examine relationships on a conditional basis. In order to illustrate the power of conditioning, consider one of the most commonly used variables in traditional tactical asset allocation mod-

---

[2] This technique was first introduced as a computational-statistics approach to finding optimal decision trees. See, L. Brieman, J.H. Friedman, R. Olshen, and C. Stone, *Classification and Regression Trees* (Belmont, CA: Wadsworth International Group, 1984).

[3] See Joseph J. Mezrich, "When Is a Tree a Hedge," *Financial Analyst Journal* (December 1994), pp 75-81. Also see Eric H. Sorensen, et al., *Decoupling Strategies*, Salomon Brothers Inc. (May 1996) and Eric H. Sorensen, et al., *Decoupling of U.S. Stocks and Bonds — Modeling When it Happens*, Salomon Brothers Inc. (September 1994).

els — relative value. We define relative value as the earnings yield on the S&P 500 minus the long bond yield. High relative value is indicative of higher future equity market performance. This variable is generally considered to be mean-reverting and consequently, often looked upon as a market performance predictor. On a monthly basis, since the early 1950s, last month's relative value exhibits a weak statistical relationship with next month's S&P 500 excess returns; the monthly correlation between these two variables is only 0.08.

Suppose, however, we hypothesize that investors only care about relative value in low growth, as opposed to high growth, economic environments. The relative performance of small stocks is a good indicator of the strength of the economy.[4] We might therefore condition our use of the relative value measure on the small stock premium. When the small stock premium is in its lowest decile, the correlation between relative value and subsequent excess market returns jumps to 0.26. This conditional relationship between relative value and S&P 500 excess returns would not have been fully captured by traditional models. The ability to uncover this type of conditional relationship over multiple variables simultaneously is what makes CART such a powerful tool.

PLANTING THE TREE

Since CART is extremely adept at identifying hidden relationships among data, it places a special burden on us to choose explanatory variables carefully. Our model only utilizes variables which possess theoretical underpinnings as determinants of equity returns (see Exhibit 1). Another key feature of our analysis is that we use only capital markets data, rather than government or private statistics. This enables us to generate a forecast on any given day without having to wait for periodically-released data.

In order to evaluate multiple business cycles, we use data starting in 1954. We divide the dependent variable, S&P 500 total returns minus T-bill total returns, into three discrete categories: "underperformance," "outperformance," or "neutral" (that is, too close to call). Given our set of explanatory variables, we attempt to classify the state of next month's return, that is, to predict the probability of the dependent variable falling into each of these three categories.

Exhibit 1: List of Explanatory Variables

Yield Curve	Long bond minus 3-month T-bill yield
Credit spread	Baa corporate yield over treasury bond yield
Equity risk premium	S&P 500 total return minus 3-month T-bill return
Relative value	S&P 500 earnings yield minus long bond yield

Source: Salomon Brothers Inc.

[4] See Eric H. Sorensen, et al., *Small-Cap Prospects*, Salomon Brothers Inc. (May 1996).

Exhibit 2: Classification Tree for June 1996

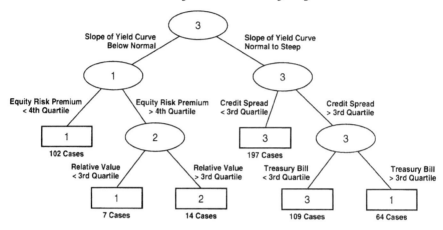

1 Underperformance (S&P 500 underperforming cash by 100 bps)
2 Neutral (S&P 500 performance is within 100 bps of cash)
3 Outperformance (S&P 500 outperforms cash by 100 bps)

Although the actual classification process is mathematically complex,[5] the basic idea behind it is simple. Initially, we attempt to divide the dependent variable into two separate groups, each of which is as homogeneous as possible. This division is accomplished by determining a critical level for an explanatory variable by which to divide the dependent variable. For example, consider our current classification tree as of June 1996, which we present in Exhibit 2. The initial division of the dependent variable takes place on the yield curve. If the slope of the yield curve is "steep to normal," most of the time the dependent variable falls into the "outperformance" category (right branch). If the slope of the yield curve is below normal (left branch), we have a subgroup of occurrences that places the dependent variable, by and large, in the "underperformance" category. However, the two initial subcategorizations are not entirely homogeneous, and they can be refined further.

The CART algorithm will continue splitting each of these two subgroups into finer statistically-distinguishable subgroups until it can no longer improve the statistical homogeneity of each subgroup by splitting on additional explanatory variables. The hierarchy of explanatory variables that results is the one that generates the minimum misclassification rate for the entire tree. The end result of this procedure is a tree-structured hierarchy of nonlinear if-then rules, where each rule is conditioning its behavior on the preceding rules. The final output from our tree is a set of probabilities for reaching each of the three states of the dependent variable.

---

[5] It is based on a recursive binary partitioning algorithm.

Exhibit 3: Success of Model Given Forecast Probability of "Outperformance"

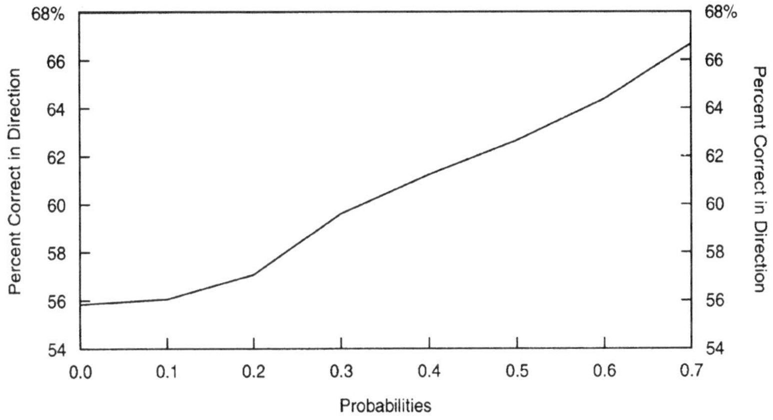

MODEL RESULTS

We reestimate our tree each month to derive the probabilities for each of the potential states of our dependent variable on an *ex-ante* basis. The actual shape of the tree and its decision rules tend to be relatively stable, but they do change slowly over time, with most of the changes occurring at the bottom of the tree structure. Next, we take these probabilities and test them to determine the success of our model.

In Exhibit 3, we plot the model's accuracy at forecasting up-moves. On the horizontal axis, we have the *ex-ante* forecast probability of being in the "out-performance" state. On the vertical axis we present the percentage of the time that next month's S&P 500 return outperforms cash. Observe how, as the probability of being in the "outperformance" state increases, the percentage of the time that we correctly forecast next month's S&P 500 excess return also increases.

Naively, since 1963, the S&P 500 has outperformed cash approximately 55% of the time. In order for any model to add value on the upside, therefore, it has to be correct more than 55% of the time. From Exhibit 3, we can see that if our model assigns a likelihood greater than 50% to the "outperformance" state, next month's S&P 500 excess return is positive approximately 62% of the time. When the forecast probability of "outperformance" exceeds 70%, our model is correct almost 70% of the time. In Exhibit 4, we display the accuracy of our model's forecast for down moves.

In Exhibit 5, we graph the *ex-ante* probability of being in the "outperformance" category over time. Over the past 30 years, the model has correctly assigned a high probability to S&P 500 outperformance during bull markets. These periods include the extended market rallies of the early and mid-1970s, the market run-up of the mid-1980s, and the current bull market. The signal from our model can be persistent and last several years at a time (as do the bull markets). Moreover, our model correctly captured the market crash of 1987 by assigning the highest probability to S&P 500 underperformance. More recently, our model has been correct in direction in 19 of the last 24 months.

In Exhibit 6, we graph the value of a dollar invested in a portfolio that utilizes our model to switch from a benchmark portfolio of 50% cash and 50% equity, into 100% cash or 100% equity. Since it is vital that any test be as unbiased as possible with respect both to the benchmark allocation and the size of permissible shifts, a 50/50 benchmark portfolio with 50% swings to either cash or equity is the best way to measure the value added by a two-asset allocation model.

Exhibit 4: Success of Model Given Forecast Probability of "Underperformance"

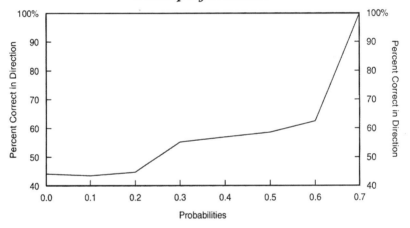

Exhibit 5: Probability of "Outperformance" Over Time

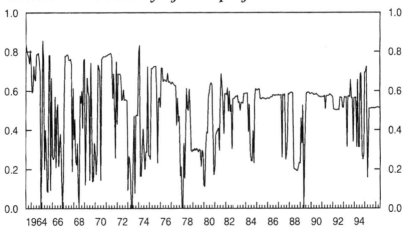

Exhibit 6: Wealth Curves

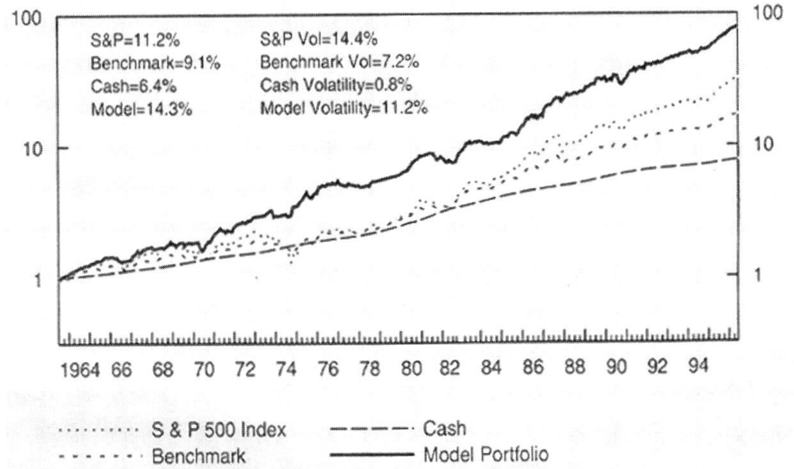

S&P=11.2%   S&P Vol=14.4%
Benchmark=9.1%   Benchmark Vol=7.2%
Cash=6.4%   Cash Volatility=0.8%
Model=14.3%   Model Volatility=11.2%

1964 66 68 70 72 74 76 78 80 82 84 86 88 90 92 94

· · · · · · · · · · S & P 500 Index   — — — —· Cash
· - · - · - · - Benchmark   ———————— Model Portfolio

In Exhibit 6, each month we shift from our 50/50 benchmark to 100% equity if the *ex-ante* probability of the "outperformance" state is higher than the underperformance or neutral states. If the highest probability is assigned to the "underperformance" category, we shift into 100% cash. If the highest probability is assigned to the "neutral" state, we stay with our 50/50 benchmark. Observe from Exhibit 6 how our model returns are far superior to the 50/50 benchmark portfolio, or even to the S&P 500. Since June 1963, the 50/50 benchmark returned an average 9.0% a year and the S&P 500 11.1%. Utilizing our model, we would have received 14.3% a year on average. Moreover, the volatility of our model returns (annualized standard deviation) is lower than that of the S&P 500 (11.2% versus 14.4%); the value added in risk-return space is significant.

A SPECIFIC FORECAST

In order to find the expected state for the dependent variable, such as, our example forecast, we simply follow each decision rule down the tree for June 1996 in Exhibit 2 until we reach a terminal node. Notice how the initial node (topmost node) on the tree is classified as "outperformance." This indicates that with no information (that is, prior to the classification process), our tree would categorize next month's S&P 500 excess returns as "outperformance." This is because out of the three possible states for the dependent variable, most fall into this category. Since the slope of yield curve is within its "normal state," we would initially branch to the right where the second split is based on credit spreads. Given that credit spreads are below the third quartile, we would branch to the left and reach a terminal node which is classified as "outperformance."

Our model assigns a probability of 52% for this "outperformance" state to occur next month, 28% for an "underperformance" and 20% for the "neutral" state. Post-1989, a 52% probability for the "outperformance" state has not been uncommon and would have led to being fully invested in equities. Observe that if credit spreads had been wide (above the third quartile), the final determination of out- versus underperformance would have been made by 6-month changes in T-bill yields.

In order to reach the final terminal node on the tree depicted by Exhibit 2, we conditioned over only two variables: the shape of the yield curve and credit spreads. This resulted in two very basic decision rules. Using such basic rules of thumb from our model can lead to significant equity market outperformance over time.

Chapter 13

The Use of Derivatives in Managing Equity Portfolios

Roger G. Clarke, Ph.D.
Chairman
Analytic/TSA Global Asset Management

Harindra de Silva, Ph.D., CFA
Managing Director
Analytic/TSA Global Asset Management

Greg M. McMurran
Chief Investment Officer
Analytic/TSA Global Asset Management

INTRODUCTION

The growth of the derivatives markets in recent years has given the investment manager an important set of tools to use in managing the risk and return characteristics of equity portfolios. In this chapter we will discuss some of the common strategies available using three different derivatives contracts: index swaps, futures, and options. Each of these derivatives has their own special characteristics which make them useful for adjusting the payoff profile of the portfolio to reflect a manager's expectations or view of the market.

One of the main characteristics of derivatives contracts is that little, if any, up-front money is required to initiate the contract. This feature allows the manager to maintain the principal involved in the transaction in other securities while increasing or decreasing exposure to the market through the derivatives contract. This separation of market exposure from the need for immediate cash outlays is what makes hedging possible, for example. Market exposure generated by holding underlying securities can be hedged with a derivative without having to sell the underlying securities themselves.

A major difference between the types of derivative contracts is the shape of the payoff structure that results when the market moves. Both index swaps and futures contracts have linear payoff patterns. That is, the payoff is symmetric around current market levels. The payoff as the market goes up or down mirrors the movement of the market itself. As a result, swaps and futures are often referred to as *portfolio substitutes* since their effects can substitute for the market return on a well-diversified portfolio of stocks. However, options generate non-linear payoff patterns. Put options are more sensitive to down market moves while call options are more sensitive to up market moves. This asymmetry allows options to create special effects in managing the risk of a portfolio not available by using swaps or futures contracts. The choice of the optimal derivative strategy is naturally a function of the manager's objectives, risk preferences, and market view.

This chapter is organized as follows. We first outline the use of derivative strategies which have linear payoffs including swaps and futures. Call and put options, along with other combination strategies which have non-linear payoffs are reviewed in the next section. In the final section we discuss the typical framework used to price options and the limitations of using this approach to select an optimal derivative strategy. We illustrate a basic framework for selecting a particular strategy given a manager's risk and return expectations. Examples are provided for one of the more commonly used derivative strategies — the covered call strategy.

LINEAR PAYOFFS: SWAPS

The simplest index swap contract is structured between two parties where the counterparties agree to exchange the return between an equity index and a fixed interest rate (usually LIBOR) scaled by the principal or notional amount of the swap. We shall refer to the investor who pays the fixed rate and receives the market return as the swap buyer; the counterparty is the swap seller. The swap allows the investor buying the swap to gain exposure to the market without having to purchase the underlying equities themselves. The investor's funds can be left in cash reserves earning interest which is exchanged with the counter party who has agreed to pay the investor the return on the equity index.

This arrangement is illustrated in Exhibit 1. Investor A who has purchased the equity index swap receives the equity index return from Investor B while paying the agreed upon fixed rate. No principal is exchanged between the two parties, only the agreed upon return tied to the notional amount of the swap is exchanged. This allows the investors to achieve returns in one market without actually having to hold securities in that market. Swaps are usually negotiated, private-party transactions. Though the specific terms of a swap may vary, it is not unusual for the maturity or *tenor* of a swap to run for a year or more with returns being exchanged at quarterly intervals.

A simple way to look at the impact of using a swap to achieve equity market returns is illustrated in Exhibit 2. The purchaser of the swap holds the notional amount of the swap in cash which earns interest. When the return on the investor's cash reserve is combined with the return on the equity index less the payment of the promised fixed rate, the investor is left with the return on the equity index plus the difference in return earned on the underlying cash reserves less the fixed return paid to the counterparty. The purchaser of the swap has created a synthetic equity return on the investment without having to actually purchase equity securities.

The seller of the swap receives the fixed return and pays the return on the equity index. If the seller holds underlying stocks which mirror the return on the equity index, the net return to the seller will be the fixed rate received plus any difference in return between the actual return on the stocks and the return on the equity index. The seller of the swap has effectively created synthetic cash while the actual underlying portfolio is invested in equities as illustrated in Exhibit 3. This is part of the power of using derivatives to manage portfolios. Since derivative contracts do not require the exchange of principal, underlying assets may be held in one type of security but the net result may be the return on another type of security.

Exhibit 1: Equity Index Swap

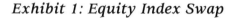

Exhibit 2: Return Equivalency from the Purchase of an Equity Index Swap

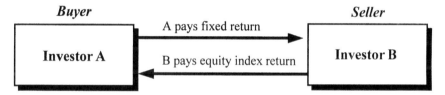

Exhibit 3: Return Equivalency from the Sale of an Equity Index Swap

Exhibit 4: Payoff of an Equity Index Swap as a Function of the Return on the Index

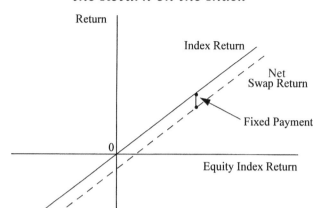

The return on the swap contract is referred to as being *linear* because it bears a straight line relationship to the return on the underlying equity index as shown in Exhibit 4. If the market goes up, the return on the swap contract will also go up. If the market goes down, the return on the swap contract also goes down. The difference between the index return and the swap return is the fixed rate the purchaser of the swap pays to the seller. When the swap return is added to the return the buyer earns on the underlying principal, the net result reflects the return on the equity index plus or minus the spread between what is earned on the cash reserve and what is paid to the seller.

Since swaps are usually entered into for an extended period of time, they are used primarily for either gaining or reducing market exposure. It may not be convenient or cost effective for the purchaser of a swap to buy actual equity securities. Entering into the swap agreement is an alternative for achieving equity exposure without the actual purchase of underlying equity securities. It has become popular in recent years to use swaps to create enhanced index funds. The investor may have a specific expertise in managing cash portfolios but no expertise in managing equity portfolios. If more can be earned on the cash portfolio than has to be paid to the seller of the swap, the investor ends up with an index-like return in the equity market but adds a spread generated by the difference in return between the actively managed cash portfolio and the fixed rate in the swap. This is sometimes referred to as *transporting alpha*. The alpha or differential return generated in one market can be converted to a differential return in another market.

Any type of equity index can be used in a swap as long as it is well defined and is agreed upon by both parties. It has become increasingly popular in recent years to use a swap on an international equity index. This saves the purchaser of the swap the difficulties of transacting in international markets and avoids directly paying for the accounting and custody fees. To the extent that the seller of the swap has potential economies of scale in assuming these costs and builds this reduced cost into the fixed return in the swap, the buyer of the swap may be able to generate international equity market returns at somewhat lower cost than purchasing the securities directly.

To illustrate an equity index swap transaction, suppose two investors agree to swap the return on the S&P 500 index in exchange for LIBOR plus 20 basis points on a $20 million notional value. The buyer of the swap pays the seller LIBOR plus 20 basis points in exchange for the total return on the S&P 500 index. If annualized LIBOR is 5.25% and the return on the S&P 500 index is 6.3% for the quarter, the buyer pays

$$\$20,000,000 \ (0.0545/4) = \$272,500$$

and the seller pays

$$\$20,000,000 \ (0.063) = \$1,260,000$$

In practice, the two amounts would usually be netted out against each other with the seller paying $987,500 to the buyer in this case.

Furthermore, suppose the buyer has invested $20 million in cash reserves earning an annualized rate of 5.85% for the quarter. The buyer of the swap has effectively earned a net return of

$$6.3\% + (5.85\% - 5.45\%)/4 = 6.40\%$$

or 10 basis points more than the index for the quarter. The extra 10 basis points comes from earning an annualized 40 basis points more per year than is required to be paid in the swap contract. If the seller of the swap has hedged the market obligation using a portfolio of stocks which has returned 6.5%, the seller's net return for the quarter will be

$$5.45\%/4 + (6.5\% - 6.3\%) = 1.56\%$$

or 6.25% at an annualized rate. The extra 100 basis points return over LIBOR with little market exposure is generated by receiving an extra 20 basis points from the fixed return in the swap plus an annualized differential return over the index of 80 basis points from the underlying equity portfolio.

LINEAR PAYOFFS: FUTURES

Futures contracts work much like swaps in their payoff pattern but there are some important institutional differences. One of the differences comes from the fact that futures contracts are traded on organized exchanges and are not negotiated directly between two counterparties. With a swap contract each counterparty is exposed to the credit risk of the other. With futures contracts the trading exchange and its members stand in the middle between two investors who have bought and sold futures contracts. The exchange plays the role of guarantor of the contract to ensure that all contract obligations are met. To help assure the financial integrity of the exchange and minimize the possibility that investors could build up losses beyond their ability to pay, investors initiating a position must deposit a performance bond with the exchange as *initial margin*. In addition, gains and losses are settled up on a daily basis between investors through the exchange (called *mark to market*) in contrast to swap contracts which are typically settled only quarterly. Finally, the interest rate which is fixed in the terms of a swap contract is embedded directly in the price of the futures contract so that it is not required to be independently specified up-front. The rate embedded in the futures contract is an implied market rate called the *implied repo rate* and matches the maturity of the contract in contrast to the fixed rate in the swap which usually resets each quarter when payments are exchanged

Exchange traded futures contracts typically carry a shorter term maturity than swap contracts. Maturities are usually staggered in three month segments with most of the liquidity found in the nearest maturity contract. There is often poor liquidity beyond the first two or three contracts. The shorter maturity of futures contracts allows them to be used with greater flexibility in managing equity portfolios, though like a swap, there are still only two things to do with a futures contract: buy it or sell it.

Applications of Buying Futures

The purchase of an equity index futures contract accomplishes the same thing as the purchase of an equity index swap. It adds equity exposure to the manager's portfolio. There are a variety of situations where a manager may want to add equity exposure. One of the most common is referred to as *cash equitization*. Equitizing cash through the purchase of futures contracts creates equity exposure synthetically without having to actually purchase underlying securities as illustrated in Exhibit 5. Many equity portfolios contain frictional amounts of cash that are difficult to keep fully invested. Dividends may be received from time to time or there may be new contributions that increase the cash in the portfolio. If the market moves up before these frictional amounts of cash can be invested in stocks, the portfolio performance will be exposed to *cash drag* and will not track the market as closely as it might. In a year when the market returns in excess of 25%, holding 5% cash would reduce portfolio performance by over 100 basis points. Since the market generally trends up over time, any frictional cash in the portfolio will tend to hurt performance.

Futures contracts might be purchased for more than just equitizing frictional amounts of cash. An entire portfolio could be left in cash reserves and futures contracts could be purchased to create a synthetic index fund. The combination of the cash reserve plus the futures contracts will behave as if a manager had purchased all of the stocks in the index. This creates tremendous liquidity in the portfolio. If funds are needed quickly, the futures contracts and the cash reserves are often easier to liquidate at lower cost than the underlying stocks. Furthermore, if the underlying cash reserve is actively managed to yield more than the implied repo rate in the futures contract, the index fund will have an enhanced return greater than the index itself. Futures contracts have been used to create enhanced index funds not only in the United States but in other countries that have actively traded equity index futures contracts. This achieves the same effect as purchasing a swap but with a shorter maturity.

Futures contracts are also useful in the trading process by helping manage the net market exposure of a portfolio as stocks are purchased or sold. It is not uncommon for slices of a portfolio to be traded involving multiple securities. These trades could be caused by the addition or withdrawal of funds in a portfolio or by a restructuring of positions internal to the portfolio. As long as the purchase or sale of securities leaves the portfolio temporarily overexposed or underexposed to the market while the trades are taking place, the portfolio manager can maintain market exposure until all of the security positions are in place by selling or buying the requisite number of futures contracts. The positions can then be closed out when they are no longer needed.

Applications of Selling Futures

The most common motivation for selling a futures contract in managing an equity portfolio is to temporarily hedge its market exposure. Like a swap, the sale of a futures contact against an underlying portfolio of stocks is equivalent to creating synthetic cash as illustrated in Exhibit 6. In essence, creating a hedged position is an attempt to counteract the market risk in the underlying securities and shift the risk to others willing to bear the risk. The risk can always be shifted by doing away with the underlying security position, but this may interfere with the nature of the investor's business or disrupt a continuing investment program. The futures market provides an alternative way to temporarily control or eliminate much of the risk in the underlying securities while continuing to hold the stocks.

Exhibit 5: Creating Synthetic Equity Exposure Using Index Futures Contracts

Exhibit 6: Creating Synthetic Cash Using Equity Index Futures Contracts: Hedging

| Underlying Stocks | - | Equity Index Futures Contracts | = | Synthetic Cash Reserve |

Exhibit 7: Return Profiles for Hedged Portfolios

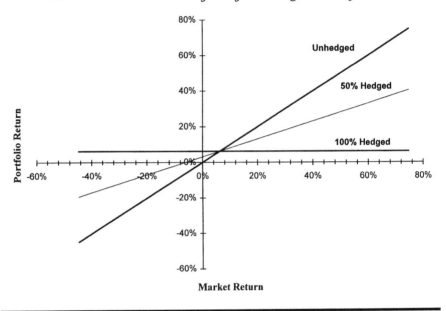

Market Return

The impact of hedging can be seen by examining the effect of hedging on a portfolio's return profile and probability distribution. Exhibit 7 illustrates the return on the hedged portfolio relative to the return on the underlying market index. A partially hedged position reduces the slope of the return line, so that the hedged portfolio does not perform as well as the market when returns are high, but it also does not perform as poorly when returns are low. The greater the portion of the portfolio that is hedged, the less slope the line will have. A full hedge produces a flat line, indicating that the hedged portfolio will generate a fixed return no matter what the underlying market does. This fixed return should be equal to the riskless rate if the futures contract is fairly priced. The slope of the return line for an equity portfolio is often referred to as the portfolio's market sensitivity or beta. Hedging effectively reduces the market beta of the portfolio as it amounts to selling the equity exposure of the portfolio.

Exhibit 8: Return Distributions for Hedged Portfolios

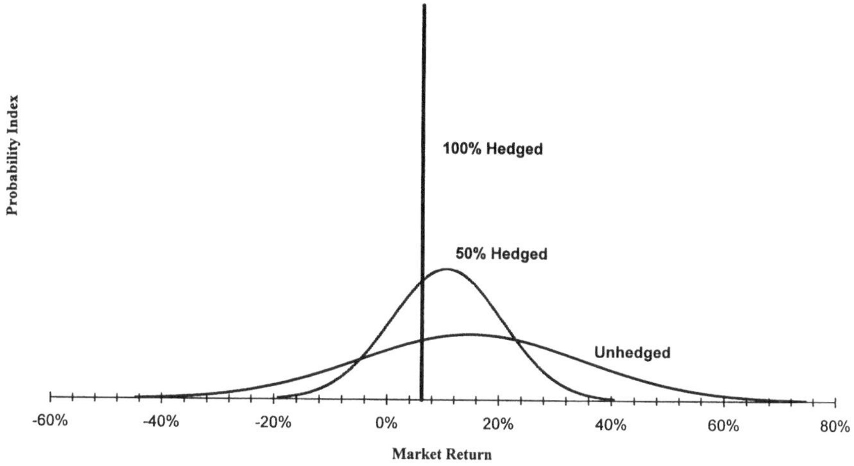

Exhibit 8 shows how the futures hedge changes the probability distribution of returns. If the return distribution for the market is symmetric with a wide dispersion, hedging the portfolio with futures gradually draws both tails of the distribution in toward the middle, and the mean return shrinks back toward the riskless rate. A full hedge draws both tails into one place and puts all of the probability mass at the riskless rate (the implied repo rate in the contract).

Hedging with futures will affect both tails equally. One of the main differences between options with their non-linear effects and futures is that options can affect one tail more dramatically than the other, so the distribution becomes quite skewed. Exhibit 9 illustrates the difference in the return distributions caused by a partial futures hedge versus a partial hedge created by using a put option. The put option hedge reduces the downside risk while leaving much of the upside potential. The use of options for hedging will be explained in more detail later.

Hedge Ratios Using Futures

A *hedge ratio* represents the amount of the futures used to construct a hedge relative to the amount of the underlying portfolio being hedged. In some cases there is a direct way to calculate the appropriate hedge ratio between futures and the portfolio. This technique can be used when the futures contract used for hedging is tied closely to the underlying portfolio being hedged as is the case when equity index futures are used to hedge a well diversified portfolio. Hedge ratios can be calculated easily because there is a direct link between the change in the value of the underlying portfolio and a change in the value of the associated futures contract.

To develop this idea, suppose an investor holds one unit of a portfolio containing securities S and wants to hedge it with a futures contract F. The change in the value of the combined position V as the portfolio value changes is

$$\Delta V = \Delta S + h\Delta F \tag{1}$$

where h (the hedge ratio) represents the number of units of futures F used to hedge portfolio S. Solving for the hedge ratio directly from equation (1) gives

$$h = \frac{\Delta V - \Delta S}{\Delta F} \tag{2}$$

For a complete hedge, or market neutral hedge ($\Delta V = 0$), the hedge ratio would be equal to the negative of the ratio of relative price changes between the portfolio being hedged and the futures contract. That is,

$$h = -\frac{\Delta S}{\Delta F} \tag{3}$$

To illustrate this concept suppose S is a diversified equity portfolio, F is a futures contract on the S&P 500 Index, and $\Delta S/\Delta F$ is assumed to equal 0.95. That is, when the S&P 500 futures contract moves by $1, the underlying equity portfolio moves by only $0.95, indicating that the portfolio is slightly less volatile than the broad market represented by the S&P 500 Index. For a market neutral hedge, the hedge ratio is

$$h = -\frac{0.95}{1.00} = -0.95$$

Exhibit 9: Return Distributions for Hedged Portfolios
Options versus Futures

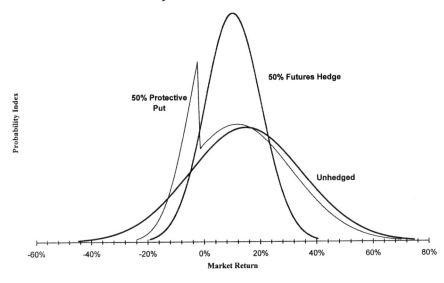

An investor would sell futures contracts worth 95% of the value of the equity portfolio to create the hedge. If the investor wanted only a partial hedge ($\Delta V = \frac{1}{3}\Delta S$, for example), the hedge ratio is

$$h = \frac{\frac{1}{3}\Delta S - \Delta S}{\Delta F} = \frac{-2}{3}\left(\frac{\Delta S}{\Delta F}\right) = -0.63$$

The investor would sell futures contracts worth only 63% of the value of the equity portfolio. With the hedge in place, the hedged portfolio would move only $\frac{1}{3}$ as much as the underlying portfolio.

Because the equity portfolio does not move one for one with the S&P 500 futures contract in the example, the investor does not want to use a hedge ratio of −1.0 to hedge the market risk in the underlying securities. A market-neutral hedge requires fewer futures contracts to be used because the underlying equity portfolio has only 95% of the movement of the futures contract.

The example above also shows what the hedge ratio must be if only a partial hedge is created to protect against the price movement in the underlying securities. If the combined hedged position is targeted to have $\frac{1}{3}$ of the movement of the underlying securities, a hedge ratio of −0.63 is needed. The investor would sell futures contracts worth only 63% of the value of the equity portfolio to create the partial hedge.

The arbitrage pricing relationship between the futures contract and the underlying market index links the two price changes together. This relationship can be used to calculate how the fair price of the futures contract will change as the price of the equity index changes. To see how this relationship can be used to estimate the hedge ratio directly, suppose that the price change of both the portfolio to be hedged and the futures contract are proportional to the change in the market index I in the following way:

$$\Delta S = \beta_S \Delta I, \text{ and } \Delta F = \beta_F \Delta I$$

where β_S and β_F represent the sensitivity to the index (market betas) of the portfolio being hedged and the futures contract, respectively.

Because portfolios and futures contracts are tied to the same underlying index, the hedge ratio is proportional to the ratio of their respective market betas. That is,

$$h = \frac{-\Delta S}{\Delta F} = -\frac{\beta_S}{\beta_F} \tag{4}$$

If the investor has an estimate of the market betas of the futures contract and the portfolio relative to the market index, the investor can calculate the appropriate hedge ratio directly.

For example, consider the calculation of the hedge ratio and the number of S&P 500 futures contracts required to hedge a $50 million equity portfolio with a beta of 1.05 relative to the S&P 500 Index. If the futures contract has a beta of 1.01 and the current level of the index is 900, the hedge ratio is

$$h = \frac{-1.05}{1.01} = -1.04$$

The contract size for the S&P 500 is 500 times the value of the S&P 500 Index, or \$450,000 (500 × 900), so the number of futures contracts required to be sold is

$$n = \frac{h(\text{Hedge value})}{\text{Contract size}} = \frac{-1.04(50,000,000)}{450,000} = -116 \text{ contracts}$$

Notice that the hedge ratio is slightly less than the beta of the portfolio. The short-term hedge ratio accounts for the slightly larger volatility in the index futures contract caused by its arbitrage pricing relationship. This additional volatility will shrink towards zero as the contract gets closer to maturity, reflecting a beta for the futures contract which converges to 1.0 at expiration. For longer term hedges with an investment horizon equal to the expiration date of the futures contract, a futures beta of 1.0 is typically used to calculate the hedge ratio.

NON-LINEAR PAYOFFS: OPTIONS

Simple options come in two forms: put options and call options. Unlike futures contracts and swaps, options require a small premium to be paid when purchased. Depending on the maturity of the option and the exercise price, the premium may range from less than 1% to more than 10% of the value of the underlying security or index. The payoff from an option at expiration depends on whether the security is above or below the level of the exercise or strike price. This lack of symmetry creates a non-linear payoff for the option at expiration. Put options have a non-zero payoff when the security price is less than the exercise price and call options pay off when the security price is greater than the exercise price. To see how options can be used in managing equity portfolios it is useful to review the payoff profile of put and call options.

Payoff Profiles for Options

Insight into the characteristics of options can be obtained by looking specifically at how options behave and what value they have at expiration. The matrix below is a simple technique for showing the value of option positions at expiration where S represents the value of the individual security or index and K represents the exercise price of the option:

	Payoff at Expiration	
	$S < K$	$S > K$
Call	0	$S - K$
Put	$K - S$	0
Security	S	S

At the expiration of the put or call option, its payoff depends on whether the security price is less than or more than the exercise price. The value of the underlying security is the same, S, whether it is below or above the option's exercise price. These payoffs form the basic building blocks for option strategy analysis.

Exhibit 10 illustrates the payoff pattern at expiration for a call option. On the horizontal axis is plotted the security price. The vertical axis measures the payoff at expiration. The trivial case representing the security's value is shown by the dashed line. For example, if the security ends with a value of K dollars, then the security will have a payoff of K dollars. The call option has a value of zero until the security price reaches the exercise price K, after which the call option increases one for one in price as the security price increases. The investor, however, must first purchase the option. So the net payoff from buying a call option is negative until the security price reaches the exercise price, and then it starts to rise (the dotted line). This line represents the payoff the investor receives net of the cost of the option. The investor breaks even with zero net profit at the point where the security price equals the exercise price plus the call option premium, C.

Note that the call option has a kinked or asymmetric payoff pattern. This feature distinguishes it from a futures contract. The future has a payoff pattern that is a straight line, as does the underlying security. This asymmetry in the option's payoff allows the option buyer to create specialized return patterns that are unavailable when using a futures contract.

Exhibit 11 illustrates the behavior of a put option. The put option has an intrinsic value of zero above the exercise price. Below there, it increases one for one as the security price declines. If an investor buys a put option, the net payoff of the option is the dotted line. The investor breaks even, with zero net profit, at the point where the security price equals the exercise price less the put option premium, P.

Exhibit 10: Payoff Profile of a Call Option

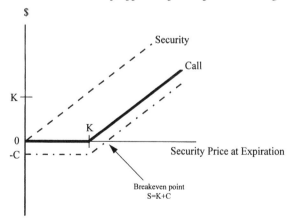

Exhibit 11: Payoff Profile of a Put Option

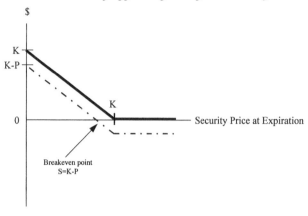

— · — · Net of option premiums

Selling Call Options: Exchanging Appreciation for Income

One of the most popular option strategies is known as a *covered call*. A covered call is constructed by holding the underlying security and selling a call option. The payoff matrix at expiration for this strategy is

	Covered Call Payoff at Expiration	
	$S < K$	$S > K$
Security	S	S
Short Call	0	$-(S - K)$
Total Payoff	S	K

The value of the security is S whether it finishes above or below the exercise price. The value of the call option is zero below the exercise price and $(S - K)$ above the exercise price. Since the call option has been sold by the investor, the payoff of the call option is owed and serves to reduce the total payoff below the value of the security itself. The total payoff of the covered call is found by adding up the value in each column. Below the exercise price, the portfolio is worth S dollars since the call has expired worthless. Above the exercise price, the portfolio is worth K dollars since the short call neutralizes the appreciation in the security above the exercise price.

The covered call strategy is shown graphically in Exhibit 12. The dashed line again represents the security value. The solid line represents the value of the security plus the payoff from the short call option. Below the exercise price the investor is left with the value of the security. Above the exercise price the security's appreciation is capped at the exercise price. In exchange for this limit on the security's appreciation, the investor receives the premium of the call option. The investor has traded the possibility of upside appreciation above the exercise price for income in the form of the option premium. The break-even point occurs when the security price is equal to the exercise price plus the call option premium. Below this point the covered call strategy gives a better payoff than holding the security by itself.

To demonstrate the result of a covered call strategy, consider an investor who holds a position in a stock worth $10 million. Assume that the current stock price is $100. The following example illustrates the effect of selling call options if the stock appreciates or depreciates 10% over the next six months.

	Stock Price	Underlying Portfolio Value	Portfolio Percentage Change
Current	$100	$10,000,000	
After six months	$110	$11,000,000	10.0
After six months	$90	$9,000,000	−10.0

Suppose the investor sells 100,000 6-month call options, each covering 100 shares with an exercise price of $105 to bring in premium income of $300,000. If the stock price declines by 10% to $90, the call options will expire worthless and the investor keeps the income from the sale of the call options giving a portfolio value of

$9,000,000 + $300,000 = $9,300,000

representing a decline of 7.0%. The value of the portfolio has declined by less than the 10% decline in the stock price because of the premium income received from the call options. If the stock price appreciates by 10%, the payoff of the call options owed by the investor will be

$100,000 (105 − 110) = −$500,000

Exhibit 12: Payoff Profile of a Covered Call

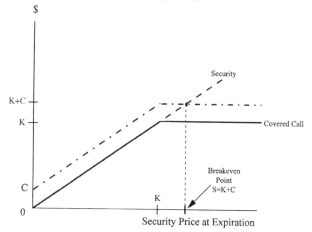

which when combined with the value of the stock and the premium income from the sale of the call options gives a portfolio value of

$$\$11,000,000 + \$300,000 - \$500,000 = \$10,800,000.$$

This represents a return of 8.0% on the value of the stocks in the portfolio compared to the stock price appreciation of 10.0%. The premium income from the call options has helped to offset the loss on the exercise of the options but the stock has appreciated beyond the break-even point so the net return on the portfolio is less than the appreciation in the stock itself.

Asymmetric Hedges: Protecting the Downside

The construction of an asymmetric hedge which responds to positive market returns differently than to negative market returns usually requires the use of an option. The most common strategies to hedge market exposure are (1) the protective put, (2) the protective put spread, and (3) the collar, range forward, or fence.

Protective Put

A *protective put* is constructed by holding the underlying security and buying a put option. The payoff matrix at expiration for this strategy is

	Protective Put Payoff at Expiration	
	$S < K$	$S > K$
Security	S	S
Put	$K - S$	0
Total payoff	K	S

The value of the security is S whether it finishes above or below the exercise price. The value of the put option is $(K - S)$ below the option's exercise price and zero above the exercise price. The total value of the protective put is found by adding up the value in each column. Below the exercise price, the portfolio is worth K dollars at expiration. Above the exercise price, it is worth S.

This strategy is depicted graphically in Exhibit 13. The dashed line again represents the security value. The solid line represents the value of the security plus the put option. Below the exercise price, the put option compensates for the decline in the security price. Once the original cost of the put option is accounted for, the net payoff is represented by the dotted line. The break-even point occurs when the security price is equal to the exercise price less the cost of the put option. Below this point, the protective-put strategy gives a better payoff than holding just the security by itself.

The benefit of this strategy occurs below the break-even point. If the security price falls below this level, the portfolio is always worth more than the security itself. This protection is of great benefit if the market is going down. The market does not give this protection for free, however. Above the break-even point, the protected portfolio is always worth a little bit less than the security. The price paid for the option results in a slightly lower return on the upside. This strategy has sometimes taken on another name, portfolio insurance, because the put option protects the value if the security price falls while maintaining some market exposure if the price rises.

To illustrate the impact of put options to hedge equity exposure, consider the same investor who holds a stock position worth $10,000,000. Assume that the current stock price is $100 and can appreciate or depreciate by 10% over the next six months. Suppose also that the investor hedges the market risk by purchasing 100,000 6-month put options, each covering 100 shares with an exercise price of $100 at a cost of $600,000. If the stock price declines to $90, the payoff of the put options at expiration will be

$$\$100,000 \, (100 - 90) = \$1,000,000$$

The net value of the portfolio will be

$$\$9,000,000 + (\$1,000,000 - \$600,000) = \$9,400,000$$

representing a decline of 6%. The value of the portfolio has declined by less than the 10% decline in the stock price because of the net payoff of the options. The options will finish in the money and contribute some value to the portfolio. Without the option position, the unhedged value of the portfolio would have declined by the full 10%.

Exhibit 13: Payoff Profile of a Protective Put

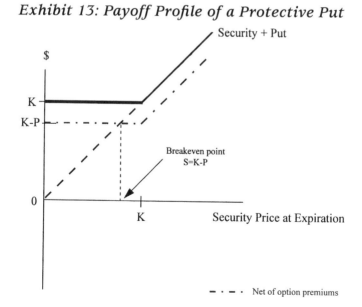

If the stock price increases to $110, the value of the put options at expiration will be zero giving a net value of the portfolio of

$11,000,000 − $600,000 = $10,400,000

representing an increase of 4%. Due to the cost of the options, the hedged portfolio will underperform the unhedged portfolio which returns a full 10.0%.

Protective Put Spread

The *protective put spread* is constructed by purchasing a put option and selling a put option farther out of the money. The payoff matrix at expiration for this strategy is

Protective Put Spread Payoff at Expiration			
	$S < K_l$	$K_l < S < K_u$	$S > K_u$
Security	S	S	S
Put Purchased	$K_u - S$	$K_u - S$	0
Put Sold	$-(K_l - S)$	0	0
Total Payoff	$S + (K_u - K_l)$	K_u	S

The total payoff of the protective put spread is split into three pieces corresponding to whether the security price is below the lower exercise price (K_l), in between the two exercise prices, or above the higher exercise price (K_u). Below the exercise price the hedged portfolio is worth the value of the stock plus the difference between the higher exercise price and the lower exercise price. If the stock price falls in between the two exercise prices, the payoff is just equal to the higher exercise price. Finally, if the stock price is above both exercise prices, the payoff is equal to the stock price since both put options expire worthless.

The strategy is shown graphically in Exhibit 14. The dashed line represents the security value. The solid line represents the value of the security plus the payoff from the two put options. In between the two exercise prices, the put spread protects the value of the portfolio as before. Below the lower exercise price the portfolio is again exposed to the decline in the market price of the stock. Once the net cost of the put option spread has been accounted for, the net payoff is represented by the dotted line. The break-even point occurs when the security price is equal to the exercise price of the protective put less the net cost of the put option spread. The cost of the protective put option spread is less than that of the protective put by itself because of the premium brought in from the put option which has been sold. As a result the break-even point is higher. The stock has to decline less in order for the protective put spread to be better than leaving the security unhedged.

The previous example can be expanded to incorporate the put spread. Suppose that 100,000 put options with an exercise price of $90 were sold to bring in premium of $100,000 to help pay for the cost of the protective puts. Now the net cost of the option positions would be $500,000. If the stock price rises 10% to $110, the payoff of the hedged portfolio will be

Exhibit 14: Payoff Profile of a Protective Put Spread

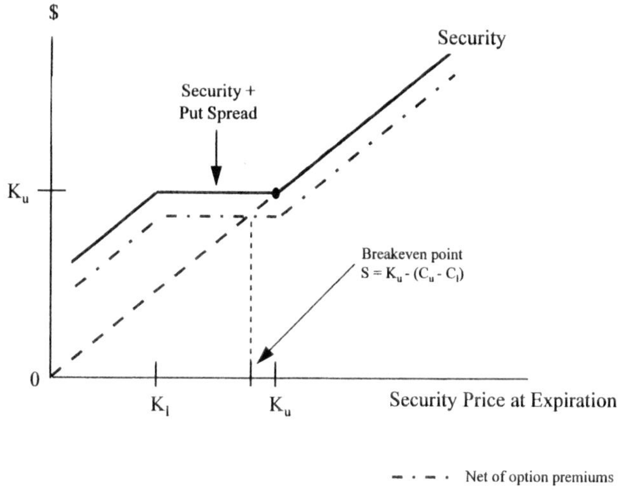

$$\$11,000,000 - (\$600,000 - \$100,000) = \$10,500,000$$

resulting in a portfolio return of 5%. If the price of the stock falls 10% to $90, the payoff of the hedged portfolio will be

$$\$9,000,000 + \$100,000\,(100 - 90) - (\$600,000 - \$100,000) = \$9,500,000$$

resulting in a portfolio return of −5% compared to the 10% decline in the stock and the 6% decline if only the protective put is used. The additional benefits resulting from the protective put spread come because the portfolio is not completely protected if the stock price falls below the lower exercise price. For example, a 20% decline in the stock price would result in a 15% decline using the protective put spread while resulting in only a 6% decline using the protective put by itself.

Collar (Range Forward or Fence)

The *collar, range forward, or fence* is constructed by selling a call option in addition to the purchase of a put option. The sale of the call again brings in cash which reduces the cost of purchasing the put option. The maturity of the call option is typically the same as that of the put, but has a higher exercise price. The sale of the call option eliminates the benefit of positive security returns above the level of the call's exercise price. If the exercise price of the call option is set close enough to that of the put, the cost of the put option can be offset entirely by the sale of the call option. This is typically referred to as a *zero cost collar*.

To accommodate the difference in exercise prices between the put and the call options, the payoff matrix must again be expanded. As a result, the payoff matrix for the collar is

Exhibit 15: Payoff Profile of a Collar

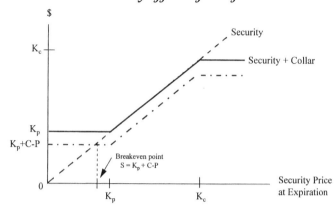

	Collar Payoff at Expiration		
	$S < K_p$	$K_p < S < K_c$	$S > K_c$
Security	S	S	S
Put	$K_p - S$	0	0
−Call	0	0	$-(S - K_c)$
Total payoff	K_p	S	K_c

K_p represents the put exercise price and K_c represents the exercise price of the call option. If the security is below the exercise price of the put at expiration, the payoff will be equal to the exercise price of the put. If the security is above the exercise price of the call option, the payoff will be equal to the exercise price of the call option. In between the two exercise prices the payoff will be equal to the underlying security price.

The payoff of the collar is shown graphically in Exhibit 15. The solid line represents the value of the security plus the payoff from the options. The dotted line represents the value of the strategy once the net cost of the options is considered. A zero cost collar would have no net option cost so the dotted line would converge to the solid line. The dashed line represents the value of holding the security unhedged. The benefit of this strategy occurs below the exercise price of the option similar to the protective put. The exact break-even point depends on the price of the call option sold to truncate some of the upside potential. This loss of upside potential beyond the break-even point of the short call position is the disadvantage of using the collar.

To continue the previous hedging example, suppose that call options are sold with an exercise price of $105 for $300,000 in addition to the purchase of put options with an exercise price of $100. If the stock price declines to $90, the put options will have value, but the call options will expire worthless. The net value of the portfolio will be

$$\$9,000,000 + \$100,000\,(100 - 90) - (\$600,000 - \$300,000) = \$9,700,000$$

representing a decline of 3% compared to the stock price decline of 10%. The sale of the call option has helped offset the cost of the put option hedge which previously showed a decline of 6%.

On the other hand, if the stock price increases to $110, the put options will expire worthless and the value of the call option at expiration will detract from performance giving a portfolio value of

$$\$11,000,000 - \$100,000\,(110 - 105) - (\$600,000 - \$300,000) = \$10,200,000$$

representing a net increase of only 2% compared to the 10% increase in the stock price.

Comparing the protective put strategy with the collar shows that the investor is better off using the collar if the stock price declines, but could be worse off if the stock price increases sufficiently beyond the exercise price of the call option. In the example here the loss on the value of the call option is more than the premium received when the option was sold so the investor has done slightly worse than the protective put strategy even though the stock price increased. In general, the collar or range forward works well as long as the market does not increase beyond the exercise price of the call option. If the market rallies much beyond that point, the investor will not participate in the upside market gains.

Buying Call Options: Creating Market Exposure

Two common option positions used to create market exposure are buying calls and buying call spreads. To add equity market exposure to a portfolio, the investor can buy call options on an equity index. If, for example, extra exposure to the U.S. equity market is desired, the investor can buy call options on the S&P 500. If the market appreciates, the option will increase in value. If the market declines, all the investor can lose is the cost of the option. The cost of the call option is the price the investor must pay to participate in the upside market potential while avoiding a loss in a declining market.

An alternative strategy would be to buy a call spread to create the market exposure. With a call spread, an investor buys calls with a lower exercise price than the call options sold. For example, if the market has only moderate upside potential, an investor might buy a call option with an exercise price at current market levels and sell a call option with a higher exercise price — at an exercise price above where the market is expected to be at expiration. Using a call spread, the investor participates in the market only up to a point, but at a reduced cost because the sale of the out-of-the-money call option offsets the cost of the long call option.

Exhibit 16: Payoff Profiles from Buying Calls and Call Spreads

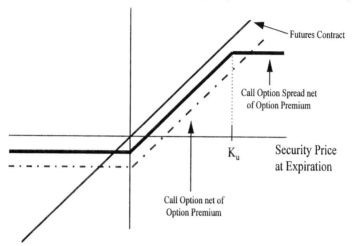

The payoff profiles at expiration for these two strategies, compared to buying a futures contract, are illustrated in Exhibit 16. If investors buy futures contracts, they will participate to the full extent of the market increase or decrease. If they buy a call option to create exposure, they participate if the market goes up, but if the market goes down, they will not suffer the full decline. The gap between the option and futures payoff on the upside represents the cost of the call option. If an investor's view about the market is positive, but not excessively bullish, the lower-cost call spread creates additional exposure but caps the market participation beyond a certain point.

Probability Distribution of Returns

In addition to using payoff diagrams to describe the effect of options, an investor can look at the probability distribution of returns for various strategies. Consider first the covered call strategy. Exhibit 17 shows the probability distribution of returns for an underlying security with and without the sale of call options. Note how the shape changes as an increasing proportion of call options are sold relative to the underlying security position. Selling call options draws the portfolio distribution back gradually on the right side and increases the chance that an investor will receive only moderate returns. Selling call options on 100% of the portfolio completely truncates the right-hand side of the probability distribution: the investor has a high probability of receiving moderate returns and no probability of receiving high returns. Most of the probability of receiving low returns is preserved, however.

Next consider the protective put strategy. Exhibit 18 shows the probability distribution of returns for an underlying security with and without the use of put options. Note how the shape changes as an increasing proportion of put options are purchased relative to the underlying security position. Purchasing put options draws the portfolio distribution back gradually on the left side and increases the chance that an investor will receive only moderate returns. Buying put options on 100% of the portfolio completely truncates the left-hand side of the probability distribution: The investor has a very high probability of receiving moderate returns and no probability of receiving low returns. Most of the probability of receiving high returns is preserved, however.

Exhibit 17: Return Distributions for Covered Calls

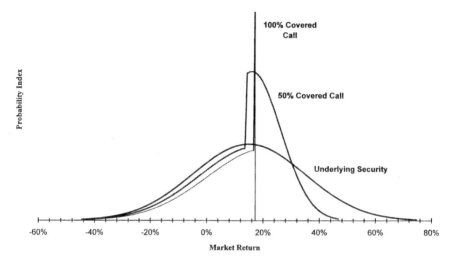

Exhibit 18: Return Distributions for Protective Puts

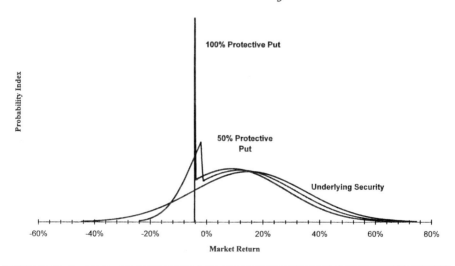

Exhibit 19: Return Distributions for Collars

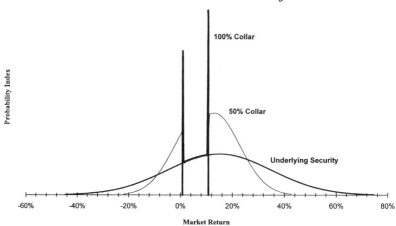

Exhibit 20: Creating a Synthetic Cash Reserve Using Options

| Underlying Security | + | Put Option | - | Call Option | = | Synthetic Cash Reserve |

Exhibit 19 illustrates the effect of selling call options and buying put options simultaneously (a fence or collar). The combination causes quite a severe misshaping of the probability distribution in both tails. The distribution is no longer smooth and symmetric. The asymmetry of options allows an investor to shape and mold the probability distribution by truncating some parts and adding to others. Call options affect the right-hand tail most dramatically, while put options affect the left-hand tail.

Notice that the collar provides similar downside protection but loses its upside participation if the security return is positive beyond the level of the call's exercise price. Selling the call option with the same exercise price as the put option would protect against downside losses but would also eliminate any upside participation. This would make the hedge symmetric similar to selling a futures contract or swap. Indeed, the short call and long put position with the same exercise price creates a synthetic futures contract which produces a symmetric hedge. This can be seen from the stylized put/call parity relationship in Exhibit 20 which indicates that a combination of the underlying security, the purchase of a put option, and the sale of a call option with the same exercise price and maturity will behave the same as a cash reserve. The short call option and the long put option work to create a synthetic futures contract which offsets the risk in the underlying security resulting in a cash equivalent position.

Exhibit 21: Creating Synthetic Equity Exposure Using Options: Put/Call Parity

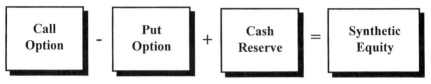

Exhibit 22: Creating a Synthetic Covered Call Strategy: The Collateralized Put

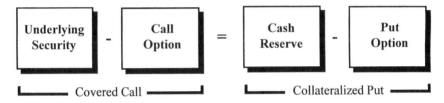

Exhibit 23: Creating a Synthetic Protective Put

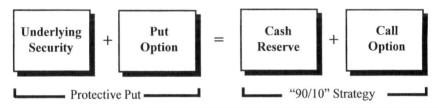

Rearranging the relationship to create a synthetic security instead of a synthetic cash reserve indicates that the combination of the cash reserve minus a put option plus a call option creates a market position as shown in Exhibit 21. In this case the long call option and the short put option work to create a synthetic futures position which adds market exposure to the cash reserve creating a synthetic security.

One last comment about the put/call parity relationship. Rearranging the components allows us to create the same payoff for the covered call and the protective put strategies in another way than previously described. The covered call strategy is normally constructed by purchasing the underlying security and selling a call option. An equivalent way to achieve the same payoff is to sell a put option and invest equivalent funds in an interest bearing cash reserve as shown in Exhibit 22. This alternative is sometimes referred to as a collateralized put and produces the same return profile as a covered call. In like manner, an equivalent way to create the same payoff as the protective put strategy is to purchase a call option and invest the remainder of the funds in an interest bearing cash reserve as illustrated in Exhibit 23.

This alternative is sometimes nicknamed the "90/10" strategy since roughly 90% of the investor's funds are held in a cash reserve with 10% used to purchase call options to give upside market participation. These configurations give equivalent payoffs because the arbitrage relationships between put and call options with the same maturities and exercise prices ensure that the payoff patterns will be preserved.

Automatic Changes in Market Exposure

Changes in market exposure can be triggered automatically as the market moves by selling options. The sale of a call option will truncate market participation above the option's exercise price. Selling some index call options against a long futures position or against exposure in the underlying stocks effectively pre-sells a portion of the exposure at the option's exercise price if the market reaches that level by the expiration date of the option. The receipt of the option premium effectively pays the investor for making the decision to sell in advance.

Conversely, the sale of a put option will allow the investor to prepurchase a position in the market at the put option's exercise price. The sale of options are frequently used in asset allocation and trading strategies to automatically reposition the portfolio if certain market levels are reached. Selling call options on 10% of the portfolio's exposure will automatically reduce the exposure by 10% if the market rallies up to the level of the call option's exercise price. Selling put options on 10% of the portfolio exposure will automatically increase the exposure by 10% if the market falls to the level of the put option's exercise price. At that point the investor can replace the option position by selling stocks for a gain and repurchasing the calls or by purchasing stocks at a discount and repurchasing the puts in order to make the shift permanent. The advantage is that the investor gets to keep the option premium for having made the decision in advance. The premium effectively increases the sale price of the appreciated stocks or reduces the purchase price of the depreciated stocks.

The purchase of additional market exposure by buying call options or the hedging of existing market exposure by buying put options can also be thought of as creating automatic changes in market exposure. The purchase of call options allows the investor to increase market exposure as the market rises while the purchase of put options allows the investor to decrease market exposure as the market falls. The options automatically adjust their levels of participation as the market reaches the options' exercise prices and go in the money. The non-linear payoff pattern of an option creates this automatic adjustment feature.

A VALUATION FRAMEWORK FOR SELECTING DERIVATIVE STRATEGIES

Since the advent of the listed equity option market in the United States in 1973, investors have used options both to reduce risk and enhance return. The majority of investors use options in combination with other securities — option covered-call writing strategies are an example of such a strategy, where options are sold on a portfolio of underlying stocks in order to generate incremental returns. In spite of the fact that options are used in such a fashion, there is no generally accepted framework to evaluate the impact the options have on the return of the overall portfolio. The most widely used option pricing models such as the model developed by Black and Scholes[1] or the model of Cox, Ross, and Rubinstein[2] are geared more to valuing options as opposed to computing the expected return from a combined stock and option position. These models do not help an investor in selecting an optimal choice of option or the optimal structure — i.e., how does an investor choose between the various covered call alternatives?

In this section we outline a framework which can be used to evaluate the combinations of stock and option positions. We do not cover the fundamentals of option pricing as there are a number of books that provide an introduction to this topic.[3] We do, however, briefly cover the assumptions underlying the Black-Scholes model in order to highlight the conditions under which actual option prices may significantly differ from their theoretical Black-Scholes prices. The primary focus of this section is to outline a valuation framework to be used in choosing the optimal trade-off between risk and return when deciding to invest in an option in combination with another security (such as a stock or bond). We focus on covered call or overwriting strategies in our examples, although the framework is applicable to any security and option combination.

The Problem with Black-Scholes

The typical investor has a specific view on the future outcome for an equity security in which he is considering making an investment. Option valuation models, however, take the current price of the stock as given and then price the security using the key assumption that it is possible to combine the option and the underlying security to form a risk-free security. This combination should in equilibrium earn the risk-free rate. These models, as we show using a simple example below, do not allow an investor to estimate the value or expected return from a particular option conditional on the investor's expected return distribution. In order to compute such an expected return it is necessary to compute the actuarial value of the option.

This actuarial value can then be used to compute the expected return from investing in a particular combination of stock and options. We illustrate this below using a simple example for a manager considering using a strategy of selling calls on stock he owns as a means of increasing the return on the portfolio.

---

[1] See F. Black and M. Scholes, "The Pricing of Options and Corporate Liabilities," *Journal of Political Economy* (May/June 1973), pp. 637-657 for the original derivation of this pricing model.
[2] This more general approach to option pricing was first presented in J. Cox, S. Ross, and M. Rubinstein, "Option Pricing: A Simplified Approach," *Journal of Financial Economics* (September 1979), pp. 279-263
[3] See for example R. Clarke, *Options and Futures: A Tutorial*, The Research Foundation of the Institute for Chartered Financial Analysts or J. Hull, *Options, Futures and Other Derivative Securities: 2nd ed.* (Englewood Cliffs, NJ: Prentice Hall, 1993).

Exhibit 24: Expected Stock Return

Current Value		Future Value	Probability	Future Price × Probability
$50		60	0.65	39
		40	0.35	14
Expected Value				$53
Return				6.00%

For example, consider a stock at $50 that can go up or down. This is shown graphically in Exhibit 24, where in a period of say one quarter the stock can move up to $60 or down to $40. Given this set of outcomes, how do we price a call option with an exercise price of $50. The Black-Scholes approach is to first create a riskless position — i.e., a position whose final value is independent of whether the stock price moves up or down. In this simple example, such a riskless position can be constructed by a buying one share of stock and selling two options. On expiration day, if the stock has appreciated to 60 the position will be worth the value of the stock less the value of the two call options (worth $20 at a price of $10 each) for a net position value of $40. Conversely, if the stock moves down, the two options expire worthless, so the net position is again worth $40. Given that this position is guaranteed to have a value of $40 at the end of the quarter, the current value of this position must be equal to $40 discounted at the risk-free rate. If we assume a risk-free rate of 5%, this amounts to $39.50. As the position is equivalent to buying the stock and selling two calls, both calls must be worth $10.50 — or $5.25 per option.

Notice that this does not require us to know the likelihood of outcomes to value options. The key observation in the Black-Scholes model and other risk neutral models is that information about the future outcomes is reflected in the price. From the perspective of a manager proposing to make an equity investment in a security about which he believes to have superior information, this valuation process is not very insightful.

One approach to overcoming this problem is to compute the actuarial return from investing in an option. Suppose in this case that the manager believes — based on his or her internal analysis — that the probability of the stock rising is 65% and the probability of the stock falling is 35% (the probabilities have to sum to one). Given the manager's analysis, the expected return from investing in the security as shown in Exhibit 24 is 6%. Using the Black-Scholes approach, if the manager observed the option selling at $6, he could sell the overpriced call option. However, selling the call would result in the expected return falling to 5.68%. (See Exhibit 25.)

Exhibit 25: Stock + Covered Call (at $6.00) Return

Current Value		Future Value	Probability	Future Price × Probability
$44		54	0.65	32.5
		40	0.35	14
Expected Value				$46.5
Return				5.68%

The expected return is reduced because given the manager's expectations, the expected value of the call is $6.50. This is because there is a 65% probability that the option will be worth $10 and a 35% probability that it is worth zero. Note that this is more than the Black-Scholes value. This actuarial value is the criterion the manager should use in evaluating whether the option should be sold. Indeed, selling the option at a price less than the actuarial value will consistently reduce the expected return from the combined stock and option position *vis-à-vis* the stock position.

This does not imply that the Black-Scholes value is incorrect. However, it does highlight the notion that the Black-Scholes model is not useful when evaluating alternative option strategies given a view (in terms of expected return and risk) on a security. It also highlights the fact that an option's price being above that of the Black-Scholes does not assure that the seller should expect to gain from selling the option. The difference between the Black-Scholes value and the actual market price can only be earned if the seller of the option implements the complete Black-Scholes trade and re-balances the trade to maintain its risk neutrality until the expiration of the option. Transactions costs may often prevent such a strategy from being workable in the presence of limited liquidity and non-continuous markets or some of the other key assumptions underlying the Black-Scholes and other risk neutral models of option pricing as discussed below.

Why Observed Prices May Differ from Black-Scholes

The Black-Scholes model is one of the most widely used models to price securities. However there are key assumptions underlying the model which often result in observed option prices being different from their theoretical values. The factors which affect this usually arise from the violation of one or more of the economic assumptions underlying Black-Scholes. We discuss each of these briefly below.

Perfectly Liquid Markets

In order to construct the riskless hedge which underlies the Black-Scholes pricing model, we have to be able to buy or sell shares of the underlying stock and sell or buy a zero-coupon bond in the proportions required by the hedge. We must be able to trade at precisely the same price as we assumed in estimating the hedge parameters. In reality, when we actually make the purchase or sale, there is no guarantee that we will achieve our target price.

In addition, if the underlying stock is thinly traded the purchase or sale of shares will have a significant effect on the price. In such a case the cash flow of the purchase would not equal the amount required by the Black-Scholes formula.

Constant Interest Rates

The risk-free rate of interest is not constant as assumed by the Black-Scholes formula. In other words, the costs built into the formula are not equal to the actual costs in carrying out the strategy. Whenever this happens it is no longer true that the total cost of constructing the hedge will be equal to the risk-free price.

Continuous Markets

The Black-Scholes hedging strategy works if the investor can continuously rebalance the hedge. This is seldom possible in the presence of transactions costs.

Geometric Brownian Motion

In computing the Black-Scholes hedge, it is necessary to assume that stock prices follow a geometric Brownian motion. In reality we observe serial correlation in stock prices and we also observe that the volatility of stock returns changes over time and often overreacts to new information. Stock returns also exhibit a tendency to "jump" — so Black-Scholes hedge positions will be susceptible to such jump risk.

Short Selling Assumption

The Black-Scholes hedge for an investor who is short call options consists of a bond sold short and a certain number of shares of the underlying security. The short position is used to finance the long position. If this money is not available, an opportunity cost (in terms of borrowing cost or foregone return) has to be incurred. In such a situation, the strategy will not be self financing.

Whenever one or more of these assumptions is violated, we would expect to see the implied volatility on an option being systematically greater than the expected actual volatility. Unless the assumptions are satisfied, however, it is not possible for an investor to attempt to capture the mispricing as he is unable to engage in the Black-Scholes riskless hedging strategy. The valuation approach identified here can then be used to identify the optimal option structure to exploit this mispricing without resorting to an active hedging strategy.

A Generalized Actuarial Model

In the example given above, we illustrated the concept of using an actuarial value approach. Here we outline a generalized approach under the usual assumption that stock returns follow a log normal distribution. We will use the following notation:

S_0 = initial stock price
C_0 = initial call price
W_0 = initial investment
D = dividends received over the time period of the option
S_f, C_f, W_f = values of the stock, call and investment on the expiry day of the option
$dS_f P_T(S_f/S_n)$ = probability density of stock price changing from S_0 to S_f in time T assuming log normal distribution

$$= \frac{dS_f}{S_f\sqrt{2\pi\sigma^2 T}}\exp\left(-\frac{\left(\ln\left(\frac{S_f}{S_0}\right)-\mu T\right)^2}{2\sigma^2 T}\right) \tag{5}$$

T = time to expiration (T_{yr} = 1 year in same units)
σ^2 = variance of log of stock price return (ln (S_f/S_0))
μ = mean per unit time of stock log price return

Given this distribution, the expected return from an investment in the combination of stock and option is given by:

$$\int dS_f P_T(S_f/S_0)\ln\left(\frac{W_f(S_f)}{W_0}\right) \tag{6}$$

For the covered call position:

$W_0 = S_0 - C_0$
$W_f = S_f - \max[0, S_f - E] + D$

The integral can be done numerically or approximated analytically. A similar approach handles any complex combination of stock, cash, and options, allowing an investor to identify the optimal security and option combinations. Note that using numerical techniques this same framework can be adapted to handle any arbitrary distribution. For example, the "fat tailed nature of stock price returns" can be taken into account. Transactions costs, including commissions and bid-ask spreads, are also easily incorporated into this valuation framework.

Examples of Actuarial Valuation
We illustrate the benefits of using the actuarial valuation approach to assess alternative covered call strategies — arguably one of the most popular option strategies. In this example, we assume that options on a $50 stock are priced at an implied volatility of 30% per annum. Given this assumption, call options with a maturity of one year on such a stock would take values similar to those shown in Exhibit 26. Our hypothetical investor forecasts the volatility on the stock to be 20% with an expected return of 12%. These forecasts can be derived using a variety of methods based on historical data, a factor model, or scenario forecasting.

Obviously, given this volatility forecast, every option on the stock is overvalued because the implied volatility at 30% is greater than the forecast volatility of 20%. If the investor could trade the stock under the assumptions implicit under Black-Scholes, he could essentially engage in a continuous trading strategy to try and exploit the difference. However, for most investors this is not a feasible alternative — especially if the stock is not actively traded.

The actuarial value approach described above, however, can be used to identify the preferred covered call position. Using equation (6), we compute in Exhibit 27 the expected return from the various covered call positions. Also computed is the standard deviation of the returns associated with each position, as well as the negative semi-deviation. Since selling the call "caps" the maximum return from the covered call position, this results in a non-symmetric distribution, and therefore standard deviation is not an appropriate measure of risk. To accurately capture the risk of loss, we compute the negative semi-deviation. This is a measure of downside risk. The data from Exhibit 27 demonstrate that the sale of an overpriced covered call should not necessarily be expected to generate incremental returns.

Selling of the calls with exercise prices of $52.5 or less actually decreases the expected return. However, it should be noted that the expected risk (assuming that negative semi-deviation is the appropriate risk measure for this investor) of each position is also lower. In contrast, the position with an exercise price of $60 has a higher expected return (15.3% versus 12%) and a lower downside risk (5.5% versus 8.5%) than simply investing in the stock.

Differing expectations for the volatility and return of the security will obviously generate differing expected returns from following this strategy. Using the same example as before, the expected return under the assumption that the investor forecasts volatility to be 25% per annum is recalculated — i.e., closer to the implied volatility of 30%. The resulting returns and risk measures are shown in Exhibit 28.

Exhibit 26: Call Option Prices

Strike Price	Call Price
40.00	13.19
42.50	11.42
45.00	9.80
47.50	8.35
50.00	7.06
52.50	5.93
55.00	4.95
57.50	4.11
60.00	3.40

Prices computed using Black Scholes model using a 30% annualized volatility, a risk-free rate of 5%, three months to maturity, and an underlying stock price of $50.

Exhibit 27: Gain from Alternative Stock Option Combinations
Expected Stock Return = 12% Standard Deviation = 20%

Strike Price	Stock + Covered Call Return (%)	Standard Deviation (%)	Negative Semi-Deviation (%)
40.00	7.8	3.6	2.4
42.50	9.3	4.6	2.9
45.00	10.3	6.3	3.8
47.50	11.4	7.2	3.8
50.00	12.6	8.8	4.3
52.50	13.8	10.2	4.4
55.00	14.6	12.4	5.4
57.50	15.0	13.7	5.5
60.00	15.3	14.8	5.5
Stock Only	12.0	20.0	7.5

Exhibit 28: Gain from Alternative Stock Option Combinations
Expected Stock Return = 12% Standard Deviation = 25%

Strike Price	Stock + Covered Call Return (%)	Standard Deviation (%)	Negative Semi-Deviation (%)
40.00	7.2	6.1	4.4
42.50	7.9	7.8	5.5
45.00	8.6	9.3	6.2
47.50	9.6	10.4	6.4
50.00	10.6	12.5	7.6
52.50	11.4	13.5	7.4
55.00	12.0	15.5	8.4
57.50	13.1	16.7	8.3
60.00	13.6	18.1	8.5
Stock Only	12.0	20.0	10.4

In this case it is only the sale of those call options with an exercise price greater than $55 that can be expected to generate incremental returns. Changes in the expected return for a stock can also have a dramatic impact on the expected return from entering into a covered call position. For example, suppose that the investor has an expected return forecast of 8% with a volatility forecast of 20%. The resulting expected returns from a covered call position are shown in Exhibit 29. With the exception of the option with the lowest exercise price, every covered call strategy has the potential to generate incremental returns and reduce risk. The magnitude of the value added is also substantially greater in this instance.

Exhibit 29: Gain from Alternative Stock Option Combinations
Expected Stock Return = 8% Standard Deviation = 20%

Strike Price	Stock + Covered Call Return (%)	Standard Deviation (%)	Negative Semi-Deviation (%)
40.00	7.6	4.8	3.3
42.50	8.6	5.4	3.3
45.00	9.5	7.2	4.3
47.50	10.4	8.7	4.9
50.00	10.9	10.6	5.6
52.50	11.5	12.2	6.1
55.00	12.1	13.7	6.6
57.50	12.1	15.2	6.8
60.00	12.4	16.6	7.3
Stock Only	8.0	20.0	10.4

In addition to highlighting the use of the actuarial valuation process, the examples in this section also illustrate the importance of forecasting both the mean and standard deviation when attempting to exploit option market mispricing though the use of covered call writing option strategies. In each example presented here, the options were overvalued; however, it was only in the case when the return on the underlying security was low (8% per annum) that the choice of any of the call options would have added value. Without such forecasts with some demonstrated predictive power, it is doubtful that value can be added though a traditional covered call writing strategy considered here.

The implication of the examples presented above is that managers considering the use of option strategies to enhance the performance of their equity portfolios cannot simply rely on using a simple Black-Scholes or risk neutral valuation approach to attempt to add incremental returns to a portfolio. As the analysis in this chapter demonstrates, the observation that the implied volatility on an option is greater than the actual volatility is not a necessary condition to ensure that the sale of the option will generate incremental returns to a portfolio.

More generally, the valuation framework presented here can be utilized as a tool to identify optimal derivative strategies and test the implications of alternative return and volatility outcomes on expected returns. As outlined in this chapter, the potential for modifying the risk and return profile of a portfolio using derivatives is vast. Only by using such a formal valuation framework can managers systematically identify those strategies that efficiently exploit their risk and return forecasts of asset classes or individual securities.

Chapter 14

New Applications of Exchange-Traded Equity Derivatives in Portfolio Management

Gary L. Gastineau
Senior Vice President
American Stock Exchange

INTRODUCTION

Much has been said and written about the growing use of derivative financial instruments in recent years. The most highly publicized growth has been in derivatives linked to fixed income and currency markets, but a number of changes in the regulatory environment and market structure and some important cost reductions have accelerated the development of equity derivatives applications.

This chapter is divided into three sections. We begin with an introductory discussion of derivatives applications for equity portfolio management, offering a few examples to illustrate some of the opportunities and obstacles. This introduction is followed by a brief discussion of the evaluation and pricing of equity derivatives. This section highlights what an equity manager needs to think about in terms of market efficiency and inefficiency and price/value discrepancies. Arbitrageurs exploit temporary or permanent market inefficiencies and assure continuing opportunities for investors whose objective is to use derivatives in a risk management or cost reduction strategy that is not sensitive to relatively small changes in valuation of derivative instruments. The chapter concludes with a more extensive discussion of equity derivative products traded on organized exchanges — with specific focus on stock index futures contracts, exchange-traded options, and structured products.

Some paragraphs and longer segments of this chapter have appeared previously in articles written or co-written by the author. These articles include: James A. Angel, Gary L. Gastineau, and Clifford J. Weber, "Flexible Friends," *Risk* (October 1997); James A. Angel, Gary L. Gastineau, and Clifford J. Weber, "Reducing the Market Impact of Large Stock Trades and Other Applications of Equity FLEX Options," *Journal of Portfolio Management* (Fall 1997); Gary L. Gastineau, "Exchange-Trades vs. OTC Derivatives Markets," *Financial Derivatives and Risk Management* (November 1995), pp. 17-24; and, Gary L. Gastineau, "A Changing Perspective on Teaching Options," *Financial Practice and Education* (Fall/Winter 1997), pp. 55-59.

Exhibit 1: U.S. Withholding Tax Savings with Equity Derivatives (basis points)

Net Withholding Tax Rate	Dividend Yield:		
	1%	2%	3%
15%-Tax Treaty	15	30	45
30%-Non Tax Treaty	30	60	90

SOME FUNCTIONS OF DERIVATIVES

Somewhat arbitrarily, we divide the functions of derivatives into three categories. While the reader will note considerable overlap in practice, we divide the functions into cost reduction, risk management (including asset allocation), and regulatory problems and opportunities. The latter category includes examples of situations where there are obstacles to the use of derivatives as well as circumstances in which derivatives offer an opportunity to solve a regulatory problem.

Cost Reduction

An important cost reduction opportunity, particularly for cross-border equity investors, is the ability to avoid dividend withholding taxes. Taking the United States market as an example, non-resident investors, whether their accounts are taxable or not in their home country, almost invariably pay a non-recoverable withholding tax on dividends they receive from U.S. stocks.[1] U.S. investors face similar taxes when they invest in other countries, so our examples apply to nearly all cross-border investors. If the investor is a resident in a tax treaty country, the net withholding tax rate after a partial recovery is typically 15%; if the investor resides in a non-treaty country, the rate is 30%. A 2% dividend yield to an investor in a 15% (treaty) country will generate a 30 basis point annual withholding tax. Exhibit 1 shows the potential annual savings that foreign investors may enjoy by avoiding the U.S. withholding tax with a synthetic long stock position.

Apart from potential tax avoidance, the principal opportunity for true cost reduction with derivatives arises from valuation discrepancies, i.e., where a particular derivative instrument is overpriced or underpriced relative to its fair value. When the derivative is or contains an option, valuation is largely dependent on the price volatility of the underlying financial instrument. Because volatility estimates are an art, not a science, a derivative which includes an option may appear undervalued to one observer and overvalued to another.[2] Ultimately, differences of opinion are what make all markets work. Given different views on val-

---

[1] The reason for the qualifying "almost" is that foreign government funds and a very few other foreign portfolios are exempt from the U.S. dividend withholding tax.

[2] The author acknowledges the existence of a substantial body of work applying the tools of "science" to the volatility estimation process. The results of these efforts are often useful, but they are still more art than science.

uation and different tax effects (like the dividend withholding tax effect) for different groups of investors, the ultimate determinant of trading volume in most derivatives markets is transaction cost. The lower the transaction costs, i.e., commissions, fees, and trading spreads, the higher trading volume is likely to be and the better the pricing of an instrument will reflect the valuation perspectives and differential economics of all market participants. We discuss valuation issues in the next section, but several trading cost issues are worth noting here.

Market efficiency for derivative instruments often turns on the creation of an efficient and active trading environment within an arbitrage complex. A classic example of an arbitrage complex is the trading in futures contracts, stock baskets, fund shares (SPDRs traded on the American Stock Exchange), and options on the S&P 500 index and other S&P 500 related products. The number of related product markets and the level of trading in each of these markets contributes to market efficiency and liquidity in financial instruments tied to the S&P 500. A similar complex will develop in the near future in portfolios and derivative products on the Dow Jones Industrial Average. To a greater or lesser extent, arbitrage complexes on other domestic and international stock indexes and other market sectors create portfolio liquidity.[3]

The growth of arbitrage complexes based on individual stocks, while unlikely to approach the importance of the major indexes, has grown markedly in recent years, partly as a result of substantial changes in the structure of the equity options market and the reduction of transaction costs in these markets. Specifically, the introduction of Equity FLEX options with no position limits invites large institutional investors into the equity options market for the first time. The resulting increase in liquidity, particularly for large positions, is accompanied by a substantial reduction in transaction charges.[4] These changes plus the high degree of transparency brought to the Equity FLEX marketplace by wide dissemination of requests for quotation (RFQ's) have been a significant factor in transaction cost reduction in this segment of the derivatives market. These options cost reductions, linked to already low transaction costs for stock index futures contracts and basket or portfolio trades, open up equity derivatives markets to a wide range of investors looking to trade in the most cost effective manner.

---

[3] Most of these arbitrage complexes are based on indexes underlying successful futures contracts, but an important exception is worth noting. The success of Morgan Stanley in securing adoption of its MSCI indexes as portfolio benchmarks combined with the introduction of WEBS funds in the United States and OPALS in other countries has opened an arbitrage complex based on portfolio baskets rather than futures contracts on MSCI country indexes.

[4] For example, the American Stock Exchange has capped exchange transaction fees imposed on brokers who handle standardized and Equity FLEX option transactions for large customers. Specifically, these fees which might have become quite large under the old per-contract fee structure are now capped at 2,000 contracts for a customer trade. Prior to the AMEX fee capping, an investor's broker would have paid 100,000 times the single contract exchange fee for a 100,000 contract transaction in a single option series. The broker will now pay only 2,000 times the single contract fee, no matter how many contracts the customer trades in a single option series on a given day.

Generalizations as to the cost of trading in cash equity markets versus derivatives markets are difficult to make, but it is safe to say that stock index futures transactions are generally extremely low cost trades followed closely by trades in funds such as the S&P 500 SPDRs, by portfolio or basket trades on standardized portfolios, and by index options transactions. All of these index trades should carry lower costs than most transactions involving single stocks or a subset of the stocks in an index. In general, particularly when measured in underlying equivalents, costs in options markets will exceed transaction costs in stock markets, which in turn will exceed transaction costs in portfolio or fund markets and in the stock index futures market. Nonetheless, applications involving options on individual stocks may be very attractive in a specific portfolio management application. The opportunity to enhance return in a variety of ways and even to use options to cut the cost of stock trading may overwhelm a simplistic transaction cost analysis.

Risk Management and Asset Allocation

Apart from opportunities for cost reduction, the most widespread use of equity derivatives is in risk management and asset allocation applications. These applications fall into three basic categories. The first is the use of index vehicles like stock index futures or funds to adjust asset allocation and market exposure in a symmetric and aggregate way. Specifically, an investor may find it more economical to use stock index futures or exchange-traded funds, or to a lesser extent, a portfolio trade as an alternative to stock-by-stock or group-by-group changes in a portfolio. Cross-border investors in particular, for reasons highlighted in the discussion of dividend withholding taxes, will often find that the use of futures contracts in a variety of countries offers the opportunity to adjust cross-border exposures on a more attractive basis than would be possible with cash market securities alone. Transaction cost savings, withholding tax avoidance issues, and a host of other cross-border regulatory and economic issues combine to support this application.

Often, a portfolio manager will want to create an asymmetric risk exposure — where the commitment to a particular market has an embedded or separate option characteristic.[5] For example, if the manager is a believer in momentum, he or she will prefer to hold a position with market exposure increasing as the market moves in a favorable direction and decreasing when the market moves against the structure of the portfolio. In this case, the purchase of calls or puts can incorporate the desired change in exposure as the underlying market goes up and down. Because options are available on a wide variety of fixed income and equity market issues, a broad range of risk management and asset allocation structures can be based largely on synthetic or derivative instruments. The exposure offered by these structures can be principally symmetric — based on futures contracts and

---

[5] An asymmetric return pattern is an irregular, even discontinuous, pattern of changes in settlement valuation that does not translate all linear changes in the value of the underlying instrument, index, or rate into a continuous linear settlement value. Asymmetric payoff patterns are characteristic of traditional securities with embedded options and of option contracts themselves.

funds; principally asymmetric — based on a variety of options and options-like structures; or it can be a combination with symmetric risk exposure in some markets and asymmetric exposure in others.

A third risk management application can be described broadly as risk decomposition. While traditional portfolio managers will find a host of these applications, the classic risk decomposition application is the work of the risk arbitrageur who will use options of various maturities and strikes to divide and reallocate the risk of a position, allowing him to accept certain risks and avoid others. Comparison of options premiums on contracts with expiration dates before and after the expiration of a tender offer, a shareholder vote, or a board meeting is a common method of measuring the market's expectation for the outcome of an event. With a variety of standardized and Equity FLEX options, portfolio investors and arbitrageurs with different perspectives on economic events or corporate developments can allocate the risk among themselves in a way that reflects each entity's expectations and/or risk preferences. Relatively "pure" risks can be taken and avoided with a range of option contracts.

Regulation

Rather ironically, regulation has not only been the greatest reason why the development of equity derivatives markets has lagged behind the development of fixed income and currency derivatives markets, it has also presented some of the greatest opportunities for derivatives applications. Regulation promises to offer a similar mix of obstacles and opportunities in the years ahead.

Regulation creates obstacles to the use of derivatives because equity markets are by far the most intensely regulated of financial markets. In part, this close regulation is due to the wide range of issuers, and in part, to widespread public participation in equity markets. The Securities and Exchange Commission (SEC), the primary regulator of equity markets in the United States, has imposed a variety of rules, including customer suitability requirements, which restrict the use of option contracts by many small investors.

Regulatory restrictions are no less significant on the portfolio side than on the customer side. While state gaming laws and similar prohibitions on the trading and use of options and futures have been largely preempted by federal legislation, many older trust agreements and many of the older, larger mutual funds have prospectuses which restrict or forbid the use of options and futures. These prospectuses are sometimes hard to change. A provision of the tax code that limited a fund's ability to realize short term gains, the "short-short" rule, restricted the use of derivatives in mutual funds, but it was repealed by the Tax Payer Relief Act of 1997.[6] Many pension trusts and other aggregations of investable assets

---

[6] The 30% or "short-short" rule disqualified a mutual fund from the pass through tax treatment accorded regulated investment companies if the fund got more than 30% of its gross income from gains on positions held less than three months. This rule is now an historic curiosity. Its repeal will probably be credited for most of the growth in institutional use of options over the next several years.

have modified their governing documents since the early 1980s in response to the development of stock index futures markets. Many of these modifications were not extended to options because the SEC imposed low and strict options position limits until some recent relaxation of these limits. A consequence of this regulatory history is that far more portfolios are permitted to use futures contracts than are permitted to use options. In recent years, most new fund documents permit the use of a variety of derivative instruments, and a few funds have added options to their futures approval as option position limits have increased.

With some important exceptions, the adverse derivatives publicity of the mid-1990s has not led to major restrictions on portfolio applications of exchanged-traded equity derivatives. The derivatives image problems of the mid-1990s have been concentrated in the over-the-counter markets and in fixed income and currency products. While some criticism of stock index arbitrageurs surfaced at the time of the 1987 market crash, exchange-traded equity derivatives have been relatively free from major criticism for a number of years. A few tax issues like the "short-short" rule have attracted legislative attention, but the recent pattern of regulatory initiatives in equity derivatives has been in the direction of less, rather than more, intense regulation. The combination of a relatively benign regulatory environment and the trend toward an increasing number of equity portfolios obtaining greater flexibility in their use of a variety of instruments has been an important factor in market development.

In some respects, the regulatory environment has been an area of opportunity rather than strictly an area of occasional difficulty. Opportunities come from ways to do indirectly what a portfolio manager cannot do directly — either as a result of a legal obstacle or due to costs associated with an adverse regulatory structure. It is useful to illustrate a few of the regulation-based opportunities.

Many institutional investors are prohibited from selling short. Usually, however, they face few obstacles to using equity linked notes (ELNs) with values that increase as the value of a security, a basket of securities, or an index *declines*. The functional equivalent of a short position can be embedded in a note with an implied credit for the use of proceeds from a short sale. A built-in cap on losses from rising prices (a floor on the value of the note) could make the note structure considerably more attractive to many institutions than a true short position.

A derivative can skirt a regulatory obstacle in the creation of instruments providing access to markets that are otherwise difficult to access because of local restrictions on foreign ownership. While most of these instruments are over-the-counter, some listed securities like closed-end funds and structured notes designed to provide access to otherwise closed markets have traded on exchanges. Embedding the functional equivalent of a futures contract or an option in an equity-linked note is very useful for a wide variety of institutional investors. This instrument, usually with a minimum value guarantee for the note at maturity, is the most common structured note.

The significance of these regulatory opportunities lies primarily in the fact that regulations generally view financial instruments and applications of financial instruments in terms of "pigeon holes." An instrument meets regulatory requirements if it fits into the pigeon hole or description regulators have created for a particular purpose. In most cases, a derivative instrument embedded in a debt instrument fits in an entirely different kind of pigeon hole than a stock index futures contract or an option. The structured note is seen as a variation on a simple debt instrument. As a consequence of this pigeon hole perspective, something which may be difficult to do directly is relatively easy to do when an ineligible instrument is embedded in a structured note.

VALUATION OF DERIVATIVES

Because it has a limited purpose, this section offers a very brief discussion of the principles behind the valuation of the two basic equity derivatives contracts: stock index futures and options. Structured products usually embed the functional equivalent of a futures or options contract in an equity-linked note or an index fund portfolio. Our purpose in discussing valuation is simply to provide the reader with some comfort that arbitrage traders who attempt to profit from small valuation discrepancies will eliminate or prevent large discrepancies, thus making the exchange-traded derivative markets safe for investors who are interested in risk management and specific return patterns to trade futures and options with little concern for valuation discrepancies. We will spend more time on the simpler valuation principles of futures contracts than on the valuation of options because our purpose is to highlight the significance of arbitrage pricing. Arbitrage pricing is easier to describe in futures markets.

Futures

A futures contract is an agreement to make or take delivery of the object of the contract at a specified time and at a market determined price. Many financial futures contracts differ from commodity futures contracts in that they are characterized by cash settlement. Actual delivery of the object of the contract is not common in futures markets, but many financial contracts do not call for actual delivery under any circumstances. Cash passes between the buyer and seller of the futures contract based, ultimately, on the spot market price of the underlying object of the contract on the settlement date.

Cash settlement and, more importantly, the fact that some form of "money" is the commodity behind the contract simplify fair value computations for financial futures contracts. Pricing and evaluating futures contracts on agricultural and industrial commodities can be extremely complex. A new harvest of grain or cotton; a new gold or copper mine; scarcity induced by a drought or by hoarding: all of these make it difficult to make definitive statements about the appropriate price of commodity futures contracts. Financial futures contracts, by comparison, tend to be easier to evaluate, at least relative to the underlying object or instrument.

The principle behind the pricing of financial futures contracts can be illustrated with a hypothetical common stock transaction. Assume for a moment that Apex Equipment common stock is selling for approximately $100 a share and you decide to purchase some of the stock for your portfolio. For purpose of this illustration, we assume the stock pays no dividend. Your broker accepts your order to buy at $100. Moments later he calls to say that you can buy the stock at $100 a share for settlement under the normal 3-day settlement process, or you can purchase the stock for that price and not pay for it until 3 months and 3 days have passed. Which would you choose? Obviously, you would prefer to own the stock today, yet not have to pay for it right away. The $100 stock price could be invested at interest over the 3-month period. If the interest rate was 8% annually (to keep the calculations simple), you could earn $2 in interest over the 3-month period. (The 8% annual rate is divided by 4 to reflect the fact that you will not have to pay for the stock for a quarter of a year.)

When you commit to buy the stock today, but defer payment for three months, you have bought a forward contract. A forward contract is not quite the same thing as a futures contract, but both types of commitments assure the parties to the agreement that they will receive all the gain (or loss) from price changes in the underlying instrument between now and the contract's final settlement date. The difference is that the variation margin mechanism of the futures market provides for a series of daily settlements of the futures contract. Variation margin flows have little impact on the value or pricing of a futures contract, so we will not discuss this feature of futures markets in detail.

The $2 interest you could earn on the cash you do not have to pay out immediately has important implications for the price you could afford to pay for the three month "deferred delivery" contract on Apex Equipment. If someone offered you Apex Equipment at $100 today for delivery in three months, you could afford to pay more for that contract than the current price of the stock. In fact, you could pay any price up to $102 and still be better off than if you simply bought the stock and paid for it under normal terms. In market equilibrium, the deferred payment contract for Apex Equipment would sell at approximately 2 points over the cash price for current delivery. The difference between the forward price and the cash price is called the *basis*. Unlike commodity contracts, where basis is often a function of storage, production, crop expectations, and financing costs, the appropriate basis on a financial futures contract is uniformly a function of the cost of carrying the underlying position. The equilibrium financial futures price is equal to the price of the underlying instrument plus the net carrying cost. Correspondingly, the equilibrium price basis of a financial futures contract is equal to the net carrying cost of the underlying position.

Options

Options share the forward pricing characteristic of futures, but add an additional element to valuation. Whereas the pricing of a financial futures contract and the range of opportunities for arbitrageurs is determined by differences in financing costs, evaluation of options is somewhat less precisely defined because the value of an option also depends on the *volatility* of the underlying instrument. In the case of an option on a stock or stock index, the option's price is dependent on stock price volatility. If the price of the underlying stock or basket is highly volatile, the option is worth more than an option on an underlying instrument with a price that rarely moves beyond a narrow range. Since volatility is generally two-sided, an instrument that is highly volatile usually will have more valuable puts as well as more valuable calls. While differences in perspective on the valuation of a futures contract are ordinarily constrained by differences in the cost of funds for various market participants, different perspectives on likely market volatility can lead to substantial differences of opinion on the appropriate valuation of an option contract.

A comprehensive discussion of valuation of various derivative instruments is well beyond the scope of this chapter, but the point of this discussion is that an arbitrageur will nearly always be looking at a very small price discrepancy in the futures market. Price discrepancies in option markets are partly in the eye of the beholder; thus, an investor with extremely good or extremely poor vision may have an extreme view of option value. As a consequence of the less determinant nature of option prices, applications based on options frequently have very different characteristics and pricing risks than those based on futures, funds or other symmetric market exposure instruments.

One essential conclusion of the less determinant pricing of options is that transparent price discovery in an open market environment is the investor's best protection from mispricing — unless the investor is prepared to evaluate any option instrument based on his own volatility analysis. Transparent pricing is one of the key advantages of exchange-traded versus OTC derivatives.

EXCHANGE-TRADED VERSUS OTC DERIVATIVES MARKETS

An important misconception held by some observers of financial markets is that derivatives traded on exchange markets are in strong and persistent competition with customized over-the-counter (OTC) derivative instruments. Such competition is assumed to affect cash securities markets and futures as well as markets in options and more complex derivatives. In truth, most types of financial instruments are either traded predominantly on an exchange market or predominately OTC. Within a specific category of derivatives, competition between exchange-traded and OTC products is more the exception than the rule.

One important example of exchange/OTC competition illustrates several key issues particularly well. OTC swaps may compete with listed futures in some functions, particularly in interest rate markets. Listed trading in swaps has not been successful, but the safety of the futures clearing houses has stimulated interest in collateralizing swaps positions at some of the same clearing houses which handle futures. Interest in collateralization of swaps is not universal. Some end-user counterparties (corporate liability managers) use swaps because they need more pricing and product flexibility than a futures exchange can provide. These users might not be able to meet the collateralization requirements of a clearing house, or they might not feel that this credit-risk protection is worth its cost. They often choose swaps because they do not want a clearing house. In contrast to liability managers, asset managers who have portfolios they can use freely as collateral may value the collateralization of futures, but need more pricing and structure flexibility than they can get in a standardized product. These asset managers value the collateralization of swaps. Collateralization makes swaps fully competitive with futures for these managers and, for some users, tips the balance between the use of an exchange-traded instrument and an OTC product. In each case, it is the combination of features that determines the product choice, with the collateralized swap filling a niche as an intermediate product between a futures contract and a traditional swap.

Regulation will play an occasional role in determining where an instrument will be traded, but relatively simple economics usually determines the structure of a market. Subject to some qualifications, exchange markets dominate when a large volume of transactions in standardized instruments characterizes a market. If a market needs diverse instruments, some of which are created specifically to meet the requirements of one party to the transaction, the market will be an OTC market. Exchanges tend to be more successful if secondary trading over the life of an instrument is useful to market participants.

Ordinarily, if an exchange lists a financial contract, that specific instrument will be traded on the exchange as long as the exchange fosters an active market. If the exchange's volume is inadequate to support an efficient market because the exchange product does not meet a broad enough set of needs, the exchange may delist the instrument and the market will revert to OTC trading. The exchange contract specifications will merge with those of similar OTC products, each of which meets a specific set of needs better than any viable exchange-traded product.

Comparing the Markets

Exhibit 2 provides a simplified and admittedly incomplete comparison of exchange-traded and OTC derivatives markets. With the caveat that the exhibit's generalizations are not infallible, a common characteristic of exchange-traded derivatives is that their developers hope they will be used by investors of all sizes. The developers succeed in the aggregate, but it may take several different exchange markets to satisfy investors of all sizes. Market segmentation by customer size and type is particularly common in the United States where few SEC-regulated derivatives have large institutional constituencies. Among SEC-regulated instruments, only S&P 500 index options on the Chicago Board Option Exchange (CBOE) and Standard & Poor's Depository Receipts (SPDRs) on the American Stock Exchange (AMEX) have achieved significant institutional penetration. Correspondingly, relatively few individuals use CFTC-regulated financial derivatives markets.

Exhibit 2: Comparing the Markets

	Primary Users	Product Type	Underlying Market	Liquidity	Transaction Costs
Exchange-Traded	Investors of all sizes	Standardized	Highly regulated, good price information, underlying more likely to be exchange-traded	Depends on underlying market and related markets	Usually low to moderate
Over-the-Counter	Institutional investors	Customized	Less regulated, limited or restriced price information, underlying more likely to be traded OTC	Depends on underlying market and related markets	Highly varied

In an effort to bring both individuals and institutions to the same products, the notional size of an exchange-traded derivative contract may be relatively large by the standards of most individual investors and small relative to the minimum transaction size in the institutionally dominated OTC market. With the exception of recently introduced FLEX products, exchange-traded contracts have been highly standardized. The FLEX products depart from this tradition of standardization in a limited way, but FLEX contracts are much closer to other exchange products than to highly customized OTC contracts. FLEX contracts provide relief from strict standardization, but are just one small additional stage in a continuum that ranges from standard exchange products through FLEX contracts to "plain vanilla" OTC products and to truly one-of-a-kind customized OTC instruments.

By far the largest volume of OTC derivatives transactions is in plain vanilla instruments, which may be distinguished from standard exchange-traded derivatives and FLEX contracts more in product structure and credit management than in function. Plain vanilla means something quite different from standardization. The terms of these instruments can be remarkably diverse along any of several scales, but the instruments themselves can be described clearly by an easily recognized name (such as interest-rate swap, reverse floating-rate note, collar, etc.) and by specific terms expressed as prices or rates (or as ways to measure prices or rates such as 3-month LIBOR), reset or expiration dates, and strike or limit prices or rates. Combinations of terms permit great variety in spite of the widely used structure of most of these instruments. Standardized exchange trading is not practical for these instruments because few market participants are interested in primary, let alone secondary, trading at each of the almost innumerable price, rate, strike, and term-to-maturity combinations that are available. Someone may want a swap that terminates on March 1 but have no interest in one that terminates on March 2.

There is little to be said about single or few-of-a kind instruments that are small in number but potentially important in their impact on the course of financial market development. Most of these specialty products will never see widespread usage, but some will be adapted eventually to regular use in the OTC markets. Many new products get their start as custom-tailored instruments, but very few custom-tailored products are useful on a large scale.

As Exhibit 2 suggests, it is possible to make some useful generalizations about the underlying markets behind exchange-traded and OTC derivatives. Other things equal, the markets underlying exchange-traded derivatives tend to be highly regulated and to offer standardized products in their own right. These markets usually provide reliable and consistent price information and are likely to be exchange markets themselves. In this context, exchanges enjoy a much higher market share in cash and derivatives markets in equities and physical commodities than they do in less intensely regulated interest rate and currency instruments.

Exchange-traded derivative instruments may or may not enjoy a liquidity advantage relative to OTC instruments. Any apparent difference in liquidity in exchange-traded or OTC products is usually a function of the liquidity characteristics of the underlying market, combined in some cases with differences in transaction costs. Because the products tend to be standardized, transaction costs in exchange-traded markets are usually low to moderate. Transaction costs are much more variable in OTC derivatives markets. To the extent that an OTC contract is a plain vanilla instrument like an interest rate swap, transaction costs may be very low. These instruments are priced off futures and forward markets and have to compete with the latter markets in function. In contrast, a highly customized structured product may involve complex hedging by the dealer who creates it. If the product is hard to hedge or hard to evaluate, the dealer may price in a high profit margin. High transaction costs embedded in such an instrument become most apparent if the buyer of the instrument attempts to close out the position prior to its scheduled maturity. The dealer's reluctance to give up profit in the early close-out is often characterized as illiquidity.

Transaction cost and liquidity issues deserve considerable attention, not only because they reveal differences between exchange-traded and OTC markets, but also because they play a major role in many decisions to use derivatives instead of traditional cash market instruments. It is possible to illustrate the cost and liquidity issues with examples from many markets, but several examples from equity markets illustrate the key points.

Transaction Costs: A Key To Market Success

On a global basis, the principal types of exchange-traded derivatives instruments which have enjoyed the greatest success have been stock index futures, stock option contracts, and sovereign bond futures and option contracts. The relative success of exchange-traded and OTC contracts and the ability of exchanges to dominate important segments of equity and debt derivative markets illustrate some of the issues which determine where the line between exchange-traded and OTC derivatives contracts falls.

The nature of the customer often determines where an instrument trades. In most countries, individual investors do not use most OTC derivatives contracts. Customers for OTC products may or may not have to be financially sophisticated, but they must have the financial resources to interest a dealer. Retail products tend to trade on an exchange secondary market even if they are created by an OTC dealer. Examples of the latter type of product include covered warrants and some public issues of equity-linked notes.

Exchange-traded stock option contracts have gained market share relative to OTC stock-option trading in most countries. The exchanges have created standardized stock options which provide adequate flexibility, a reasonable measure of liquidity for an investor who wants to close out an option position before expiration, and acceptable transaction costs. For reasons detailed below, exchange-traded stock options are usually retail products.

Exchange-traded stock index futures have been extremely successful in most markets. The ability to take a position on the market (an index) as opposed to a position in an individual stock, combined with a dramatic reduction in transaction costs relative to the cost of taking or eliminating a position in a cash market portfolio, has been highly popular. As a broad generalization, total transaction costs in stock index or bond futures contracts are about 5% to 10% of the cost of making a similar transaction in cash markets without the aid of futures. This dramatic transaction cost reduction has stimulated the growth of these exchange-traded derivatives more than any other single factor.

Exchange-Traded Equity Derivatives — Market Structure and Applications

There are three principal categories of exchange-traded equity derivatives products: futures, options, and structured products. This categorization simplifies things a bit because structured products include a wide range of instruments with a correspondingly wide variety of market exposure and risk characteristics. Our description and discussion of products and markets will not attempt to draw a complete picture or to show all possible applications. The focus, appropriately, will be on applications for portfolio management. However, some applications that are peripheral to portfolio management will be described when necessary to provide a clear picture of the product or when the product may be used in lieu of a traditional portfolio product.

Stock Index Futures

A stock futures contract is equivalent to an index fund with no cash investment and with a fixed maturity or expiration date. The fact that a stock index futures contract will track the underlying index extremely closely — almost precisely when adjustments for the pattern and timing of dividends and modest valuation discrepancies are taken into account — makes the most important portfolio applications of stock index futures readily apparent. Futures have been widely used to create synthetic long and short stock portfolio positions. They have been used as temporary positions to take or reduce stock market exposure at a low transaction cost and without disturbing other positions.

The most interesting application of stock index futures in the portfolio context is probably in asset allocation, particularly in cross-border portfolios. As indicated, a major drawback to cross-border equity investment is the almost universal imposition of dividend withholding taxes on cross-border dividend payments. An investor can use a combination of stock index futures contracts and money market or other debt instruments in a variety of currencies to create a tax advantaged, multinational portfolio without suffering the penalty of withholding taxes. In some European countries domestic dividend tax reduction provisions cause stock index futures contracts to be consistently undervalued relative to the valuation calculations of a tax-exempt domestic investor. In these countries the futures offer an enhanced index return to the cross-border investor. A "synthetic" portfolio composed of a variety of futures and money market or other fixed income positions taken to provide a wide variety of cross-border equity market exposures can be passive in the sense that allocations to different indexes remain essentially unchanged over time or perhaps move slightly reflecting price changes in certain underlying indexes. They can be active in the sense of an active allocation strategy that attempts to move among domestic equity and fixed income markets on the one hand, and equity and fixed income markets in an international context on the other.

Exchange-Traded Options

Several varieties of exchange-traded options play important roles in equity portfolio management strategies. Index options traded in securities markets and stock index futures options traded in futures markets play roles related to the roles played by futures contracts. These index option contracts provide aggregate portfolio exposure adjustments, supplemented by an opportunity to profit from correct judgment of market volatility or to obtain a degree of protection or a somewhat different return pattern than would be available with a symmetric market instrument like a futures contract. Interestingly enough, in spite of the substantial growth in indexing in recent years, the use of index options in the United States has not kept pace with the growth in index funds. Index option volume has been static and even weak when viewed in the aggregate. A significant part of this weakness is probably attributable to brokerage firm litigation and compliance problems which surfaced in the aftermath of the 1987 crash and continue to affect securities' firms attitudes toward this product.

The use of index options has never really caught on in a large way with major institutional investors — despite rather significant increases in index option position limits and the introduction of index FLEX options. In addition to the compliance issues noted above, the fact that these options are cash settled and, for the most part, settled at the market opening rather than at the close has tended to reduce investor interest.

We expect growth in options on exchange-traded index funds to ultimately make up for the lack of index option growth. The only example of a fund option which we can point to today has hardly been a rousing success.[7] However,

---

[7] The option on the Toronto Stock Exchange's TIP fund is undersized relative to competing index options and suffers from small position limits.

we expect fund options to be a major product line in the period ahead, largely because they will eliminate many of the weaknesses of cash-settled index options. They will be physically settled into the shares of the fund and they will expire at the market close rather than at the opening. Also, because there is an underlying instrument and physical settlement, it will be more difficult for investors and their advisors to lose track of the risk exposure of a short position in a fund option.

Individual investors and, increasingly, institutional investors have shown a growing interest in equity (stock) options. Both standardized equity options and Equity FLEX options which permit a high degree of customization in response to investor demand should grow dramatically. Most importantly for institutional investors, Equity FLEX options are available without position limits. Position limits have been the major obstacle to institutional use of options.

Largely because of position limits, standardized equity options have not been a major institutional product. Equity option position limits started at 1,000 contracts in 1973. While position limits have grown, there are many option stocks trading today with option position limits of only 4,000 contracts on standardized options. The most actively traded stocks have option position limits as high as 25,000 contracts with hedge exemptions that permit an increase beyond this level in some applications, but the increase has not been adequate. The fact that major U.S. stock indexes are now at levels more than ten times their 1973-1974 lows illustrates how little position limits have been liberalized on standard equity options.

Large institutions find that position limits severely constrain their opportunity to use options. As a consequence, institutions have not made the expenditure and effort to undertake significant options programs. Apart from modest operations at a number of major investment organizations, most institutional options market participants are hedge funds and small investment advisors. There is reason to believe that institutional options market participation will increase in the period ahead, and much of this increase will undoubtedly be due to the introduction of Equity FLEX options and the elimination of position limits on these contracts. Many of the applications of these options will be in the nature of portfolio applications; consequently, this product merits attention from portfolio managers.

On October 24, 1996, the American Stock Exchange and several other exchanges introduced Equity FLEX options trading on a small group of listed option stocks. Additional names have been added and will continue to be added in response to investor demand. The SEC initially approved position limits covering purchase or sale of Equity FLEX options on up to 7,500,000 underlying shares on some large cap, actively traded stocks. SEC approval of complete elimination of Equity FLEX position limits on the American Stock Exchange came in the third quarter of 1997. To further encourage institutional use of options, the American Stock Exchange announced a cap on option transaction charges effective July 1, 1997. The combination of Equity FLEX position limit elimination and reduced transaction charges opens up many new options applications. To understand these new applications, we need a different perspective of where options fit into the range of investment tools — and particularly how they fit into the portfolio manager's toolbox. The first step in developing a useful perspective is to see options as tactical tools rather than as the centerpiece of a portfolio manager's investment strategy.

Strategies versus Tactics — Changing the Image of Options Long calls, short puts or spreads, straddles, and strangles, as well as collars, seagulls, and Christmas trees are invariably called *options strategies*. This terminology goes back to the conventional or over-the-counter options market that preceded exchange-traded options. We live in an era of strategic planning, strategic weapons, and strategies for success. Inevitably, we try to wrap the connotations of "strategy" around some non-strategic things.

In a military context, commanders refer to large-scale planning or global activities as strategy. Smaller scale actions taken to implement a strategy usually fall under the heading of tactics. The relevance of this distinction to options is that, perhaps as much as any other single factor, the use of the word "strategy" in connection with options has led some investors and pedagogues to focus too much on the theory of options and the aggregate impact of options on portfolio performance and too little on tactical options applications. The introduction of Equity FLEX options offers an opportunity to redress the balance.

If options are strategic, it is too easy to see them as inherently more important than the underlying instrument. We can lose sight of the risk/reward characteristics of an unoptioned portfolio. Focusing on an option strategy's payout pattern rather than on the usefulness of an option application may be akin to a military commander choosing his weapons before he learns the nature of his mission. It is probably easier to view Equity FLEX options from a tactical perspective than it is to attain this perspective with index options that can affect the risk/return characteristics of an entire portfolio. Tactical option applications not only address the importance of thinking small in terms of position or portfolio impact, but they also extend the usefulness of options to problems often ignored by big-picture option users.

We still need to understand option evaluation; however, increasingly, the emphasis will be on integrating option evaluation with the economics of other techniques and applications. These applications include trading cost reduction, asset allocation, return enhancement, and cost of capital reduction. In a number of these applications, buyers or sellers of an option may be willing to buy or sell a somewhat mispriced option to accomplish some other objective. The acceptability of some mispricing is the best indication that the option is being used as a tactical tool.

A Trading Application A relatively simple example of a tactical option illustrates a market impact reducing application of Equity FLEX options. Suppose that a portfolio manager notes with satisfaction that his position in Technomarvel, Inc. common stock has performed very well in recent months. It has contributed to the manager's outperformance of his benchmark index. In spite of (or perhaps because of) this recent record, the manager now feels that the stock is not likely to continue its outperformance over the intermediate term. At current prices he would like to replace the position with a stock that is more likely to outperform the benchmark in the months ahead. The logistics of selling the Technomarvel position outright without substantial market impact are daunting. The manager is responsible for 10 million shares with a current market value of approximately $500 million — not an uncommon position in institutional portfolios. If the institution's trader simply indicates a selling interest the size of this block, any corresponding buying interest is likely to be well below the currently quoted bid.[8]

Any investor who is a candidate for purchase of all or a substantial fraction of a half billion dollar block of stock recognizes that the sell decision which brings the block to market may be based on specific adverse information. The seller may know or think he knows something that makes the stock a dangerous holding during the period ahead. The possibility of an earnings disappointment or of bad news affecting the company's product line or its management could cause the shares to underperform — or even to fall sharply. The possibility that such information is behind the decision to sell, makes any potential buyer reluctant to purchase the block except at a significant discount. In a traditional stock transaction, the seller has no obvious way to assure the buyer that the sale is not based on adverse information.

Equity FLEX options provide a simple way to send a signal — and even offer an enforceable "guarantee" — that the seller does not have stock specific information that could hurt the buyer. The trader for the selling institution can indicate that, as an alternative to selling the shares outright, he is willing to sell calls with a strike price near the current market price of the stock. The calls are sold in the expectation that the option will be exercised if the stock price moves up (or is unchanged) over the life of the option.

What better way to indicate the absence of adverse information than to offer a potential buyer a call option on the shares? Whether the would-be buyer elects to buy call options (perhaps priced at a modest discount in implied volatility points to the price of standardized exchange-traded options) or simply makes a more competitive bid for the stock in reliance on the option offer, the fact that the alternative was available sends a signal to any buyer that the sale is not based on adverse information. The buyer of the option knows that if the stock declines over the life of the option, the seller will collect an option premium. However, any loss on the stock greater than the amount of the option premium can affect the seller's portfolio significantly. If the stock is simply dull, as the seller anticipated, he collects the option premium. The premium might make the stock a better contributor to portfolio performance than it would have been without the option. If the stock is above the strike at expiration, the seller will succeed in moving the block with negligible market impact.

---

[8] The seller may be able to sell a small quantity of the stock through a crossing network or similar system, but even such anonymous sales will soon begin to have an impact on the stock price.

The buyer's decision to buy the option rather than the stock will be based on such issues as the expected cash flow into and out of his portfolio, his fund's authorization to purchase call options, his judgment on the likely future volatility of the underlying stock, and, of course, the pricing and credibility of the option offer.

How Equity FLEX Options Trade Before we look further at Equity FLEX applications we need to look more closely at how the Equity FLEX market works. The institutional investor who wants to use Equity FLEX options in the management of a portfolio will go to a broker or dealer, much as an OTC option trade is initiated. From the client's perspective, the interaction with the broker or dealer is similar to an OTC option trade, but the process is very different from the dealer's perspective. A brief description of the price discovery and trading process will help illustrate the advantage of the Equity FLEX process to the cost conscious client.

Once the client, alone or working with the broker or dealer, has developed an idea for an Equity FLEX transaction, the broker will go to the floor of the AMEX and complete a *request for quote* (RFQ) form, describing the terms of the contracts for which bids and/or offers are being solicited. The broker representing the client is called the *submitting member*. If the submitting member is a dealer, the submitting firm may be prepared to cross a trade on the Exchange if its facilitating bid or offer is the best available on the floor.

The RFQ goes to the specialist responsible for options in the designated underlying stock and the specialist reviews it for completeness and accuracy. The Equity FLEX request must be for a minimum size of 250 contracts if the series is not currently open or 100 contracts if this series has already been traded and continues to be outstanding. Smaller trades may take place only to close out an entire position in a series. The specialist fixes a request response time from 2 to 20 minutes for responsive quotes to be reported to the post and assigns an alphanumeric identifier to the trade. The information on the proposed trade is disseminated over the Options Price Reporting Authority (OPRA) tape. This information also will be displayed on special pages created for the purpose by the leading quote vendors. At present, this information is available from Bloomberg, ILX, Reuters, and Track Data. Potential Equity FLEX participants will see the RFQ announcement on the trading floor, over OPRA, or from one of the data vendors that publishes information on Equity FLEX RFQs. If they elect to do so, off floor dealers or their customers may prepare responsive bids or offers and send them to their brokers for representation to the specialist, who is responsible for maintaining a temporary "book" on this proposed trade, consistent with the time and price priority rules of the Exchange.

Any participating member may modify his or her customer's responsive quote at any time during or at the end of the request response time. The submitting member also may enter a responsive bid or offer to facilitate the customer's trade. The submitting member's bid or offer ranks with any other bid or offer according to the time and price priority rules. If the submitting member indicates a desire to cross a trade, he is guaranteed the right to at least 25% of the non-customer side of the trade at the trade price. At the end of the response time, the specialist gives the post supervisor the best bid and offer (BBO) with size for dissemination. The submitting member then must either accept or reject the BBO within a reasonable time period. The submitting member may accept all or part of the BBO subject to minimum requirements, reject the entire BBO, or attempt to negotiate a better price during a BBO improvement interval. Messages on revised BBOs will be disseminated as they change. At the end of any BBO improvement interval, the submitting member must promptly accept or reject the BBO. If the entire BBO is not accepted, the participating members may accept any part of the unfilled balance, subject to minimum requirements. Trading may continue as long as there is interest on the floor. When the specialist determines that there is no further interest in the specific RFQ, he announces that the market is closed for that particular RFQ, and the post supervisor sends an administrative message to that effect over OPRA. If a customer subsequently wishes to trade in this series, a new RFQ must be submitted and the process repeated.

In some Equity FLEX trades, option terms such as premium, strike price, and size will not be expressed as dollar amounts or number of contracts, but can be converted into these forms at the completion of the Equity FLEX trade. For example, the strike may be set at 10% over the last sale at time of trade or the premium may be reflected as a percentage of the underlying stock price. These terms are converted into dollar prices by the parties to the trade and disseminated over OPRA. If the terms cannot be specified in dollar amount and number of contracts immediately (for example, 10% out of the money puts on a $10 million notional amount based on the closing stock price), dissemination is made in notional and percentage terms agreed upon at the time of the trade. Once all contingencies are determined, prices are set at the nearest minimum trading increment. The midpoint of a price range is rounded up.

Any member of the Exchange can participate in Equity FLEX transactions. The specialist in the option is required to provide a bid or an offer, or both (depending on the terms of the RFQ), but other participating members in the Equity FLEX process are not required to respond to a given RFQ. Members who do respond are required to do so for at least 100 contracts. To avoid contributing to the crush of OPRA tape traffic at the 9:30 a.m. opening of option trading, Equity FLEX trading hours are 10:00 a.m. to 4:00 p.m., New York time.

One purpose of this chapter is to describe how the new Equity FLEX structure — without position limits and with a sharp reduction in transaction charges on large trades — provides important new opportunities for large institutional portfolio managers and their trading desks. Our objective is simply to highlight some applications that are sufficiently important and universal that most institutional investors will find them useful. After institutional investors and traders begin to use this market, the list of applications will grow. Investors not currently able to use listed options may conclude that, in contrast to earlier efforts, an attempt to loosen constraints on their options usage will be worthwhile because options can enhance investment performance and cut transaction costs.

We have already described one way in which options can reduce market impact from the sale of a block of stock. We will go on to describe applications to:

- Reduce market impact from the purchase of a block of stock.
- Facilitate portfolio cash management and risk management by separating market risk from the size of a cash commitment.
- Create synthetic long positions that may provide better returns, perhaps by letting a non-U.S. investor side-step the dividend withholding tax.
- Create synthetic short positions with greater protection from buy-ins and/or lower net costs than traditional short selling.
- Permit an investor to use more of the information developed by stock or market analysis to profit from volatility forecasts or to structure payout or profit/loss patterns to reflect a more sophisticated forecast than the simple directional forecast which underlies most stock portfolio selections. These applications involve event and surprise risk management opportunities.
- Accept some risks and hedge others in risk arbitrage situations.
- Use special purpose applications at the fund and position level to limit or control risk exposure or to control the timing of realization of a gain or loss for tax or regulatory purposes.

Reducing the Market Impact of a Stock Purchase Decision We illustrated an application of Equity FLEX call options which reduced the market impact of an investor's decision to sell a large block of stock. To demonstrate that such opportunities are not limited to calls or to stock sales, we describe here an opportunity to reduce the market impact of a stock purchase by selling an Equity FLEX put. These transactions have an important characteristic in common: they provide a mechanism for the investor who is trading on statistical research rather than event-specific knowledge to reduce transaction costs. The option provides a way for this investor to signal and even "guarantee" the level and nature of the conviction behind the decision to trade.

Analysts of trading costs often describe and evaluate the demand for execution immediacy in terms of options.[9] They describe the entry of a limit order to buy or sell a stock as giving other market participants a free option to sell stock to or buy stock from the party entering the limit order. Of course, the option given by the limit order may be exercised after an event has rendered the bid or offer more attractive, because the option offered by the limit order may be, suddenly, "in the money." The sale of a call to initiate a stock sale or the sale of a put as a

---

[9] This approach appears to have originated in Thomas E. Copeland and Dan Galai, "Information Effects on the Bid-Ask Spread," *Journal of Finance* (December 1983), pp. 1457-1469. A well-developed option analysis of limit orders appears in Evan Schulman, "Shackled Liquidity: An Institutional Manifesto," *Journal of Portfolio Management* (Summer 1992), pp. 42-46.

way to establish a position in a stock is simply a more explicit use of an option. The limit order that is built into an exchange-traded option is good for a defined interval — the life of the option — in contrast to the option in a simple limit order that is subject to cancellation at the discretion of the party entering the limit order. The explicit sale of an Equity FLEX option also differs from the free options granted by investors using limit orders in that the investor selling an Equity FLEX option is paid a cash premium for the option. No cash premium is paid the investor who enters a limit order.

Selling a put to facilitate a possible stock purchase may be useful when an investor decides that a company's shares are undervalued — and may well stay that way for a period of time. The investor is interested in taking and holding a position in the stock if the position can be acquired on favorable terms. The stock is attractive at current or lower levels, but the manager cannot justify purchase if entering a buy order will cause the stock to trade up. In contrast to a traditional buy order, sale of a put may express just the degree of interest and patience which the would-be buyer feels. Adjustments in the option premium, strike price, or expiration date of the put can refine the expression of buying interest.

In emphasizing the possible sale of options to facilitate stock purchases and sales, we do not mean to imply that there will be no market impact from a stock purchase or sale decision implemented with options. The purchase or sale of options in large size will almost certainly have some impact on option premiums and on underlying stock prices. The sale of an at-the money put indicates buying interest at present or lower prices. This expression of buying interest may prevent a price decline or even stimulate a modest price advance as other buyers see an indication of buying "support."

Use of options should help reduce stock price volatility in some cases. The investor who sells a put will send a message to the market that the stock purchase intention reflected in the put sale (see Exhibit 3) is certainly not based on an expectation that a particular event will cause the price of the stock to rise sharply in the period immediately ahead. Instead, the put seller is giving the put buyer most or all of any near term upside in an associated stock position. The seller of the put is accepting downside exposure to the stock price in exchange for the option premium. If the put seller's judgment is correct, the options will be exercised when the stock is slightly in the money. The stock will then rise to reflect the value that this patient investor is looking for.

Traders continually wrestle with the difficulty of communicating the strength or weakness of a purchase or sale decision to the market. The party on the other side of the market cannot safely accept a statement that the party initiating an order has no specific knowledge of coming events. However, willingness to sell a put as an alternative to immediate purchase of the stock or to sell a call against a long stock position is an eloquent and enforceable statement of the option seller's lack of the kind of specific information which is likely to affect the stock price in the short run.

Exhibit 3: Selling a Put versus Buying Stock Outright

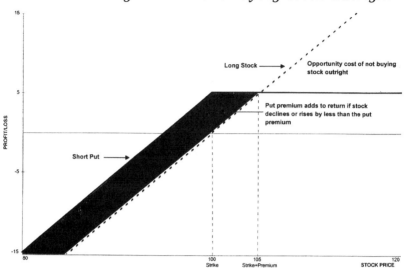

As an aside from portfolio applications, corporate stock repurchase programs have used put sales as a way to buy stock patiently. Most such transactions have relied on over-the-counter put transactions because of restrictions on the use of exchange-traded puts. The introduction of Equity FLEX options eliminates any advantages the over-the-counter market had and accentuates the advantages of exchange traded options.[10]

Options and Cash Management   The options literature is replete with examples of alternate ways to take risk-equivalent positions using very different amounts of cash. From a risk perspective and assuming European-style exercise, a short put is the equivalent of a covered call. A long call is the risk equivalent of a long stock position plus a long put. Buying a call and selling a put at the same strike price creates a synthetic long stock position. Setting aside the differences between European and American options and some margin and credit issues, the major difference between these paired risk equivalent positions is the cash commitment that an investor must make. The covered call writer who is long the stock and short a call is making a substantial cash commitment to a position which can have relatively modest market exposure. The investor who takes a risk-equivalent position by selling a put will deposit collateral as security and receive cash from the sale of the option. The fact that the sale of a put generates cash rather than absorbing it provides opportunities and requirements for cash management that are very

---

[10] See Angel, James, Gary Gastineau and Clifford Weber, "Using Exchange-Traded Equity-FLEX Put Options in Corporate Stock Repurchase Programs," *Journal of Applied Corporate Finance* (Spring 1997), pp.109-113.

different from the cash management position of the covered call writer. Any investor taking a short option position is required to post a performance bond in any of a variety of forms (an option guarantee letter, an escrow receipt, or direct deposit of collateral). Credit issues are rarely significant because the exchange-traded option counterparty, the Options Clearing Corporation, is rated AAA. Exhibit 4 illustrates the risk comparability of alternate ways of taking various positions.

Exhibit 4: Alternative Ways to Take a Position — Short Put versus Covered Call

(A) Short Put

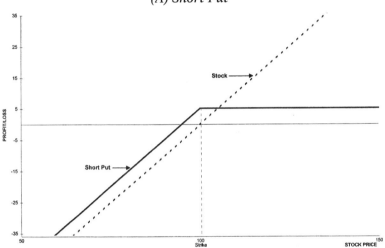

(B) Covered Call (Long Stock, Short Call)

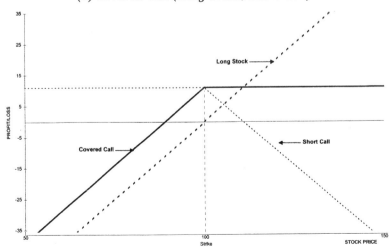

Exhibit 4 (Continued)
(C) Long Call

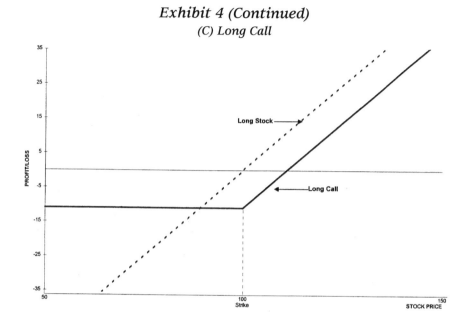

(D) Long Synthetic Call (Long Stock, Long Put)

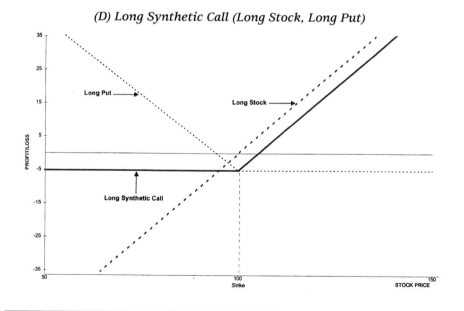

Exhibit 4 (Continued):
Long Stock versus Long Synthetic Stock
(E) Long Stock

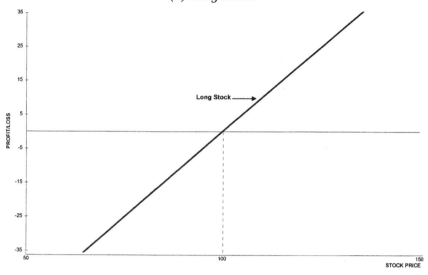

(F) Long Synthetic Stock (Long Call, Short Put)

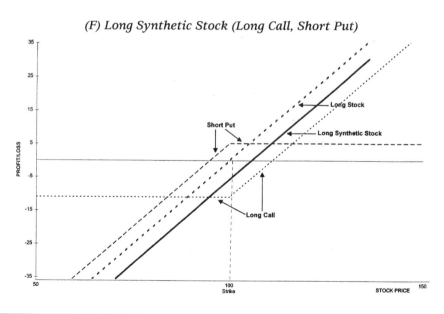

Assuming there are no significant valuation discrepancies among the options involved, alternative equivalent positions can play a useful role in adjusting the composition of a portfolio to actual or expected cash flows. For some portfolios, the ability to take a sizable position with little cash can help anticipate cash flow, control leverage, or generate cash for an enhanced money-market return strategy. Index funds combining enhanced money market return strategies with stock index futures have become almost commonplace.[11] The availability of Equity FLEX options lets active equity managers combine their stock selection skills with the skill of managers who run enhanced money market portfolios.

Creating an Efficient Synthetic Long Position For a wide variety of reasons, an investor may wish to take a long position in a specific underlying stock, yet be faced with obstacles or costs which do not apply to certain other investors. As noted earlier, most non-U.S. investors are subject to a 15% to 30% withholding tax on any cash dividends distributed by a U.S.-based company. One way to avoid liability for this tax is to take a synthetic stock position by buying a call and selling a put struck at the same price. For analytical purposes, the cash not used in the synthetic position is invested in money market instruments. The cash flows of this synthetic stock position are slightly different from the cash flows associated with outright ownership of the stock, even after the money market adjustment. The investor analyzes the implicit financing costs and returns associated with the alternate positions by calculating an implied repo rate (IRR) or return to the hedged portfolio (RHP) for the money market position associated with the synthetic. The choice of actual stock or the synthetic is dictated by a comparison of this implied repo rate with the investor's best cash-equivalent investment alternative. Even if the synthetic position is not quite as attractive as the traditional position on a pre-tax basis, it may still be advantageous to a non-U.S. investor because the withholding tax on the stock's dividends can be avoided. The advantage of the synthetic long to the non-U.S. investor is particularly interesting in light of the opportunity to create a corresponding synthetic short position.

Creating a Synthetic Short Position An investor who is only an occasional short seller may find buying puts and selling calls more attractive than an outright short sale. The ability to set up a synthetic short stock position with European options offers complete protection against a buy-in if the underlying stock becomes hard to borrow. While the value of buy-in protection may be reflected in the option premiums, avoiding the risk of having to cover the short prematurely may be worth any additional cost of using options — particularly if the investor is not active in the stock loan market. Investors who are active and experienced short-sellers may find it profitable to take the actual short position and the synthetic long position (the other side of the options necessary to create the short position in the alternate

[11] See, for example, Karen Damato, "Pimco Fund Beats S&P 500 With Bonds," *Wall Street Journal* (December 5, 1996).

option form. These investors are, in effect, selling "buy-in insurance" to a less comfortable short seller.

Volatility Analysis Most institutional investors use only a small fraction of the information that they acquire through their in-house research efforts and from street research. The integration of Equity FLEX options into the portfolio management process, however, makes more of this information useful to an investment manager. Most stock research focuses on the outlook for corporate earnings reports and on specific corporate and product developments. The emphasis is on the likely *direction* of stock price movement. Relatively few analysts and portfolio managers stress the historic and prospective volatility of common stocks and the impact of earnings reports and other events on *volatility* because it has not been easy for large portfolios to profit from being right on volatility. If investors can profit from informed judgments on likely future volatility, they are using more of the research information they have developed. They can add value by virtue of the fact that there is less competition in volatility estimation than in, for example, earnings estimation. If research provides a detailed expectation of a volatility pattern or of a definite pattern of price behavior, options can be useful in structuring a payout pattern tailored to the expectation.

Exhibit 5 illustrates one example of a structured payout. In this specific example, the investor has concluded that the most likely price for the stock at the time the component options expire is close to the peak in the pattern illustrated. The investor also believes that the chance of a large stock price decline is limited and, if there is any volatility risk, it is on the upside. These expectations suggest a payout structure that provides neutral results if the stock price runs away on the upside. Obviously, this pattern is only illustrative. We expect most institutional investors to use options primarily to reflect general volatility views rather than highly specific expectations for price patterns, but many possibilities are available. Opportunities include the simple sale of a call on a stock that an investor expects to be less volatile in the near term than its option premium implies, or purchase of a put to provide downside protection on a position which the manager feels has excellent long-term prospects and significant near term risk — with the risk not fully reflected in the pricing of the options.

Temporary Market Exposure Reduction and Tax Deferral Several option techniques can be used to maintain a position in an underlying stock during a period when the investor wishes to reduce exposure to that stock's price behavior. Selling calls and buying puts are the traditional option transactions used to reduce exposure to an underlying stock held in a portfolio. Occasionally these transactions are combined to create a collar or risk reversal as illustrated in Exhibit 6. Equity FLEX options are easy to use to create a zero-premium collar, a market risk control structure that has been popular in the OTC options market.

Exhibit 5: A Structured Payout with Options

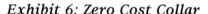

Exhibit 6: Zero Cost Collar

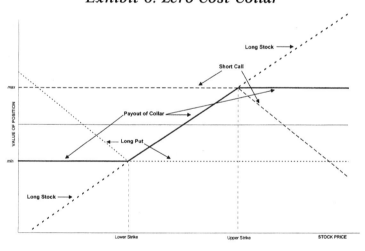

Collars and other options positions may be used to defer taxes and delay the recognition of gains for other purposes. For taxable accounts, a degree of care must be exercised in taking risk offsetting options positions because the tax treatment of these positions can be tricky. Certain option positions will interrupt an investor's holding period if the position is not yet long term, acting as the equivalent of a short sale. Other option positions have no effect on holding period or cost basis. Consultation with professional tax counsel is always a good idea if a position has significant tax exposure.

Risk Arbitrage Exchange-traded options are used frequently by risk arbitrageurs as a way to divide and reallocate the risk of a position and to permit the risk arbitrageur to accept certain risks and avoid others. Comparisons of option premiums on contracts with expiration dates before and after expiration of a tender offer, a shareholder vote, or a board meeting are common methods of measuring the market's expectation for the outcome of these events. With Equity FLEX options, investors or arbitrageurs with somewhat different perspectives on an event or corporate development can allocate the risk among themselves in a way that reflects each entity's expectations and risk preferences. The limitations on expiration dates with standardized options and the credit issues which often cloud OTC option contract discussions can be eliminated and relatively "pure" risks can be taken and avoided with Equity FLEX contracts.

Special Return Structures A variety of special return structures are possible with Equity FLEX options that were cumbersome at best with standardized options and difficult to implement with low position limits in place. Some structures can provide a type of position or portfolio loss insurance. Others can provide a relatively stable return under most circumstances. Some of these positions and portfolios have been feasible for some time, but the economics have not been attractive. With Equity FLEX options, a greater degree of flexibility and lower transaction costs improve the bottom line on most structures. These techniques can be either formulaic in the sense that a fixed trading or position adjustment rule is followed, subject to specified market parameters, or they can incorporate the judgment of a portfolio manager to modify the structure over the course of a market cycle. Exhibit 5 illustrates one such return structure.

Renewing Corporate Capital Losses In the United States, a corporation cannot deduct capital losses against ordinary income, but it can carry capital losses forward against the day when it generates capital gains. Corporate capital loss carry forwards are generally limited to five years, but regulated investment companies can carry losses forward for eight years. Corporations can carry foreign expropriation capital losses forward ten years. While the straddle rules limit opportunities to defer gains, there seems to be no objection to realizing a gain to use an expiring capital loss carry forward and deferring an offsetting loss to the next tax year. The new loss starts the capital loss aging process anew. From a portfolio perspective the opportunity will be most useful to a mutual fund or unit trust taxed as a regulated investment company. Here, as noted above, consultation with a tax advisor is appropriate.

Structured Products

In some ways a discussion of structured products is a natural extension of Equity FLEX options because some structured products will be built around Equity FLEX options. Just as structured products have been the vehicle through which OTC equity options have been embedded in notes to create equity-linked notes of incredible variety, Equity FLEX options will be the raw material for many future equity products structured to meet specific investor needs.

Exhibit 7 shows the payoff patterns for several types of equity linked notes. This exhibit is meant to be illustrative, not exhaustive. While many other structures are possible, the most common structured products are designed to provide a predetermined minimum return, most often zero, and varying degrees of participation in embedded underlying equity instruments determined by the risk appetite of the investor and/or the investor's expectations for volatility in the underlying stock basket, or index. Structured products usually involve an underlying minimum return structure — either because of investor preference or because they are designed to meet a specific legal, regulatory, or policy requirement. These requirements usually permit ownership of fixed income or convertible securities. Credit concerns relating to the issuers and providers of the equity option cover embedded in the note structure are extremely complex and worthy of study for the would-be issuer or user of these products. Many investment banks which create these products have produced large quantities of material which they are ordinarily happy to provide to potential customers and issuers.

Open-End Exchange-Traded Funds

While not strictly a derivative product, exchange-traded funds are generally associated with derivatives in part because of their innovative nature and the fact that they tend to be traded on an exchange alongside derivative instruments. These funds now trade on the American Stock Exchange in the United States and the Toronto Stock Exchange in Canada. One reason for discussing them in the context of this chapter is that they are often used as a group and in conjunction with a variety of futures and options applications in asset allocation strategies. They can also serve as the underlying for options contracts. In many respects, fund options seem likely to replace many broad-based index options because they can provide physical rather than cash settlement and settlement at the market close rather than at the opening. Exhibit 8 lists the exchange-traded funds available at the time this chapter was written; additional funds are likely to be created in the months and years ahead.

A brief description of the S&P 500 SPDR fund traded on the American Stock Exchange illustrates the general structure of exchange-traded funds. The specification sheet, shown as Exhibit 9, illustrates some of the features of the SPDRs, but the trading mechanism deserves more attention. The S&P 500 SPDRs, rely on two different mechanisms to eliminate purchase and sale impact on established investors' positions. For most orders, SPDR transactions are executed like stock transactions on the American Stock Exchange. The investor's purchase or sale does not increase or decrease the number of shares in the fund; consequently, it has no impact on ongoing shareholders. If a single transaction or accumulated transactions are largely on the buy side or the sell side, SPDRs are created or redeemed by deposits or withdrawals of portfolio stock baskets in multiples of 50,000 SPDR shares by certain securities dealers, including the AMEX specialist responsible for making a market in SPDRs.

Exhibit 7: Composition of an Equity-Linked Note

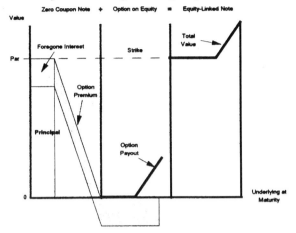

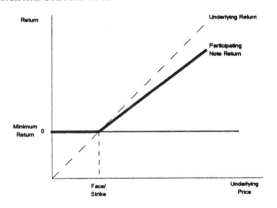

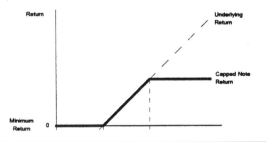

Exhibit 8: EXchange-TRAded Funds as of 6/30/97

Name	Launch Date	Fund Assets	Trading Volume (Jan-June 97)
AMERICAN STOCK EXCHANGE			
SPDRS:			
500 SPDR	January-93	$2,910,956,500	2,239,833
MidCap SPDR	April-95	$239,457,000	80,762
WEBS Index Series:			
Australia	March-96	$46,327,541	35,680
Austria	March-96	$4,192,904	3,868
Belgium	March-96	$35,841,344	22,250
Canada	March-96	$24,303,638	11,285
France	March-96	$15,782,368	12,655
Germany	March-96	$20,029,446	16,070
Hong Kong	March-96	$19,869,264	24,463
Italy	March-96	$29,998,628	27,695
Japan	March-96	$179,553,576	144,774
Malaysia	March-96	$18,625,047	19,079
Mexico	March-96	$10,304,254	14,960
Netherlands	March-96	$10,334,048	3,450
Singapore	March-96	$14,171,200	15,654
Spain	March-96	$9,527,185	6,155
Sweden	March-96	$7,221,770	3,367
Switzerland	March-96	$13,414,805	10,061
United Kingdom	March-96	$26,515,342	21,460
		$486,012,359	
TORONTO STOCK EXCHANGE			
Participation Units			
TSE 100 Index - HIPs	August-95	$543,006,082	200,000
TSE 35 Index - TIPs	March-90	$2,534,028,381	1,150,000

Dealers notify the SPDR trustee or distributor when they are planning a SPDR creation or redemption as of the day's close. These dealers act for their own account or for the account of a large customer. Rather than making stock transactions on behalf of the fund, the SPDR trustee simply accepts or delivers a portfolio of stocks reflecting the S&P 500 Index composition to complete a creation or redemption order. The commissions and the market impact of transactions related to creation and redemption do not disappear. These costs occur outside the fund, for the account of the creating or redeeming dealer, and do not affect ongoing shareholders. The trustee collects fees from the depositing or redeeming dealer to cover the modest expenses of handling these deposits or withdrawals.

Exhibit 9: Specification for S&P 500 SPDR

SP·DR®

Specifications
Standard & Poor's
Depositary Receipts®
Symbol: SPY

Description of SPDRs	SPDRs — Standard & Poor's Depositary Receipts — are Exchange-traded securities that represent ownership in the SPDR Trust, a long-term unit investment trust which has been established to accumulate and hold a portfolio of common stocks that is intended to track the price performance and dividend yield of the Standard & Poor's 500 Composite Stock Price Index. SPDRs are designed to provide a security whose market value approximates 1/10 the value of the underlying S&P 500 Index. Holders of SPDRs are entitled to receive proportionate quarterly distributions corresponding to the dividends which accrue on the S&P 500 stocks in the underlying portfolio, less accumulated Trust expenses.
Sponsor and Trustee	The sponsor of the SPDR Trust is PDR Services Corporation, a wholly owned subsidiary of the American Stock Exchange, Inc. The trustee for SPDRs is State Street Bank and Trust Company of Boston. The distributor for SPDRs is PDR Distributors, Inc., a registered broker-dealer and wholly owned subsidiary of Signature Financial Group, Inc.
Trading Unit	A round lot is 100 SPDRs. Odd lots (i.e., fewer than 100 SPDRs) trade as well.
Price Quotations	Quotations in dollars and fractions per SPDR; fractions of a dollar in minimum increments of 1/64. Example: a quote of 92 1/64 represents a price of $92.0156 (or $9,201.56 for a SPDR round lot).
Settlement of Trades	Three business days. All SPDRs are book-entry only held in The Depository Trust Company (DTC).
Dividend Equivalent	Dividend equivalent amounts — a pro rata amount (less accumulated Trust expenses) of regular cash dividends for the stocks in the Trust which have gone ex-dividend — are paid quarterly on the last business day in April, July, October and January. SPDRs' ex-dividend date is the third Friday in March, June, September and December. Quarterly accrual periods begin on the ex-dividend date and extend to the next ex-dividend date. DTC's Dividend Reinvestment Service will be made available to DTC participant brokers for quarterly reinvestment of cash distributions received by SPDR holders.
Creations and Redemptions	SPDRs can be created in "creation unit" block sizes of 50,000 SPDRs by the deposit into the SPDR Trust of a specified portfolio of stock closely approximating the composition of the S&P 500 Index and a specified cash amount. Conversely, a creation unit of 50,000 SPDRs can be redeemed for a specific portfolio of stocks and specified cash amount. The shares of component stocks in a creation unit are determined by the trustee prior to the opening of trading each business day. The required cash amount is determined on the same day following the close of trading.
Net Asset Value	The net asset value (NAV) per SPDR is computed each business day at the close of trading, normally 4 p.m. New York time. NAV represents the aggregate closing market value of the underlying portfolio of S&P 500 securities in the SPDR Trust plus any accrued dividends, minus accumulated Trust expenses on a per SPDR basis.
Initial Customer Margin	Regulation T margin requirements for exchange-traded securities apply. Long positions require 50 percent margin; short positions require 150 percent margin.
Symbols	**SPY** Trading Symbol **SXN** Net Asset Value **SXD** Quarter-to-Date Accrued Dividend Equivalent Amounts **SXP** Dividend Amount Payment*
Product Description	Amex Rule 1000 requires members to provide all purchasers of SPDRs in the secondary market a written Product Description for SPDRs in a form provided by the Exchange not later than the time a confirmation of the first transaction in SPDRs is delivered to such purchaser. The Product Description must also accompany SPDR sales material sent out by members. See Amex Rule 1000, Commentary .01.
Trading Hours	9:30 a.m. to 4:15 p.m. New York time.
CUSIP Number	78462F103

*Displayed beginning on the ex-dividend date. "Standard & Poor's®," "S&P®," "Standard & Poor's 500®," "Standard & Poor's Depositary Receipts®" and "SPDRs®" are trademarks of The McGraw-Hill Companies, Inc., and have been licensed for use by PDR Services Corporation and the American Stock Exchange, Inc. SPDRs are not sponsored, endorsed, sold or promoted by Standard & Poor's ("S&P"), a division of The McGraw-Hill Companies, Inc., and S&P makes no representation regarding the advisability of investing in SPDRs.

An investor buying or selling SPDRs in the secondary market on the American Stock Exchange will pay a negotiable commission to a stockbroker. There is also a possible market impact cost in AMEX SPDRs transactions, but it is surprisingly small relative to most stock transactions. SPDRs are traded with a minimum tick of $1/64$ of a point, and the bid-asked spread in 1996 was $1/16$ or less on more than 60% of the quotes and $1/8$ or less on about 95% of the quotes. A typical SPDR market order would experience an impact cost of half the spread.

Buying and Selling Fund Shares There is more to SPDRs transactions than the comparison of commissions and market impact. The difference in entry and exit techniques gives a SPDR investor more flexibility in timing orders. The SPDR investor can enter an order to avoid — or even benefit from — the market impact of other investors' orders. With simple limit orders an investor might buy SPDR shares slightly below their intraday net asset value or sell them slightly above intraday net asset value during the course of most trading days.

Like many financial instrument prices, SPDR prices are linked to net asset value by an arbitrage mechanism. If the price is more than a few cents above or below net asset value, a dealer will sell the overpriced SPDRs or buy the underpriced SPDRs, buy or sell the underlying stock portfolio, and do a creation or redemption transaction with the trustee. The pricing mechanism is virtually identical to the mechanism for stock index arbitrage between the stock market and S&P 500 futures contracts.

SPDRs offer a contrast to conventional funds where the investor can purchase or sell only at the day's closing price — whatever that eventually turns out to be. An investor using SPDRs can buy or sell these instruments at their prevailing price at any time over the course of the trading day. The investor who places an order with a conventional fund at noon has no assurance that the price at 4:00 p.m. will be near the price at noon. The price might be significantly higher or lower. The cost or proceeds from a transaction might be better or worse, but the investor has no choice about the price.

In contrast to most funds' single time and uncertain execution price, market orders to buy or sell SPDRs can be executed in a matter of seconds throughout the trading day. The investor may place an order and receive an execution report during a single telephone conversation with a broker. If a SPDR investor does not want to chance the short-term vagaries of the market, a whole host of order types is available. Any type of order that can be used to purchase or sell a stock can be used to purchase or sell a SPDR.

The combination of the ability to buy or sell at an intraday price and to use any type of stock order gives SPDR investors a wide range of opportunities to reduce their transaction costs and/or to implement any price sensitive or market timing strategy. There is no certainty that investors will reduce transaction costs or that their strategies will be successful, but they do have a chance to try to improve their results. While other exchange-traded funds have slight differences in structure and in their creation and trading mechanism compared to SPDRs, the general characteristics are similar. Because of their prices and trading features, most funds of this type are widely used as portfolio components in asset allocation strategies and basket components of other portfolios.

Many users of exchange-traded funds use them as a stand alone substitute for a conventional mutual fund, but they are also components of index arbitrage complexes. For example, the SPDRs and the WEBS in the United States and the TIPs in Toronto all serve as active components of arbitrage groups. The presence of arbitrage opportunities improves pricing efficiency and lowers transaction costs for all of the associated products.

The most interesting area for the development of funds in the overall derivatives product structure probably lies in the development of fund options. The only existing fund option on the Toronto TIPs is not an active trader — in large part because the contract size is too small and the fund option position limits are substantially smaller than the limits on comparable index options. Increasing the contract size by a factor of 10 and increasing the position limits to the same size as those available on index options, would create interesting competition between the cash-settled and physically-settled options in Toronto. Fund options hold considerable promise to support a variety of structured products in the years ahead.

Chapter 15

The Use of OTC Derivatives in Equity Investment Strategies

Bruce Collins, Ph.D.
Associate Professor of Finance
Western Connecticut State University

INTRODUCTION

The purpose of this chapter is to review the uses of OTC equity derivatives. Particular attention is given to how OTC derivatives can benefit traditional equity investment strategies. The discussion is deliberately kept at a basic level and emphasizes general practical applications of OTC equity derivatives, avoiding a rigorous discussion of pricing derivatives.

DEVELOPMENT OF OTC EQUITY DERIVATIVES

The development of financial futures and stock options in the 1970s represents one of the most important financial innovations in the modern financial era. The creation of currency futures and interest rate futures at the Chicago Mercantile Exchange (CME) and the Chicago Board of Trade (CBT) and options on individual stocks at the Chicago Board Options Exchange (CBOE) provided market agents with new methods for managing risk. This was followed by the development of stock index futures and options in the 1980s. By the mid-1980s, a multitude of exchange-traded derivative securities were available to portfolio managers for the purpose of implementing various risk-reduction or hedging strategies.

 The modern over-the-counter (OTC) derivatives market has its roots in the exchange-based markets and in the development of currency and interest rate swaps in 1981. OTC equity derivatives emerged as a major force only after the development of listed options and futures markets and the creation of currency and interest rate swaps. The modern OTC equity derivatives market was born in 1987 with the creation of an OTC market for put options on the Nikkei 225 Index.[1] In 1990, the techniques developed in the Nikkei put market expanded to a

---

[1] Companies in Japan issued debt instruments with an embedded put option linked to the performance of the Nikkei 225 Index. Banks subsequently separated the put option and sold it in the secondary market primarily in London.

multitude of markets causing the market for OTC equity derivatives to grow rapidly. However, the OTC derivatives market did not experience rapid growth until extraordinary advancements in computer technology provided market makers with the means to analytically manage and price risk. This development combined with experience in the listed market and the swap market stimulated the growth of OTC equity derivatives. Additional stimulus was derived from the globalization of capital markets, which caused the demand for global market diversification to move quicker than financial deregulation. OTC derivative structures provided the wherewithal to circumvent the problems imposed by strict financial regulation.

Historically, investors have allocated their wealth among three basic asset classes — equity, bonds, and cash. The proportion allocated to each asset class was part of a strategic asset allocation decision. Equity was regarded as the riskiest asset class and managing risk was accomplished by making marginal shifts among stocks, bonds, and cash. Since the development of derivatives markets, however, investors can use a combination of listed and OTC derivatives to manage the risk of their investment strategies without the need to conduct all or even any transactions in the cash market.[2] The OTC equity derivatives market has extended the benefits of the listed market by providing investors access to more risk/reward combinations. The bottom line for investors is that equity derivatives provide a direct and cost effective means to manage risk.

In the past, the method that pension funds used to implement and manage an investment strategy was a function of management style and was carried out in the cash market. Pension funds managed risk by diversifying among management styles. The first risk management tools available to investors were limited to the listed futures and options market. Although providing a valuable addition to an investor's risk management toolkit, listed derivatives were limited in application due to their standardized features, limited size, and liquidity constraints. The OTC derivatives market, in contrast, gives investors access to longer-term products that better match their investment horizon and provides flexible structures to meet their exact risk/reward requirements. The number of unique equity derivative structures is essentially unlimited.

The development of the OTC market has been affected by other factors. One factor is the lack of trading size available to investors in the listed market due to both position limits and liquidity constraints. Investors with sizable portfolios, such as a pension fund with $1 billion dollars or more in assets, were not able to meaningfully impact their overall position with listed derivatives.[3] Transactions in the OTC market can be of any size and are often in excess of $100 million. The trend toward global investing has also facilitated the growth of the OTC equity

---

[2] The term "Cash" is often used to refer to transactions in the financial assets underlying a derivatives contract. For equity derivatives, this would involve the purchase or sale of the physical stocks.

[3] Listed derivatives are subject to both position limits and liquidity constraints, which limit the usefulness of listed products for large institutional investors. The most successful stock index futures contract has an average daily dollar volume of $38 billion dollars, while the combined value of equity assets on the balance sheets of U.S. pension funds and mutual funds is over $3 trillion.

derivatives market because OTC structures can be created to give investors access to foreign markets without assuming currency risk or dealing with the regulatory and administrative procedures associated with a particular market. The market's growth was further enhanced by the market maker's ability to warehouse products through sophisticated risk management techniques. Market makers, by holding large portfolios of the underlying securities, have transferred costs and risk to the margin, which allows investors to gain access to markets at a lower cost than direct investment. The OTC derivatives markets have established a network of channels among global financial markets. Through the participation of commercial and investment banks, an efficient mechanism for transferring risk was established. The competition among market makers has resulted in a large market for OTC equity derivatives. In a global financial marketplace characterized by high levels of competition, equity derivative products are valuable tools for investors to create finely tuned investment portfolios and to optimize their tactical and strategic asset mixes.

EQUITY DERIVATIVES MARKET

Equity derivatives are divided into two main categories: listed equity derivatives and OTC equity derivatives. Although the main focus of this chapter is the OTC market, it is instructive to compare it with the listed market. The listed market primarily consists of options, warrants, and futures contracts.[4] The primary listed options market consists of exchange-traded options and warrant contracts with standardized strike prices, expirations, and payout terms traded on individual stocks, equity indexes, and futures contracts on equity indexes. A Flexible Exchange Option™ (FLEX) was introduced by the CBOE in 1993 that provides the customization feature of the OTC market, but with the guarantee of the exchange.[5] The listed futures market consists of exchange-traded equity index futures with standardized expiration and settlement terms.

The listed market for equity options on individual stocks began trading in 1973 and the equity index option market came into being in 1983. Stock index futures began trading in 1982 and are now traded domestically on 11 indexes across four exchanges. The indexes have expanded from the broad market indexes to style

---

[4] There are other derivative product listings such as equity-linked notes listed on the CBOE and index-linked notes listed on the American Stock Exchange. However, the volume is low and the products are retail oriented. In contrast, S&P 500 Depositary Receipts (SPDRs) trade at substantially higher volume compared with listed equity-linked notes, but not compared with index futures or index options. In addition, SPDRs are subject to Regulation T, which requires a 50% margin payment for long positions.

[5] According to the CBOE, the FLEX option was designed to broaden institutional investor access to customized derivative products. FLEX options initially required $10 million of notional principal and provided similar features to OTC products without the trading counterparty credit risk. The contract terms can be customized along four dimensions: underlying asset, strike price, expiration, and settlement style. The value of FLEX options is that the CBOE provides a secondary market to offset or alter positions and an independent daily marking of prices.

and sector indexes.[6] Nonetheless, the daily trading value of S&P 500 futures contracts is still the largest of any listed stock index futures contract.[7] In addition, equity index futures contracts are traded on exchanges in several other countries.[8]

OTC equity derivatives are not traded on an exchange and thus exact market size and volume are difficult to determine. Nonetheless, trade size is considerable.[9] OTC equity derivatives have an advantage over listed derivatives because they provide complete flexibility and can be tailored to fit an investment strategy rather than having to fit an investment strategy to satisfy the constraints of listed options or futures. One of the keys to the success of OTC equity derivatives is the flexibility of its structure. A fundamental difference between listed and OTC derivatives is that listed options and futures contracts are guaranteed by the exchange while in the OTC market the derivative is guaranteed by the issuer. Thus, the investor is subject to credit or counterparty risk.[10]

The OTC equity derivatives market can be divided into three main groups: OTC options and warrants, equity-linked debt investments, and equity swaps. OTC equity options are customized option contracts that can be applied to any equity index, basket of stocks, or an individual stock. OTC options are privately negotiated contractual agreements between an investor and an issuing dealer. The structure of the option is completely flexible in terms of strike price, expiration, and payout features. OTC warrants are long-term options on equity indexes, basket of stocks, or an individual stock and have the same flexible structure capability as OTC options.

An example of how OTC options can differ from listed options is exemplified by an Asian option. Listed options are either European or American in structure relating to the timing of exercise. Asian options are options with a payout that is dependent on the average price of the underlying spot over the life of the option. Due to the averaging process involved, the volatility of the spot price is reduced. Thus, Asian options are cheaper than similar European or American options.

Equity-linked debt investments are debt instruments with principal or coupon payments linked to the performance of an established equity index, a basket of stocks, or a single stock. Equity swaps are similar in structure to interest

---

[6] The CME lists stock index futures on a value index, a growth index, a small capitalization index, and a technology sector index.

[7] The average daily trading volume for the first half of 1997 was around 80,000 contracts or over $30 billion in volume.

[8] As of July 1997 there were 74 contracts listed across 31 countries and trading on 34 exchanges throughout the world. All of these currently extant contracts are listed in *The Salomon Brothers Global Stock Index Futures Handbook* (Salomon Brothers, 1997).

[9] It is not uncommon for deal sizes to exceed $100 million. The size of the OTC equity market is over $1 trillion in notional principal, but is a fraction of the total OTC market. Interest rate swaps still dominate the market in terms of volume. The listed equity market is a larger share of the total listed derivatives market than OTC equity products are a proportion of the total OTC market. Nonetheless, the market is growing more rapidly than the market as a whole.

[10] The CBOE's FLEX options are the exchanges attempt to address the problem of credit risk and liquidity risk associated with OTC structures while providing the same flexibility. The limitation of FLEX option is the underlying is limited to a few indexes.

rate or currency swaps. They are contractual agreements between two counterparties providing for the periodic exchange of a schedule of cash flows over a specified time period where at least one of the two payments is linked to the performance of an equity index, a basket of stocks, or a single stock.

PRODUCT FUNDAMENTALS AND APPLICATIONS

The three basic groups of OTC equity derivatives offer an array of product structures that can assist investors in developing and implementing investment strategies that respond to a changing financial world. The rapidly changing investment climate has fundamentally altered investor attitudes toward the use of derivative products. It is no longer a question of what can be gained from the use of OTC derivatives, but how much can be lost by avoiding this marketplace. OTC derivatives can assist the investor with cost minimization, diversification, hedging, asset allocation, and risk management.

In this section, we examine the product fundamentals across each category of OTC equity derivatives in more detail and illustrate how investors can more effectively implement equity investment strategies through the use of equity derivative products. Exhibit 1 summarizes various OTC equity derivative structures, their use, and benefits. A broad spectrum of equity investment activities can benefit from these three basic categories of OTC equity derivative structures.

Exhibit 1: OTC Equity Derivative Applications

Derivative Structure	Application	Benefit

OTC options	Risk management
	Return enhancement
	Equity investment
	    Single stock
	    Stock portfolio
	Sector rotation
	Traditional option strategies
	Currency hedged investment
		Customization
		Cost reduction
		Leverage
		Accessibility

Equity swap	Asset allocation Diversification Accessing foreign markets Index fund alternative Currency hedged investment	Cost reduction Leverage Customization Simplicity of deal

Equity-linked debt	Risk management
	Accessing foreign markets
	Equity investment
	    Single stock
	    Stock portfolio
		Customization
		Leverage
		Debt instrument

Exhibit 2: OTC Equity Derivatives
Institutional Investor Application Example

Investor	Product	Application	Structure	Benefits
Pension fund	Equity swap	Asset allocation	Pay long bond Receive S&P 500 (total returns)	•Avoids cash market costs •Superior return
Pension fund	Equity-linked debt	Accessing foreign market	3-year ELD linked to CAC-40 Index	•Principal protected •Diversified •Avoids tax (withholding)
Insurance co.	Equity-linked debt	Equity exposure	2-year ELD linked to Russell 2000	•Avoids risk-based capital rules
Money manager	OTC option	Hedging	Buy collar on stock portfolio with December 31 expiration	•Customization •Create option where no listed option exists •Protects portfolio through years end

Exhibit 2 provides some examples of how an institutional investor can use specific products and structures to implement an equity investment strategy and how they might benefit. The concern of most investors is to perform better than an appropriate benchmark. Saving 50 basis points in cost or enhancing returns by that amount through taking advantage of derivative markets can go a long way to facilitate equity investment performance.

Derivative securities have a variety of applications for investment management. Among the considerations for equity portfolio management, for example, are ways to take advantage of promising returns through reallocation of funds within the portfolio. This might include sector rotation, international diversification, style rotation or return enhancement. These strategies focus in some way on stock selection. Another example is diversification into the global equities market. This investment can be considered the result of an asset allocation decision through investment in a new asset class referred to as a "foreign equity security." On the other hand, the decision may be regarded as expanding the existing equity asset class. Nonetheless, these types of decisions address the question of how to structure the investment portfolio in order to maximize risk-adjusted returns.

OTC equity derivatives have numerous applications to support this decision-making process in ways that cannot easily be achieved in the cash market. A second consideration is concerned with risk management. Although risk cannot be separated from return, it can be decomposed into its market and non-market components. OTC derivatives can help effectively hedge market risk or other components of risk to meet the objectives of the portfolio manager. Here again, OTC equity derivatives can play a constructive and perhaps vital role for overall investment management.

EQUITY INVESTMENT AND RISK MANAGEMENT ISSUES

The key to the development of any new financial product or security is its applications. The demand for a financial product is derived from its applicability in solving a financial problem. In this section, we focus on the landscape of the equity investment world in order to make the connection between OTC equity derivative products and equity investments. There are two interrelated issues that all investment managers must address: risk and return. Applications of OTC derivatives can emphasize return enhancement or risk management issues or both. For example, a zero-cost collar structure in the OTC market can hedge market risk by selling off a piece of the investment's upside potential. A barrier option can isolate the precise conditions that the investor believes are most likely to occur without the need to buy all possible outcomes. In both cases, the manager is focusing on risk management. On the other hand, an OTC structure such as an equity swap may be designed to take advantage of higher expected returns in a foreign market. In either application, one cannot separate return from risk, but we can separate the choice of an asset within an asset class from managing the market risk associated with the asset class itself. Thus, we can view equity investment as part of a strategic asset allocation strategy that utilizes OTC structures when necessary to manage a fund's exposure to equities.

Equity investing can be implemented through active or passive management styles. Active investment management pre-dates the 1960s efficient markets hypothesis and is based on the premise that markets have anomalies that can be profitably exploited. Managers with superior skills and methodology can "add value" to a passive strategy of comparable risk. Active equity management comes in many styles and flavors except, perhaps, plain vanilla. Active strategies range from traditional value-based and growth-based strategies to highly quantitative and technologically intensive strategies. OTC derivative structures offer active managers of all persuasions a means of cost-effective risk management. Furthermore, the OTC market may provide an alternative means of implementing active strategies. Regardless of the orientation or the style of management, OTC derivatives expand the universe of risk management tools and investment vehicle choices for active managers beyond the listed market or the cash market.

Passive equity management, on the other hand, embraces the efficient markets hypothesis. Consequently, passive strategies are designed to mimic the performance of an asset class. One vehicle to accomplish this objective is an index fund. An index fund is an investment strategy designed to exactly replicate the risk/return characteristics of an asset class benchmark. In practice, equity index funds are investments in a portfolio of stocks designed to track an equity benchmark or stock index. The most common equity index fund is benchmarked against the S&P 500 stock index. Traditional equity index funds implicitly subscribe to the single-period capital asset pricing model by investing in the market portfolio. Contemporary index fund management has gone beyond traditional index funds to include benchmarks representing non-market factors such as value, growth, or capitalization. Narrowly defined indexes or style indexes based on value, growth, or capitalization apply standard index fund investment methodologies to establish a replication portfolio designed to track the corresponding cash index. Contrary to traditional indexing, which makes no attempt to time the market or identify undervalued securities, style index funds are designed to do so at the market level, but not the factor level. In other words, the style index fund is created to track the benchmark, which may perform better than the market as a whole. Style indexing provides a link between active and passive approaches to investment management. In either case, the index fund is designed to exactly track the benchmark, but not necessarily track the market.

The listed and OTC derivatives markets provide portfolio managers with a set of tools to improve index fund management. Stock index futures can be used to create a synthetic index fund at a lower cost than in the cash market.[11] For other indexes, however, equity-linked debt (ELD) structures or equity swap structures may be a preferred investment vehicle. OTC derivative structures add a valuable dimension to the equity investment process by offering flexibility to the way a manager chooses to implement an investment strategy.

OTC Options and Warrants

The basic type of first generation OTC options either extended the standardized structure of an existing listed option or created an option on stocks, stock baskets, or stock indexes without listed options or futures. Thus, OTC options were first used to modify one or more of the features of listed options: the strike price, maturity, size, exercise type (American or European), and delivery mechanism. The terms were tailored to the specific needs of the investor. For example, the strike price can be any level, the maturity date at any time, the contract of any size, the exercise type American or European, to include any stock, stock portfolio, equity index or foreign equity index, and to be settled as physical, in cash or a hybrid.

The differences between listed and OTC derivatives prior to the arrival of the FLEX option are summarized in Exhibit 3. The flexibility of OTC option structures allows the manager to choose the features that meet their investment requirement. Although the FLEX option products provide similar advantages of OTC options, they are limited to a few standard indexes and a group of large capitalization stocks. Furthermore, there are some restrictions on settlement and FLEX products are subject to the customer margin rules of the CBOE and Regulation T of the Federal Reserve Board. Nonetheless, the FLEX group of products has moved the listed market closer to the OTC market.

---

[11] For a review of the many applications of stocks index futures, see *The Salomon Brothers Introductory Guide to Stock Index Futures* (Salomon Brothers, 1997).

Exhibit 3: OTC versus Listed Derivatives

	Listed	OTC

Features	Standardized contracts
	• strikes
	• maturities
	• contract size
	• limited stocks and indexes
	  with listed options
	
	• exercise type
	• delivery
	• payouts(put or call)
		Terms are flexible and negotiable
		• strikes at any level
		• any maturity date
		• varying contract sizes
		• underlying security can be any
		  single stock, portfolio or index
		  domestic or foreign
		• American, European or Asian
		• physical, cash or hybrid
		• payouts are flexible may be complex

Trading	Exchange-traded Highly liquid	Private placement agreement Limited liquidity
Guarantee	Options Clearing Corp.	Option writer

OTC Option Applications

In this section, we present a series of OTC derivative solutions to common equity investment problems. We first present a situation and then follow it with the listed solution, a comment on the listed solution, and the OTC solution with brief commentary.

Hedging Application: Hedging a Stock Portfolio

Situation A manager's portfolio has outperformed the benchmark considerably year-to-date, say in the first 9 months of the year. The manager believes that there is a significant risk of a market reversal and would like to lock in gains today through the end of the calendar year, but also acknowledges that a year-end rally is possible.

Conventional Solution Purchase an index put option using OEX or S&P 500 options. Alternatively, purchase a CBOE FLEX option on the OEX or S&P 500.

Comments on the Conventional Solution Before the arrival of FLEX options in 1993, the investor may not have been able to purchase a listed index option with the desired strike price or with an expiration on the last day of the year. Thus, the cost of a hedge increased and the level of protection was less than desired. The investment was also subject to market volatility between the expiration of the listed contract and the end of the year. Moreover, the manager's hedging strategy may be subject to tracking error that would depend on the correlation between the manager's portfolio and underlying index. FLEX options are an alternative investment vehicle because they are designed to provide institutional access to the customized derivatives market while eliminating the counterparty credit risk associated with OTC products. However, the FLEX option solution is still limited to a few specific indexes and therefore may not be adequate to address the hedging needs of all investors.

OTC Solution Purchase a put option on the exact portfolio with the desired strike price and a maturity date set on December 31. This solution allows complete flexibility in setting the cost of the hedge and eliminates tracking error until the end of the year. The manager avoids the regulatory complications and other limitations associated with FLEX options. In addition, the OTC solution could include a knockout feature that would provide a way out of the position without the need to make a secondary market transaction.

Next, we look at a few additional traditional investment strategies that can utilize OTC options. The strategies are familiar ones, but the solutions are customized to meet the specific needs of the investor.

Hedging Application: Hedging Selected Stocks in Core Holdings

Situation A pension fund's research team has identified 25 stocks within the fund's core portfolio that have high fundamental valuation. The team believes these stocks are due for a correction and recommends hedging the group. Moreover, the pension fund wants to maintain its voting rights in the shares and wants to minimize the cost of the hedge.

Conventional Solution Purchase listed put options on each of the 25 stocks. Alternatively, purchase an index put option with the lowest tracking error to the basket of 25 stocks held in the proper proportions. Writing OTM call options can finance the put options.

Comments on the Conventional Solution The listed solution is subject to the same problems discussed in the previous hedging example. The problem of tracking error can be significant using the index put solution, and the other regulatory considerations associated with listed options also apply.

OTC Solution Purchase a put option on the exact 25 stock portfolio, financed in part with written call options on the same basket of stocks. When the puts are fully financed, it is called a *zero-cost collar*. The OTC solution also provides complete flexibility in determining the exact features of the options. The combined position can be obtained with a single transaction and without the risk of exercise.

Overwrite Application

Situation A manager is long a portfolio of drug stocks and phone companies and is neutral to slightly bullish on both sectors. The manager wants to earn incremental returns and gain some downside protection.

Conventional Solution Write calls on individual stocks with listed options or write index call options against the portfolio. More recently, a number of listed options on industry groups have emerged.[12] The manager could write PHLX Phone Sector call options combined with AMEX Pharmaceuticals call options.

Comments on the Conventional Solution Writing individual call options changes the risk profile of the actual position versus the desired position because not all stocks may have listed options. In the case of index calls, the manager assumes the risk that the overall market may rally while one of the two sectors declines. Using the sector options reduces the problem of tracking error, but is subject to liquidity constraints, problems of size, and the restrictions of standardization.

OTC Option Solution Write a call on the exact portfolio which eliminates the risks associated with the conventional solution while taking a position consistent with the investment outlook for the two sectors. Moreover, the investor can choose the strike price, expiration date, delivery mechanism, and option style to exactly meet their investment objectives.

Market Timing Application

Situation A manager would like to invest funds in regional banks, but would be prepared to do so only after a 5% pullback in this sector.

Conventional Solution Write 5% out-of-the-money(OTM) put options on individual stocks with listed options in the sector. The alternative is to write OTM put options listed on the PHLX Bank Sector or the CBOE's put options listed on the S&P Banking Sector.

Comments on the Conventional Solution The conventional solution is exposed to significant stock specific risk. The basket of stocks represented by the sectors may not contain the desired set of regional bank stocks. The problems of standardized options contracts and liquidity also apply in this case.

OTC Solution Sell put options on S&P's Regional Bank Stock Index struck at 5% OTM. If the index drops below 95% of its current value, the manager is effectively long the financial services sector at the desired level. Alternatively, the manager can select a basket of stocks that he wants to hold and can design an OTC structure that achieves the investment objective.

---

[12] The AMEX has an option series in Computer Technology and another in Telecommunications. The CBOE has a listed option on the Technology Sector and on the NASDAQ 100, which is dominated by technology stocks. There are also options on the Phone Sector, Oil, Biotech, and a host of others that are listed on the AMEX, the CBOE, and the PHLX.

Accessing the Market

Situation A manager is bullish on a set of emerging markets and wants to incorporate a basket of emerging stocks into the strategic asset allocation mix. However, the manager wants to avoid the short-term volatility associated with owning the stocks.

Conventional Solution As of this writing, there is no conventional solution. That is, there are no listed index options on this group of stocks. The only alternative is to purchase the stocks directly, which the manager prefers to avoid or is restricted from doing so.

Comments on the Conventional Solution A missing investment opportunity results in a sub-optimal strategic asset allocation plan.

OTC Solution Investor purchases long-dated OTC call warrants on the desired basket of stocks and achieves the desired equity exposure. The warrants provide long-term commitment to an investment in emerging stocks, while avoiding the problems of direct investment in the stocks. In addition, the call warrants provide downside protection from the volatile movement of emerging market stocks. The funds that are not invested in warrants can be invested in an aggressive cash management vehicle to help pay for the warrants and achieve the highest return.

      The first generation of OTC options offered the type of solutions to investment situations illustrated in the examples above that listed options did not. In one example, the manager achieves total risk protection for a specific time horizon through a customized OTC option. We can see that the first generation of OTC options allows managers to fine tune their traditional equity investment strategies through customizing strike prices and maturities, and by choosing any underlying equity security or portfolio of securities. Managers are now able to improve the risk management through customized hedging strategies. Furthermore, managers can enhance returns through customized buy writes, invest in foreign stocks without the need to own them, profit from an industry downturn without the need to short stocks, or implement an intermediate asset allocation strategy through the purchase of warrants. In addition, some exotic features, a characterization of "second generation" OTC options, can provide additional benefits in pricing. Exotic options are OTC derivatives with specific rules that govern the payouts. In many cases, the payouts are path-dependent, which means the payout depends on the specific price behavior of the underlying security. OTC structures can embed a path-dependent characteristic into the option to deal with adverse contingencies. One example is a barrier put or knockout option that will automatically terminate the option without the need for a secondary market transaction. We will discuss "exotic" options in more detail in the next section. While some exchanges have jumped into the customized derivatives market, their products address these first generation features of OTC equity derivatives.

EXOTICS: SECOND GENERATION OTC OPTIONS

The second generation of OTC equity options include a set of products that have more complex payoff characteristics than standard American or European call and put options. These second-generation options are sometimes referred to as "exotic" options and are essentially options with specific rules that govern the pay-off. Some exotic option structures are on a stand-alone basis while others are part of a bond issue. Competitive market makers are now prepared to offer a broad range of derivative products that satisfy specific requirements of managers. The fastest growing portion of this market involves products with option-like charac-teristics on major stock indexes or stock portfolios. Mark Hudson describes the market as the over-the-counter stock index option market (OTCSIO).[13] It is derived from investor demand for long-dated European options and for options with more complex option structures. There is virtually no limit to the types of payouts.

In this section we review selective product structures that are applied to the implementation of traditional equity investment strategies. Exhibit 4 provides a partial listing of exotic options together with a brief description and an accompanying equity investment strategy application.[14] Before using exotic options, it is important for the manager to understand the impact that a specific exotic structure will have on the risk/reward profile of the current investment and the cost of implementing the strategy.[15]

The use of exotics are many and varied. What makes these options so attrac-tive is that they provide all the flexibility of first generation OTC options and the addi-tional feature of special payouts. It is important for managers to understand the nature of the exotic derivative in question, including the pricing, the risks, and the expected benefits. Moreover, an understanding of what could go wrong is necessary, including the potential costs, the tax implications, and the impact on the performance of the manager's portfolio. Consider, for example, a situation where the manager chooses a put option with a barrier structure that is designed to knock out at some level above the current price. If the barrier is hit suddenly and the put option is "knocked out," the risk is that the market reverses just as suddenly leaving the portfolio unprotected. Therefore, it is crucial that the manager understand that the savings of the barrier option compared to a standard put option has a risk component.

---

[13] See Mark Hudson, "How to Play OTC Index Options," *Euroweek* (April 1991).

[14] For an extensive discussion of exotic option products see, Israel Nelken (ed.), *The Handbook of Exotic Options* (Burr Ridge, IL: Irwin Professional Publishing, 1996). Another good source of OTC derivatives is: J. C. Francis, W. Toy, and G. Whittaker (eds.), *The Handbook of Equity Derivatives* (Burr Ridge, IL: Irwin Professional Publishing, 1995.) In addition, Mark Hudson, "The Value of Going Out," *Risk* (March 1991) provides a description of several of the most common structures. See Mark Rubinstein, "Exotic Options," (Working Paper Manuscript, March 1991) for a categorization of a set of exotic options into 11 classes and addresses pricing considerations of exotics. An overview of specific types of exotic options together with various approaches to pricing is provided in John Hull, *Options, Futures, and Other Derivative Securities*, (Englewood Cliffs, NJ: Prentice Hall, 1993).

[15] For example, in the latter case, a lookback option that guarantees the optimal exercise value of the option seems very attractive. However, due to the expense of such an option, the investor may not be better off than if she had purchased the underlying security.

Exhibit 4: Description of Some Basic Exotic Options

Option	Description	Use	Pricing Comment
Knockout call	One of a class of barrier options Option is canceled if the spot price violates barrier target price	Overwriting	Less expensive than standard call option
Knockout put	One of a class of barrier options Option is canceled if the spot price goes above barrier target	Hedging	Less expensive than standard call option
Compound option	Option on an option Call on a put gives owner the option to buy the put	Hedging Speculating	Less expensive than standard call option
Spread option	Payout depends on the difference in performance between two assets	Asset allocation	Large risk premium due to correlation
Lookback option	Option that gives the right to holder to buy or sell underlying at best price attained over the life of the option	Equity exposure to volatile sectors Market timing	More expensive than standard options
Quanto option	Quantity-adjusted option Payout depends on underlying price and size in proportional to price	Access to foreign markets with currency hedge	Pricing depends on correlation of exchange Rate and spot price
Chooser option	Holder must choose to set the option as a call or put at some specific time	Similar to straddle	Less expensive than straddle
Asian Option	Payout depends on average price of the underlying over a specified time period	Allows participation on average return Liability management	Less expensive than standard option

Second Generation OTC Options Applications

There are several traditional equity investment strategies that can be facilitated using second generation options. These include hedging, overwriting, asset allocation, sector rotation, and style management exposure. The use of exotic options should be carefully considered and should provide a degree of precision to satisfy the investment objective that can only be achieved with an OTC structure.

Hedging Application: Zero-Cost Collar

Situation A pension fund wants to hedge substantial gains in an underlying equity position, but prefers to avoid paying a put option premium and has substantial tracking error versus the indexes on listed index options.

Conventional Solution Purchase listed index option put paid for by writing index call options Alternatively, purchase a FLEX collar on the index with lowest tracking error versus the portfolio.

Comments on the Conventional Solution The investor is limited in the choice of an index to those listed and faces both liquidity constraints and payout constraints. Moreover, the conventional solution requires two separate transactions that increase transaction costs.

OTC Solution Enter into a zero-cost hedge on the target portfolio where the cost of the put is offset by the premiums from selling call options. There is a single transaction and all costs are incorporated into the structure. The put price is paid for by giving up the potential for gains should the portfolio continue to appreciate and the strategy proves to have been unwarranted. Managers can find a situation that caps the upside at a level that is comfortable and still keeps hedging costs low. The real advantage in the OTC product is the flexibility of the terms and the matching of the exact portfolio.

As indicated in Exhibit 5, the payout to a zero-cost hedge is similar to a bull spread. The put option is struck at a level of principal protection. The cost of paying for the put is the loss of upside potential. The important decision facing the manager is to ascertain the desired level of protection and the time length of the hedge. Once that is determined, a call option structure can be devised to maximize upside participation while still paying for the put. The call structure can be varied according to the amount of give-up with which the manager is comfortable.[16] Managers can also extend the protection horizon by trading-off short-term upside participation. For example, consider a manager who is bearish in the short term (over the next three months), but less bearish in the three months that follow. Moreover, the manager still wants to maintain protection over the entire horizon. A zero-cost hedge could be structured to purchase a 6-month put paid for by writ-

---

[16] The level of participation does not have to be 100%. It is a function of the issuer's financing rate.

ing 3-month call options. The cost of the put would involve giving up more upside participation in the short run. This zero-cost option solution is particularly attractive for managers who believe the portfolio is likely to decline.

Hedging Application: Barrier Put Option, Up and Out Knock-out

Alternative OTC Solution As an alternative to the zero-cost collar solution or the conventional put option solution, the manager could purchase a barrier put option which knocks out if the market continues to rise above the specified barrier. The cost of a barrier option is lower than a similar conventional option, which lowers the cost of hedging to the manager. This solution is for investors with some short-term concern of a market correction, but willing to abandon that concern if the market continues to rise. The level of the barrier can be adjusted to meet the desired amount the manager wants to pay for protection. In addition, the rebate can completely offset the cost of the put to achieve the same solution as the zero-cost collar.

Exhibit 6 compares the cost of a regular put option, a zero-cost collar and a knock-out put. The choice of using a zero-cost collar, or a regular put option comes down to the manager's conviction regarding the risk of a market correction and sensitivity to cost. The choice between a zero-cost collar and a knock-out put option depends upon the size of the rebate for the knock-out. The example in Exhibit 6 makes the strategies economically the same by using rebates that exactly offset the cost of the put option. These levels correspond to the strike price on a written call in the zero-cost collar strategy.

Exhibit 5: Zero-Cost Collar S&P 500 Portfolio

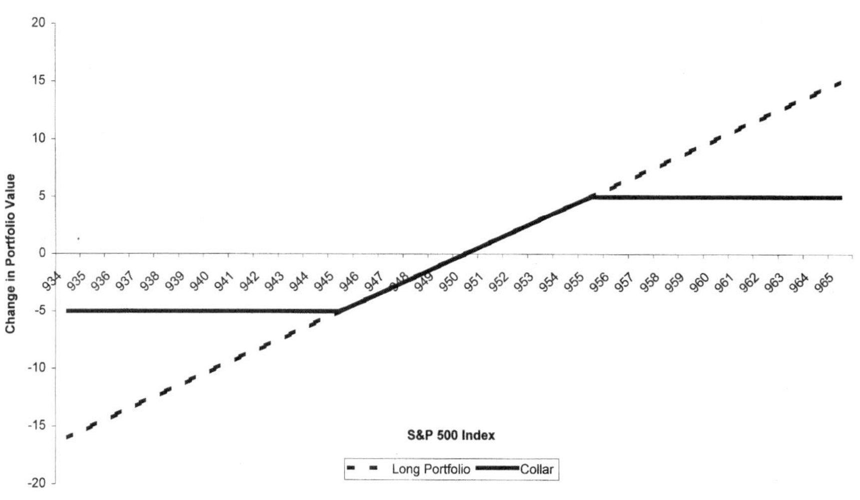

Exhibit 6: Hedging Strategy Cost Comparisons

Option	Premium	Upside
ATM put	5.32%	unlimited after paying for put
5% OTM put	3.215	unlimited after paying for put
10% OTM put	1.793	unlimited after paying for put
ATM zero-cost collar	-0-	limited to 4% by short call
5% OTM zero-cost collar	-0-	limited to 9.5% by short call
10% OTM zero-cost collar	-0-	limited to 15% by short call
ATM knock-out put 12% rebate	-0-	limited to 4% by barrier
ATM knock-out put 9% rebate	-0-	limited to 9% by barrier
ATM knock-out put 7.5% rebate	-0-	limited to 7.5% by barrier

Hedging Application: Contingency Put Option, Up and In Knock-In Option[17]

Alternative OTC Solution Purchase an OTC put option structured with a knock-in feature that is triggered when the barrier is crossed. The choice of the barrier is not restricted to the equity market. It could be related to another predictor of equity valuation such as interest rates. The equity market is inversely related to interest rates. A put option could be structured that knocks in when the rate on the long bond or some other interest rate is crossed. Alternatively, the put option could knock in when the rate of inflation rises above 3%. This put is less expensive than its conventional counterpart because there are outcomes where the conventional put has a positive payout and the contingent put does not.

Hedging Application: Compound Option

Alternative OTC Solution As an alternative to the conventional solution, the zero-cost collar solution or the barrier option, the manager could purchase a compound option. The manager who is concerned about the impact of a market correction on a portfolio, but is otherwise bullish, may purchase a call option on a put option written against the portfolio. This derivative structure gives the option to the manager of purchasing protection against the downside move. The call option is exercised if the portfolio declines. This strategy is for managers who want downside protection for as little cost as possible, but full participation on the upside.

Overwrite Application: Knockout Options

Situation A manager is long an equity portfolio and is neutral to bearish on the stock's prospects. The manager has established a upper and lower price range for

---

[17] For a more complete discussion of defensive strategies using barrier options and other derivatives see, Salomon Brothers, "Defensive Alternative," *Global Derivatives Review* (Salomon Brothers, April 1997).

realizing gains and cutting losses, respectively. The manager would like some incremental income and some downside protection.

Conventional Solution Implement an overwrite strategy by writing an index call option with a strike equal to the upper selling price.

Comments on the Conventional Solution The problem with this solution occurs when the lower price target is hit. The manager would liquidate the position by selling the portfolio and buying back the option. The risk is an increase in volatility will inflate the option premium further reducing returns.

OTC Solution Overwrite the stock with a knockout call option struck at the upper price target with a barrier price equal to the lower price target. The knockout feature will guarantee that the option will extinguish at the lower price target, thereby avoiding the need to buy back the option. However, because knockout options are priced below an otherwise equivalent standard option, the upfront premium will be less. The manager has to weigh the loss in premium against the risk of paying up to repurchase the standard call. The loss in premium is smaller, the lower the barrier price and the higher the strike price.

Exhibit 7 shows combinations of prices between 6-month regular call options and knockout call options assuming 100 is ATM, the dividend yield is 2%, interest rates are 5.25%, and volatility is 22%. We can see that the price converges when the barrier is 90 and the strike price is 115. For more reasonable numbers, however, for a 5% OTM call the price differential is $4.731 - 3.20 = 1.531$ in lost premium. This is clearly higher than the commissions of unwinding the trade, but will narrow as volatility increases the cost of reversing the trade.

Equity Exposure: Bull Spread Strategy

Situation A manager is currently out of one sector of the market waiting for a market correction to restore reasonable valuations. In the search for equity investments in a market that has reached record valuation levels, the investor is now mildly bullish on the sector. The manager is looking for a derivatives solution to the investment problem.

Exhibit 7: Price Comparisons of Regular Calls versus Knockout Calls for Overwrite Strategy

Strike	Barrier	Knockout Price	Regular Price
115	95	1.49	1.98
110	95	2.24	3.12
105	95	3.20	4.73
115	90	1.91	1.98
110	90	2.97	3.12
105	90	4.42	4.73

Conventional Solution A classic bull spread is appropriate where the manager buys the lower strike and sells the higher strike. This is comparable to a collar for managers who currently are long the equity portfolio.

Comments on the Conventional Solution The conventional solution has two disadvantages. First, the strategy requires two separate transactions, which increases costs. Second, reversing the strategy may be expensive. There are also margin considerations when using the listed market

OTC Solution Structure a bull spread in one transaction by purchasing a knock-out call option with a barrier equal to the upper strike of the short call option in the bull spread. It can be accomplished in a single transaction at a price competitive with the bull spread.

Asset Allocation Application: Spread Option
Situation A manager wants to shift $100 million in stock exposure to bond exposure.

Conventional Solution Short stock index futures and go long bond futures or buy an equity index put and a call option on bond futures.

Comments on the Conventional Solution The manager's portfolio may not be the underlying index creating tracking error risk. Bonds may actually underperform equities.

OTC Solution The manager purchases a 3-month relative performance option that will pay the return differential of bonds over the targeted equity portfolio. The manager maintains a long position in equities. The spread option gives the manager the right to the overperformance of bonds over equities even if both decline in value. If bonds underperform, the manager's returns are reduced by the cost of the option.

Spread options are also know as relative performance options. They also have applications for sector rotation because a spread option can provide the manager with the right to the overperformance of one sector relative to another sector. In addition, relative performance options can be applied to style management products by providing the manager with the right to the overperformance of one management style relative to another style. The latter application can be designed to utilize the S&P/Barra Growth Index and the S&P/Barra Value Index or customized indexes representing a particular management style. The problem with spread options is that pricing is dependent on the correlation between the two assets, which is less stable than volatility estimates. In practice, this has resulted in higher premiums than suggested by theoretical models. Issuers with superior correlation forecasting models have an advantage in pricing.

Asset Allocation Application: Quanto Options

Situation A manager wants to shift $100 million from cash to exposure in Germany equities and does not want to assume currency risk.

Conventional Solution Go long stock index futures on the DAX or alternatively purchase an index call on the DAX stock index and sell the German mark forward. In both cases, invest proceeds in domestic money market security to minimize currency risk.

Comments on the Conventional Solution This solution is reasonable, but requires separate transactions. If futures contracts are used, there are cash management issues and variation margin risk. Another consideration is whether to keep the proceeds in a domestic money market security and hedge the margin exposure to currency risk, or to transfer the funds to a foreign security and hedge the entire investment.

OTC Solution The manager purchases a quanto index call option with a fixed exchange rate at inception of the contract. The quanto will pay out the intrinsic value of the position completely hedged against currency risk.

Equity Exposure: High Volatility Portfolio Using Lookback Options

Situation An equity manager believes that a high volatility sector will be appreciably higher over the next six months, but may experience a meaningful decline before then. The manager does not want to take the chance of no correction.

Conventional Solution Purchase a sector index call option and write an OTM sector index put option to reduce the cost.

Comments on Conventional Solution If the sector goes higher without declining, then the call option preserves the upside on the investment in the sector. If the stock falls below the put strike, the investor buys the portfolio at a lower price than available today. The strategy involves two transactions and is subject to tracking error risk, as well as the other risks associated with listed options. As an alternative, the manager could purchase only call options.

OTC Solution Purchase a 6-month lookback or partial lookback option. The option could be struck at the lowest price over the 6-month life of the option or some subset of that time to reduce costs. The price of lookback options are higher than a similar conventional option. In order for this type of option to pay, the value of the portfolio must decline after the time the contract is initiated and appreciate enough above its original value to compensate for the higher cost. This is not unlikely for volatile industry sectors with tremendous growth potential but subject to significant interruptions. Examples would include biotech, computer technology, internet-related, and other sectors dominated by innovative companies.

Exhibit 8: Comparative Performance: Lookback Option versus Split Forward

Option Strategy	Scenario 1 Down 10%	Scenario 2 Down 15%	Scenario Down 20%
Long 5% OTM Call	−1.930%	−1.930%	−1.930%
Short 5% OTM Put	+18.245	+18.245	+18.245
Split Forward	+16.310	+16.310	+16.310
Lookback	+ 7.560	+12.560	+22.560

The price of a 6-month European ATM call option assuming interest rates are constant at 5% and the dividend yield is a constant 1.7% is about 6.93%. A knockout option using the same data would cost about 12.44%. If the manager expects a decline in stocks first, then writing a 5% put option would generate 3.245% in premium, which would produce a net cost of 3.685% to the manager. In order for the lookback option to be economical, the market would have to fall at least 20.685% (12.44% + 5.00% + 3.245%) to perform as well as a put strategy.

In Exhibit 8, we look at three down market scenarios with the market ending up 10% above where it began. We can see from the results that the only time the lookback makes sense is when the market has fallen the most. Thus, if the manager believes the market will be falling little and rising a lot, the manager should buy the call option and sell the put. If, in contrast, the manager expects a major correction and a reversal at or slightly above the point of origin, the lookback option might make sense for the manager in spite of its cost.

The examples demonstrate how OTC equity options and warrants can provide managers with opportunities to fine tune their risk/reward profiles by providing flexible product structures that meet very specific investment requirements. As this section has illustrated, several traditional equity investment strategies can utilize OTC products and achieve results not obtainable with conventional solutions. Some options exchanges have fought back by listing options with flexible features, but have not begun to provide the type of product diversity available in the OTC market. We have touched upon some OTC derivative applications to equity investment situations. There are numerous other possibilities such as the use of digital options, chooser options, and a mix of other complex structures available in the OTC options market.

EQUITY-LINKED DEBT INVESTMENTS

Equity-linked debt investments are typically privately-placed debt instruments. They differ from conventional debt instruments because either the principal or coupon payment or both is linked to the performance of an established equity index, a portfolio of stocks, or an individual stock. Consistent with other OTC equity derivatives, equity-linked products have extremely flexible structures. For example, the equity component of the product can assume the characteristics of a call or a put or some combination. The payouts can be more complex, mixing exotic-type option payouts with a bond. In addition to providing flexible structures, equity-linked products also offer the manager the potential for higher returns than conventional debt instruments of similar credit risk. Other characteristics include more volatile cash flows, the principal guaranteed by issuers with investment-grade credit, and the avoidance of certain regulatory restrictions that prevent managers from entering into futures contracts, options, or swap agreements.[18] Equity-linked products are typically longer-term investments and therefore have limited liquidity.

Equity-lined debt investments are also referred to as equity-linked notes. Examples of these include Equity Participation Notes (EPNs), Stock Upside Notes (SUNs), Structured Upside Participating Equity Receipt (SUPER), Synthetic High Income Equity Linked Security (SHIELDS), and numerous others.[19] Equity-linked notes are issued by financial and nonfinancial corporations and have maturities ranging from one to ten years. The coupon can be fixed or floating, linked to an equity index, a portfolio of stocks or a single stock, and denominated in any currency. The equity-linked payment is typically equal to 100% of the equity appreciation, and redemption at maturity is the par value of the bond plus the equity appreciation.[20]

The conventional ELD instrument is illustrated in Exhibit 9 and is simply a portfolio consisting of a zero-coupon bond and an index call option. This structure can be extended to include a put or an exotic option. The cash flows associated with an ELD structure are illustrated in Exhibit 10. At issuance, the investor purchases the note, which represents the initial cash flow. Periodic cash flows are derived exclusively from the performance of the linked-equity index. For example, if the index were up 10% for the year, equity participation would be 100%, and the notional amount was $1 million, the investor would receive $100,000 as a periodic cash flow. The final cash flow includes the return of principal and the final equity payment.

Exhibit 9: Equity-linked Debt Structure
S&P 500 Linked Returns
"AA" Zero-Coupon Bond + S&P 500 Index Call Option
= S&P 500 Equity-linked Note

---

[18] Some pension funds are restricted from using derivatives. ELNs are recorded as a debt instrument and circumvent the restriction.

[19] Merrill Lynch has offered EPNs and SUNs. Most large brokers or OTC dealers have their own version of the equity-linked note product. In addition, there are listed equity-linked products that are designed primarily for retail investors. For a fairly extensive list of these notes see, G. Gastineau and M. Kritzman, *Dictionary of Financial Risk Management* (New Hope, PA: Frank J. Fabozzi Associates, 1997).

[20] Equity participation is actually flexible and changes depending on whether the ELD instrument includes a coupon payment.

Exhibit 10: Equity-linked Debt Cash Flows

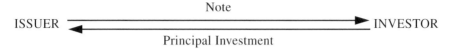

Note

ISSUER ◄─────────────────────────────────► INVESTOR

Principal Investment

Exhibit 11: SUN Performance
5-year note: Maximum appreciation: 13.3%

Year	1	2	3	4	5	Cum
S&P 500 Index(hypothetical)	−5%	15.00%	10.00%	5.00%	20.00%	51.14%
Realized Appreciation	0	13.30	13.30	6.65	13.30	55.11

Often, cash flows are subject to a cap, which limits the upside participation.[21] SUNs, for example, provide 100% of principal at maturity and pay an annual coupon based on 133% of the year over year appreciation in the S&P 500 index subject to a cap of 10%. Thus, the maximum appreciation is 13.3% per annum. If a manager believes the S&P 500 will appreciate by more, this not the appropriate investment vehicle. Consider a 5-year SUN with previously mentioned characteristics. Assume the S&P 500 is at 960 when the SUN is issued and has the year end levels given in Exhibit 11. The SUN actually outperforms the index because of downside protection and 133% appreciation up to 13.3% per annum. Here it works in favor of the manager.

Applications

The use of ELD is particularly attractive to domestic insurance companies subject to risk-based capital guidelines, which mandate higher capital requirements for equity than for debt.[22] ELDs are carried as debt but with performance linked to equity. Thus, insurance companies can maintain the capital requirements associated with debt instruments and still obtain equity market exposure. Pension funds also can benefit by using ELDs to gain access to foreign equity markets. Direct foreign equity investments subject pension funds to withholding taxes. The use of ELD structures, where the equity component is a foreign index, allows pension funds to avoid withholding taxes. The note has the same structure flexibility as conventional ELD instruments and can also include a currency hedge.

---

[21] The cost of the ELD instrument is the price of a discount bond plus the price of a call option. The cost of an at-the-money long-dated call option often exceeds the discount on the bond. In order to sell the note at par, the call option is partially financed by the sale of OTM call options which acts as a cap on the amount of equity appreciation.

[22] The National Association of Insurance Commissioners has issued risk-based capital guidelines of a 30% reserve requirement on common stock compared with 0.3%-9.0% for fixed-income instruments.

Foreign Exposure Application

Situation A pension fund is under-weighted in the UK equity market and wants to allocate some funds indexed to the FTSE-100 Index, but does not want to assume currency risk.

Conventional Solution Purchase FTSE-100 futures contract and set up a program over time to roll into a portfolio of UK stocks that track the FTSE-100. Also, design a strategy to hedge currency risk either in the forward market, the futures market, or the money market.

Comments on Conventional Solution The fund manager is faced with managing a futures position which involves an initial margin requirement and margin re-adjustments over the course of the investment. Moreover, the shift from futures to stocks involves overcoming any obstacles associated with holding foreign stocks, plus the manager must be responsible for administrative and transaction costs. Furthermore, a separate currency hedging program requires resources and incurs additional costs.

OTC Solution Purchase an equity-linked note (ELN) with a 5-year maturity, maximum equity participation in the FTSE-100 index, and denominated in U.S. dollars with full principal protection. The ELN combines a zero-coupon bond and an at-the-money call option on the FTSE-100 Index. The redemption value of the ELN is the higher of par value and the product of par value times the ratio of the value of the FTSE-100 Index at maturity and its value when the ELN is purchased. That is,

$$\text{Redemption value} = \text{Max}(\text{Par}, \text{Par} \times [\text{FT-SE}(T)/\text{FT-SE}(t)])$$

where FT-SE(T) is the value of the FT-SE(T) at time T.

This ELN creates a fixed-income instrument with payments based on the returns to the FTSE-100 Index, while eliminating all unwanted risks and costs associated with holding U.K. equities.

As in the case of OTC options, ELD structures are extremely flexible. The manager can decide upon the amount of equity participation, whether or not to include a coupon, whether or not to target levels of equity appreciation over the life of the product as the target is realized, or create a synthetic convertible bond.

EQUITY SWAPS

Equity swaps are similar in concept to interest rate or currency swaps. They are contractual agreements between two counterparties which provide for the periodic exchange of a schedule of cash flows over a specified time period where at least one of the two payments is linked to the performance of an equity index, a basket of stocks, or a single stock. In a standard or conventional equity swap one counterparty agrees to pay the other the total returns to an equity index in exchange for receiving the total return of another asset or an interest rate. All payments are based on a notional amount and payments are made over a fixed time period.

Equity swap structures are very flexible with maturities ranging from a few months to 10 years. The returns of virtually any asset can be swapped for another without incurring the costs associated with a transaction in the cash market. The real value of equity swaps to investors is that they provide 100% correlation with the underlying index or equity portfolio while avoiding the costs of transacting in the cash market. These costs include withholding taxes, custody fees, rebalancing costs, stamp taxes, market impact costs, and commissions. This makes equity swaps a very useful asset allocation tool and investment vehicle. Payment schedules can be denominated in any currency, irrespective of the equity index, and payments can be exchanged monthly, quarterly, annually or at maturity. The equity asset can be any equity index or portfolio of stocks, and can be denominated in any currency (hedged or unhedged). Variations of the conventional equity swap include: international equity swaps where the equity return is linked to an international equity index; currency-hedged swaps where the swap is structured to eliminate currency risk; and, a call swap where the equity payment is paid only if the equity index appreciates. Depreciation will not result in a payment from the counterparty receiving the equity return to the other counterparty because of call protection.

A basic swap structure is illustrated in Exhibit 12. In this case, the manager owns a short-term credit instrument that yields Libor plus.[23] The manager then enters into a swap to exchange Libor plus for the total equity returns to an index. The counterparty pays the equity total return plus a spread in exchange for Libor plus a spread. Assuming the equity index was the Nikkei 225, a U.S. manager could swap dollar-denominated Libor plus for cash flows from the total return to the Nikkei denominated in yen or U.S. dollars. The index could be any index, foreign or domestic. As indicated in Exhibit 12, the swap could also be structured to generate superior returns if the fixed income instrument in the swap yields significantly higher returns than Libor.

Applications

Equity swaps have a wide variety of applications, including asset allocation, accessing international markets, enhancing equity returns, hedging equity exposure, or synthetically shorting stocks.

Asset Allocation Application

Situation A U.S. manager expects short-term interest rates to remain low over the coming year and expects U.S. equities to offer a significantly higher return. The manager wants to shift some funds from cash to equities. The manager currently holds a portfolio of money market assets.

---

[23] Libor refers to the London Interbank Offered Rate. It is the rate at which Eurocurrency banks lend to one another and is the basis of many derivative transactions.

Exhibit 12: Equity Swaps

Basic Domestic Swap Structure

Enhanced Return Swap Structure

Exhibit 13: Swap Data

Time	Libor	S&P 500	Accrued Dividends
Settlement	3.25%	920	4.1
First reset date	3.20	945	4.1
Second reset date	3.10	970	4.1
Third reset date	3.25	940	4.1
Maturity	3.15	950	4.1

Calculation of payments:

Investor receives:
(Return on S&P 500 × Notional amount) + Accrued dividends

Investor pays: Libor × (91/360) × Notional amount

Conventional Solution Liquidate the money market portfolio and purchase a portfolio of stocks. Alternatively, purchase stock index futures contracts to create a synthetic index fund.

Comments on the Conventional Solution The conventional solution is subject to execution costs and administrative costs, which have a negative impact on returns. The second solution is comparable to an equity swap, but involves cash flow management issues and variation margin risk. Moreover, it is restricted to a few standard equity indexes.

Swap Solution Enter into a 1-year equity swap where the counterparty agrees to pay the investor the total return on the S&P 500 Index in exchange for dollar-denominated Libor on a quarterly basis. Exhibit 13 summarizes the mechanics of the swap assuming that on the settlement date the S&P 500 is 920, dividends are 4.10 index points each quarter, the current 90-day Libor is 3.25%, and the notional amount is $1 million. To illustrate the mechanics of the swap, additional assumptions are made regarding the value of the relevant variables at each reset date and at maturity.

On the first reset date the investor receives $23,415. The entire cash flow schedule based on the given assumptions is provided in Exhibit 14 and the calculations for the first cash flow are shown below.

$$[(945 - 920)/920 \times \$1,000,000 = \$27,174] + \$4,456 = \$31,630$$

$$\text{Net payment to investor} = \$31,630 - \$8,215 = \$23,415$$

The total return to the equity index at maturity consists of $10,750 in price appreciation and $17,726 in dividends. This is the same amount had the investor been able to purchase the index directly without incurring transaction costs. This type of equity swap is the economic equivalent of financing a long position in the S&P 500 Index at a spread to Libor. The advantages of using the swap are (1) no transaction costs, (2) no sales or dividend withholding tax, and (3) elimination of any tracking error or basis risk versus the index. Furthermore, there are no cash flow management issues or variation margin risk.

International Diversification Application

Situation U.S. pension fund wants to diversify its equity exposure internationally.

Traditional Solution Purchase a portfolio of stocks in the designated country of interest. Alternatively, set up an investment program using stock index futures contracts and money market securities.

Comment on the Conventional Solution U.S. investors are exposed to execution costs including stamp taxes, commissions, and market impact costs. In addition, there are custodial fees and dividend withholding taxes that are not recoverable for a tax-exempt investor. If the stock index futures solution is taken, the investment is subject to cash management issues, variation margin risk, follow-up choices, and money market investment considerations.

Equity Swap Solution Enter into an equity swap structured to meet the specific needs of the investment objective. The investor swaps a financing rate for the total returns to a foreign index, regional index, or global index.

Exhibit 14: Cash Flow Schedule

Time	Notional	Libor	Index	Accrued Dividend	Net Payment
First reset date	$1,000,000	8215	27,174	4456	23,415
Second reset date	1,023,415	8278	27,074	4440	23,236
Third reset date	1,046,651	8201	−32,371	4423	−36,148
Maturity	1,010,503	8940	10,750	4407	6,215

Exhibit 15: Estimated Cost of Direct Investing in U.S. and Foreign Stocks

	U.S.	U.K.	Germany	Swiss	France	Japan
Transaction costs*	0.70	2.19	1.53	1.54	1.64	2.16

* Including custodial fees, transfer fees, withholding taxes on dividends, commissions, and market impact.

The basic mechanics of equity swaps are the same regardless of the structure. However, the rules governing the exchange of payments may differ. For example, a U.S. investor wanting to diversify internationally can enter into a swap and, depending on the investment objective, exchange payments on a currency-hedged basis. If the investment objective was to reduce U.S. equity exposure and increase Japanese equity exposure, for example, a swap could be structured to exchange the total returns to the S&P 500 Index for the total returns to the Nikkei 225 Index. If, however, the investment objective is to gain access to the Japanese equity market, a swap can be structured to exchange Libor for the total returns to the Nikkei 225 Index. The advantages of entering into an equity swap to obtain international diversification is that the investment exposure is devoid of tracking error, incurs no sales tax, custodial fees, withholding fees, or market impact associated with entering and exiting a market. The swap is the economic equivalent of being long the Nikkei 225 financed at a spread to Libor at a fixed exchange rate.

There are numerous applications of equity swaps, but all assume the basic structure outlined above. Managers can virtually swap any financial asset for the total returns to an equity index, a portfolio of stocks or a single stock. Market makers are prepared to create structures that allow a manager to exchange the returns of any two individual or composite assets. The schedule of cash flows exchanged is a function of the assets. For example, a manager wanting to outperform an equity benchmark may be able to accomplish this by purchasing a particular bond and swapping the cash flows for the S&P 500 total return plus a spread. Asset swaps are a useful means of implementing an asset allocation strategy. An example of an asset swap would be swapping the S&P 500 total return for the total return to the DAX index. The manager can reduce U.S. equity exposure and increase German equity exposure through an asset swap and thus avoiding the costs associated with cash market transactions.

Managers have two different avenues to access international markets: the cash market (direct investing) or the derivatives market. The advantage of using derivatives is that managers can reduce costs, avoid withholding taxes, eliminate tracking error, and achieve a desired risk/reward profile. The cost advantage can provide the manager with a means to outperform benchmarks. Exhibit 15 presents estimates of the costs of direct foreign investment for tax-exempt US investors. The total costs consist of custodial fees, transfer fees, withholding taxes on dividends, commissions, and market impact. These costs can be reduced using derivatives markets thereby providing investors with an opportunity for superior returns versus a cash market investment. Equity swaps and equity-linked notes are two OTC derivative products that managers can utilize to gain international equity exposure.

CONCLUSION

The development of the OTC equity derivatives market offers managers investment opportunities that are simply not available in the listed market or cash market. The importance of the OTC market is that it provides a product line not available in the listed market. Contrary to conventional wisdom, however, in most cases the listed market is not necessarily in direct competition with the OTC market. The fact is that some derivatives are predominantly traded on listed exchanges while others are traded OTC.[24] The choice of a listed or OTC solution depends on the strategic and regulatory requirements of the manager. The international banking community has seized upon recent trends in investing, and through competition and the use of modern technology has created a marketplace that has improved the efficiency of investing. Managers can no longer ignore the value of using derivative products as major part of their overall investment strategy. It is incumbent on plan sponsors, money managers, insurance companies, mutual funds, and corporations to consider the use of equity derivatives in achieving their investment objectives. An effective global asset allocation strategy must involve cash markets, listed derivative markets, and OTC markets.

---

[24] For an excellent discussion of this issue see, G. Gastineau, "Exchange-Traded vs. OTC Derivatives Markets," *Financial Derivatives and Risk Management* (November 1995).

.

Chapter 16

Constructing a Multi-Manager U.S. Equity Portfolio

Robert F. Ploder, CFA, CPA
Senior Investment Manager — U.S. Equities
IBM Retirement Funds

DETERMINING THE INVESTMENT OBJECTIVE

For most pension funds, the amount to be allocated to U.S. equity is a function of optimizing several asset classes — within certain constraints — to achieve the highest fund return at a given level of volatility or risk. However, future returns and volatility for individual asset classes cannot be known in advance. A thinly-capitalized firm may want to manage its pension fund by closely matching funds flows and the duration of its assets and liabilities.[1] Under such a scenario U.S. equities might be held to an absolute risk constraint rather than one linked to a general market index. Expected long term returns from such a portfolio, however, would also be less.[2] Instead, almost all pension funds constrain risk by limiting U.S. equity to a certain percentage of the total portfolio. The risk/reward of this exposure is then measured by utilizing a general market index such as the S&P 500.

A common investment objective for U.S. equity is to exceed market returns over the longer term by taking on a certain amount of additional risk. Risk, in this instance, is defined as any additional volatility around the general market index or benchmark. This risk is often expressed as the standard deviation of any extra (excess) returns or, more simply, tracking error. An investor with a longer time horizon presumably has a greater tolerance for short-term risk, permitting higher volatility around the benchmark and a higher tracking error. An investor with a shorter-time horizon or with a low tolerance for any shortfall to the market would (or at least should) desire lower volatility around the benchmark and a lower tracking error.

A first step, then, is to gain an understanding of a fund's investment time horizon and corresponding risk tolerance with regard to U.S. equities. A tracking

---

[1] In such an environment, "risk free" is not a zero-volatility Treasury bill, but those investments which most closely match the liability stream under various interest rate assumptions. Diversification, to the extent it widens any mismatch, would actually be undesirable.

[2] Such a portfolio would be decidedly more conservative than current "value" benchmarks such as the Russell 1000 Value or the S&P/BARRA Value indices.

error of 2% against the Russell 3000 index, for example, indicates that the U.S. equity portfolio should post returns (before any alpha) within 2% of the benchmark two-thirds of the time,[3] or four out of six years. Stated another way, returns will likely exceed the benchmark and expected alpha by over 2% one out of six years and *lag the benchmark and expected alpha by over 2% one out of six years.*

Although a 2% tracking error does not seem overly aggressive, returns can fall below the benchmark and expected alpha two years in a row.[4] Lagging expectations for two years by perhaps 3% is not particularly comfortable, especially for a larger fund or one with a relatively low tolerance for risk. After experiencing such a shortfall it does not take long to conclude that smaller, more consistent gains are more desirable than larger advances offset by sizable declines.

A reasonable goal for a U.S. equity portfolio, then, might be a higher rate of return than the market index, achieved with reasonable consistency and without too much downside. How much excess return might one expect? An excess return ratio (information ratio) of 0.25 to 0.50 relative to the tracking error would be reasonable for most pension funds. An equity portfolio with a 100-200 basis points (bp) tracking error relative to a broad U.S. equity benchmark should be expected to generate 25-100 bp of annual excess return over the longer term.

DESIGNING THE PORTFOLIO

Before hiring active U.S. equity managers one has to decide on the probability of a particular manager or group of managers outperforming the overall market or some specific benchmark. With over a thousand institutional investment products from which to choose, this is not an easy task. It has been well-documented that the majority of professional U.S. equity managers will likely *underperform* the market over the long term, even before subtracting what can be quite sizable fees.[5]

It should be noted that this is not necessarily true in other equity markets or asset classes. For example, active managers seem to perform better in emerging countries, where markets are presumably less efficient (albeit riskier and much more expensive to trade). Some have found that custom-built quantitative models work well in other equity markets such as Japan, at least within the industrial sector. Properly designed enhanced index strategies in fixed income have also achieved reasonably consistent excess returns.

---

[3] Two-thirds of the time approximates one standard deviation in a normal bell-shaped distribution.

[4] If the distribution of returns are normal and each year is independent of the other, there is a 50% chance of underperforming in one year and a 25% chance of underperforming two years in a row.

[5] The fact that most active managers are likely to perform poorly should not be too surprising. It has been estimated such managers hold over 50% of the value of all stocks and account for over 70% of all trading. In essence, active managers *are* the market. After incurring the costs of trading and subtracting fees it can be expected that the majority of U.S. active equity managers will indeed underperform the market over the longer term.

Exhibit 1: Rolling 12-Month Excess Return
S&P 500 Equally Weighted versus S&P 500 Capitalization Weighted

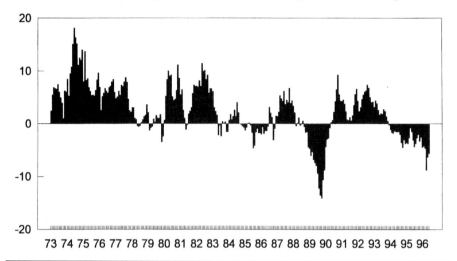

When Do Active Managers Outperform?

Although the majority of active U.S. equity managers will underperform over the longer term, as a group they can and do outperform over shorter time periods. Most active managers lean toward midcap stocks and tend to equal-weight rather than market-weight individual positions. As a result, active U.S. equity managers typically do well in broad market moves favoring lower cap size stocks. Often this occurs off major market bottoms, a particularly good period for *fully-invested* active managers.

There are several ways to determine whether the market environment is favoring active managers. These include comparing the S&P 500 index to an equal-weighted S&P 500 index, comparing midcap indices to broad market indices, or analyzing market breadth measures such as the cumulative advance/decline line. For example, at the beginning of 1997 the equal-weighted S&P 500 had underperformed the market-weighted S&P 500 for over three years (Exhibit 1) while the very largest cap stocks performed extremely well. This marked a very difficult period for active equity management in the United States.

Certain *individual* managers, of course, have demonstrated skill over longer periods of time. In designing a multi-manager portfolio, one could decide to vary the active-managed percentage depending on either the likelihood of managers as a group doing well and/or the level of confidence one has in particular managers. In the spring of 1997, a reasonable decision might have been to increase active equity. Admittedly, this would not have been an easy decision for funds already underperforming from a previous exposure to active management.

Which Active Managers Are Best?

Small Cap Managers

A close examination of past returns indicates that certain *groups* of active managers seem to do better than others. Small cap managers,[6] for example, have achieved rather consistent excess returns over small cap indices. Although market returns over the past 15 years have been extraordinary in many respects, there are several reasons to expect continuing outperformance by small cap managers. First, the smaller companies they analyze are generally researched less actively. Second, small cap stocks are more volatile, thereby creating more *opportunity* for success. Third, many smaller firms are leading-edge companies with good prospects for above-average growth. The successful small cap manager, of course, also recognizes that these companies generally have a lower return on assets and equity, often have a weak competitive position and thin management, and are more expensive to trade.

Within this sector, *small cap growth managers* have produced significantly greater excess returns against their growth benchmarks than have small cap value managers.[7] This may reflect heavier concentrations of investments in "high growth" sectors than that of the index. In recent years these high growth sectors have greatly benefited from a strong economy, accelerating growth in technology and rising market valuations. Growth stocks also have greater volatility and dispersion of return than value stocks, providing more opportunity for gain to the growth manager. By contrast, *small cap value managers* frequently have major investments in low growth sectors or turnaround situations and have a tendency to hold excess cash reserves. Excess cash has had a particularly negative effect on relative performance during the long bull market of the 1980s-1990s. Small cap value stocks also have less liquidity and are more expensive to trade than small cap growth stocks. Still, over the longer term, small cap value managers have been able to earn some excess return over their benchmarks.

Unless conditions in the U.S. economy and equity markets deteriorate significantly, it appears likely that small cap managers will continue to do well, particularly those oriented to growth.

Large Cap Growth and Value Managers

Although managers of large cap stocks in total have had mixed to poor results, certain groups have fared better than others. As in the case of small cap, large cap *growth* managers have generally performed better relative to their benchmarks than have large cap *value* managers.[8] The reasons for this outperformance appear similar to that of small cap managers, particularly since most large cap growth managers have also focused on higher growth sectors in a very favorable market environment.

---

[6] Small cap definitions vary, but a common proxy is the Russell 2000 index, which consists largely of stocks under $1 billion in market cap. This group of stocks represents about 10% of the Russell 3000, a broad general market index.

[7] Frank Russell Company small cap growth and value manager universes.

[8] Frank Russell Company large cap growth and value manager universes.

Many large cap *value* managers, on the other hand, have a strong desire to preserve capital. This has often led to higher cash reserves, a minimum yield requirement, and a desire to invest in low P/E stocks. As a consequence, many value managers have low risk or beta, even to a value benchmark. This lower risk profile has probably contributed to poor relative performance during the bull market of the last 15 years.

Another major problem for large cap value managers is that the benchmark itself is skewed to three major sectors. Value managers find it difficult to invest up to one-half of their portfolios in utility, financial, and energy stocks. Yet a number of studies show that, over the very long term, value investing has provided higher returns with lower risk than growth investing.[9] This suggests that value managers have a "tailwind" helping them outperform, yet this advantage is being dissipated by an apparent failure to invest more heavily in the particular economic sectors and individual securities that comprise this grouping.

Core Managers

Many managers believe they are equally skilled in either growth or value investing and will perform well in either market environment. After the fact, however, manager returns usually reflect a bias toward either a growth or value benchmark. For example, a manager who screens the broad market averages for "cheap" stocks and then narrows that list to those securities with rising earnings estimates will often end up with a closer fit to a value benchmark. This is true even though the manager screened for both growth and value attributes. Contrast this to the manager who first screens the universe on earnings momentum and positive earnings surprise, finally narrowing that list to "fairly priced" stocks. That manager will often end up with a closer fit to a growth benchmark.

About the only time managers do well in either kind of market environment is when sector or style weightings are kept close to those of the broad market benchmark. Quantitative model builders typically do this well, but most traditional managers find this more difficult to do. Simply underweighting utilities, integrated oils, and money center banks, for example, can easily move a portfolio into faster growing, more expensive sectors, making superior performance difficult when "deep" value is in favor. On the other hand, an orientation to low P/E can produce a tighter correlation to a value benchmark, making it difficult for a manager to outperform when high growth and momentum are in favor. Because of these innate biases most traditional managers will fall into a particular "style" category. This is the principal reason why funds separate managers by style and measure their performance against growth or value benchmarks.

Certain core managers are sector rotators or style managers. Sector rotators overweight and underweight entire sectors, typically performing top-down economic analysis combined with valuation work on individual sectors. Style

---

[9] For example, see Josef Lakonishok, Andrei Schleifer, and Robert W. Vishny, "Contrarian Investment, Extrapolation, and Risk," *Journal of Finance* (December 1994).

managers do a similar top-down and valuation analysis on the growth/value and large cap/small cap categories. In either case there is the presumption that a correct call on a sector or style will yield more value-added than correctly calling individual stocks. However, style and sector calls *must* be correct to generate excess returns whereas making many predictions on a broad number of stocks allows more room for error. In general, sector rotators and top-down style managers have had mixed results and have not accumulated significant assets.

In my experience, the best core managers are those who build quantitative, computer-driven models which are optimized to closely track a general market benchmark. These include market-neutral managers and enhanced indexers, more fully discussed below.

Market-Neutral Managers

A market-neutral portfolio is long and short equal amounts of stock such that a market move, by itself, will not impact portfolio return. That is, systematic market risk is removed so that returns generated are due entirely to specific, or stock-related risk.

Note that simply equalizing one's long and short investments does not necessarily eliminate market risk. To be market neutral, a portfolio's cap size, sector, and style weightings in both the long and short portfolios should be balanced. Even then there is the possibility of being modestly away from the market because of a mismatch in industry weightings, financial leverage, or other common factors. Moving to a closer match, however, makes it increasingly difficult to generate much excess return.

A market-neutral portfolio has the advantage of permitting portfolio holdings to be more equal-weighted than market-weighted because, if balanced correctly, there is no additional market risk. The portfolio weight of an individual holding can be more directly related to a manager's conviction regarding the possibility of positive or negative excess return, as long as corresponding offsetting positions are placed in the portfolio. This is particularly helpful on the short side, where more significant bets can be taken compared to the option in long-only of simply not owning specific issues.

Another major advantage of market neutral portfolios is that a sector's weighting need not be geared to a particular benchmark, but instead reflect a manager's analytical strength in a particular area and/or his conviction regarding certain issues within the sector. In fact, a market neutral portfolio can be quite narrow in terms of capitalization size and/or economic sectors represented, although a broader range of holdings would further reduce overall risk.

The benchmark for a market neutral portfolio is generally the 90-day Treasury bill rate. Importantly, the amount of cash buffer required to support mark-to-market moves is about 10% of the short position. By using some cash to invest in futures such as the S&P 500 or any other efficiently-traded index, any excess return from the market-neutral portfolio can be overlaid on another financial market benchmark.

Enhanced Indexing

There are two ways to enhance an index. The first uses benchmark derivatives with the remaining cash invested at a higher rate of return than the short-term interest rate embedded in the derivative. The second is a portfolio quite similar to the benchmark, but modestly overweighted/underweighted in various names.

In the derivative-based approach, excess returns are generated by investing cash in arbitrage activities, fixed income strategies, or other low risk endeavors. However, some of these products use substantial leverage. Care must be taken to avoid those strategies that appear to offer consistent excess returns over long periods of time, yet could produce a significant negative return in a particular market environment. Many managers of derivative-based products also charge relatively high performance-based fees, further reducing net returns. These strategies are basically stand-alone cash management products which can be transported to any particular index or benchmark where reasonably liquid future or options markets exist.

The second approach to enhancing an index is to simply make small bets around the benchmark. Most of these products have a tracking error of 2% or less. This is lower risk than the 4%-6% tracking error incurred by most traditional active managers. The information ratio for an enhanced indexer is typically higher, however, because larger, sometimes unintended, sector bets give way to smaller, more numerous stock bets. This is where managers tend to have more skill and *not owning* a particular security now becomes more meaningful.

This latter point is quite important. If a long-only manager believes a specific security is unattractive and it represents only 0.2% of the benchmark, he stands to achieve little excess return even if he is right. In a less volatile enhanced index portfolio, however, these small excess returns become proportionately more important. This is particularly true if the enhanced index tracking error is brought down from 2% to 1%. In the latter case, not owning certain securities becomes doubly important in calculating excess return. Looked at in this way, tightly enhanced index investing begins to take on some of the better attributes of market neutral long/short investing.

One difficulty with enhanced indexing has been finding U.S. equity managers willing to work at reduced prices per dollar of assets invested. This is particularly important at the 1% tracking error level. Since enhanced indexing should provide a higher information ratio on reduced risk, however, a proportionately higher allocation can be made to this strategy. Fortunately, most enhanced index managers are quantitative model builders who typically have lower costs and recognize that the greater amount of assets managed will still result in sizable fees.

Which Sectors Should Be Actively Managed?

Although most active managers are destined to underperform the market over the longer term because of transaction costs and management fees, there still is opportunity for generating excess return. Utilizing investment managers for the small cap sector of the market makes a lot of sense, as does using market neutral long/short managers who demonstrate a high level of investment expertise in specific areas. Enhanced indexing offers an attractive way to improve overall returns by improving the risk/return ratio.

Actively managing the large cap growth sector should also produce excess returns in a generally rising market environment. Value and traditional core managers have had a more difficult time in generating excess returns, but increasing the active/passive ratio for all large cap managers after a period of midcap underperformance should improve prospects for increased returns.

Adding small cap, large cap growth, market neutral, and enhanced indexing together could easily account for over one-half of a fund's U.S. equity exposure. Perhaps a good starting point is investing 50% of U.S. equity on an active basis. This percentage could be modified after considering the current state of the midcap (or equal-weighted) market and, more importantly, the excess return-generating capability of a particular group of managers.

CHOOSING MANAGERS

Entire books have been written on the subject of choosing and hiring managers, but it might be wise to briefly review some of the key elements to consider when adding a manager to your team.

Philosophy

How can one generate excess returns in a relatively efficient market? Interestingly, most investment managers never formally address this question. When asked, most state they simply find companies through extensive research which have favorable prospects not yet recognized in the stock price. However, this often leads to a portfolio with a growth and midcap tilt, resulting from the fact that smaller companies have greater *opportunity* for growth but are not yet closely followed by the investment community. As noted earlier, many such companies are not leaders in their field, have less management depth, are more cyclical, and have lower returns on assets and equity than their larger brethren. Consequently, most of these companies have lower dividend yields and stock multiples which will likely remain discounted to the larger cap sector, particularly in a bear market.

Far better if a firm's investment philosophy instead capitalized on less conventional approaches to stock selection or valuation. For example, one successful money manager with a number of security analysts makes no earnings estimates at all! This particular manager simply determines if consensus earnings estimates seem appropriate given current economic and industry conditions. Another successful manager, recognizing that growth investors typically become disenchanted sellers when faced with a period of flat or disappointing earnings, has a longer-term investment horizon and achieves superior returns after buying at distressed prices.

People

That managers have personal integrity and be totally committed to their clients is paramount. It is also critical that managers be knowledgeable of and experienced in the equity markets. Some academics are quite knowledgeable about the financial markets but lack the insight gained from experiencing various market cycles and emotionally distressing periods. Many traditional managers have long experience in the marketplace, yet are not open to many of the new ideas and concepts developed over the past few years.

Although the success of a product is often linked to the abilities of one key individual, a strong professional staff would likely produce even better results. If a firm has high personnel turnover it may be a sign that fresh viewpoints are not welcome, upward mobility is difficult or compensation is unsatisfactory.

Investment Process

Once a firm has a winning investment philosophy and knowledgeable, experienced people, it must have a thoughtful, disciplined investment process to achieve consistent results. If the investment process is not disciplined, there can be little confidence that any prior success will be repeated. Virtually all successful investment managers adhere to a certain investment methodology. Understanding and appreciating this methodology must be a key consideration before hiring a manager.

The investment process is normally a two-step procedure. The first step is determining which stocks are attractive. This may be done by ranking a universe of securities from best to worst, assigning individual stocks an attractiveness rating, screening out unwanted securities, or simply choosing those securities that fit a particular theme. In many cases managers may not have specific opinions on a large part of the investable universe. This often leads to taking "unintended bets" against (i.e., making no investments in) many of the stocks in their benchmark. It is better if an investment manager has a sufficiently large, qualified staff to analyze all of the sectors in a particular universe or benchmark.

The second step is constructing the actual portfolio. Most traditional managers size each investment position by its perceived attractiveness to the other holdings in the portfolio. Overall risk is then controlled by constraining each security, industry, or sector to certain limits. As noted earlier, this will generally produce a portfolio with a tendency toward equal-sized positions and a portfolio market cap below that of the benchmark. A portfolio so constructed is typically more volatile than the benchmark and, as noted earlier, will frequently have a lower return on assets, a lower return on equity, and a lower yield than that of the benchmark. A more benchmark-oriented portfolio construction process is desirable, with sector and company weightings tied more closely to index weightings.

Performance

Numerous studies have concluded that past performance, *even when measured against specific style benchmarks*, is not a good precursor of performance in the future.[10] In my experience this frequently is the result of particular sector bets being rewarded in one period but not in another. Investment managers often have strong biases, leading to a consistent overweighting or underweighting of particular sectors over time. For example, one growth manager with strong analytical capability in health care overweighted this sector and performed extremely well until the early 1990s. The firm had little capability in technology, however, and performed poorly after the market rotated away from health care to technology. In another case, a value manager with a strong bias against the "poorly managed" banking industry performed very well until the early 1990s, but completely missed the improving fundamentals and has underperformed since.

Another major reason why past performance may not be indicative of future performance is the cap size effect discussed earlier. A manager who tended to equal-weight securities may have had excellent performance through 1993, but poor performance in the very favorable large cap market since then. It is important that care be taken to attribute past performance to all factors, especially cap size and sector bets, not simply assume past performance will continue.

Studies indicate only slightly more than one-half of those managers who have outperformed the market in the past few years will continue to outperform in the future.[11] Does this mean we should exclude past performance when choosing managers? Of course not. One-half of the outperforming managers *will* continue to perform well. Through a careful analysis of manager performance and all other critical inputs, the odds of finding a successful manager should improve significantly.

Fees

The cost of managing money must be kept at competitively low levels to achieve excess returns over the benchmark. Interestingly, fee rates are often a function of recent performance despite the lack of correlation between past and future excess returns. Fees also reflect the size and maturity of an organization, the cost of doing business, and, in general, the degree to which a manager really wants a sponsor's business. Looking back, however, investors often find that the level of fees bore little relationship to the performance achieved.

Most investment managers, on any given product line, attempt to provide similar rates of return to all their institutional clients. (If this is not the case, the investment manager may not have a very disciplined investment process). Consequently, a manager's proposed fee schedule is unlikely to influence his future performance. That being the case, every effort should be made to negotiate the lowest possible fees.

In the long run, negotiated performance-based fees may be more attractive (cheaper) than fixed rates. I use the word *negotiated* because most stated per-

---

[10] For example, Josef Lakonishok, Andrei Shleifer, and Robert W. Vishny, "The Structure and Performance of the Money Management Industry," in Martin N. Baily and Clifford Winston (eds.), *Brookings Papers on Economic Activity, Microeconomics 1992* (Washington, D.C.: Brookings Institution), pp. 339-391.

[11] Slightly means 51% to 52%. When managers are measured against closer-fitting benchmarks, the percentage rises modestly to perhaps 53% to 54%.

formance fee schedules appear unattractive relative to fixed-rate schedules. It is important when negotiating performance-based fees to amortize any incentives over a period of time, not simply paying higher fees in better years while still paying healthy fees in years of underperformance. The fee should be structured so that if there are no excess returns longer term, *cumulative* performance fees will be less than *cumulative* fixed-rate fees.

Traditional versus Quantitative Managers

Most investors are familiar with traditional managers, but many are not familiar with quantitative managers. The latter design computer-driven models to rank stocks, create portfolios, or do both. In ranking stocks, most "quants" pick certain fundamental or valuation factors such as earnings momentum and P/E, then score each stock based on these attributes. Models can be very simple, such as ranking P/E's based on trailing earnings, or complex, such as using many factors specific to each industry dynamically weighted to account for the current economic or market situation.[12] Some traditional managers also create such rankings to screen stocks for further analysis. Quantitative managers, however, generally design a model to not just screen but produce a final list of attractive issues. A portfolio is then constructed with certain stock, industry and/or sector constraints so that the volatility of the portfolio relative to a benchmark will be known beforehand.

There are several advantages to a model-driven portfolio. A very large universe of stocks can be analyzed in a disciplined and consistent manner. The model can be designed to eliminate judgmental biases. Risk (tracking error) can be tightly controlled.

The major disadvantage of using quantitative models is the implicit assumption that the markets will behave in the future much as they have in the past.[13] Computer-driven models must be continually updated and improved to reflect the current state of knowledge and dynamics in the marketplace. They should not be allowed to become stale under the assumption that past relationships or anomalies will remain unchanged; many models that produced good results in past periods will not work well in the future.

Even so, experience indicates quants have as good an opportunity as traditional money managers to outperform, particularly across a wide universe. As noted earlier, traditional managers seem to do best when segmented into either a growth or a value style. Quants, however, seem to do better across a broad spectrum of securities. Accordingly, one decision may be to use traditional managers in the growth and value segments of the portfolio and to use model-driven managers in the core or "market benchmark" portion of the portfolio.

---

[12] See Bruce I. Jacobs and Kenneth N. Levy, "Investment Analysis: Profiting from a Complex Equity Market," Chapter 2 in this book.

[13] Traditional money managers also assume that past "rules of investing" will work in the future, but they can adapt to a fast-changing environment more quickly than quantitative managers.

Manager Success and Asset Growth

After careful research, a sponsor selects a firm with a small but insightful group of professionals. They have particular strengths in a segment of the U.S. equity universe and have continued to build on their excellent track record. However, they have been so successful that new money is flowing into the firm at a rapid rate, the staff needs to be expanded, administrative and client servicing needs are exploding, time is at a premium and performance is beginning to suffer.

Since superior performance is usually accompanied by growth in assets, it will become more difficult for a sponsor's best managers to maintain past levels of excess return. Recognize that some managers simply will not be able to grow and continue their success. A sponsor must be prepared to prune such managers out of its line-up on a periodic basis.

CONSTRUCTING THE PORTFOLIO

After identifying which investment managers are attractive, a sponsor will have to decide which ones to select and in what proportion in order to achieve the desired result. The fund's managers have presumably already determined the maximum risk they are willing to accept to achieve possible excess returns over the market benchmark. Still, excess returns do not necessarily rise in proportion to the risk incurred and a sponsor may choose to go with a lower level of risk. A combination of enhanced indexing, active small cap managers, active large cap growth managers, and passive value managers may provide the highest information ratio and desired consistency of result without resorting to a higher level of risk. Recognize, however, that a fund's returns may be compared to those of other funds without, perhaps, a lot of consideration being given to the amount of risk incurred elsewhere.

As noted earlier, active growth managers have generally outperformed active value managers, small cap managers have usually returned better results than large cap managers and quantitative managers appear to have performed better with less risk than traditional managers against a market benchmark. If this is also representative of a fund's "best manager" list, than the next task is to combine the active managers with passive products in such a way to maximize returns without exceeding the desired level of risk. Along the way a sponsor will need to make decisions as to whether any style or size tilts should be taken, completion funds should be used, or cash should be equitized.

Style and Size Tilts

Even if a sponsor could perfectly balance its managers by style, other tilts such as size, sector, and yield will show up in the portfolio. All of these will influence a fund portfolio's beta (systematic risk) and tracking error. Some tilts, most notably size and style, are more significant than others. Correctly predicted, style and size tilts can probably add more excess return to the portfolio in the short term than any other action that a sponsor can take.

Over the very long term, small cap stocks have realized higher returns than large cap stocks.[14] In addition, large cap value stocks have generated higher returns than large cap growth stocks[15] and small cap value stocks have performed better than small cap growth stocks.[16] These observations, however, may not hold true for periods as long as ten years,[17] a time horizon beyond that of most investment professionals.

When deciding to overweight or underweight small cap stocks, it is critical to recognize the high transaction costs in this sector. One-way transaction costs (commissions plus spread plus market impact) typically exceed 2%, and are even higher on the less liquid small cap value stocks. These high transaction costs can completely erase any advantage to trading small cap equities. Accordingly, decisions to overweight or underweight small cap stocks should be made infrequently, perhaps no more than every two years (unless significant price action has occurred). A decision to overweight small cap value stocks, which would seem appropriate, should be made even less frequently given the higher transaction costs in this category.

A key question is to what extent should bets be placed on either style or size? One way to resolve the issue is to examine what such a bet will do to a fund's tracking error.

Investing fully in either the Russell Large Cap Value or Large Cap Growth index will produce an estimated tracking error of between 250-350 bp to the Russell 1000 index. Similarly, investing totally in the Russell 2000 index produces an estimated tracking error of between 700-1,000 bp to the Russell 3000 index. A 1994 Frank Russell study[18] mathematically determined that keeping tracking error down to a level of 100 bp relative to the Russell 3000 index required constraining large cap value/growth (or growth/value) to roughly a 60/40 ratio (compared to a normal 50/50) or constraining small cap/large cap to approximately 20/80 (compared to a more normal 10/90). Performing two tilts and keeping risk down to 100 bp tracking error would allow about a 55/45 split of large cap value/growth (or growth/value) and a 17/83 small cap/large cap ratio. These findings are dependent on the volatility and correlation of inputs used, but it would seem that the above-noted tilts permit a reasonable amount of flexibility. If the

---

[14] *Stocks, Bonds, Bills, and Inflation: 1997 Yearbook*, Ibbotson Associates, p. 30.

[15] For example, Lakonishok, Schleifer and Vishny, "Contrarian Investment, Extrapolation, and Risk."

[16] For example, see Eugene F. Fama and Kenneth R. French, "The Cross-Section of Expected Stock Returns," *Journal of Finance* (1992), pp. 427-465.

[17] For example, the Russell 2000 Small Cap index returned only 12.4% annually compared to 15.1% for the Russell 1000 Large Cap index in the ten years ended 12/31/96. The Russell 1000 Growth index returned 15.4% compared to 14.7% for the Russell 1000 Value index during the same period. However, the Russell 2000 Value index returned 13.7%, exceeding the Russell 2000 Growth index return of 10.9% for the same period.

[18] Ernest M. Ankrim, "Value and Small Cap Tilts in a U.S. Equity Portfolio," *Frank Russell Company Research Commentary* (March 1994).

tracking error for the entire U.S. equity portfolio is 200 bp, these constraints on tilting would permit an additional 100 bp of tracking error on active stock selection.

Does it make sense to bet on size or style? Although a correct tactical call can be very profitable, there is not much room for error. Most style managers make one major call every two years. If one is correct 55% of the time on picking either style or individual stocks, after two years the chance of underperforming on style is 45%; the chance of underperforming over that period on a 50-stock portfolio is only 20%. This is the basic reason, of course, for diversification — and why most funds prefer to take the "less risky" avenue of stock selection over that of style.

Perhaps the best approach to betting on size or style is to make a modest tilt when the odds are strongly in your favor. This might be the case when the index level and/or certain valuation parameters are at least 1.2 standard deviations away from norm, suggesting an 88% chance of regressing to the mean. While there is no guarantee of securing excess return, the odds are certainly better. In addition, if most size/style adjustments are made as a sponsor hires, terminates or rebalances its managers, transaction costs will be reduced substantially.

What About Completion Funds?

Even a carefully balanced multi-manager portfolio in terms of style will normally still contain size and sector tilts. As noted, active equity managers typically underweight the largest cap stocks, finding their most attractive ideas in the broad middle segment of the market. Compounding the problem, managers tend to equal-weight their selections, bringing the "weighted" cap size of the portfolio down even further. For example, traditional large cap growth managers are often underweighted in names such as General Electric and Coca-Cola and over-weighted in midcap technology and business service companies.

The most common sector tilts are chronic underweightings in utilities and energy. In early 1997, utilities and integrated oil companies accounted for about 10% and 8%, respectively, of the S&P 500. It would not be unusual for an active manager to underweight utilities by 50% and oils by 25%, thus leaving a portfolio "short" 7% in these two high-yield, defensive sectors. While this may be an intended bet, more often than not the manager simply looked elsewhere for potentially more attractive and exciting names. This leaves a fund's portfolio more susceptible to underperformance in a declining market.

This situation may be alleviated through the use of completion or fulfillment funds. The first step is to periodically determine the extent of any chronic underweightings or unintended bets made by a fund's managers. There are consulting and investment management organizations that will perform this work and recommend a portfolio to resolve the situation. A typical completion fund might consist mostly of large cap names (to bring cap size up to the benchmark weight) and utility, oil, and finance companies (to bring sector weights more into balance) or both. If a fund's managers are reasonably well diversified, any remaining tilts are likely to be minor.

Completion funds can be passive or active and may include short positions. An active completion fund will attempt to add excess return, but still provide size and sector exposures necessary to reduce overall risk. A long/short completion fund can do double-duty in the sense that overweightings (such as in midcap stocks) can be reduced by shorting directly, requiring less investment funds to balance the overall portfolio.

The use of completion funds is not widespread. Perhaps this is because they are difficult to explain and appear to be a bet against the very managers who have been hired for sizable fees to provide excess returns. In addition, completion funds are used to lower risk, not increase returns, and will penalize overall returns from time to time.

One way to bypass the need for completion funds is to hire managers who are more likely to hold larger cap issues and/or more tightly structure their portfolios to benchmark sector weights. These managers focus on stock selection and avoid taking size or sector bets. More attuned to risk control, these firms generally are model-driven quantitative managers or enhanced indexers. However, a few traditional money managers have begun to embrace the advantages of tighter risk control and the resulting improvement in overall performance. As more of these "benchmark-oriented" products become available, serious consideration should be given to using such portfolios to reduce risk.

Cash Reserves

Holding cash in excess of that needed to facilitate trading has been a costly mistake, particularly in recent years. Even experts in tactical asset allocation have performed poorly on market timing, and portfolio managers generally do much worse. Managers who increase cash when securities seem temporarily unattractive or who simply want to reduce the volatility of their portfolio are generally unable to bring themselves to later reinvest these funds, even when they were correct on the initial decision. Perhaps this is because as the market declines it reinforces the "correctness" of the earlier decision to hold cash and the manager becomes increasingly unwilling to increase his equity exposure in a highly uncertain environment. Much has been written about the necessity for being fully invested in the market,[19] particularly during those few days off the bottom. It is important not to jeopardize portfolio returns by permitting a fund's managers to hold cash in excess of that needed for trading flexibility, say 3%-5%.

To the extent managers do have cash or the total portfolio temporarily has uninvested U.S. equity funds, it would be wise to equitize that cash by utilizing S&P 500 or other index derivatives. If a fund is not permitted to trade in futures, a synthetic future can be created by simultaneously buying calls and selling puts. Since the portfolio is likely to have a lower cap size than the benchmark, it may be best to utilize derivatives with a larger cap size to lower overall risk.

---

[19] For example, see Robert H. Jeffrey, "The Folly of Stock Market Timing," *Harvard Business Review* (July-August 1984).

Managing the Portfolio

When hiring a manager to fill a need in a particular style, capitalization size and/or sector, benchmark selection is very important. The benchmark should be appropriate to a fund's needs and fully understood by the manager. For example, most large cap value managers will not invest 50% of their portfolios in the utility, finance, and energy sectors, but being less-than-benchmark weighted in these sectors poses significant risks to the overall fund. Managers should understand that poor performance caused by an underweighting in these sectors cannot be tolerated for very long. They must appreciate that performance shortfalls principally attributable to capitalization size, style, or sector bets away from the benchmark are the responsibility of the manager and cannot be used as an excuse for poor performance.

Some funds require managers to limit holdings in an individual portfolio to only those securities in the benchmark, emphasizing the importance of lower tracking error and closer fit. However, this limits the opportunity for increased alpha and is not widespread. For example, although most large cap managers will typically confine their research to large U.S. common equities, they will at times see good appreciation potential in a few select international, small cap and/or convertible securities. It is often the case that these "exceptions," simply because they are exceptions, offer superior risk/reward characteristics and bring excess return to the portfolio. In order to control tracking error, it is probably wise to limit the amount of bets away from the benchmark, such as permitting no more than 5% in international stocks and/or no more than 5% in convertible securities.

Although investment managers must be knowledgeable about their benchmark, it is also important that individual portfolios not look exactly like an index. A certain degree of latitude and flexibility must be permitted to achieve additional excess return. Combining the managers into a total portfolio is where much of the risk reduction will occur. The weighting of each manager's portfolio will depend on the style, size, and sector tilts desired in the overall portfolio, the correlation of each manager's returns to the others and the confidence a sponsor has in each manager meeting return and risk goals. Balancing the need for risk control with the potential to secure excess return is the most critical and rewarding aspect of large fund management.

Adding to and subtracting from a manager's assets increases transaction costs so it is important not to make changes too frequently. As noted earlier, this is especially true in small cap. A good time to make such adjustments is when U.S. equity is being rebalanced in the total fund portfolio. Another good time is when there are valuation extremes, providing an opportunity to rebalance the portfolio on the assumption there will be a reversion to mean. For example, by the end of May 1997 small cap stocks had underperformed large cap stocks by such a significant amount for such a long time that it made increasing sense to overweight the small cap sector (see Exhibit 2).

Exhibit 2: Russell 2000/Russell 1000 Ratio

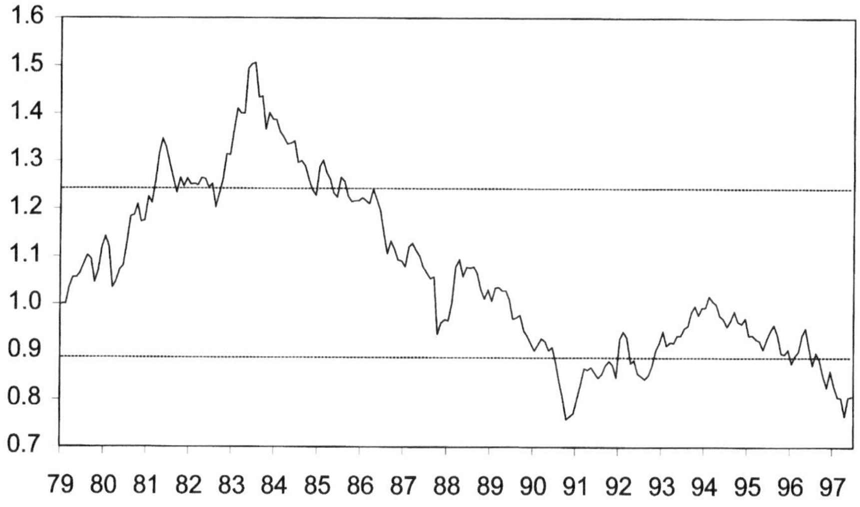

No matter how much care is taken in the selection process, some managers will ultimately fail to achieve the mandated objectives. Poor performance should be scrutinized closely to determine whether or not the manager's investment style and methodology is simply "out-of-sync" with the market (at some point to be reversed) or whether skill has been compromised because of increased assets, loss of personnel, sector biases, or other factors. Because there are several possible causes of poor performance, in most instances it is probably wise to reduce a particular manager's assets before taking the ultimate step of firing that manager. Once it is clear that a manager's skill level is not up to a fund's requirements, however, termination should not be postponed because of friendship, long time association, low fees, or the lack of ready alternatives. Although it is best to have a number of current or potential managers in the wings who can do the job, a number of index funds and derivatives now exist that can temporarily absorb assets while a careful search for a new manager is underway.

SUMMARY

In managing a large multi-manager U.S. equity portfolio, it is critically important to first understand the risk tolerance of the fund managers/trustees. Assuming the benchmark is a market index such as the S&P 500 or Russell 3000, one must understand the degree of shortfall that will be tolerated and for what period of time. It is probably wise to assume that patience will wane during any lengthy period of underperformance, so that *actual* tolerance may, in fact, be less than *stated* tolerance. Accordingly, it is probably best to construct a portfolio with not too long a time horizon or too wide a tracking error. Long-term consistency of performance is likely to prove more desirable than a higher excess return marked by periods of sizable or lengthy underperformance.

This being the case, it is probably wise to limit size, style, and sector bets by hiring more structured managers who have a broader capability to add excess return across all the primary sectors within their benchmark. They should be able to achieve acceptable excess returns with lower tracking error than managers who take more concentrated risks. The latter can be profitably used, however, if they can be balanced against other managers or their portfolios "completed" through the use of specialized funds. It is important to remember that when skilled managers with concentrated portfolios have periods of underperformance, it is often because of what they *did not own* rather than what they did own.

Because so many active U.S. equity managers are unable to beat their benchmarks, enhanced indexing is gaining increased acceptance. Of course, the higher information ratio promised is only as good as the investment philosophy and process used by these managers. Although these products should produce more consistent excess returns, it must be recognized such returns may not prove very exciting in a particularly good year favoring active managers.

Finally, success will be achieved by remaining open to new ideas and appreciating that the investment landscape is destined to change. The extraordinary bull market of the last 15 years produced a very different environment compared to the flat market of the previous 15 years, and the next 15 years will almost certainly present different return patterns compared to the most recent past. With many U.S. equity valuation parameters at very high levels, moving to a more consistent, less volatile stream of excess returns may prove to be a wise course of action at this time.

Index